Frances Stackhouse Acton

The Castles & Old Mansions of Shropshire

Fifth Edition

Frances Stackhouse Acton

The Castles & Old Mansions of Shropshire
Fifth Edition

ISBN/EAN: 9783744790444

Printed in Europe, USA, Canada, Australia, Japan

Cover: Foto ©ninafisch / pixelio.de

More available books at **www.hansebooks.com**

A TREATISE

ON

MINE-SURVEYING.

STANDARD WORKS

FOR THE USE OF

SURVEYORS, MINING ENGINEERS, AND METALLURGISTS.

TRAVERSE TABLES: computed to Four Places Decimals for every Minute of Angle up to 100 of Distance. By RICHARD LLOYD GURDEN, Authorised Surveyor for the Governments of New South Wales and Victoria. THIRD EDITION. 21s.

ORE AND STONE MINING. By C. LE NEVE FOSTER, D.Sc., F.R.S., Prof. of Mining, Royal College of Science. With very numerous Illustrations. 34s.

COAL MINING. By H. W. HUGHES, F.G.S., Assoc. R.S.M. With 490 Illustrations. SECOND EDITION. 18s.

PRACTICAL GEOLOGY (Aids in). By G. A. J. COLE, F.G.S., Prof. of Geology, Royal College of Science, Dublin. With numerous Illustrations. SECOND EDITION. 10s. 6d.

BLASTING AND THE USE OF EXPLOSIVES. By O. GUTTMANN, A.M.Inst.C.E. With Folding Plates and Illustrations. 10s. 6d.

ASSAYING. By J. J. BERINGER, F.C.S., F.I.C., and C. BERINGER, F.C.S. THIRD EDITION. 10s. 6d.

ELEMENTS OF METALLURGY: The Art of Extracting Metals from their Ores. By J. ARTHUR PHILLIPS, C.E., F.C.S., F.G.S., and H. BAUERMAN, F.G.S. With numerous Illustrations. THIRD EDITION. 36s.

NEW METALLURGICAL SERIES,

EDITED BY

W. C. ROBERTS-AUSTEN, C.B., F.R.S.,

Chemist and Assayer of the Royal Mint; Prof. of Metallurgy, Royal College of Science.

---

1. **INTRODUCTION TO THE STUDY OF METALLURGY.** By the EDITOR. THIRD EDITION. 12s. 6d.
2. **GOLD.** By T. K. ROSE, Assoc. R.S.M., D.Sc., Assistant-Assayer of the Royal Mint. 21s.
3. **IRON.** By THOS. TURNER, Assoc. R.S.M., F.I.C. 16s.
4. **STEEL.** By THOS. TURNER, Assoc. R.S.M., F.I.C.
5. **COPPER.** By THOS. GIBB, Assoc. R.S.M., F.I.C.
6. **METALLURGICAL MACHINERY.** By H. JENKINS, Wh.Sc., Assoc. R.S.M., Assoc. M.Inst C.E., of the Royal Mint.
7. **ALLOYS.** By the EDITOR.

⁎ Other Volumes in Preparation.

LONDON: CHARLES GRIFFIN & COMPANY, LTD., EXETER STREET, STRAND.

MINE-SURVEYING IN THE MIDDLE AGES.
(*Facsimile of a drawing in Agricola's de re Metallica*, 1556.)

A TREATISE

ON

MINE-SURVEYING.

BY

BENNETT H. BROUGH,

ASSOCIATE OF THE ROYAL SCHOOL OF MINES; FELLOW OF THE GEOLOGICAL SOCIETY AND OF THE INSTITUTE OF CHEMISTRY; MEMBER OF THE NORTH OF ENGLAND INSTITUTE OF MINING ENGINEERS AND OF THE MINING INSTITUTE OF CORNWALL; FORMERLY INSTRUCTOR IN MINE-SURVEYING AT THE ROYAL SCHOOL OF MINES.

FIFTH EDITION, REVISED.

With Numerous Diagrams.

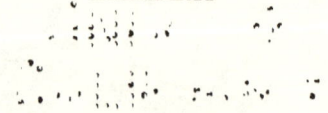

LONDON:
CHARLES GRIFFIN & COMPANY, LIMITED;
EXETER STREET, STRAND.
1896.

(All Rights Reserved.)

GIFT OF

DEAN FRANK H PROBERT.

PREFACE.

No apology is required for any well-considered attempt to provide a manual of Mine-Surveying for the use of English readers. The absence of any general work on the subject has long been a source of practical inconvenience alike to teachers and students. The text-books recommended to candidates for the examination in Mine-Surveying held by the City and Guilds of London Institute, namely, Budge's *Practical Miner's Guide*, published in 1825, and Hoskold's *Practical Treatise on Mining, Land, and Railway Surveying*, published in 1863, are too limited in their scope, the former dealing only with the mines of Cornwall, the latter only with those of the Forest of Dean; besides which both works are out of print, and increasingly difficult to procure.

The present work is intended primarily for students, and embodies the substance of the course of instruction in Mine-Surveying given at the Royal School of Mines. At the same time, it will also, it is hoped, be found useful as a companion to the standard works of reference on Land-Surveying.

In the plan of the book, the surveying of collieries and that of metalliferous mines do not receive separate treatment. The two have much in common, and the one may often advantageously borrow a method from the other. Few mine-surveyors in Great Britain appear to be acquainted with the methods and instruments used abroad. This is the more to be regretted, as no mine-surveys made in this country approach in accuracy those of the collieries of Pennsylvania, or those of the metalliferous mines of the Harz. Attention therefore has been directed to the recent improvements in foreign practice. With the exception of a few diagrams borrowed from Professor

Rankine's *Manual of Civil Engineering*, the figures elucidating the text have been specially drawn for this book.

The Appendix of examination-questions and exercises for plotting has been culled from recent papers set at the examinations of the Science and Art Department, of the City and Guilds of London Institute, of the local boards under the Home Office for granting certificates of competency to Colliery Managers, and of various Mining Schools. These will, it is trusted, be found of use to such students as have not the advantage of regular instruction in the subject. It must, however, be borne in mind that the mere reading of a text-book will never make a mine-surveyor. The most that a book can do is to help the student to obtain a knowledge of the theory of the subject. The mechanical manipulation of the instruments can only be learnt under the personal supervision of a teacher, whilst the technical skill requisite for carrying out subterranean surveys must be obtained in the mine itself.

I have taken for granted on the part of my readers an elementary knowledge of mathematics, such, for example, as would enable them to pass the second stage of the Science and Art Department's examination in that subject.

In the preparation of the work, I have received valuable help from numerous friends at home and abroad. In particular, I am indebted to Mr. H. W. Hughes, Assoc. R.S.M., F.G.S., for several important additions to the text, and to Mr. A. Pringle, M.A., B.Sc., who ably assisted me while the volume was passing through the press.

BENNETT H. BROUGH.

THE ROYAL SCHOOL OF MINES,
LONDON, *February, 1888.*

NOTE TO THE FOURTH EDITION.

This Edition has been thoroughly revised. Descriptions of appliances invented since the publication of the Third Edition in May, 1891, have been inserted, and references to some important recent papers are given. The additions cover twenty-four pages of text. Among them will be found notices of the methods of surveying in South Africa, and of making the preliminary surveys for wire ropeways and for hydraulic mining ditches. A few diagrams have also been added.

January, 1894.

NOTE TO THE FIFTH EDITION.

The Fifth Edition has been carefully revised, and much important matter has been added. References to some papers published since the last edition, and recent examination questions, have been inserted. A chapter has been added describing methods of Surveying by the aid of Photography, methods that are well adapted for such topographical surveys as mining engineers are sometimes called upon to execute. Reference is also made to the mine-surveying clauses of the recent Gold law of the Transvaal, and considerable additions have been made to the chapter on the Variation of the Magnetic-Needle.

December, 1895.

CONTENTS.

CHAPTER I.
GENERAL EXPLANATIONS.

	PAGE
Surveying,	1
Historical sketch,	1
Importance of mine-surveying,	3
Mineral deposits,	5
Mining terms,	6
Measures of length,	7
Angular measures,	8
Trigonometrical formulæ,	9

CHAPTER II.
THE MEASUREMENT OF DISTANCES.

Methods of measuring,	11
(a.) The chain,	11
Chaining on slopes,	13
Offsets,	15
Obstacles to measurement,	16
Surveying with the chain only,	18
Chain used in trigonometrical surveys,	20
(b.) Rods,	21
(c.) Steel bands,	22
(d.) Measuring wheel,	23
(e.) Pacing,	23
Accuracy of linear measurements,	24

CHAPTER III.
THE MINER'S DIAL.

Directive action of the earth's magnetism,	26
Historical sketch,	26

	PAGE
Description of the miner's dial,	28
(a.) The magnetic-needle,	29
(b.) Spirit-levels,	30
(c.) The tripod,	31
(1.) Taking underground observations with the dial,	31
Taking vertical angles,	33
Keeping the dialling-book,	34
(2.) Surface-surveys with the miner's dial,	36
(3.) Colliery-surveys with the miner's dial,	38

CHAPTER IV.

THE VARIATION OF THE MAGNETIC-NEEDLE.

Definitions,	40
(a.) Secular variations,	40
(b.) Diurnal variation,	42
Irregular variations,	44
Determination of the true meridian,	44
1. Method of shadows,	44
2. Method of corresponding altitudes,	46
3. Determination of the meridian by means of the Pole star,	48
4. Determination of the meridian by means of a map,	49
Setting out the meridian line,	49
Inclination of the magnetic-needle,	50

CHAPTER V.

SURVEYING WITH THE MAGNETIC-NEEDLE IN THE PRESENCE OF IRON.

Influence of iron rails,	52
Local attraction in the mine,	53
Surveying with the dial in the presence of iron,	54
Dialling-book,	54
Errors in compass surveys,	57

CHAPTER VI.

SURVEYING WITH THE FIXED NEEDLE.

Vernier,	59
Racking,	60

CONTENTS. xi

	PAGE
Various forms of dial,	61
(a.) Lean's miner's dial,	61
(b.) The Henderson dial,	62
(c.) Davis's miner's dial,	63
Dial-joint,	64
(d.) Whitelaw's dial,	65
(e.) Thornton's dial,	66
Traversing underground,	67
Surveying in inclined shafts,	75
The vernier compass,	75

CHAPTER VII.

THE GERMAN DIAL.

Invention of the German dial,	78
Measuring station-lines,	78
The clinometer,	79
Use of the clinometer,	80
The hanging-compass,	81
Surveying with the German dial,	81
Plotting the survey,	83
Surveying with the hanging-compass in the presence of iron,	85
Use of the German dial,	85

CHAPTER VIII.

THE THEODOLITE.

Historical sketch,	87
Description of the theodolite,	87
The telescope,	90
Various forms.—(a.) Hoskold's transit-theodolite,	91
(b.) The Everest theodolite,	91
(c.) The Hoffman tripod head,	93
(d.) American theodolites,	95
(e.) Traveller's transit-theodolite,	97
Adjustments of the theodolite,	98
Measuring horizontal angles,	100
Repetition,	101
Measurement of vertical angles,	102
The solar attachment,	103

CHAPTER IX.

Traversing Underground.

	PAGE
Use of the theodolite in the mine,	107
Comparison of the theodolite and compass,	118

CHAPTER X.

Surface-Surveys with the Theodolite.

Triangulation,	120
Computing the sides of the triangles,	123
Interior detail of the triangulation,	126
American mining claims,	127
Surveying in South Africa,	132

CHAPTER XI.

Plotting the Survey.

Scales,	134
1. Simply divided scales,	134
2. Diagonal scales,	135
3. Vernier scales,	136
Plotting scales,	137
Plotting with a protractor,	138
Plotting by means of chords,	139
Plotting by rectangular co-ordinates,	140
Calculating scales,	148
Traverse tables,	149
Combined surveying and plotting instrument,	149
Plotting colliery surveys in Scotland,	150
Calculating the co-ordinates of a triangulation,	151

CHAPTER XII.

Calculation of Areas.

Measures of area,	154
Methods of calculating areas,	154
1. Method of triangles,	154
2. Method of ordinates,	156
3. Mechanical method,	158

	PAGE
Produce of coal seams,	160
The calculation of ore-reserves,	161

CHAPTER XIII.

LEVELLING.

Definitions and principles,	164
The mason's level and boning staves,	164
The spirit-level,	165
(a.) The dumpy level,	165
(b.) The Y-level,	166
(c.) The Troughton level,	166
The adjustments of the level,	166
(d.) Cushing's reversible level,	167
The levelling-staff,	167
Mine levelling-staves,	169
Practice of levelling,	171
Section levelling,	175
Bench marks,	180
(e.) The reflecting level,	183
Sources of error in spirit-levelling,	183
Accuracy attainable in spirit-levelling,	183
Plotting sections,	184
(f.) The water-level,	185
Trigonometrical levelling,	187
The clinometer,	190
Physical levelling,	191
Determination of the depth of shafts,	193
Contour lines,	196
Applications of levelling,	197

CHAPTER XIV.

CONNECTION OF THE UNDERGROUND- AND SURFACE-SURVEYS.

Methods employed,	201
1. By means of an adit level,	201
2. By means of two shafts,	201
3. By means of one shaft,	205
4. By means of a transit-instrument,	208
4a. The Severn tunnel method,	210
5. By means of a transit-theodolite,	210
6. By means of the magnetic-needle,	213

CHAPTER XV.

MEASURING DISTANCES BY TELESCOPE.

	PAGE
Theory of telescopic measurement,	217
Calculations,	222
The protractor,	222
The tacheometer,	223
The staves,	223
The field-work,	223
The topographical stadia,	225
The theodolite and stadia,	226
Telescopic measurements in mine-surveys,	228

CHAPTER XVI.

SETTING-OUT.

Ranging straight lines,	230
Plotting the underground traverse on the surface,	231
Setting-out railways to mines,	231
Ranging curves,	231
Cross-sections,	235
Driving levels underground,	235
Curves for engine planes,	237
Setting-out tunnels,	237

CHAPTER XVII.

MINE-SURVEYING PROBLEMS.

Determination of the direction and inclination of a mineral deposit,	246
Determination of a point at the surface directly above one underground,	250
Holing from one excavation to another,	252
Sinking shafts from several levels,	256
The cubical content of a mine-reservoir,	257
Determination of the strike and dip of the line of intersection of two veins,	258

	PAGE
The search for dislocated lodes,	261
Irregularities of seams and beds,	263
Subsidence and draw caused by working coal,	265

CHAPTER XVIII.

MINE PLANS.

Plan and section,	270
(a.) Metalliferous mines,	270
(b.) Colliery plans,	273
Surface plans,	274
(c.) American colliery plans,	275
Importance of correct sections,	276
Uniformity of scale and conventional signs,	277
Preservation of plans,	278
Practical hints for constructing mine plans,	279
Copying plans,	282
(1.) Copying by tracing,	282
(2.) Copying on tracing paper,	282
(3.) Pricking through,	282
(4.) Copying by photography,	282
Reducing and enlarging plans,	283
Isometric plans of mines,	284
Relief plans and mine models,	286

CHAPTER XIX.

APPLICATIONS OF THE MAGNETIC-NEEDLE IN MINING.

Exploring for iron ore,	289
(1.) Brooks' method,	293
(2.) Thalén's method,	294
(3.) Tiberg's method,	297
Use of the magnetic-needle in surveying bore-holes,	300
Employment of a powerful magnet in cases of uncertain holing,	303

CHAPTER XX.

PHOTOGRAPHIC SURVEYING.

	PAGE
Photogrammetry,	307
Instruments used,	308
Application to mining work,	310
Advantages of photogrammetry,	314

APPENDIX I.

Examination questions,	315

APPENDIX II.

Bibliography,	327
INDEX,	329

A TREATISE

ON

MINE-SURVEYING.

CHAPTER I.

General Explanations.

Surveying is the art of making such measurements as are necessary to determine the relative positions of any points on the earth's surface. From such measurements a map, or plan, of any portion of the surface may be drawn, and its area calculated. All surveys are conducted upon nearly the same principles, the difference consisting in the style of instruments used in the work, and the amount of attention bestowed on the various details.

The branch of surveying specially applied to mining is known as Mine-surveying or, locally, as "*dialling*" or "*latching*." It consists in measuring, with a view to subsequent delineation on a plan and sections, first, the underground workings of a mine, and, secondly, the mine-buildings at the surface and the mine-concession or royalty. Thirdly, it requires an accurate method of connecting the underground- and surface-surveys. Trustworthy plans and sections are of value for giving a condensed view of all the facts connected with the works and explorations of a mine; for affording data to assist in the further prosecution of workings after temporary abandonment of the excavations; and for the avoiding of destructive and lamentable effects—such, *e.g.*, as disastrous litigation respecting trespass on adjoining royalties, loss caused by driving in the wrong direction, or irruptions of water, quicksand, or firedamp, giving rise to loss of life and property—which have too often resulted from incorrect or imperfect mine-plans.

Historical Sketch.—The origin of mine-surveying must be sought with that of mining in very early times. The oldest mine-plan known is a papyrus, preserved in the museum at

MINE-SURVEYING.

Turin, depicting the workings of an Egyptian gold-mine. It was drawn in the reign of the king Mineptah, 1,400 years before the Christian era. Land-surveying was first practised in Egypt. There the annual overflows of the Nile, and the consequent deposit of mud, destroyed the land-marks of the different proprietors, so that it became necessary to determine them by measurement every year. The oldest evidence of the solution of mathematical problems is afforded by a papyrus in the British Museum, which is believed to have been copied, 1,700 years B.C., from a much older work. It gives rules for the calculation of areas of triangles, trapezoids, and circles.

That the important mines of the ancient Greeks necessitated the solution of mine-surveying problems is shown by the fact that such problems are fully discussed by Hero of Alexandria (B.C. 285-222), several of whose works are extant. The greatest advance in survey practice made by Hero was his invention of the *diopter*, a sighting instrument for surveying purposes. The oldest instrument for measuring angles, like the cross-head which is still in use, only permitted right angles to be set out. This primitive instrument consisted of two straight-edges fastened together at right angles, a pointed vertical staff being fixed to the point of intersection. The two straight-edges were provided at each extremity with sight vanes, from which plumb-lines were suspended so as to enable the instrument to be levelled. With Hero's improved instrument, any angle could be measured. Indeed, it must be regarded as the origin of the highly perfect theodolite of the present day. It consisted essentially of a beam resting between two uprights on a pillar-like stand. The beam was movable in both directions by means of spiral screws acting on horizontal and vertical cog-wheels. It was hollowed out, and contained a metal tube, at right angles to which were glass cylinders at each end of the beam. The cylinders had special covers made of metal plate, which could be raised or lowered by means of screws. They were furnished with vertical and horizontal slits for sighting. The instrument was thus a combined theodolite and level. Two staves with sliding circular vanes were used in conjunction with it.

From the beginning of the Christian era until the Middle Ages, mining records are wanting. An ancient charter relative to the mines of the Mendip Hills is in existence. Of this Mr. Robert Hunt gives a fac-simile in his *British Mining*. It dates from the reign of Edward IV., about 1480. It is a rude attempt at plan-drawing, representing the "Myne deeps," as they were then called.

The first writer who treated mining systematically, Georgius

Agricola, in his work *De re Metallica*, published in 1556, devotes an entire section (Book V.) to mine-surveying. He states, as has been frequently repeated since, that the ancient mine-surveyors strenuously endeavoured to keep their art a secret. In the Middle Ages they were in consequence superstitiously regarded as sorcerers. The divining-rod was closely associated with the practice of their profession, and in many cases that hazel-twig was trusted more implicitly than the most scientific surveying operation.

In 1686 appeared the first treatise on mine-surveying, the *Geometria Subterranea* of Nicolaus Voigtel. This was followed by the treatises of J. F. Weidler, 1726 (in Latin); and of H. Beyer, 1749, and von Oppel, 1749 (in German). These works, by advocating the plotting of mine-surveys by means of rectangular co-ordinates, lifted mine-surveying to a higher plane.

In Great Britain, instructions for making mine-surveys were published by Thomas Houghton in 1681 for the Derbyshire miners, by William Pryce in 1778 for the Cornish miners, and by Thomas Fenwick in 1804 for the Newcastle colliers.

Importance of Mine-Surveying.—When the enormous value of mineral resources is considered, the high importance, from a commercial point of view, of the art of mining is apparent. In the United Kingdom alone, the annual value of minerals raised has approached £80,000,000, the result of the labours of some 500,000 persons directly employed in their extraction. It thus becomes a matter of the utmost importance that the extent and character of the mineral deposits should be made known. This can only be effected by careful and accurate surveys.

Mine-surveying, unfortunately, has not kept pace with the advances made in other branches of surveying; for it is to be regretted that, in many cases, mine-surveys are still made with instruments which have long been set aside as too inaccurate for surveys aboveground, although the latter rarely present such serious difficulties as are encountered underground. This is, in part, due to the conservatism of miners, a conservatism which has frequently led them to regard with contempt every kind of knowledge except that learned underground. It is a fact, as Mr. R. Hunt points out, that the untrained mind, as a rule, treasures every truth as a mystery to be carefully guarded for individual use only. Experience has often stored an individual mind with valuable facts, which are rarely recorded. The miner trusts to his memory, and, when he dies, the results of his experience die with him. The son has to begin where the father began, and this is repeated from generation to generation, so that there has been no advance. These remarks apply more particularly to the miners of the county of Cornwall, where the mining proverb, "Where it is, there it is," still holds its own.

Happily, a better system is beginning to prevail. Coal-mining is now carried on with a high degree of skill. Colliery managers, who formerly were generally ignorant of the theoretical principles upon which practice is based, are now submitted to a severe educational test before a certificate of competency is granted. It is, however, to be regretted that a similar examination has not been instituted for the agents of metalliferous mines. The mining schools which have been founded in various districts offer suitable opportunities for the necessary theoretical training, as also do the local classes held under the Science and Art Department, and under the City and Guilds of London Technical Institution.

Another cause which has retarded the progress of mine-surveying is the uncertain and speculative nature of mining. Casual failures, caused by the want of easily accessible information, frequently lead to the abandonment of highly promising mines. Mining, though speculative, is not entirely the work of chance; and he who, avoiding vague and unsatisfactory speculations, constantly stores up facts, and can grasp the extent and object of mining works, is frequently enabled to avoid expenses and difficulties, in which those who are without such data would soon be involved.

In this connection, Sir Warington Smyth, in a lecture on mining, says: "At the present time, few large collieries or metalliferous mines are conducted without the aid of a satisfactory plan, but there are very numerous mines in which this department is much neglected. Moreover, there is generally a want of uniformity in system, an absence of details which should give all the information that can be laid down on paper, a deficiency of surface-objects by which the workings can at a future day be referred to their proper position, and (what may sometimes lead to the most fatal errors) a neglect of observation or notice of the variation of the magnetic-needle, according to which mining plans are almost invariably constructed. It is too often the case when mines are worked by companies, that the shareholders are so regardless of what does not, as they conceive, lead to immediate gain, that they grudge the moderate sums needful for the employment of properly qualified surveyors, and either wink at the total neglect of plans, or leave them to be carried out by men already sufficiently tasked or incapable, although they may dial with accuracy, of representing on paper what they have measured."

As an example of an error involving great loss, serious danger, and future grave embarrassments, it may be mentioned that, according to Mr. P. W. Stuart-Menteath, at an important mine in Spain an incorrect survey caused an error of 65 metres to be made in driving a main tunnel less than 200 metres in length. In collieries, too, examples are not wanting. Thus, in 1875, at a small colliery in Nottingham there was an accident owing to some old workings. Trusting the old plans, which showed a barrier 100 yards away, the men worked into the old headings with disastrous results. Another case is recorded by Mr. J. Dickinson in 1878, when an inundation occurred by which two lives were lost, from a former working being cut into without any bore holes in advance. In this instance, there was a correct plan of the former work, but by a mistake of the surveyor, a wrong direction was set out.

Mineral Deposits.—For practical purposes mineral deposits may be divided into *tabular deposits*, including mineral veins, beds, and seams, and *irregular deposits*, including masses, stockworks, and pockets. Tabular deposits are those in which two dimensions predominate. The third smaller dimension, the perpendicular distance between the two bounding planes, is termed the thickness. The adjacent rock on both sides of these two planes is termed the *country*, the portion on which the deposit lies is the *foot-wall*, and that covering the deposit is the *hanging-wall*. With beds and seams, these are known as the *floor* and *roof* respectively. The *strike* or *course* of a deposit is the angle formed with the meridian by the direction of a horizontal line drawn in the middle plane. Its *dip* is the inclination downwards measured in degrees from the horizontal. As the dip of veins is usually great, it is sometimes measured from the vertical, and is then termed *underlie* or *hade*. The portion of a mineral deposit occurring at the surface is known as the *outcrop, basset*, or (U.S.) *apex*.

Mineral veins or lodes are defined by Dr. C. Le Neve Foster as tabular deposits of mineral, which have been formed subsequently to the rocks by which they are surrounded. Usually, they occupy fissures in the earth, frequently cutting across the planes of stratification of the rocks. They may occur in eruptive or in sedimentary rocks. Their contents vary, some parts containing worthless vein-matter or *gangue*, others being filled with ore. The productive portions are termed shoots or courses of ore, bunches, or ore-bodies. Cross courses are veins coursing nearly at right angles to the chief lodes of any particular mining district.

The characteristic feature of beds and seams is, that they are members of a series of stratified rocks. They may be interstratified deposits, or superficial ones, such as peat, bog iron ore, gold placers, and tin stream-works. In the former case, they are younger than the floor, and older than the roof. As stratified deposits, they were originally deposited in a more or less horizontal form, and follow all the contortions of their country rock. The minerals occurring in bedded deposits are coal, anthracite, lignite, iron ore, cupriferous-shale, lead-bearing sandstone, gravels containing diamonds, or gold, or tin, sulphur, salt, clays, limestone, gypsum, oil-shale, alum-shale, and slate. Miners often erroneously speak of "veins" of coal or ironstone; these, geologically, are true "beds" or seams.

"Masses" are deposits of mineral of irregular shape, which cannot be recognised as beds or as veins. Such, for instance, are the red hæmatite deposits of Ulverston, the brown hæmatite of the Forest of Dean, the iron ore deposits of Missouri, the iron mountains of Gellivara and Taberg in Sweden, and the pipes of diamond-bearing rock in South Africa. They may be filled-in cavities or metamorphic deposits, such as the zinc ore deposit of Altenberg, which is 260 yards long and 65 yards broad and deep. When the whole rock is permeated with mineral matter, accumulated in minute veins, the deposit is termed a *stockwork*. Examples of such deposits occur at Carclaze and other places in Cornwall, and at Altenberg in Saxony.

No classification of mineral deposits can be quite satisfactory in all cases. A bed, for instance, even of coal may be so folded and contorted as to lose its original tabular form, and to assume the shape of an irregular mass.

Mining Terms.—Many local as well as technical terms are used in mining. The following are definitions of some of the objects most frequently named on mine-plans:—A *shaft* is a pit sunk down from the surface. In the mining of stratified deposits, the shafts sunk are usually perpendicular. In vein-mining, they may be sunk perpendicularly to cut the vein, or they may follow its underlie. *Levels* are horizontal excavations along the course of a vein, or horizontal passages, by which access is gained to the workings of the mine. A level driven from the surface, to draw off the water, is termed an *adit level*, or (U.S.) a *tunnel*. A drift or gallery driven across the usual direction of the veins generally for the purpose of searching for a new vein, or of connecting two known veins, is termed a *cross-cut*. The extreme end of any level or cross-cut is called the *forebreast* or end. A *stope* is the working from which the ore is extracted. Above a level, the working is an "overhand" or back stope; an "underhand" stope is the working downwards from the floor of the level. A *winze* is a shaft which connects two or more levels, but does not come to the surface. A *rise* is an upright winze commenced from a level; a *sump* is a winze worked downwards. Surface workings include open cuts, pits, and excavations of limited extent. A tract of land let for mining purposes is known as a *sett, royalty, concession,* or *claim.*

In coal-mining, the pair of galleries driven from the shaft are variously known as *drifts, headings, levels, way-gates, gate-roads,* and *rolley-ways.* The winning of the coal is effected in different ways, following a variety of modifications between the two extremes, namely, the "*post and stall*" system, otherwise known as the "*bord and pillar,*" or in Scotland as "*stoup and room,*" and the "*long-wall*" system. In the former a given district is at first worked by narrow excavations, so that no considerable fall from above shall take place; in the latter, the whole of the available mineral is removed in successive slices, and the roof allowed to fall in.

Measures of Length.—The standard measure of length in the United Kingdom is the *yard.* In addition to the yard, the following units of length are used for surveying purposes:—

The *inch,* one thirty-sixth part of the standard yard. The *foot,* one-third part of the standard yard. The *fathom* of 6 feet or 2 yards. The *chain* of 66 feet or 22 yards; divided into 4 *poles* of 5½ yards, and 100 *links* of 7·92 inches. The *statute mile* of 1,760 yards or 5,280 feet or 80 chains, divided into 8 *furlongs.*

The standard yard is the distance between two fixed points on a certain metal rod at the temperature of 62° F., and under the mean atmospheric pressure. The British and United States standards are identical.

To obviate the inconveniences of the innumerable units of length used in different countries, attempts were made towards the middle of the 17th century to introduce a natural unit, which could at any time be again determined if the standard should be lost. Two proposals were considered; one being based on the length of a pendulum vibrating seconds, the other on the magnitude of the circumference of the earth. The former suggestion was due to Huygens, who proposed to divide the length of a pendulum vibrating seconds into three parts, and to term each part a foot. This method was found impracticable, since the length of the seconds-pendulum varies with the latitude at different places; thus, at London it is 39·1393 inches, whilst at New York it is 39·1017 inches.

The second plan was therefore adopted—that is, a fraction of the earth's meridian was taken as the standard. For this purpose, at the time of the French Revolution, the distance from Dunkirk to Barcelona was determined. Both these places are in the same meridian as Paris. The measurement was subsequently extended to the Island of Formentera, and, from the length determined, the distance of the pole from the equator was calculated to be 5130740·74 French fathoms (toises). The tenmillionth part of this length (0·513074 toise) was termed the *metre*, and was adopted as the French unit of length. In 1799, two similar rods of platinum were constructed as standards, having that length at 0° centigrade. The given length of the metre being thus determined, it ceased to be a natural measure. With the present improvements in measuring-instruments, it is possible for us to determine the circumference of the earth with greater accuracy, whilst the length of the metre is fixed. Indeed, it is now known that the metre was determined a not inconsiderable fraction too small.

The French measures of length are multiples and submultiples of the metre. The value of the latter in British measure is 3·2808693 feet, or 39·37043 inches. For mine-surveys the metre is the unit now almost exclusively used in continental European countries. It is also employed on Government surveys in the United States.

Special units of length used for mining purposes in various countries are the following:—

	British Fathom.	Feet.
Fathom,	1·000	6·000
Metre,	0·546	3·280
Swedish Famn,	0·973	5·844
Russian Sashon,	1·166	7·000
Austrian Klafter,	1·037	6·222
Bavarian Lachter,	1·062	6·372
Württemberg Lachter,	1·096	6·576
Hanoverian Lachter,	1·050	6·300
Saxon Lachter,	1·093	6·558
Prussian Lachter,	1·144	6·864
Spanish Vara,	0·463	2·782
French Toise,	1·065	6·394

Angular Measures.—The circumference of a circle is divided into 360 parts; each part being termed a "degree." The degree is divided into 60 minutes, and the minute into 60 seconds. This is known as the sexagesimal division.

The French centesimal division of the quadrant into 100 degrees, instead of 90 degrees, is rarely used except for surveys with the tacheometer. Each centesimal degree is divided into 100 minutes, each of 100 seconds.

GENERAL EXPLANATIONS.

Trigonometrical Formulæ.—The following is a summary of the principal trigonometrical formulæ used in surveying:—

The trigonometrical functions of a given angle may be defined as the ratios to each other of the sides of a right-angled triangle possessing the given angle. Assuming that A, B, C represent the three angles of a right-angled triangle, C being the right angle, and that a, b, c represent the sides respectively opposite to these angles, c being the hypothenuse; then the trigonometrical functions of the angle A are—

$$\sin A = \frac{a}{c}\,; \quad \operatorname{cosec} A = \frac{c}{a}$$

$$\cos A = \frac{b}{c}\,; \quad \sec A = \frac{c}{b}$$

$$\tan A = \frac{a}{b}\,; \quad \operatorname{cotan} A = \frac{b}{a}$$

The following equations give the most important relations amongst the trigonometrical functions of the angle A:—

$$\sin A = \frac{1}{\operatorname{cosec} A} = \sqrt{1 - \cos^2 A} = \frac{\tan A}{\sec A}$$

$$\cos A = \frac{1}{\sec A} = \sqrt{1 - \sin^2 A} = \frac{\operatorname{cotan} A}{\operatorname{cosec} A}$$

$$\tan A = \frac{1}{\operatorname{cotan} A} = \sqrt{\sec^2 A - 1} = \frac{\sin A}{\cos A}$$

$$\operatorname{cosec} A = \frac{1}{\sin A} = \sqrt{1 + \operatorname{cotan}^2 A} = \frac{\sec A}{\tan A}$$

$$\sec A = \frac{1}{\cos A} = \sqrt{1 + \tan^2 A} = \frac{\operatorname{cosec} A}{\operatorname{cotan} A}$$

$$\operatorname{cotan} A = \frac{1}{\tan A} = \sqrt{\operatorname{cosec}^2 A - 1} = \frac{\cos A}{\sin A}$$

The complement of an angle is that angle which must be added to it to make a right angle, and

$$\sin (90° - A) = \cos A\,; \quad \operatorname{cosec} (90° - A) = \sec A$$
$$\cos (90° - A) = \sin A\,; \quad \sec (90° - A) = \operatorname{cosec} A$$
$$\tan (90° - A) = \operatorname{cotan} A\,; \quad \operatorname{cotan} (90° - A) = \tan A$$

The supplement of an angle is that angle which must be added to it to make two right angles. Compared with the trigonometrical functions of the angle A, those of its supplement are—

$\sin (180° - A) = \sin A$; $\operatorname{cosec} (180° - A) = \operatorname{cosec} A$

$\cos (180° - A) = - \cos A$; $\sec (180° - A) = - \sec A$

$\tan (180° - A) = - \tan A$; $\cotan (180° - A) = - \cotan A$

The formulæ for the solution of plane triangles are deduced from the principles that the sum of the three angles of a plane triangle is equal to two right angles, and that the sides of the triangle are proportional to the sines of the opposite angles. For right-angled triangles the most useful formulæ are—

$$b = a \sin B \qquad c = a \cos B$$
$$b = c \tan B \qquad c = b \tan C$$
$$b = c \cotan C \qquad c = b \cotan B$$

For oblique-angled-triangles, the most useful formulæ are—

$$b = \frac{a \sin B}{\sin A} \qquad c = \frac{a \sin C}{\sin A}$$

$$\cos A = \frac{b^2 + c^2 - a^2}{2bc}.$$

CHAPTER II.

The Measurement of Distances.

Methods of Measuring.—The straight lines which have to be measured by the mine-surveyor may be horizontal, vertical, or inclined. The measurement of horizontal lines is of the most frequent occurrence. When a line inclined towards the horizon has to be measured, the operation is, as a rule, performed with the object of determining the horizontal and vertical projections of the line. It is then necessary, in each case, to determine the angle of inclination formed by the measured line and the horizon.

Lines are usually measured with chains, tapes, or rods, divided into fathoms, yards, links, feet, or some other unit of measurement.

(*a.*) **The Chain.**—The instrument most frequently used in surveying is the chain. In coal-mines and in field-surveying, Gunter's chain is employed. It is 66 feet in length; 80 chains being equal to 1 mile. This length was chosen by the inventor, Edmund Gunter, in 1620, with the object of facilitating the computation of areas; 10 square chains being equal to 1 acre. The chain is composed of 100 links of iron or steel wire, each bent at the end into a ring, and connected with the ring at the end of the next piece by means of three rings. The chain is thus prevented from becoming twisted or *kinked*. A couple of swivels are also inserted in the chain, so that it may turn round without twisting. Every tenth link is marked by a piece of brass with one, two, three, or four points, corresponding to the number of tens that the brass represents, counting from the nearest end of the chain. The middle, or fiftieth, link is marked by a brass circle. A swivel-handle is provided at each end of the chain. The wire used in the construction of iron chains is usually No. 8 W.G.; that used for steel chains is No. 12, or No. 8 W.G.

The hundredth part of the chain is called a *link*, and is equal to 0·66 foot or 7·92 inches. All calculations with chains and links can thus be easily performed by means of decimals. The following table will be found useful for converting chains into feet and feet into links :—

Chains into Feet.		Feet into Links.	
Chains.	Feet.	Feet.	Links.
0·01	0·66	1·00	1·515
0·02	1·32	2·00	3·030
0·03	1·98	3·00	4·545
0·04	2·64	4·00	6·060
0·05	3·30	5·00	7·575
0·06	3·96	6·00	9·090
0·07	4·62	7·00	10·606
0·08	5·28	8·00	12·121
0·09	5·94	9·00	13·636

For colliery use, the chain is sometimes made with ten links in brass at each end, in order to prevent the compass-needle being attracted.

It must be remembered that any error in the length of the chain will cause erroneous measurement throughout the entire survey. It should, therefore, be tested and adjusted before the commencement of every survey, or at any rate from time to time. This is best done by having a standard marked on a level pathway or on the top of a wall, showing not only the accurate length of the chain, but also the length of every ten links. Standard 66-feet and 100-feet chains have been fixed by the Government in Trafalgar Square and Guildhall, for the use of surveyors in London. For rough colliery surveys, the chain may be left half-an-inch longer than the true length, since it is rarely stretched perfectly horizontally, or drawn out into a perfectly straight line. If a line has been measured with an incorrect chain, the true length of the line may be found from the proportion:—As the length of the standard given by the incorrect chain is to the true length of the standard, so is the length of the line given by the measurement to its true length.

Accompanying the chain are ten *arrows* or iron pins, which are used in succession to mark the end of the chain in measuring a line. They are a foot long, and are made of stout iron wire sharpened at one end and bent into a ring at the other. A piece of red tape is usually attached to the rings to render the arrows visible from a distance. The chain is folded by taking it by the 50-link mark, and folding the two ends simultaneously, taking care so to cross the links that the body of the chain when folded may be smaller in the middle than at the ends. The chain is opened by taking both handles in one hand, and throwing the chain out with the other.

The chain is used by two persons, the *leader* and the *follower*. The former having been supplied with the ten arrows, stretches the chain in the required direction, while the follower holds one end of it at the starting-point. An arrow is then driven perpendicularly into the ground by the leader at the point where the chain ends. He then proceeds onward, drawing the chain after him, and repeats the same operation throughout the length of the line; the arrow last put down serving as the mark to which the follower has to bring his end of the chain. The arrows are taken up by the follower as he advances, until he has them all, when they are returned to the leader to be used over again. The arrows are thus changed from one to the other at every 10 chains' length; care being taken to note each change in the field-book. At the end of the line, the number of changes added to the number of arrows in the follower's hand, and to the number of links extending from the last arrow to the end of the line, gives the total length of the line measured. If the ground is so hard that an arrow cannot be driven in, the leader marks the ground and lays the arrow down. Eleven arrows are usually preferred. The eleventh is used to mark the end of the eleventh chain; another being substituted for it before the leader goes on. During the operation, the follower has to see that the chain is tight, straight, and unentangled, and to direct the leader so as to enable him to place the arrow in the ground exactly in the alignment.

In measuring lines in a colliery, the arrows are usually dispensed with; the end of each chain being marked with a piece of chalk.

The chain used in metalliferous mines is 10 fathoms or 60 feet in length, and is provided with brass marks at every fathom. Each link of the chain is 6 inches in length. The chain is sometimes made entirely of brass. No advantage is gained by using Gunter's chain in a metalliferous mine, since acreage has never to be calculated, and measurements have to be made with such precision that the inch is to be preferred to the link as a unit.

Chaining on Slopes.—In chaining up or down a slope, the distance must be reduced on the plan to the projection of that

14   MINE-SURVEYING.

distance on a horizontal plane. If the slope is gentle, the lower end of the chain may be raised until the chain is level. To

Angle. Degrees.	Slope.	Gunter's Chain. Correction in Links.	10-fathom Chain. Correction in Feet.	100-foot Chain. Correction in Feet.
3	1 in 19·08	0·14	0·08	0·14
4	1 in 14·30	0·24	0·14	0·24
5	1 in 11·43	0·38	0·22	0·38
6	1 in 9·51	0·54	0·32	0·54
7	1 in 8·14	0·74	0·44	0·74
8	1 in 7·11	0·97	0·58	0·97
9	1 in 6·31	1·23	0·73	1·23
10	1 in 5·67	1·52	0·91	1·52
11	1 in 5·14	1·83	1·09	1·83
12	1 in 4·70	2·18	1·30	2·18
13	1 in 4·33	2·56	1·53	2·56
14	1 in 4·01	2·97	1·79	2·97
15	1 in 3·73	3·40	2·04	3·40
16	1 in 3·48	3·87	2·32	3·87
17	1 in 3·27	4·37	2·62	4·37
18	1 in 3·07	4·89	2·93	4·89
19	1 in 2·90	5·44	3·26	5·44
20	1 in 2·74	6·03	3·61	6·03
25	1 in 2·14	9·37	5·62	9·37
30	1 in 1·73	13·39	8·03	13·39

The rate of slope (the ratio of the hypothenuse to the perpendicular) is the cosecant of the angle of inclination. The rate of inclination (the ratio of the base to the perpendicular) is the cotangent of the angle of inclination.

ensure the raised end being exactly above the right spot, the chain may be raised along a vertical staff, or an arrow may be carefully dropped, or, better still, a plumb-line may be employed. The process is called *stepping*, and, on steep ground, may be carried on by half-chains, or even shorter distances. A more accurate method is to measure the angle of the declivity. The cosine of this angle, multiplied by the measured hypothenuse, gives the length of the horizontal distance.

The most convenient method is by means of a *correction* to be deducted from each chain. This correction, being known, may be applied mechanically during the chaining by pulling the chain forward at each chain-length through a distance equal to the required correction.

The preceding table gives the correction for each chain measured on the slope.

In order to save calculation, many mining dials and theodolites have the correction for declivity marked on the graduated arc on which angles are measured.

Offsets are ordinates or transverse distances measured from known points on a station-line to objects the position of which is to be ascertained. Offsets, as a rule, are measured at right angles to the chain. The length of the offset having been determined, the position of the object is fixed with reference to the main line.

Offsets may be measured with an *offset rod*, 10 links in length, painted black and white in alternate lengths, or, preferably, with a *measuring-tape*. This is divided on one side into links and on the other into feet and inches. It should be tested frequently, particularly after use in a wet mine. It is not advisable to use offsets more than a chain in length. When the offset does not exceed this length, with practice the eye may be relied upon to give a right angle with precision. The *cross-staff* and *optical square*, recommended by some surveyors for erecting perpendicular lines, are rarely necessary in mine-surveying practice.

The *optical square* consists of two small mirrors placed in a brass box at an angle of 45°, thus reflecting an object through an angle of 90°. The unsilvered half of one mirror gives a direct view of the object, whilst the reflected and true object can be exactly superimposed in the observer's field of view when they are at right angles to each other. The *cross-staff* has two pairs of sights fixed at right angles to each other on the upper end of a staff having a spike at its lower end for fixing into the ground.

In taking offsets, the surveyor reads the tape at the chain.

16 MINE-SURVEYING.

The ring of the tape is held at the point to which the offset is required. The surveyor then turns the tape in a horizontal plane until he obtains the shortest measurement, and ascertains the link on the chain where the offset forms a right angle.

In cases where additional accuracy is required, *oblique offsets* may be used. From two points in the chain, offsets are measured obliquely to the object, and the triangle thus formed, when plotted, shows the accurate distance of the object from the station-line. When the object is the corner of a building, such as D in Fig. 1, it is convenient to make each of the offsets, if possible, lie in a straight line with a face of the building.

Obstacles to Measurement.—Obstacles sometimes occur in a long station-line, rendering it impossible to chain along the line with accuracy. In some cases it may even be impracticable to range the line directly across the obstacle. These difficulties may easily be obviated by the use of angular instruments. It is, however, possible to use the chain alone.

When the impassable obstacle can be seen over, a ranging pole is planted in the station-line at the further side D (Fig. 2) of the obstacle. At two marks, A and D (the nearer and further sides of the obstacle respectively), two lines, A B and D C, are ranged at right angles to the station-line. These perpendiculars are made equal to each other, and the distance B C is measured.

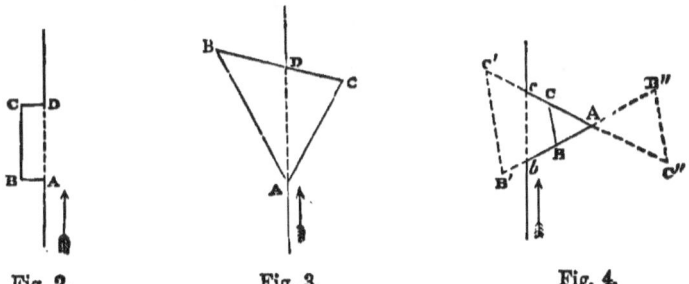

Fig. 2. Fig. 3. Fig. 4.

This measured distance will then be equal to the required distance, A D.

In order to erect a perpendicular to a line at a given point, Euclid's proposition (I., 47) may be applied in the following way :—Measure 40 links along the line, and let one end of the chain be held at that point, and and let the 80-link mark be held at the given point where the perpendicular is to be erected. Then take the 50-link mark, and tighten the chain, drawing equally on both portions of it. The 50-link mark will then give the perpendicular required. It is advisable to repeat the operation on the other side of the line, so as to test the accuracy of the result.

When the obstacle can be seen over, the length of the gap in the station-line may be determined by setting out a triangle A B C (Fig. 3) enclosing the obstacle. The triangle may be of any form or size, provided that B and C are in one straight line with D, and that the angles are not very obtuse nor very acute. The lengths A B, A C, B D, and D C are measured. Then the inaccessible distance will be found either by plotting the triangle and the point D in its base, or from the formula:—

$$AD = \sqrt{\left(\frac{AB^2 \cdot CD + AC^2 \cdot BD}{BC} - BD \cdot CD\right)}$$

The figure of the obstacle may be surveyed by offsets from the sides of a triangle. Let b and c, in Fig. 4, be points in the station-line on opposite sides of the obstacle. From a convenient station A, chain the lines A b, A c, being two sides of the triangle A $b c$. Connect these lines by a line BC to form the triangle A B C. Then the inaccessible distance is obtained from the following formula given by Rankine:—

$$bc = \sqrt{\left\{Ab^2 + Ac^2 - \frac{Ab \cdot Ac}{AB \cdot Ac} \cdot (AB^2 + AC^2 - BC^2)\right\}}$$

This formula will apply if the points B and C are taken in the prolongations of A c and A b beyond the station-line, as at B′ and C′, or in their prolongations beyond A, as at B″ and C″. The formula is greatly simplified if A B and A C are set off so as to be respectively proportional to A b and A c. Then the triangles A B C and A $b c$ are similar, B C is parallel to $b c$, and the inaccessible distance $b c$ is equal to $BC \cdot \frac{Ab}{AB}$.

When the obstacle can be chained round, but not chained across nor seen over, the inaccessible distance may be determined by means of parallel lines. Thus in Fig. 5, from A and B two points in the station-line on the nearer side of the obstacle, set off the equal perpendiculars A C, B D, of length sufficient to enable a straight line to be ranged parallel to the station-line, and to be chained past the obstacle. Commence the chaining of this line at D, in continuation of that of the station-line at B. As soon as the obstacle is passed, set off the perpendicular E G equal to A C and to B D. Then G will be a point in the station-line beyond the obstacle, and the inaccessible distance B G will be equal to D E. By repeating the process, an additional point H in the station-line may be found.

The problem may also be solved by means of similar triangles. At A (Fig. 6) two diverging lines A F and A E are ranged past the two sides of the obstacle. In these lines, measure the distances A D and A C of two points D and C, which lie in one straight line with B. Continue the chaining of A F and A E, and make those distances respectively proportional to A D and A C. Measure D C, noting the position of B, and measure E F, in which line take the point G, dividing E F in the ratio in which B divides C D. Then G will be a point in the station-line beyond the obstacle. Other points may be found in a similar manner. The inaccessible distance is equal to $\dfrac{A B \cdot C E}{A C}$.

When the obstacle can be seen over, but neither chained across, nor chained round, as in the case of a station-line interrupted by a river or ravine, a pole must be ranged and fixed at D (Fig. 7) in the station-line beyond the obstacle. B D being the inaccessible distance, at B set out B C perpendicular to the station-line. At C range C A perpendicular to C D, cutting the station-line at A. Measure A B, B C; then B D is equal to $B C^2 \div A B$.

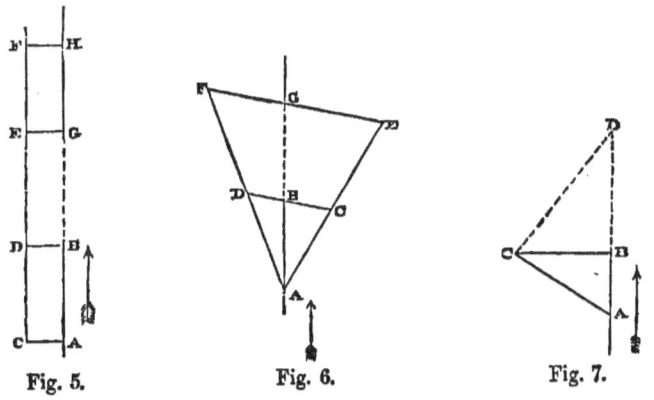

Fig. 5.　　　　Fig. 6.　　　　Fig. 7.

Surveying with the Chain only.—In this method of surveying, the surface is to be divided into a series of imaginary triangles;

the triangle being the only plane figure of which the form cannot be altered, if the sides remain constant. The triangles should be as large as the nature of the ground will allow, and as nearly equilateral as possible. The sides of these triangles are first measured, and a straight line is measured from one of the angles to a point in the middle of the opposite side. This fourth line is called a *tie-line* or proof-line, and is an efficient means of detecting errors. Within the larger triangles, as many smaller triangles and tie-lines are measured as may be required for determining the position of all the objects included in the survey. The directions of the lines forming the sides of these secondary triangles are so placed that the offsets to be measured from them may be as short and as few in number as practicable. Pickets are placed in the ground at each angle of the triangles, the general form and position of which are noted for reference in a hand-sketch, distinctive letters being written at each point of intersection. The points of intersection of all straight lines, as well as the angles of the triangles, are always points measured to or from. They are called *stations*, and the lines connecting them *station-lines*. Secondary stations are best marked by *whites*, which are cleft sticks holding small pieces of white paper, on which a number may be pencilled.

In carrying out a survey with the chain only, it is necessary to attend to the following rules :—Walk two or three times over the ground in order to get a good idea of it, helping your memory with a rough sketch. The first line should be made as long as the place to be surveyed will allow, so that it may form a convenient base with which the other lines may be connected. Select a suitable station on each side of the *base-line* near the boundary of the work. To these stations, lines should be measured from each end of the base-line, thus forming two large triangles, one on each side of the base-line. On the sides of these triangles, smaller triangles must be marked out, so as to cover all the ground to be surveyed.

The rough sketch is usually made in the *field-book*—a book in which every step of the operations gone through in the survey is to be carefully entered *at the time*. The field-book is ruled with a column down the centre of the page. In this are set down the distances on the station-line at which any offset is made, and on the right and left of the column are entered the offsets and observations made on those sides respectively of the station-line. The middle column represents the chain. It is, therefore, advisable to begin the entries at the bottom of the page; the chain and field-book being thus placed in the same position at the station-line with respect to the surveyor, who keeps his face directed towards the distant station. The crossing of fences, roads, or streams is to be shown by joining lines in a way similar to the form which they present on the ground.

The following example shows the manner in which the field-notes may be entered in the survey of a triangular piece of ground :—

From B	687	to D, tie-line
	862	to A
From D	⊙	
	956	to D
From C	⊙	
	1265	to C
	800	to B, point for tie-line
From A	⊙	

In booking, certain conventional signs are adopted for the remarks that occur frequently. The commencement of a station-line, for example, is represented by a small circle or a triangle, and its termination by a line drawn across the page. A station left in a line, to or from which another line is to be measured, is usually represented by its number enclosed in a circle. A turn to the right or left is indicated thus ⌈ , ⌉.

Proper attention in keeping the field-book saves much time in plotting, and guards against errors likely to arise from reference to confused notes. In fact, notes ought to be kept so clearly that a draughtsman should be able to plot the survey without further instruction from the surveyor

In spite of its apparent want of accuracy, the method of surveying with the chain alone gives, in the hands of an accomplished surveyor, very satisfactory results. At the same time, though sometimes used for the surface-surveys of small collieries, it is not considered sufficiently accurate for surveys of metalliferous mine royalties.

Chain used in Trigonometrical Surveys.—Before compensating bars were invented, steel chains were employed for base-measurement in the Great Trigonometrical Survey of the

United Kingdom. In using the steel chain, a drawing-post and a weight-post were used; a 56-lb. weight being always applied to one end of the chain, whilst the other was fixed to the drawing-post. The chain was made to rest in deal coffers supported by trestles, in order to obtain a perfectly level surface, and thermometers were placed at different distances in order to ascertain the temperature of the chain, so that the base might be reduced to its value at a given temperature. The chain was 100 feet long, and consisted of 40 links, each ½ inch square.

(*b.*) Rods.—When very accurate measurements were required, deal rods were at one time largely used instead of the chain for measuring long lines. They were, however, soon discarded in exact operations, as experience showed that they were liable to sudden and irregular changes in length from dryness or humidity. Saturated with boiled oil, and afterwards covered with a thick coat of varnish, well-seasoned wooden rods will be found sufficiently exact for ordinary purposes. Such rods are usually made of lance wood, and are 5 feet in length. They must be placed in line very carefully end to end. They are rarely placed directly on the ground, which, as a rule, is too uneven. A horizontal line may be constructed along the base to be measured, by means of a stretched cord.

On the Trigonometrical Survey of the United Kingdom, glass rods were substituted for wood in the measurement of the Hounslow base in 1784. Their ends were protected with metal caps. The results obtained were perfectly satisfactory, measurements with the glass rods and a check measurement with a steel chain of perfect workmanship, giving results that differed by little more than half an inch in the base-line of 27,404 feet. Steel rods also have been found useful for geodetic measurements.

For the measurement of the Loch Foyle base, an apparatus was devised by Colonel Colby. In this he obtained an unalterable linear measure by using compensating expansions. Two bars, one of iron, the other of brass, 10 feet long, were placed parallel to each other, and rivetted at the centre, it having been found by numerous experiments that they expanded or contracted in the proportion of 3 to 5. The brass bar was coated with some non-conducting substance, in order to equalise the susceptibility of the two metals to change of temperature. Across each end of these combined bars was fixed a tongue of iron, with a minute dot of platinum so situated on this tongue that, with every change of contraction or expansion, the dots at each end always remained at the constant distance of 10 feet.

On the Continent, rods 3 to 4 yards in length are employed,

terminated by two points, and provided in the middle with a builder's level and a handle. This apparatus is known as the *field-compasses*, and is often used for filling in the details of a survey.

(c.) **Steel Bands.**—The most suitable instrument for measuring lengths in mine-surveys is the steel band. It is more convenient and less liable to inaccuracy than the chain. It is usually 100 feet, or 100 links, in length, with feet etched on one side and links on the other. It is provided with a handle at each end, and is wound on a steel or wooden cross. It is employed in precisely the same way as the chain. Like that instrument, it presents the advantage of rapidity; but it has the additional advantage of representing a length of which the variations are dependent only on the temperature, since it does not kink, stretch, nor wear so as to change its length.

In surveying the anthracite mines of Pennsylvania, Mr. E. B. Coxe * uses a measuring-tape made of a ribbon of tempered steel, 0·08 inch broad and 0·015 inch thick. It is 500 feet long, and weighs 2 lbs. 7½ oz. At each tenth foot a small piece of brass wire is soldered across the tape, the white solder extending about an inch on each side of the wire. In the latter is filed a small notch which marks the exact spot where the tenth foot ends. The distances from the zero point of the tape are marked upon the solder by counter-sunk figures. The white solder enables the 10-feet notches to be found very easily, and the counter-sunk figures, being filled with dirt, stand out upon the white ground of solder. The tape is wound upon a simple wooden reel, 10 inches in diameter, which can be held in one hand and turned by the other. Two brass handles, which can be detached, accompany the tape, and are carried upon the reel.

The advantages of the tape are—(1) the greater facility in measuring up and down slopes, or along the face of the coal; (2) greater accuracy in measuring from one station to another, as the tape forms a straight line from one station to the other, and there is no error from the use of arrows; (3) the tape does not stretch appreciably. Its disadvantages are—(1) it is liable to break, unless carefully handled; (2) it is necessary to roll it up and unroll it again when the distances vary very much. The tape, however, can be easily mended when it breaks. For this purpose, a small sleeve of brass is made tinned inside, in which the broken ends of the tape are slipped and then soldered by heating the sleeve with a red-hot poker.

There are three sources of error in the use of the steel tape,

* *Trans. Amer. Inst. M.E.*, vol. ii., 1874, p. 219.

(1) the extension of the tape by stretching; (2) the shortening of the tape in consequence of its assuming the form of the catenary curve; and (3) the contraction or expansion due to change of temperature. The tape does not stretch to any appreciable extent, and any error thus caused is compensated by the shortening due to the formation of the catenary curve by the tape. The true distance indicated by a 500-foot steel tape, when subjected to the usual tension of 40 lbs., is calculated to be 499·9185 feet. With regard to the expansion caused by change of temperature, a tape measuring 500 feet in length at 32°F. becomes 500·6 feet in length at 212°, so that a variation of 60° causes a variation of only two-tenths of a foot in a 500-foot tape.

The steel band is to be recommended for all important work in mine-surveying, whilst the chain should be used for filling in details, and where extreme accuracy is unnecessary.

(d.) **Measuring-Wheel.**—The viameter, or measuring-wheel, is sometimes used for measuring station-lines. The wheel is rolled over the ground to be measured, and its motion is communicated to a series of toothed wheels so proportioned that the index-wheel registers their revolutions, and records the whole distance passed over. On very even ground the results are fairly satisfactory.

(e.) **Pacing.**—A line may be measured by pacing, with tolerable accuracy. This method consequently is frequently employed on explorations, preliminary surveys, and in levelling with the aneroid barometer. In order to obtain accurate results, the surveyor must accustom himself to an accurate pace. This may be done by pacing a distance of 200 to 300 yards repeatedly, until the same number of paces is always obtained. An instrument, called a *passometer*, made in the form of a watch may be conveniently used for registering the number of paces, thus precluding the absorbing attention required for accurately counting a considerable number of paces. The distance may be registered direct by a similar instrument, the *pedometer*, which can be adjusted with facility to long or short steps.

The usual step is the military pace of 30 inches, 108 of these paces per minute representing a velocity of 3·07 miles an hour. If no unfavourable conditions come into play, for example, slope of the station-line or fatigue, a distance may be determined by pacing accurately to within 2 per cent. The pace of the surveyor should be re-measured from time to time, since after the age of 25 to 30 years, the length of the pace diminishes considerably with increasing age.

On slopes, the pace is always shorter than on level ground. Professor W. Jordan gives the following averages:—

Rise.	Pace.	Fall	Pace.
	Inches.		Inches.
0°	30·3	0°	30·3
5°	27·5	5°	29·1
10°	24·4	10°	28·3
15°	22·0	15°	27·5
20°	19·7	20°	26·3
25°	17·7	25°	23·6
30°	15·0	30°	19·7

The relation between the height of the individual and the length of his pace, may be seen from the following averages:—

Height.		Pace.	Height.		Pace.
Feet.	Inches.	Inches.	Feet.	Inches.	Inches.
5	0	29·5	5	8	31·5
5	2	30·3	5	10	32·2
5	4	30·7	6	0	32·6
5	6	31·1	6	2	33·0

Accuracy of Linear Measurements.—Professor F. Lorber, of the Leoben School of Mines, has made a careful study of the accuracy of linear measurements. From 6,000 measurements, he deduces the following table showing the mean error of each method employed. The error is proportional to the square root of the length, according to the theory of probabilities. The mean error m in measuring a line L by five different methods is as follows:—

Square root of L multiplied by

Two rods along a stretched cord, . . $m = 0·000535$
Two rods, without cord, ... $m = 0·000927$
Chain, ... $m = 0·003000$
Steel band, ... $m = 0·002160$
Field-compasses, ... $m = 0·002120$
Measuring-wheel, ... $m = 0·003600$

The mean error is thus approximately—

$$1 : 2 : 6 : 4 : 4 : 7,$$

according to the method employed. Thus, a measurement with rods along a stretched cord is six times as exact as a measurement of the same line with the chain. From the results given above, it is evident that measurements with rods along a stretched cord are the most exact, whilst, with the exception of the measuring-wheel, the chain gives the most untrustworthy results. The steel band, too, gives results one and a half times more accurate than those given by the chain.*

Normal errors, such as those due to defects in the instrument, and errors in allignment, increase in proportion to the length. For the various instruments, with the exception of the rods along a stretched cord, where the normal error r is reduced to a minimum, these errors are as follows:—

Two rods, without cord, ... $r = -0.00008\ L$
Chain, ... $r = +0.00046\ L$
Steel band, ... $r = -0.00032\ L$
Field-compasses, ... $r = -0.00079\ L$

In the case of the chain only is the error positive; that is to say, the length measured is longer than the true length.

The rapidity of measuring is shown by the following averages:—

Instrument.	Assistants.	Mean Speed per Minute.	
		Absolute.	Per Assistant.
Rods, ...	2	Feet. 45	Feet. 22
Chain, ...	2	59	29
Steel band, . . .	2	65	32
Field-compasses, . .	1	85	85

* Improved methods of chaining are described by W. M. Thompson, *Min. Proc. Inst. C.E.*, vol. xcii., 1888, p. 268.

CHAPTER III.

THE MINER'S DIAL.

Directive Action of the Earth's Magnetism.—In determining the linear direction of mineral deposits, and in acquiring information to aid in laying down on paper the position and extent of mine-workings, the magnetic-needle has long been employed.

The action of the earth on a magnetic-needle is directive, that is, it determines the position of the needle with relation to the cardinal points of the horizon, but causes no strain on the point on which the needle is balanced. Thus, if a magnetic-needle is supported at its centre of gravity, it assumes a certain direction; one pole pointing towards the north and the other towards the south. The pole of the needle directed towards the north is called the *north pole* or, more correctly, the north-seeking pole, and that directed towards the south is called the *south pole* or south-seeking pole. The magnetic force acts through rocks, glass, and liquids as instantaneously and with as great intensity as through the air.

Historical Sketch.—To Flavio Gioja (1302–1320) is usually assigned the credit of having first enclosed a magnetic-needle in a box. The use of the magnetic-needle for surveying mines is first described by Georgius Agricola in the fifth book of his *De re Metallicâ*, published in 1556. The compass there described is of a very primitive character. It consists of a series of seven concentric circles filled with wax of different colours; in the middle is a depressed receptacle to contain the magnetic-needle. An old compass of this type is preserved in the collection of the School of Mines of Clausthal in the Harz. It bears the date 1541, and consists of a wooden plate, $\frac{3}{4}$ inch thick and $6\frac{1}{2}$ inches in diameter, in the middle of which is a small brass compass-box, 2 inches in diameter. The whole is placed in a circular receptacle in a wooden box, which may be closed by a lid, and which is provided with a hole in its base, probably to enable it to be placed on a stand. The compass has only a north and south line marked, and round its raised edge a double ruler revolves. The wooden plate has several concentric circular depressions, filled with wax of different colours. When in use, the instrument was so placed that the needle pointed to the north, and the ruler revolved until it pointed in the direction, the bearing of which was required. A scratch was then made on one of the wax circles to indicate this direction. The laying down of the results was effected by repeating the survey at the surface, commencing at the mouth of the shaft. The object of such surveys was merely to determine how near the underground workings were to the boundary of the concession.

In the 17th century, mines were surveyed in this country in a somewhat similar manner. Thomas Houghton, writing in 1681, describes the method of surveying adopted in the Derbyshire mines, as follows:—" Having provided yourself of a *Dial* in a square Box, or a long square Box, which is better; and also of a Two Foot Rule, and a String or Cord with a Plummet at the End: first plum the Shaft: Now suppose you come to take a Length forwards into the Drift at the Shaft Foot, having first made a Mark there where the Plum fell, let a Boy hold one End of the String therein, and bid another Man take the Plummet, and go as far back into the Drift as he can, till the Plum he hath in his Hand touches the Side; and stretching the String streight, observe that it touches no where betwixt that End he holds in the Mark, and the Plummet the other Man hath in his Hand, (if it touches the Side bid him come nearer) then apply the *Dial* to the Side of the String, and when the String and *Dial* lie exactly streight together, take the Point the Needle stands on, which suppose here to be 44; set down the Point, bid him make a mark at the Plummet; then pull back the String and measure it, which suppose here to be 12 rules and 14 inches: Then go to the Mark he hath made, hold one End of the String in it, bid him go back into the Drift with the Plummet as far as he can, till the middle of the String begins to touch the Side; then stretching the String streight, observe that it touches no where betwixt them that hold it, apply the *Dial* to the Side of it, and take the Point the needle stands on."

The process was then repeated until the end of the level was arrived at. The lengths and bearings thus obtained were pegged out at the surface, and thus a mark was obtained above ground exactly above that left at the end of the level underground. "You must observe," says Houghton, "that your Rule and String lie parallel with the Edge of your Dial, that is, equally at both Ends; or else you will miss in taking the true Point. Under Ground the Dial is guided by the String; but above Ground the String is guided by the *Dial*."

Even in the middle of the last century, dialling was carried on with appliances of a very primitive character. "The instruments used," writes Dr. W. Pryce in 1778, "are, a compass without a gnomon or style, but a center pin projecting from the middle of the compass to loop a line to, or stick a candle upon, fixed in a box exactly true and level with its surface, about 6, 8, or 9 inches square, nicely glazed with strong white glass, and a cover suitable to it hung square and level with the upper part of the instrument: a twenty-four inch gauge or two-foot rule, and a string or small cord with a plummet at the end of it: a little stool, to place the dial horizontally: and pegs and pins of wood, a piece of chalk, and pen, ink, and paper."

The author warns "those who take no account of the points or angles of the compass, but in lieu thereof, chalk the bearing of the line they measure with, on the board the compass lies in; for if they are not exceedingly careful and precise in their operations, they may commit almost unpardonable and irretrievable blunders: yet formerly, before penmanship and figures were so generally understood and practised among the common Tinners, as they are at present, most of our Mines and Adits were dialled for in this manner."

Towards the end of the last century, the dial was fitted with sights, by means of which the direction of the station-line could be taken with precision.

Description of the Miner's Dial.—In its simplest form, the miner's dial consists of a box of brass or wood, on the base of which is fixed a brass ring divided into 360°. The base of the box within this ring is also graduated, but each division contains 10°, and the numbers proceed from the north and south points to 90° on each side, thus dividing the inner circle into four quadrants of 90° each. On a finely pointed pin fixed in the centre of the circle, a magnetic-needle is freely suspended, so that when the dial is placed in a horizontal position and the needle unchecked, one end points towards the north. This north-seeking end is distinguished by some mark. The instrument is supplied with a glass cover, and also with a brass lid to protect it when not in use. Perpendicular to the horizontal plane of the instrument, are two brass plates, called *sights*, one at the north, and the other at the south point. These sight vanes are divided into two parts, the upper one on one side having a fine slit cut throughout. The corresponding division of the opposite sight carries a plain wire. In the lower divisions, the relative positions of the slit and wire are changed. The compass-box is attached to a tripod-stand by a socket fitting on to a corresponding plug; an intermediate ball and socket joint furnishing the means of levelling the instrument.

(a.) **The Magnetic-Needle.**—In shape, the magnetic-needle is usually rhombic (Fig. 8) or rectangular (Fig. 9), or its height may be greater than its breadth, in which case the edges are bevelled (Fig. 10). Magnetic-needles of the rhombic form have the advantage of lightness. It is, however, not advisable to make the needle pointed, as it retains its magnetism longer when the ends are square. In the form shown in Fig. 9, the points are replaced by a fine etched line, representing the magnetic axis.

Fig. 8.

Fig. 9.

Fig. 10.

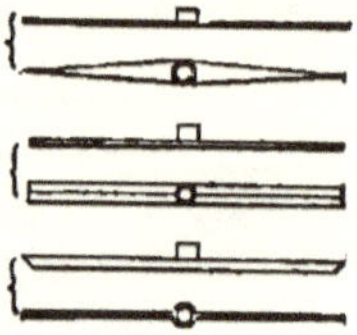

The needle is drilled through in the centre, and carries above the aperture a hollow brass cap, lined with some hard stone conically hollowed out. Agate or carnelian is usually employed for the purpose; but ruby is best. The cap must be as light as possible, and it must be firmly fixed to the needle in such a way that its axis forms a right angle with the axis of the needle. The interior of the cap must be accurately conical. Caps made of brass, silver, or steel should be avoided, as they cannot be polished so well as those of agate, and they are very soon bored through by the centre pin. This pin is made of good steel with a hard, smooth, round point, the angle of which is not too great. The more pointed the pin and the more obtusely conical the interior of the cap, the less is the friction of the needle on its pivot.

The needle must be made of very hard steel, and so constructed that its geometrical centre line passes exactly through the centre of the cap. It must be sufficiently magnetised, and, when placed on its pivot, must assume a horizontal position. A needle which is horizontal before being magnetised, will dip after having been subjected to that treatment. It is, therefore, necessary to make one end of the needle heavier than the other.

In order to preserve the pin from unnecessary wear, and from being broken off when the instrument is carried, a contrivance is employed for fixing the needle. This consists of a slide, pressed from outside, which raises the needle and presses it against the glass lid of the dial. When required to be used, the needle should be lowered carefully, so that it gently rests and does not fall upon the centre pin.

Much depends upon the sensitiveness of the needle. A sluggish needle is utterly useless. The needle may be tested by bringing a piece of iron near it when at rest, observing whether it returns exactly to its former position after a few oscillations.

The test should be made at several points round the dial. The needle should not move when the dial is gently revolved.

All parts of the dial, with the exception of the magnetic-needle and the centre pin, must be made of metal free from iron or nickel. They may be tested by bringing them near a sensitive magnetic-needle balanced on a centre pin fixed in a piece of wood, and noting whether the needle moves, as each separate portion of the dial is brought near it.

In making a survey with the dial, care must be taken that nothing capable of attracting the needle is carried about the person, such as penknives, keys, steel watch-chains, spectacles, nickel-plated studs, or iron rivets in the magnifier used to read the graduations. Watches in which the movements are made of nickel, attract the needle almost as much as when the movements are made of iron. The brims of felt hats are sometimes stiffened by inserting an iron wire round the edge. The surveyor should therefore examine both his watch and his hat before commencing a survey. Sometimes the needle persistently sticks to the under side of the glass. This is caused by the glass becoming electrified from rubbing against the clothes, or from being cleaned with a silk handkerchief. The electricity may be at once removed by touching the glass with the moistened finger or by breathing on the glass. An unsuspected source of error in magnetic-needle readings has recently been discovered to arise from the magnifying glass used for reading the graduations becoming electrified. The magnifier generally used for that purpose has a hard, highly-polished, black frame, which is peculiarly liable to become electrified, even by the mere carrying in the pocket, so that, when brought near the magnetic-needle, it draws it sometimes as much as half a degree from its true resting place.

In a good dial the centre pin of the needle should be exactly in the centre of the graduated circle, and the needle should be straight. If this is not the case, there will be an error of eccentricity in every observation. The *constant eccentricity*, when the centre pin and the ends of the needle are not in one vertical plane, and the *variable eccentricity*, when the centre pin is eccentric to the graduated circle, may be detected by the readings at the two ends of the needle not agreeing. In both cases the error may be corrected by reading both ends of the needle, and by taking the mean of the two results. Cases of *irregular eccentricity* are sometimes met with—that is, when the point of suspension of the needle in the cap is variable. Needles presenting this error are useless.

(*b*.) **Spirit-Levels.**—On the dial-plate are two small spirit-levels, consisting of glass tubes slightly curved and nearly filled with some limped liquid, a bubble of air being left. One of the spirit-levels is parallel to the direction of the sights, whilst the other is at right angles to it. They are so adjusted that when the bubbles are in the centres of the tubes, the dial is level.

Spirit-levels are usually filled with alcohol or ether. The bubble, being specifically lighter than the liquid, always assumes the highest possible position; and if the tube has been ground to a perfectly circular longitudinal section, the tangent to its inner surface at the centre of the air bubble is a horizontal line.

(c.) **The Tripod.**—The dial is usually supported on three legs, shod with iron, and connected at the top in such a way that they

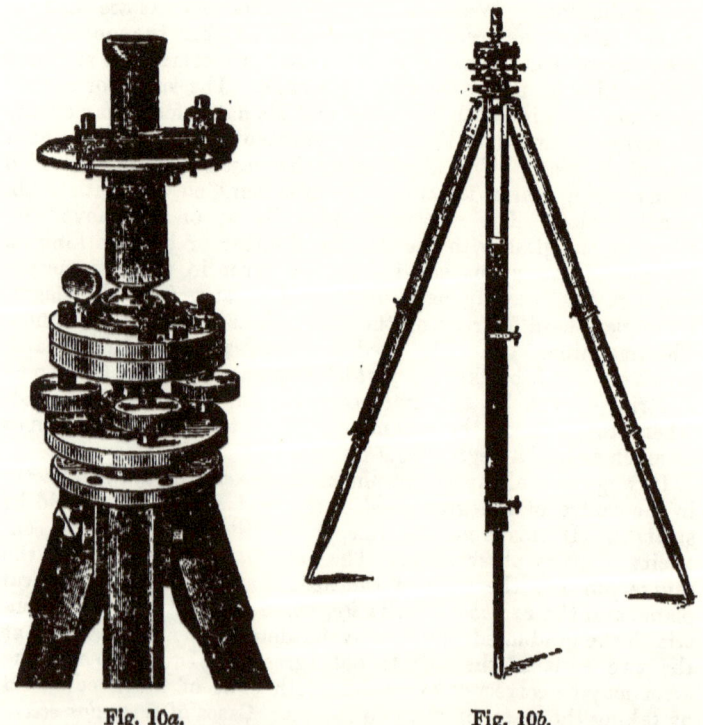

Fig. 10a.   Fig. 10b.

are movable in any direction, lightness and rigidity being the qualities desired. Usually the legs are made with a screw-joint in the middle, and a set of extra points is provided to screw on, when the workings are low. The dial is connected with the tripod by means of a *ball and socket joint*, which consists of a ball at the end of a covered spindle fitting into a corresponding cavity under the dial-plate. The ball turns in a socket, and can be loosened or tightened at will. It thus admits of motion in any direction.

In order to ensure accuracy, it is advisable in underground surveys to use three tripods, one for the instrument and the others for the lamp or candle. The latter is fitted in a special holder (Fig. 10a) provided with two spirit-levels, and capable of being levelled by a ball and socket joint and levelling screws. One of the best forms of tripod is that made by Messrs. E. T. Newton & Son, of Camborne, who employ slotted legs with thumb-screws for tightening them when any wear takes place owing to the shrinkage of the wood under climatic influences. For surveying over very irregular ground, these tripods (Fig. 10b) are provided with sliding adjustable slotted oak legs, a device that greatly economises time in levelling the instrument.

(1.) **Taking Underground Observations with the Dial.**—The *bearing* of a line is the angle which it forms with the direction of the magnetic-needle. To take the bearing of any line, set the compass exactly over any point in the line by means of a plumb-line suspended from beneath the centre of the dial; level the instrument, and direct the sights to an object at the other end of the line. Then measure the line, and note the distance measured in the dialling-book. The needle will thus have been allowed sufficient time to come to rest. A second look along the line may now be taken in order to test the accuracy of the observation, the eye being applied to the south sight. The number of degrees to which the north-seeking end of the needle points is then carefully noted. This method of taking an observation with the north sight in advance is that generally employed. The results are called *fore-observations*. Sometimes, however, it is desirable to place the eye at the north sight, and look back in a direction contrary to the order of the survey. Observations taken in this way are called *back-observations*. The angle is read from the north-seeking end of the needle, and entered in the dialling-book as if it had been a fore-observation. This method is employed in dialling a line from the centre of a shaft, where the instrument cannot conveniently be set up. By using the back-observation throughout a survey, taking back-observations and fore-observations alternately, the instrument is moved only half the number of times it would otherwise be.

THE MINER'S DIAL.

The lettering of the miner's dial differs in an important particular from that of the mariner's compass or pocket geological compass. When we face the north, the east point is on our right hand, and the west on our left, and the graduated card of the mariner's compass is marked accordingly. In the miner's dial, however, the letters representing east and west are transposed.

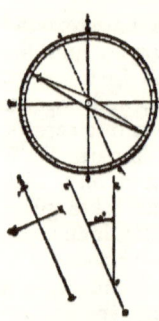

Fig. 11.

The reason of this will be seen from Fig. 11. Here the dial is represented with the east and west points in their true position. The line of sight in which the observation is taken lies over the north and south line marked N S. This is to be placed in any required direction, and being fixed, the magnetic-needle is found to rest, we will suppose, in the position indicated by the dotted line A B, the north-seeking end of the needle coming to rest at 24° distant from the north and south line. The reading of this is not N. 24° W., as might at first be supposed, but N. 24° E. The reason is apparent on considering that the needle is the only representative of the magnetic bearing. If then a corresponding line C D is drawn upon paper, the end C will represent the magnetic north. The line N S coincides with a line in the direction of the road to be surveyed, which on the plan will be represented by a line E F parallel to N S, and this line of direction is clearly seen to be on the *east* side of the magnetic meridian, forming with it an angle of 24°.

In order to prevent confusion, miner's dials are, as a rule, graduated from right to left, the east and west points being transposed. An illustration of the necessity of this change may be afforded by imagining a watch in which the dial-plate moves from left to right, whilst the hand remains immovable. It is evident that the hours must count from right to left for the watch to indicate the right time. Similarly, in the case of the miner's dial, the magnetic-needle always points to the north, and may consequently be compared with the fixed hand of the supposed watch.

In some of the older patterns of miner's dial the letters are not transposed, the east being on the right and the west on the left. In using a dial of this kind, the letters must be mentally reversed before the bearing is noted. The best method to adopt for entirely avoiding all confusion is to disregard the lettering of the dial, and read the azimuth or meridian angle, remembering that 90° represents the east, 270° west, and 180° south.

Taking Vertical Angles.—In the old type of miner's dial, the brass cover protecting the glass fitted on in one position only. The edge was graduated to 45° on each side of a zero-point, a pin being fixed on the edge directly opposite that point. The line joining the pin and the zero-point was at right angles to the line of sight. Vertical angles were measured by turning the instrument, by means of its ball and socket joint, until it was in a plane at right angles to its proper position for taking horizontal angles, the graduation of the cover being at its lower edge. A plumb-line was then suspended from the pin in the upper edge of the cover. This line coincided with the zero of the graduation when the sights were horizontal. On turning them upwards or downwards from that position, the number of degrees indicated by the plumb-line was found to represent the angle of elevation or depression.

Miner's dials are now made with a semicircular vertical arc which may be fixed at pleasure across the central line of the compass. It is provided with a movable limb carrying a horizontal bar with a pair of sights. The semicircle is, as a rule, divided into single degrees, marked from 0° in the centre to 90° on the horizontal line on each side. Frequently a long spirit-level is fastened to the bar of which the sights are part. The sights are directed to the object, of which the bearing is required, and inclined the requisite amount. The horizontal and vertical angles can then be read.

This vertical arc is in general use in metalliferous mines. In collieries where the vertical angles required to be measured are never excessive, a side arc is usually employed. This has the advantage of leaving the face of the dial quite free. Fig. 12 illustrates the best form of side arc. In

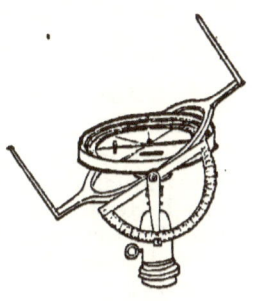

Fig. 12.

the dial here shown the sights are carried by an outer ring concentric with the dial. This arc was invented in 1850 by John Hedley, H.M. Inspector of Mines.

The side arc with sights attached to it should be avoided. If the sights are directed to the forward or back object when taking a vertical angle, the bearing will be incorrect, as the deviation from the true line on looking through the side-sights amounts to half the diameter of the dial—that is, the distance from the centre of the dial to the line of sight.

Keeping the Dialling-Book.—The survey is noted in the following manner:—

WORK AND REST MINE.—ADIT LEVEL.

From perpendicular line in engine shaft 3/- W. and 2/- N. of centre.
Shaft (90°) 14 by 7.

No.	Bearing.	Distance.			Offsets.		Remarks.
		fms.	ft.	ins.	R.	L.	
A	359° 45'	12	2	6	2/-	3/-	
B	346° 00'	13	4	10	3/6	2/9	
C	332° 21'	10	3	0	2/-	3/-	N. 2/6 S. 3/-
D	275° 03'	5	0	2	4/-	5/-	
E	254° 06'	3	5	9	6/6	3/-	
F	292° 15'	32	0	0	4/2	6/-	
G²	184° 00'	12	0	0	3/-	3/-	END of × cut.
G	272° 00'	16	0	6	3/9	3/9	
H	264° 06'	5	4	0	2/6	2/-	
J*	232° 00'	3	5	9	2/-	2/6	Peg and nail, N. wall, 2/- N. of J.
K	232° 00'	1	0	0	2/6	2/6	END.

The above are the notes of the survey of the adit level of a supposed metalliferous mine, the name of which was suggested by Mr. J. Henderson, M.Inst.C.E., as showing the intermittent nature of many metalliferous mines, which are so frequently abandoned when the metal falls in price, and re-opened in better times.

The survey is made in the adit level, and starts from a perpendicular line in the vertical engine shaft, which is rectangular in section, 14 feet long by 7 feet wide. The dial is set up at A, and a back-observation is taken to the perpendicular line, the observer looking through the north sight of the instrument. The bearing indicated by the north-seeking end of the needle is read and entered as the first bearing. It will be found advisable to write the degrees and minutes as if the latter were decimals; in this way any confusion between such numbers as 30' and 3' is avoided. The length of the station-line is measured, and the result, 12 fathoms 2 feet 6 inches, entered in the distance column. The best form of book to use is an ordinary account-book, the £, s., and d. columns serving for fathoms, feet, and inches.

In plans of metalliferous mines, it is highly desirable to represent the variable width of the level after the ore has been extracted, so as to clearly indicate the position of the various courses of ore. Offsets should therefore be taken at the end of each station-line at right angles to it. They are measured in feet and inches, and, in order to necessitate as little writing as possible—an important matter in a wet mine—may be written in a way similar to the abbreviated mode of writing shillings and pence.

At C the survey line leaves the cross-cut driven from the shaft to the lode, and continues on the lode. As there is a sharp turn at this point, offsets are measured to the north and south, as well as to the right and left. At F a cross-cut is driven south of the lode. The dial being set up at F, an observation is taken to a candle at the end of the cross-cut. The bearing is then read, and the distance, 12 fathoms, measured. This line is a branch from the main survey line, and is distinguished by a small figure 2 attached to the letter that would have been assigned to the station had it belonged to the main line. With the dial still at F, an observation is next taken to G, and the survey continued as before. At K, the *end*, or *forebreast*, is reached, and a permanent mark has to be left, from which the survey may be continued at a future date. The mark should not be placed at the end, where it is liable to be shattered in the next blasting operation. The usual practice is to measure a fathom back along the line of sight, and to insert a peg and nail in the wall of the level, carefully noting its position for future reference.

The offsets to the walls of the level are sometimes omitted, the level being shown in the plan as a double coloured line. In this case, care must be taken to keep the line of sight exactly in the middle of the level; otherwise an incorrect representation of the workings will result.

(2.) **Surface-Surveys with the Miner's Dial.**—For making the surface-survey of a mine-royalty, the dial may be used in the same manner as it is underground. There is, however, the advantage that opportunities frequently occur of checking the work during its progress by means of tie-lines.

The manner in which the results should be entered in the field-book may be seen from the accompanying record of a survey of a four-sided field connected with the shaft of a mine.

The measurements in this survey are made in links. The dial was placed at A, and, when the instrument had been carefully levelled, the sights were turned in the direction of the shaft. An assistant having by this time placed a staff at the

FIELD RECORD OF SURVEY.

	A	512	6
		460	10
		400	
	(12	370	
	10	250	
	6	130	
		120	
5.		100	5
	115° 00′	☉	13
	D	433	6
		400	12
		250	11
4.		130	17
	220° 00′	☉	9
	C	450	8
		340	17
		260	31
		200	35
3.		100	23
	285° 18′	☉	17
	B	496	12
		400	18
		290	35
		270	24
2.		200	27
	30° 00′	☉	15
		630	☉ **A**
1.	Shaft to **A**	☉	
	13° 33′		

centre of the shaft, the sights were turned until the vertical hair of the back-sight exactly cut the staff. This being a back-observation, the observer looked through the sight at the north end of the dial. When the needle had settled, the bearing indicated by its north-seeking end was read, and entered as 13° 33' in the field-book. The distance from the shaft to A, 630 links, was then measured, and noted. The sights were then directed to a staff held at B. This was a fore-observation, and therefore the observer looked through the sight at the south side of the dial, turning the instrument until the vertical hair of the fore-sight exactly cut the staff. The needle was then read, and the bearing, 30° 00', entered in the field-book. The distance from A to B, 496 links, was measured, and offsets taken at the bends in the hedge along that line. The instrument was then removed to C, and a back-observation taken to the staff still standing at B. This gave the bearing of line No. 3, 285° 18'. Line No. 4 was a fore-observation from C to D. In order to obtain the bearing of line No. 5, the instrument was centred over the point at D, where the staff stood, and a fore-observation taken to a staff held at the original station A. In this way, by going round the boundaries, the outline of the field is obtained. In extensive surveys, this would not be sufficient; a number of tie-lines would have to be measured in order to check the survey during its progress.

In the field-book, the date of the survey should be inserted, all the station-lines should be numbered, and the booking should begin at the last line of the page, and be written upwards. In this way, the notes follow the direction of the survey and offsets to the right or left are noted on the corresponding side of the page. All objects, whether hedges, houses, or ponds, or whatever offsets have been taken to, may thus be sketched in with facility. The notes should be kept so clearly and accurately that if necessary the survey may be plotted after the lapse of years, without trusting to the surveyor's memory for its details.

(3.) **Colliery Surveys with the Miner's Dial.**—In surveying a colliery where safety-lamps are used, the surveyor must provide himself with a safety-lamp made of copper or brass, entirely free from iron, for reading the magnetic-needle. The method of conducting the survey is essentially the same as that adopted at the surface. Instead of the staves used in the surface-survey, lights must of course be used as signals.

The usual method of surveying a colliery is to start from the centre of the shaft and continue along one of the levels to the face, thence through the workings to the other face, and finally back to the starting point at the centre of the shaft. For all other roads that require to be surveyed, marks are left to return to. In this way tie-lines are obtained, which are of great value in checking the accuracy of the survey. The size and direction of all faults must be carefully noted in the survey-book.

A colliery survey, when no offsets are taken, may be booked in the way shown in the following example:—

Station-Line.	Distance. Chains.	Magnetic Bearing.	Inclination, Descending.
Shaft to A	4·58	98° 25′	0° 00′
A B	8·55	175° 00′	9° 50′
B C	17·75	178° 13′	11° 15′
C D	7·59	256° 57′	0° 00′
D E	8·84	277° 53′	0° 00′
E F	9·50	5° 08′	7° 15′
F G	14·46	8° 08′	5° 45′
G H	9·10	78° 45′	0° 00′

When offsets are taken, it is best to begin booking at the bottom of the page and write upwards as in the example of a surface-survey. Except against ribs and in main gateroads, offsets are seldom taken in a coal-mine, since the position of the face has probably changed before the surveyor reaches the surface. In the method of booking generally adopted, both bearings and distances are entered in the ruled column, and the line drawn across the page at the end of each draft, as shown in the preceding field-record, is always omitted.

The accuracy of a closed survey made with the magnetic needle may be tested by reducing the observed bearings to included angles. To do this, from the fore-bearing, increased by 180°, the back-bearing is subtracted, the difference being the included angle between the two lines. The sum of the included angles should, with four right angles, be equal to twice as many right angles as the polygon has sides.

CHAPTER IV.

The Variation of the Magnetic-Needle.

Definitions.—A magnetic-needle when suspended finds its position of rest in a line joining two fixed points on the horizon. At certain places on the earth's surface, these points correspond with the north and south points of the horizon; but, as a rule, though near, they do not coincide with these. A vertical plane passing through the points on the horizon indicated by the needle, is called the *magnetic meridian,* in the same way as a similar plane passing through the north and south poles is known as the *true meridian* of the place. The angle formed by the magnetic and true meridians is termed the *declination* or *variation* of the needle.

A knowledge of the declination is of the utmost importance in preparing mine plans, as this does not remain constant in the same place, but is subject to continual, though slight, variations. These variations are either regular or irregular. Under regular variations are included *secular* and *diurnal* variations.

(*a.*) **Secular Variations.**—Observations of the amount and direction of these variations have been made in all parts of the world. The first observation appears to have been made in Paris in the year 1541. The declination of the needle was at that date easterly, and amounted to 7°. In 1550 it was 8°, whilst in 1580 it amounted to 11° 30′. Thus, between the years 1541 and 1580 the magnetic meridian veered 4° 30′ further towards the east. From 1580 the declination decreased, the magnetic meridian moving towards the west, until in 1666 there was no variation; the magnetic and true meridians coinciding. Ever since that date, the variation has been westerly, attaining its maximum of 22° in 1820, and then gradually decreasing, so that the magnetic meridian is now gradually approaching the true meridian.

The magnetic history of Paris does not apply to London; every place, as far as has been ascertained, has a magnetic history of its own. The following table shows the change in the position of the magnetic-needle near London from the earliest observations up to the present time :—

Date.	Declination.	Date.	Declination West.	Date.	Declination West.
1580	11° 15′ E	1817	24° 36′	1871	20° 10′
1622	6° 00′ E	1818	24° 38′	1872	20° 00′
1634	4° 06′ E	1819	24° 36′	1873	19° 58′
1657	0° 00′	1820	24° 34	1874	19° 52′
1665	1° 22′ W	1858	21° 54′	1875	19° 41′
1672	2° 30′ W	1859	21° 47′	1876	19° 32′
1692	6° 00′ W	1860	21° 40′	1877	19° 22′
1723	14° 17′ W	1861	21° 32′	1878	19° 14′
1748	17° 40′ W	1862	21° 23′	1879	19° 06′
1773	21° 09′ W	1863	21° 13′	1880	18° 57′
1787	23° 19′ W	1864	21° 03′	1881	18° 50′
1795	23° 57′ W	1865	20° 59′	1882	18° 45′
1802	24° 06′ W	1866	20° 51′	1883	18° 40′
1805	24° 08′ W	1867	20° 40′	1884	18° 32′
1806	24° 15′ W	1868	20° 33′	1885	18° 25′
1809	24° 22′ W	1869	20° 26′	1886	18° 17′
1812	24° 28′ W	1870	20° 19′	1887	18° 10′

From this table it appears that the magnetic-needle has required 300 years (1580–1880) to move an arc of 11° 15′ + 24° 38′ + (24° 38′ − 18° 58′) = 41° 33′. The average annual movement is consequently $8\frac{1}{4}'$. The figures given in the table from 1858 are the mean values of the magnetic declination as determined at the Kew Observatory.

At Newcastle and Swansea the declination is about 1° 45′ greater than at London; at Liverpool 2°, at Edinburgh 3°, and at Glasgow and Dublin about 3° 50′ greater. At Yarmouth and Dover the declination is about 40′ less than at London.

The mean value of the magnetic declination for any particular place in Great Britain, at which no magnetic observations are made, can generally only be inferred from the map prepared in

1872 by Sir F. J. Evans, Hydrographer to the Admiralty. This is given in the *Philosophical Transactions*, 1872, vol. 162. Allowance must be made for the change which has since occurred. Values found in this way are approximations only.

In certain parts of the earth, the magnetic and true meridians coincide. The irregularly curved imaginary line joining the points where there is no declination is called the *agonic line*. Such a line cuts the east of South America, and, passing east of the West Indies, crosses the United States, passing just east of Charleston, South Carolina, and just west of Detroit, Michigan. It then passes through the North Pole, crosses Lapland to the Caspian, cuts the east of Arabia, and passes through Western Australia to the South Pole.

Isogonic lines are imaginary lines joining the places on the earth's surface whose declinations are equal at any given time. Maps on which such isogonic lines are shown are called *declination maps*, and a comparison of these in various years shows the variation to which the declination is subject.

The great variation in the declination shows the necessity of recording the date and declination of the needle on all mine-plans, with a note stating whether the bearings given were magnetic bearings, or were reduced to the angles, which the lines would form with the true meridian.

The antiquity of the workings on an old undated plan may be approximately ascertained from the meridian line shown on it. Thus, if a plan is found to be constructed to a meridian with a declination of 24° west, it is reasonable to suppose that it was drawn about the year 1800, for, according to the table, the declination in 1802 was 24° 6' west.

(*b*). **Diurnal Variation.**—On observing a magnetic-needle throughout an entire day, it will be found that the variation does not remain constant, but changes more, and in a different way, than is demanded by the secular change. Observations at London show that at about 8 a.m. the needle reaches its furthest point east, and that at 1 p.m. it shows the greatest westerly deviation from the mean magnetic meridian. The declination then decreases until 10 p.m., when it remains stationary until 4 a.m. It then decreases again until 8 a.m., by which time it has again reached its furthest point east. The needle stands at its mean position a little after 10 a.m., and a little before 7 p.m. The diurnal changes are much the same over the whole of the northern hemisphere, though the amount differs.

The following table shows the diurnal variation for London (Kew), Trevandrum, in Madras, and Hobart Town, in Tasmania. Of these places, the first is a station in middle latitude (northern

DIURNAL VARIATION.

Hour.	London.	Trevandrum.	Hobart Town.
	Minutes.	Minutes.	Minutes.
12 a.m.	−5·13	−0·61	+1·35
1 p.m.	−6·19	−0·45	+3·50
2 p.m.	−5·81	−0·15	+4·55
3 p.m.	−4·28	+0·13	+4·40
4 p.m.	−2·60	+0·28	+3·35
5 p.m.	−1·26	+0·24	+2·00
6 p.m.	−0·39	+0·13	+1·15
7 p.m.	+0·22	+0·04	+0·50
8 p.m.	+0·68	−0·05	+0·00
9 p.m.	+0·99	−0·08	−0·55
10 p.m.	+1·24	−0·06	−0·90
11 p.m.	+1·37	+0·01	−1·00
12 p.m.	+1·43	+0·09	−0·95
1 a.m.	+1·29	+0·13	−0·75
2 a.m.	+1·39	+0·15	−0·55
3 a.m.	+1·51	+0·09	−0·40
4 a.m.	+1·88	+0·02	−0·40
5 a.m.	+2·51	+0·01	−0·75
6 a.m.	+3·07	+0·18	−1·30
7 a.m.	+3·58	+0·32	−2·15
8 a.m.	+3·80	+0·24	−3·25
9 a.m.	+2·95	+0·06	−3·70
10 a.m.	+0·46	−0·22	−3·00
11 a.m.	−2·68	−0·50	−1·15

In this table deflections towards the magnetic east are reckoned positive, deflections towards magnetic west negative.

hemisphere), the second is an equatorial station, and the third a station in middle latitude (southern hemisphere).

The diurnal variations are found to vary with the seasons of the year. They are much greater in summer than in winter. The cause of the variations is frequently ascribed to the influence of sunlight. Other influences appear to be at work, as is shown by the fact that the variations of the declination of a magnetic-needle at a place on the earth's surface coincide with the variations observed simultaneously underground. This was found by Professor Borchers to be the case at Clausthal, in the Harz, where a magnetic observatory was erected at the Eleonore mine, 1,788 feet below the surface. Similar results were obtained at a magnetic observatory established, at a depth of 3,280 feet below the surface, in the deepest mine in the world, at Przibram in Bohemia. The slightest movements of the magnetic-needle observed at the earth's surface occur at the same time and to the same extent even at the greatest depths to which mining is able to penetrate.

Irregular Variations.—The magnetic-needle is subject to violent and irregular disturbances, which are sometimes considerable, amounting in extreme cases to 1 or 2 degrees. These irregular disturbances or *magnetic storms* appear to be coincident with the appearance of the aurora borealis, earthquakes, and volcanic eruptions. The cause of these storms has not yet been determined. Sabine, however, found that they are most frequent every eleven years when the spots on the sun are most numerous. Experience shows that places of the same longitude have similar disturbances at the same time, that those on opposite sides of the globe differing by 180° of longitude, have disturbances equal in amount but opposite in direction, and that places situated 90° west or east of the disturbed regions have practically no disturbance. Atmospheric storms have no effect on the needle.

Notices of the occurrence of magnetic storms are published by the Superintendent of the Magnetic Department at Greenwich in the mining journals, and deserve the careful attention of mine-surveyors.

Determination of the True Meridian.—In order to find out the extent of the declination of a magnetic-needle, it is necessary to determine the true meridian. For this purpose various methods are employed.

1. Method of Shadows.—This method is based on the fact that, at equal distances of its passage across the meridian, the sun is at equal altitudes above the horizon. Consequently at these times it gives shadows of equal lengths.

A staff is planted vertically in the ground, and the ends of its shadows are joined when they are of equal length. On joining these points to the projection of the axis of the staff, an angle is obtained, the bisectrix of which is the true meridian. The observation may be made more accurately by describing a number of concentric circles (Fig. 13) with the foot of the staff as centre,

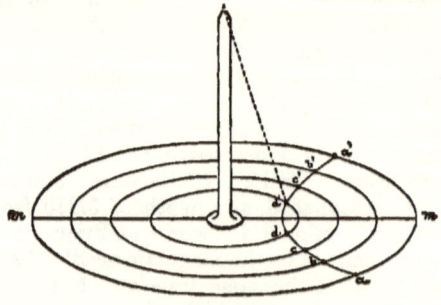

Fig. 13.

and marking the points, a, b, c, d, d', c', b', a', where each of them is touched by the shadow. The arcs thus obtained are bisected, and the points of bisection are joined to the centre of the circle. The line $m\ m$ thus obtained is the meridian. This method, though a fair approximation, is absolutely correct only at the time of the solstices (June 21, December 22). It is the oldest method known; it was used by the early Christians for determining the east for their churches.

The method is considerably improved by placing a thin metal plate provided with a small aperture, at the top of the staff. The latter is inclined so that the aperture is perpendicularly above the centre of the concentric circles. In the shadow of the metal plate, a bright spot appears, the centre of which can be found with considerable accuracy. This method has been used on a large scale by placing perforated metal plates in the roofs of high buildings, a notable example being in the dome of the cathedral at Florence (1467, A.D.)

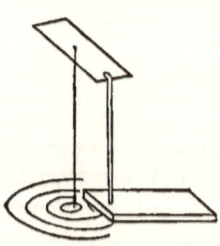

Fig. 14.

The shadow method may be applied on a small scale by employing a vertical pin placed in the centre of a number of concentric circles on a drawing-board. A more convenient apparatus may be made of a brass rod about 7 inches in length, provided at its lower end with a screw and at the top with a very thin plate of brass about 2 inches long and $1\frac{1}{2}$ inch broad, so arranged that it forms with the pin an angle of about 120°. In the middle of the plate a fine hole is drilled. The pin being screwed into a board, half an inch square, near the edge, a portable instrument, Fig. 14, termed a *gnomon*, is formed. This can be placed on a table or drawing-board in the open air, and used in the manner described.

2. **Method of Corresponding Altitudes.**—If a good theodolite (see Chapter VIII.) is available, the meridian of a place may be determined in the following manner:—The theodolite, after careful adjustment, is set up at the point, the meridian of which is to be determined, a station commanding a free view being selected. Vernier I. of the theodolite is then brought to zero, and the position of vernier II. observed. The limb is then turned horizontally, and the telescope moved vertically until it is brought to bear upon a fixed star of the first or second magnitude several hours before its culmination. As soon as the star passes the cross-wires of the telescope, the latter is clamped, and both the horizontal and vertical circles of the instrument are read. The telescope is then allowed to remain with its inclination unchanged, and after a time the star will not be visible through it. After its culmination, the star will, in the course of time, have the same altitude that it had at the first reading. The star is followed with the telescope, and at the instant it crosses the wires of the latter, the horizontal circle is read a second time.

Assuming that at the second reading the telescope had the same inclination that it had during the first reading, the direction of the meridian will be represented by half the sum of the two readings on the horizontal circle. The limb being turned horizontally until vernier I. gives the calculated angle, the axis of the telescope will give the direction of the meridian. The method is based upon the fact that a star at equal altitudes above the horizon of a place is equally distant from the plane of its meridian.

It is evident that the accuracy of the result depends upon the perfection of the instrument employed. The best results are always obtained by observing the star at various altitudes before and after its culmination, and by reading the horizontal circle each time with the telescope clamped at the corresponding altitude. Both verniers should always be read, and the arithmetical mean of the readings taken if they are not identical. The direction of the meridian is thus obtained repeatedly, and if there is no error, the result will be the same with each inclination of the telescope. If the results differ slightly from one another, the mean must be taken; with larger differences, the observations must be repeated. As a check, the observations should be repeated on the following night with the telescope inverted. The result should not differ from that obtained on the previous night. If there is a slight difference, the mean of the results of the observations on the two nights will give the direction of the meridian.

As an example of this method of determining the meridian, some of the observations may be given which were made for fixing the meridian for the magnetic observatory belonging to the Clausthal mines. The determination was effected with an 8-inch theodolite. The instrument was set up on a stone foundation, and accurately levelled. The vernier I. was brought to zero, and the position of vernier II. noted. With the upper plate clamped in this way, the telescope was brought to bear on a signal on the top of the tower of Clausthal Church. The following observations were then made with the stars β and γ Virginis:—

Altitude of the Star.	Readings on the Horizontal Circle Calculated from the Position of the Two Verniers.		Angle formed by the Meridian and the Direction of Clausthal Church.
	Before the Culmination.	After the Culmination.	
β Virginis)			
18° 20'	56° 15' 37"	196° 22' 05"	126° 18' 51"
19° 40'	58° 15' 12"	194° 22' 45"	126° 18' 58"
21° 00'	60° 18' 52"	192° 18' 50"	126° 18' 51"
21° 40'	61° 21' 42"	191° 15' 20"	126° 18' 31"
22° 20'	62° 25' 57"	190° 11' 45"	126° 18' 51"
(γ Virginis)			
15° 20'	57° 40' 32"	194° 57' 25"	126° 18' 58"
16° 40'	59° 40' 02"	192° 57' 53"	126° 18' 59"
17° 20'	60° 41' 47"	191° 56' 15"	126° 19' 01"
18° 00'	61° 43' 57"	190° 53' 55"	126° 18' 56"
18° 40'	62° 47' 07"	189° 50' 05"	126° 18' 36"

The zero of the horizontal circle represented the direction of Clausthal Church. The arithmetical mean of the results shows that the meridian formed an angle of 126° 18′ 51″ with the direction of Clausthal Church. Observations made the next night gave exactly the same results. The same number of observations were made on the two following nights with the telescope inverted. The mean of all the results obtained during the four nights gave 126° 18′ 49″. It must be noted that in these observations the stars employed were not first sighted and the angle of altitude then read. The vertical circle was clamped at a given division, and the star then brought on to the vertical wire of the telescope, and followed by means of the tangent screw of the upper plate until it also passed the horizontal wire.

If the theodolite is set up on a fixed point, and if the terrestrial object, the azimuth of which is determined, is also a secure point, a further marking-out of the meridian is not absolutely necessary. In the preceding case, however, it was thought advisable to mark out the meridian by means of a large square stone buried in the earth on a mountain in the vicinity. A hole drilled in the surface of this accurately in the meridian served for the reception of a signal staff.

The meridian may be determined during the daytime by sighting the upper edge of the sun before and after mid-day, a dark glass being placed before the objective of the telescope. A correction has, however, to be made on account of the obliquity of the ecliptic—a correction that is not taken into account in the shadow method. This method of determining the meridian is not to be recommended, as the astronomical almanacks required for making the correction are not always available. The cross-wires, too, may be directed to a star with far greater precision than to the sun.

3. **Determination of the Meridian by Means of the Pole-Star.**—Of the bright stars of the northern heavens, the nearest to the pole is the first star in the tail of the Little Bear, or the Pole-star (α Ursæ Minoris). It is a star of the second magnitude, and may easily be found by imagining a straight line to be drawn through the stars β and α of the Great Bear, and continued for about five times the distance from β to α, counting from α. These two stars are known as the *pointers*.

The meridian may be determined by observing the pole-star either when it is in the meridian, or when it is at its extreme elongation. The pole-star is not situated exactly at the north pole of the heavens, but is now about 1° 15′ from it. Twice in each sidereal day (23 hours 56 minutes) it is in the meridian.

A very simple method of determining the meridian of a place consists in sighting the pole-star, marked A in Fig. 15, when it appears in the same vertical line with the star Alioth in the Great Bear (ε Ursæ Majoris). This may be done by watching for the moment, when a suspended plumb-line will cover both stars. They will then be approximately in the meridian. The pole-star is exactly in the meridian about 29 minutes after it has been in the same vertical plane as Alioth. In the southern hemisphere a similar process may be applied to the stars α' Crucis and β Hydri.

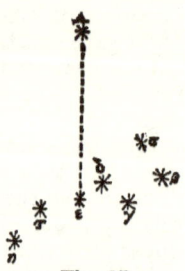

Fig. 15.

The meridian may also be determined by observing the pole-star at its extreme elongation, that is, when it is at its greatest apparent angular distance east or west of the pole. At this instant, the horizontal projection of the apparent movement of the star alters its direction, and the motion of the star appears to cease for a short time. The greatest and least horizontal angles made by the pole-star with any given line when the star is at the greatest distances east and west of the pole, are observed and the mean of the angles taken. This will be the angle made by the given line with the meridian. This method is rarely practicable with an ordinary theodolite, as one of the observations must generally be made by daylight.

4. **Determination of the Meridian by means of a Map.**—For an approximative determination of the meridian, a large-scale map may be employed. The direction of the meridian is shown by joining the degrees of longitude marked at the top and bottom of the map. The angle formed by the meridian and some line easy to determine on the ground, is measured on the map. With the aid of this line, the angle is marked off on the ground. The approximation thus obtained is at most 15 minutes.

Setting-out the Meridian Line.—In every mining district it is very desirable that all difficulty in ascertaining the true meridian should be at once removed by the erection of two conspicuous objects placed exactly on a meridian line, to remain for permanent reference. T. Sopwith, writing in 1822, urged that it would be a work of enormous advantage to the prosperity of mining districts to have meridian lines carefully set-out at distances of 1 mile from each other, and tall posts placed on these meridian lines at every mile in length, the undulating surface of the country being truly reduced to a horizontal base, so that these posts or stations should indicate squares of exactly 1 square mile.

The best method of permanently marking out the meridian is to insert, to a depth of 3 to 5 feet in the ground, a hard stone, 6 to 8 feet long and 2 feet square. The portion of the stone projecting from the ground is faced, and the top plane is made at right angles to the axis. To avoid as much as possible the action of frost, it is advisable to give the stone a good foundation and to fix it in cement. On the top of the stone a brass plate, a foot square, is fastened, so that it is exactly horizontal, and on this the direction of the meridian line is shown by a fine engraved line.

When the direction of the meridian is to be shown by two stones a distance apart, points must be marked on them exactly in the meridian. For this purpose, it is best to drill holes into which staves can be inserted

For practical purposes, a simple method of ascertaining the annual variation is to take the bearing of some remote permanent object, such as a church steeple, from a fixed point. The bearing of this so-called *line of orientation* is recorded from year to year, the difference in the readings giving the annual variation.

This line is also of great value if several dials are used in the same mine. In consequence of small errors in the construction of the instruments, the bearing of one and the same line is found to vary when determined with different dials. By observing the line of orientation, the error of each dial may be determined, and applied as a constant correction to all subsequent readings.

Inclination of the Magnetic-Needle.—If a magnetic-needle is free to move vertically, it does not, at most places on the earth's surface, rest in a horizontal position, but inclines more or less from it. The angle between the needle and the horizontal line is called the *dip* or *inclination* of the needle, provided that the vertical plane in which the needle moves is the magnetic meridian of the place. The dip varies at different places; at the magnetic equator there is no dip, whilst at the magnetic poles the needle stands vertically.

The dip is not of great importance to mine-surveyors in Britain, as the needles of dials are carefully compensated when sold. Surveyors going abroad with an English dial should be provided with a small sliding balance for the needle, which may be adjusted when necessary, should the dip prove at all troublesome.

Like the magnetic declination, the dip is subject to secular variations. The following are results of observations near London extending over a series of years:—

THE VARIATION OF THE MAGNETIC-NEEDLE. 51

Year.	Inclination.	Year.	Inclination.
1576	71° 50′	1880	67° 35′
1600	72° 00′	1881	67° 34′
1720	74° 42′	1882	67° 34′
1800	70° 35′	1883	67° 31′
1830	69° 38′	1884	67° 30′
1850	68° 48′	1885	67° 27′
1865	68° 09′	1886	67° 27′

The following are the values of the magnetic elements observed at Greenwich during recent years:—

Year.	Mean declination.	Mean inclination.
1881	18° 27·1′	67° 34·6′
1882	18° 22·3′	67° 34·1′
1883	18° 15·0′	67° 31·6′
1884	18° 8·0′	67° 30·0′
1885	18° 1·7′	67° 27·8′
1886	17° 54·5′	67° 27·0′
1887	17° 49·1′	67° 26·4′
1888	17° 40·4′	67° 25·4′
1889	17° 34·9′	67° 24·9′
1890	17° 28·6′	67° 22·9′
1891	17° 23·4′	67° 21·4′
1892	17° 17·4′	67° 19·8′
1893	17° 11·4′	67° 17·8′
1894	17° 4·6′	67° 16·5′

MINE-SURVEYING.

Mr. C. Chree, Superintendent of the Kew Observatory, has published* the following summary of recent values of declination at the principal magnetic observatories of the world:—

Place.	Latitude.	Longitude.	Year.	Declination.
Pawlowsk, ...	59° 41' N.	30° 29' E.	1893	0° 4'·4 E.
Katharinenburg, . .	56° 49' N.	60° 38' E.	1893	9° 34'·6 E.
Kasan, ...	55° 47' N.	49° 8' E.	1892	7° 30'·8 W.
Copenhagen, ...	55° 41' N.	12° 34' E.	1893	10° 47'·7 W.
Stonyhurst, ...	53° 51' N.	2° 28' W.	1894	18° 44'·1 W.
Hamburg, ...	53° 34' N.	10° 3' E.	1893	11° 54'·3 W.
Wilhelmshaven, . . .	53° 32' N.	8° 9' E.	1892	13° 10'·1 W.
Potsdam, ...	52° 22' N.	13° 4' E.	1891	10° 42'·2 W.
Irkutsk, ...	52° 16' N.	104° 16' E.	1893	2° 9'·4 E.
Utrecht, ...	52° 5' N.	5° 11' E.	1893	14° 28'·5 W.
Kew, ...	51° 28' N.	0° 19' W.	1894	17° 23'·0 W.
Greenwich, ...	51° 28' N.	0° 0'	1894	17° 4'·6 W.
Uccle (Brussels), . .	50° 48' N.	4° 20' E.	1893	14° 48'·7 W.
Falmouth, ...	50° 9' N.	5° 5' W.	1893	19° 6'·4 W.
Prague, ...	50° 5' N.	14° 25' E.	1893	9° 42'·3 W.
Parc St. Maur (Paris),	48° 49' N.	2° 29' E.	1892	15° 26'·9 W.
Vienna, ...	48° 15' N.	16° 21' E.	1893	8° 49'·7 W.
O'Gyalla (near Buda Pest), ...	47° 29' N.	19° 3' E.	1894	7° 58'·2 W.
Pola (on Adriatic), . .	44° 52' N.	13° 50' E.	1894	9° 52'·6 W.
Nice, ...	43° 43' N.	7° 16' E.	1893	12° 32'·7 W.
Toronto, ...	43° 39' N.	79° 30' W.	1893	4° 36'·4 W.
Perpignan, ...	42° 42' N.	2° 53' E.	1892	14° 16'·0 W.
Rome, ...	41° 54' N.	12° 27' E.	1891	10° 45' W.
Tiflis, ...	41° 43' N.	44° 48' E.	1892	1° 33'·6 E.
Madrid, ...	40° 25' N.	3° 40' W.	1893	16° 14'·2 W.
Coimbra, ...	40° 12' N.	8° 25' W.	1893	17° 51'·7 W.
Washington, ...	38° 53' N.	77° 0' W.	1891	4° 9'·7 W.
Lisbon, ...	38° 43' N.	9° 9' W.	1893	17° 49'·4 W.
Zi-ka-wei, ...	31° 12' N.	121° 26' E.	1892	2° 14'·4 W.
Hong Kong, ...	22° 18' N.	114° 10' E.	1893	0° 31'·2 E.
Colaba, ...	18° 54' N.	72° 49' E.	1893	0° 40'·3 E.
Manila, ...	14° 35' N.	127° 11' E.	1892	0° 50'·1 E.
Batavia, ...	6° 11' S.	106° 49' E.	1893	1° 30'·6 E.
Mauritius, ...	20° 6' S.	57° 33' E.	1892	10° 5'·1 W.
Melbourne, ...	37° 50' S.	144° 58' E.	1893	8° 9'·6 E.

The observatories are arranged according to their latitude. The longitude is in all cases referred to Greenwich.

* *Science Progress*, vol. iii., 1895, p. 392.

In the years 1884 to 1888 Dr. T. E. Thorpe and Professor A. W. Rücker made magnetic observations at 205 places in the United Kingdom. The work was subsequently extended, and the magnetic constants have now been determined at 882 places in Great Britain and Ireland. The results have been published by Professor Rücker,* who gives a map showing the true lines of equal declinations for January 1st, 1891. By means of the table of secular change it will be possible to determine the value of the declination at any place in the United Kingdom for some years to come.

The neglect of the secular variation of the magnetic-needle resulted in a sad catastrophe at Wheal Owles in Cornwall, where, on January 10th, 1893, an irruption of water from an abandoned portion of the workings led to the loss of twenty lives. According to Mr. J. Henderson,† this catastrophe was found on investigation to have been due to ignorance of the secular variation, as in the plan of the underground workings, periodically kept up to date with care, the same magnetic meridian was used for a period of forty years. Thus, the levels of some extensive old workings full of water were holed at a point where the plan showed a safe barrier of solid ground.

* *Trans. Fed. Inst. M.E.*, vol. ix., 1895, p. 417.
† *Ibid.*, vol. viii., 1895, p. 273.

CHAPTER V.

SURVEYING WITH THE MAGNETIC-NEEDLE IN THE PRESENCE OF IRON.

Influence of Iron Rails.—The method of surveying described in the preceding chapter cannot be used in mines where magnetic substances deflect the needle. On account of the increasing use of iron and steel in mines in the form of rails, props, &c., the number of mines in which the magnetic-needle is not affected is extremely small.

Rails placed end to end on the ground become, in the course of time, permanently magnetised, and if a magnetic-needle is brought near the junction of two rails, it assumes a position parallel to the two rails. Some interesting experiments to determine the influence of iron rails on the magnetic-needle were made by Professor Combes of the Paris School of Mines. He found that the nearer the direction of the rails approached that of the magnetic meridian the more highly polarised they became. The following deflections were observed when a miner's compass was brought near rails which were placed in the direction of the magnetic meridian:—

Distance from the Rails.	Height above the Rails.	Azimuth Observed.
	Inches.	
19 ft. 8 ins. on one side,	58	80° 00′
5 ft. 3 ins. on one side,	47	83° 30′
Above the first rail,	43	83° 15′
Between the two rails,	43	83° 30′
Above the second rail,	43	83° 45′
6 ft. 6 ins. on the other side,	43	83° 30′

With the rails placed at right angles to the magnetic meridian, the following angles were obtained :—

13 feet 1 inch on one side, ...	329° 45'
Above the first rail, ...	328° 00"
Between the two rails, ...	330° 00'
1 foot 10 inches on the other side, . .	328° 30'

When the compass was only 15 inches above the rails, deviations amounting to 7° 30' were observed.

Experiments made at Freiberg, in Saxony, by Professor Junge confirm these results, and permit the following conclusions to be drawn :—

1. Iron rails identical as regards weight and dimensions may act differently on the compass, the deviation caused by one being sometimes double that by another. The influence of two parallel rails on the magnetic-needle cannot be neutralised. It is not sufficient, as so many miners imagine, to place the dial exactly midway between the two rails.

2. The influence of the rails on the needle is increased by sharp blows. Four blows on a rail with a hammer was found to increase by 2° the deviation produced.

3. The influence of the rails is greatest when they form an angle of 45° to 67° 30' with the meridian. The deviation then decreases until the rail is at right angles with the meridian, when the deviation is intermediate between the maximum and that observed when the rails make an angle of 22° 30' with the meridian.

4. The influence is very considerable when the compass is as much as 47 inches above the rails. In such a case with rails at an angle of 45° with the meridian, deviations amounting to 3° 25' have been observed.

No experiments appear to have been made with iron or steel sleepers. There can, however, be no doubt that their influence on the magnetic-needle is at least as considerable as that of iron rails.

The only practical conclusion that can be drawn from the results obtained by Professors Combes and Junge, is that an accurate survey cannot be made with the miner's dial in the manner described in the preceding chapter, unless the rails are taken up.

Local Attraction in the Mine.—In many metalliferous mines, local attraction, due to the presence of magnetic iron ore in the lode, is very considerable. At Botallack mine, in Cornwall, for example, the needle has been known to be deflected to the extent of 60° from its proper bearing. Experience shows that certain eruptive rocks, notably those of a dark colour with a base of hornblende or augite, affect the needle in the same way as magnetite or magnetic pyrites. In districts composed of magnetic rocks, the dial cannot be employed, as is shown by observations made at Ammeberg in Sweden, where at equidistant points along a straight line, the following bearings were obtained:— 3° 5¾′, 3° 4′, 3° 2¼′, 3° 1′, 2° 7¾′, and 2° 6′. To make a number of observations along a straight line is the best method of finding out if there is any local attraction affecting the needle. The influence of magnetic deposits on the compass has been utilised in Sweden and the United States in exploring for iron ore.

Surveying with the Dial in the presence of Iron.—With the general employment of iron rails in mines, the question arises to what extent may surveys be made with the ordinary dial without fear of deflections of the needle giving rise to error? As a matter of fact, the magnetic-needle may be used for the purpose of obtaining the true bearings of the traverse lines in places where attraction exists, provided that the mode of procedure is slightly modified. The method is based upon the fact that the deviation of a magnetic-needle remains the same, if the relative positions of the dial and the attracting object remain unaltered. All that is necessary is to note the back- and fore-bearing at each station, however much the magnetic-needle may be deflected. Then, if the needle is attracted on looking to the back object, it is attracted to precisely the same extent on looking forward, so that the difference of bearing of the two lines is unaltered. Consequently, if a correct bearing of any one line of the traverse can be obtained, an accurate survey may be made.

Dialling-Book.—The best form of dialling-book to adopt is an ordinary account-book, the £, s., and d. columns serving for fathoms, feet, and inches. If the measurements are made in links, only one column is required. The date column of the account-book serves for the number of the draft. In the space between the date and money columns, two lines are ruled, giving three columns, which may be used for the back-bearing, the fore-bearing, and the calculated true bearing.

The method of booking a survey is shown by the following example of a closed traverse, surveyed in the presence of a very large amount of iron. The bearings and distances were as follows:—

No.	Back-Bearing.	Fore-Bearing.	Correct Bearing.	Fms.	Ft.	In.
A	...	3° 36'	3° 36'	6	4	1
B	3° 36'	1° 36'	1° 36'	3	4	10¼
C	5° 27'	327° 44'	323° 53'	5	3	5½
D	319° 15'	224° 53'	229° 31'	6	1	7½
E	202° 57'	156° 44'	183° 18'	6	0	1½
F	167° 48'	165° 03'	180° 33'	4	1	8
G	166° 15'	79° 48'	94° 06'	8	0	3
H	79° 34'	349° 04	3° 36'	...	...	...

The instrument was set up at B, where there was no attraction, and a back-bearing was taken. This was found to be 3° 36'. This bearing being correct, it was also entered as a fore-bearing at A. A fore-bearing was then taken at B; this was found to be 1° 36'. This also is correct, as there was no attraction when the back-bearing was taken, and the dial was not moved to take the fore-bearing. The instrument was then moved to C, and a back-bearing to B taken. This should have read 1° 36', the correct fore-bearing from B to C. It was, however, found to be 5° 27', showing that the needle was considerably deflected from its true position. Back- and fore-bearings were taken at each of the following stations, and in each case the needle was found to be seriously deflected. Consequently, before the survey could be plotted, the correct bearings had to be calculated.

The bearings 3° 36' and 1° 36', being known to be correct, might be inserted in the correct-bearing column. The back-bearing at C was found to be 5° 27' instead of 1° 36'. It was therefore 3° 51' too great, and as the dial was not moved, the attraction remained the same, so that the fore-bearing at C was also 3° 51' too large. The correct fore-bearing at C, then, was 327° 44' − 3° 51' = 323° 53'. The back-bearing at D, which should be the same as this, was found to be 319° 15', that is, 4° 38' too small. The fore-bearing taken at the same station under the influence of the same attraction must also have been 4° 38' too small, so that its correct value is 224° 53' + 4° 38' = 229° 31'. The back-bearing at E should be identical with this. It was, however, found to be 202° 57', that is, 26° 34' too small. The fore-bearing at the same station must also be 26° 34' too

56   MINE-SURVEYING.

small. Its correct value, then, is 156° 44′ + 26° 34′ = 183° 18′. This should be identical with the back-bearing at F, which was found to be 167° 48′, or 15° 30′ too small. The fore-bearing at F is also 15° 30′ too small, and its correct value is 165° 03′ + 15° 30′ = 180° 33′. This should be identical with the back-bearing at G, which was found to be 166° 15′, or 14° 18′ too small. The fore-bearing is also 14° 18′ too small, and therefore the correct bearing is 79° 48′ + 14° 18′ = 94° 06′. This should be identical with the bearing at the last station, which was found to be 79° 34′, or 14° 32′ too small. The fore-bearing at the same station is also 14° 32′ too small, and therefore its correct value is 349° 04′ + 14° 32′ = 363° 36′, that is, 3° 36′. The last line of this traverse is identical with the first, so that the first and last bearings should be identical. Thus, in a closed traverse the surveyor is able to check the accuracy of his work.

The following page from the dialling-book at a metalliferous mine may be taken as an example for calculation:—

No.	Back-Bearing.	Fore-Bearing.	True Bearing.	Fms.	Ft.	Ins.
A	...	245° 12′	245° 12′	9	3	6
B	245° 12′	254° 30′	254° 30′	8	5	6
C	254° 30′	164° 45′	164° 45′	9	5	8
D	164° 06′	169° 24′	170° 03′	4	0	9
E	178° 12′	161° 00′	152° 51′	5	0	8
F	157° 45′	174° 00′	169° 06′	4	1	0
G	171° 27′	186° 42′	184° 21′	4	4	6
H	183° 39′	178° 18′	179° 00′	5	4	9
J	177° 33′	221° 00′	222° 27′	8	2	7
K	221° 00′	79° 18′	80° 45′	1	5	7
L	89° 33′	80° 00′	71° 12′	2	1	5
M	71° 12′	82° 48′	82° 48′	5	3	0
N	82° 48′	84° 24′	84° 24′	3	5	1
O	84° 24′	90° 06′	90° 06′	7	5	2
P	90° 06′	91° 30′	91° 30′	2	5	3

If the first and last bearings are not identical, and if the difference does not amount to more than a few minutes, the slight error, due possibly to the imperfections of the instrument employed, may be to a great extent eliminated by dividing the error by the number of station-lines, and adding the result to, or subtracting it from, each bearing. Thus, in the example given, if the observed fore-bearing at H had been 349° 00′ instead of 349° 04′, the final error would have been 4′. It would be assumed that no error occurred in reading the first bearing. The error in each bearing would consequently be about ½′, and the calculated bearings could have been corrected for this error by adding ½′ in each case, that is to say, ½′ to the calculated bearing of B, 1′ to that of C, 1½′ to D, 2′ to E, 2½′ to F, 3′ to G, and 4′ to H.

In applying this method to colliery and surface-surveys, it will be found advisable to book upwards in the usual manner, noting the back-observation (B.O.) at each station. A tabulated statement of the bearings may then be made, and the true bearings calculated.

Errors in Compass Surveys.—In all cases where the dial is used for surveying in the presence of iron, the greatest care must be taken in making the observations; otherwise very serious errors may arise, especially in long traverses. This may be illustrated by an example.

In making a survey in the ordinary way with the dial, any error in the readings will cause the next draft to have a false position when plotted. Assuming that a survey is made between the points A and E, Fig. 16, and that the bearings are read direct from the dial without error, the plan of the traverse will be correct, as shown by the line A B C D E in the figure. If, on the other hand, a mistake is made during the progress of the survey, and the bearing, N A B, of the line A B incorrectly determined to the extent of the angle B A B′ or α, then the following drafts will have the same error.

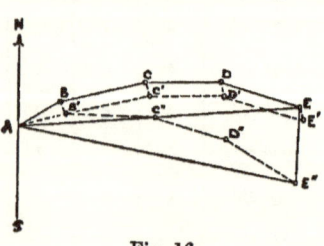

Fig. 16.

B′ will be the end point of the first draft when plotted, thus giving a lateral error of B B′. The other bearings of the traverse being correctly determined, on plotting, the lines B′ C′, C′ D′, D′ E′ will be obtained. These lines must be equal and parallel to the lines B C, C D, D E, and therefore B B′ = C C′ = D D′ = E E′. In other words, the lateral error B B′ caused by the incorrect determination of the bearing of the line A B is carried uniformly throughout the traverse, whatever its length may be. The magnitude of this error is found by trigonometry to be $2\,AB \cdot \sin \frac{\alpha}{2}$.

The magnitude of the error is entirely different when the dial is used as an angle-measurer in surveying over iron. Again, assuming that the bearing of the line A B has been incorrectly determined to the extent of the angle α, the angle N A B' having been read instead of the angle N A B, if now the dial is employed for measuring the angles, the bearing of the next line, B C, is obtained by adding or subtracting the exterior angle at B, according as the line B C is to the right or left of A B. The other bearings in the presence of iron may be assumed to have been correctly taken. The bearing of the line A B being incorrect, the bearing of the line B C will also be incorrect to the extent of the angle α. Each of the following bearings will be incorrect to the extent of the same angle, so that on plotting the calculated bearings, the line A B' C'' D'' E'' will be obtained. The error α thus affects the whole traverse from A to E, and increases in proportion to the distance apart of those points. The length from A to E being represented by L, the lateral error, E E'' is equal to $2\,L \sin \frac{\alpha}{2}$.

It is thus evident that a survey may be very inaccurate, when the angles are not correctly measured. In applying the method of surveying with the needle over iron, the surveyor should not fail to make a check-survey, or reverse course of dialling, selecting fresh points for his stations. Not only in this method, but in all other surveying operations, it is highly desirable that the mine-surveyor should adopt the practice of always checking and verifying every part of his work.

CHAPTER VI.

Surveying with the Fixed Needle.

Vernier.—In the improved forms of the miner's dial, the compass-box is connected with the plate that carries it, in such a way that it can revolve on this plate. Motion is given to it by a circular rack and pinion worked from below. Modified in this way, the instrument is known as the *circumferenter*, or *rack-dial*. When the rack-screw is turned, two marks, made opposite to each other, one on the projecting portion of the compass-box, and the other on the plate, will separate. Their angular distance apart is measured by means of a *vernier*, which may be defined as a contrivance for measuring smaller portions of space than those into which a line is actually divided.

The principle of the vernier is as follows:—If a line containing n units of measurement is divided into n equal parts, each part will represent one unit; and if a line containing $n - 1$ of these units is divided into n parts, each part will be equal to $\frac{n-1}{n}$ units. The difference between one division in the former case, and one in the latter will be $1 - \frac{n-1}{n} = \frac{1}{n}$ of the original unit. Similarly, the difference between two divisions of the one, and two divisions of the other, will be $\frac{2}{n}$ of a unit; between three of the one, and three of the other, $\frac{3}{n}$, and so on. Hence, in order to obtain a length of $\frac{x}{n}$ of a unit, a division of one scale has to be made to coincide with one on the other scale, and the space between the two corresponding xth divisions from the coinciding divisions, on both scales will be the required length of $\frac{x}{n}$ of a unit.

The same reasoning applies if n divisions of the vernier are made equal to $n + 1$ divisions of the limb. In this case, however, the vernier must be read backwards. There are thus two kinds of vernier, called *direct* or *retrograde*, according as they are read forwards or backwards from the zero points. Most verniers in surveying instruments are of the direct type. In all cases, the zero of the vernier scale marks the point on the limb, the reading of which is required.

The difference between a limb division and a vernier division is $\frac{1}{n}$ of the value of a limb division. This difference is known as the *least reading* of the vernier, and expresses the degree of minuteness to which readings can be effected.

The circle divided to 30' is a common graduation for the miner's dial. If 30 divisions on the vernier are made equal to 29 on the circle, each division on the vernier will be equal to $\frac{29 \times 30}{30} = 29'$, or 1' less than a division on the circle. The vernier will therefore read to an accuracy of one minute.

As an example of more minute division, the sextant used in marine-surveying may be cited. The limb of this instrument is divided at every 10 minutes, and 59 of these parts are made equal to 60 divisions on the vernier. The least reading in this case is $\frac{n}{60} = \frac{10}{60} = 10''$.

The rule for reading an instrument provided with a vernier is as follows:—Read the circle, in the direction of the graduation, up to the line preceding the zero of the vernier. This gives the number of whole units of the circle. The line on the vernier coinciding with a line on the circle gives the number of fractional parts of one unit of the circle to be added to the former reading.

Racking.—Provided with a vernier, the compass may be used to measure angles in a horizontal plane, or *azimuths*, without the aid of the magnetic-needle. This method of surveying is known as *fast-needle* dialling or *racking*.

The word *azimuth* used without qualification, usually means the number of degrees, minutes, and seconds by which the direction of a vertical plane passing through a station and a given object deviates to the right of a vertical plane passing through the station and the north pole. The *relative azimuth* of any two objects may be measured at any given station; that is to say, the angle by which a vertical plane passing through the station and one of the objects deviates to the right of a vertical plane passing through the station and the other object. An azimuth exceeding 180° denotes that the direction of the object to which it is measured lies to the left of the direction from which azimuths are measured, by an angle equal to the difference between the azimuth and 360°.

The horizontal angle between any two directions is the difference of their azimuths, if the difference is less than 180°. If it is greater than 180°, the angle between the directions is the excess of 360° above the difference of the azimuths. Thus, in Fig. 17, the dial being set up at A, and A B having the azimuth of 0°, the azimuth of C, an object to the right of A B, is equal to the angle B A C. On the other hand, the azimuth of D, an object to the left of A B, is the angle subtended by the arc $b'd$, that is, the difference between the angle B A D and 360°.

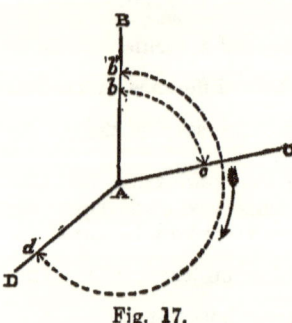

Fig. 17.

Various Forms of Dial: (*a.*) **Lean's Miner's Dial.**—There are a great number of different types of mining circumferenters adapted for surveying without the use of the needle. They differ merely in details of structure; the essential parts are the same in all.

Fig. 18 represents Lean's dial, as manufactured by Mr. W. F. Stanley of London. This form of dial is that most frequently used in metalliferous mines. Like the ordinary miner's dial, it consists of a brass compass-box attached to a tripod-stand by a socket fitting on to a corresponding plug. In addition to the levels, sights, and magnetic-needle of the ordinary dial, it has, above the main plate, a divided vernier plate by which horizontal angles may be measured independently of the needle. The same graduation thus serves for the vernier and for the needle. The movement of the circle is effected by a concealed rack and pinion, the head of which projects from the under side of the main compass-plate. The instrument is provided with a vertical arc for measuring vertical angles, and a telescope so that the instrument may be used as a theodolite for surface-surveys. The vertical arc and the telescope may be removed, and the sights used. The latter are made to fold down for convenience in packing. Underneath the compass-box is a pin to fasten the two plates together

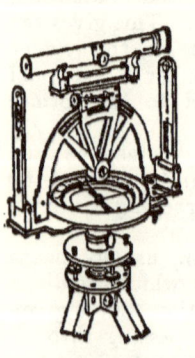

Fig. 18.

at 360°, and a spring to throw the needle off its pivot so as to preserve it when not in use.

(b.) **The Henderson Dial** is an improved form of the Lean dial. It is 6 inches in diameter, well divided, and graduated to the left. This instrument is represented in Fig. 19.

In the construction of the sights, the use of horse hairs is avoided, as they are continually getting burnt by a flaring candle underground. In place of the ordinary horse-hair sights, the *split-sight* is adopted. There is a narrow slit in each sight, through which the object can be distinctly seen, and its bearing determined with precision. On the other hand, if the vertical hair is used, it covers to a certain extent the object, which should be seen sharply defined.

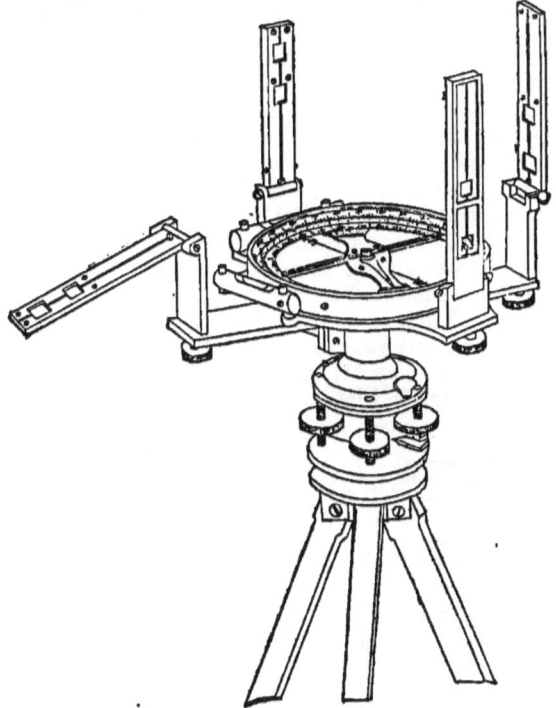

Fig. 19.—Henderson Dial.

The needle is mounted on a ruby instead of the ordinary agate. Care must, consequently, be taken to throw off the needle when not required, as the shock, caused by placing the tripod suddenly on the ground, is apt to crack the ruby, which, though extremely hard, is brittle.

To the north-seeking end of the needle, an aluminium vernier is fixed, the needle being counterbalanced at its other end. By the aid of this contrivance, a bearing can be read to three minutes, a degree of precision sufficient for general purposes.

The special feature of the dial is the attachment to the instrument of two sets of folding sights, one revolving within the other. The fixed sights are always in a line with the back object in fast-needle surveying; whilst the inner or revolving sights adjusted to the forward object give the angle of deviation from the original direction. The sights are made to fold over so as to be out of the way, in case the new line should too closely approach the direction of the old one. From the joints of a dial working loose, an imperceptible movement will sometimes take place in the body of the instrument on turning it in a new direction. There results, of course, an error in the angle obtained when looking towards the forward object. In the Henderson dial, however, the back object can be again sighted through the fixed sights, and re-adjusted should any deviation be observed.

For taking vertical angles, a semicircular vertical arc is fixed across the central line of the dial, when required. It is provided with a movable limb, to which a vernier is attached, as well as a horizontal bar carrying a pair of sights and a long spirit-level. A folding shutter is fitted to each sight, with the object of precluding the possibility of the eye being directed to the wrong orifice.

This dial was invented by Mr. J. Henderson, M.Inst.C.E.,[*] and is manufactured by Mr. Letcher, of Truro.

(c.) *Davis's Miner's Dial.*—This improved form of Hedley dial is the best instrument for colliery use. As represented in Fig. 20, the dial combines all the latest improvements of the Hedley dial with the outside vernier of the theodolite.

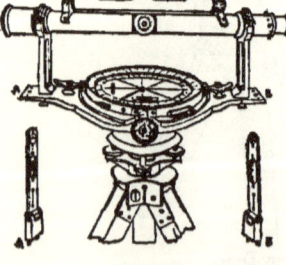

Fig. 20.

It consists of a compass-box 5 or 6 inches in diameter, divided into 360° on the compass-ring, and into four times 90° on the plate, 0° being at the north and south points, and 90° at the east and west points. The needle is mounted on an agate cap, and when not in use is thrown off by a spring. There are two spirit-levels at right angles to each

* *Proc. Min. Inst., Cornwall,* vol. i., 1883, p. 317.

other in the face of the instrument, protected by the glass cover of the compass-box. The sights are the same as those of the older form of Hedley dial previously described.

Underneath the main-plate, there is a circle or limb divided into 360°. A vernier attached to the outside of the compass-box enables horizontal angles to be read with great precision. Being placed on the outside circumference of the dial, the vernier is more easily read than when placed inside the compass-box, and the necessity of raising the head above the dial-face is obviated. The upper and lower limbs of the instrument may be fixed together at 360°, if required, by means of a pin under the body of the instrument. This dial, it will be seen, differs from the Lean and Henderson dials, in that the vernier is not movable, but remains rigid with the sights.

The Hedley form of side arc for taking vertical angles is replaced by a fixed circular box 1¼ inch in diameter, with a hand traversing a dial-plate divided into 90°. This new form of arc presents the advantages of always being in position, and of being so compact that it does not interfere with the manipulation of the screws under the body of the dial.

For surface-surveys, a telescope may be substituted for the sights. The tripod on which the dial is supported is made of mahogany, with a brass screw-joint at the centre of each leg. For very shallow seams, it is necessary to have an extra set of joints in the legs. All the joints in the legs are made interchangeable, and great rigidity is obtained by increasing the diameter of the legs towards the centre.

The special feature of the Davis dial is the arrangement by which bearings may be taken simultaneously with the magnetic-needle and with the vernier, the latter automatically checking the former. Thus any error arising from incorrect reading or from local attraction is at once detected. The graduations of the vernier ring and of the needle ring are so arranged that the readings correspond. This is effected by numbering the dial from the north from left to right, and by numbering the vernier ring from the vernier also from left to right.

Dial-Joint.—The miner's dial is usually fitted to a slightly conical spindle, having on its lower end a ball, which is confined in a socket in such a way that it can be moved in any direction in the operation of levelling the instrument.

For facilitating the setting up of the instrument, an American invention, the Hoffman joint,* has been adopted in conjunction

---

* *Trans. Amer. Inst. Min. Eng.*, vol. vii., p. 308.

SURVEYING WITH THE FIXED NEEDLE.

with the Davis dial. This tripod head combines the play of the ball and socket joint and the accuracy and rigidity of the theodolite parallel plates.

The ordinary form of tripod has the disadvantage that it is almost impossible to level up a sensitive bubble, so that it will remain in the centre of its run long enough to take a satisfactory sight. On levelling the instrument and sighting, a second glance at the bubble almost invariably shows that it has changed its position, and it is necessary to level up again. This defect is due to the fact that the levelling screws, when moved in or out to a considerable extent, do not stand perpendicular to the plate on which they rest, but on an inclined plane, so that, on turning them, their points have a tendency to slide down the plane. In this position, they spring, and turning them is apt to bind or bend them.

Another imperfection in many tripod heads, is that the plummet is attached to some point on the axis above or below the centre of the ball and socket. In either case, the plummet, after being set over a station, will, during the operation of levelling up, travel away from the point in a degree proportionate to the distance of the attachment of the plummet from the centre of the ball, and the deviation of the axis from the perpendicular at the time the instrument is placed over the centre.

The Hoffman joint (Patent 1878, No. 2084) is free from these defects. Fig. 21 shows the form supplied with the Davis dial.

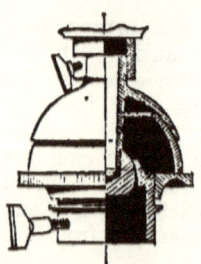

Fig. 21.

It is claimed to possess the following advantages over the ball and socket joint:—1. The plumb-line is suspended from the actual centre of the dial. 2. The rubbing-surface is some ten times greater, and consequently the joint is more rigid. 3. The joint is manipulated with greater ease and rapidity. A slight turn of the milled flange from right to left liberates the two concentric hemispheres. The dial is then levelled up, and a slight turn of the flange from left to right secures the joint. 4. Only one hand is required to manipulate the joint. 5. The total height of the Hoffman joint is 3 inches; that of the ball and socket joint $3\frac{3}{8}$ inches. The length of the centre is $2\frac{1}{2}$ inches, that of the ball and socket is barely $1\frac{1}{2}$ inch. The Hoffman joint is not heavier than the ball and socket joint.

(*d.*) **Whitelaw's Dial.**—In this instrument (Patent 1878, No. 1592) the compass and lower limb are of the same diameter

(Fig. 22). The vernier is attached to the outside of the compass-box, and is placed close to the right of the line of sight, so that readings can be taken by the surveyor directly after sighting the object, without moving aside. The graduated lower plate is covered by the compass-box except at the vernier. A circular spirit-level placed inside the compass-box serves for approximately levelling the instrument before final adjustment with the long level suspended below the vertical arc.

The special feature of this dial is the manner in which the vertical arc is supported. In order that the compass graduation shall not be obstructed, the standards are entirely dispensed with. In their place is a movable semicircular arc carrying the bar with the sights, or telescope if required. This arc is at right angles to the graduated vertical arc, and the axis, on which it turns, corresponds with the east and west points of the compass-box. Angles of elevation or depression up to 90° can be taken simultaneously with horizontal angles. The dial is thus well suited for surveying in metalliferous mines. It is manufactured by Mr. W. H. Harling, of London.

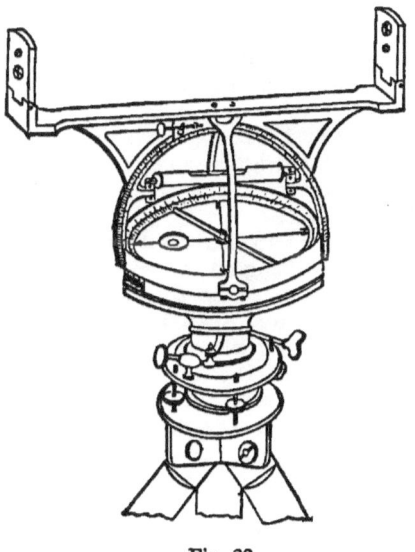

Fig. 22.

(e.) **Thornton's Dial.**—This dial is the patent of Messrs. A. G. Thornton and Co., of Manchester. Its special feature is a graduated semicircular folding arc for taking vertical angles. This vertical limb is fixed by hinge joints to the edge of the compass-box, and may be folded down out of the way of injury when the dial is being carried about in the mine. A groove is cut in the vertical limb, in which slides the bridge carrying the sights. The bridge may be fixed at any angle by a clamping screw, and to it a vernier is attached for reading vertical angles. In order to ensure the rigidity of the hinged vertical limb, a pin is provided to fix it securely, and when folded down it rests upon a ledge, and so relieves the hinged joints of strain.

The compass-plate is 6½ inches in diameter, and its edge is bevelled; the divisions are thus clearly seen, and readings can be taken very readily. The dial is provided with a vernier within the compass-box, and with two spirit-levels let into the compass-face at right angles to one another. It is attached to the tripod in the usual way by a ball and socket joint with clamping screw.

Traversing Underground.—A traverse is a series of consecutive courses, the lengths and azimuths of which have to be determined. With the vernier-dial or circumferenter, the mode of procedure is as follows:—

1. Three tripods should be provided, and two candles or lamps on stands fitting on the tripods of such a height that when the light is replaced by the instrument, the axis of the telescope when horizontal shall be of the same height as the top of the wick. Having placed a tripod with a lamp at station 1 (say, the centre of the shaft), set up the second tripod with the circumferenter at the second station, and send on the third tripod with the other lamp on it, as far forward as the light can be seen. With the pin of the circumferenter keeping the vernier at zero, take a back-observation to the lamp at station 1. Clamp the vertical axis of the instrument, carefully measure the distance from station 1 to station 2, and enter in the dialling-book the distance and the horizontal angle 0° 00′. Then take out the pin, unclamp the vernier, and take a fore-observation to the lamp at station 3, moving the sights by means of the rack-work. Clamp the vernier, measure the distance from station 2 to station 3, and note the distance and the angle indicated by the vernier.

Then take up the first tripod, and send it forward, with the lamp on it, to a station beyond the third tripod, place the second lamp on the second tripod and the instrument on the third tripod, and observe the angle as before, by first bringing the vernier to zero by means of the pin. In this way any number of angles may be measured, a back-observation being in each case first taken with the vernier clamped at zero. Thus, the last course is always taken as the base-line for the following angle.

This method of surveying is illustrated by the accompanying notes of a survey of a portion of a Durham colliery:—

No. 4.—131° 15′	365 250 225 100 365	Dipper W. 3 ft.
No. 3.—138° 20′ from $\frac{305}{1}$	90	N. headways, 20 yards.
Continued 63 links to face W. bord W. bord No. 2.—343° 45′ (or N. 16° 15′ W.)	⊙ 299 160 100 60 299	of ridding. Permanent mark left in roof. 20 yds. E. bord and holed. 30 yds. E. bord and holed.
No. 1.—340° 00′ (or N. 20° W.)	⊙ 305 ⊙	Permanent mark left in roof and thill. From winding shaft.

Survey from winding shaft to north face, round west and east face to pumping shaft, main coal seam.

SURVEYING WITH THE FIXED NEEDLE.

No. 10.—94° 15′	30	Bord continued east.
No. 9.—93° 00′	200 100 200	20 yds. to rise hitch.
No. 8.—255° 32′	160	Continued 3 yds. to rise hitch.
No. 7.—87° 20′	212 100 82 212	20 yds. to hitch.
No. 6.—89° 07′	60	100 links to hitch, rise not proved.
No. 5.—273° 21′	412 330 202 110 412	Continued 150 links to rise hitch, not proved.

No. 13.—273° 20′	⊙ 400 315 300 225 160 115 400	Left permanent mark.
No. 12.—131° 22′	⊙ 160 110 105 160	Continued 20 yds. to face. Permanent mark left. crosses dip hitch of 2 ft. 6 ins. going east. Headways continued 20 yds
No. 11.—251° 16′	⊙ 412 300 205 100 412	to permanent mark left some 20 years ago. 35 yds. to rise hitch. 30 yds. to rise hitch.

SURVEYING WITH THE FIXED NEEDLE. 71

End of	☉	survey.
	327	to centre of pumping shaft.
Water level.	220	Water level, narrow place.
	170	
	100	
No. 14.—95° 53'	327	

The local mining terms occurring in these survey notes have the following meanings:—A *bord* is a passage driven across the grain of the coal. A *headway* is a passage driven in the direction of the grain of the coal. A *stenton* is a passage between two winning headways. The *thill* is the floor of the mine. A *hitch* is a slight dislocation of the strata, which does not exceed the height of the seam. *Ridding* is clearing away a fall of rubbish. The *face* is the extremity of the workings.

The distances are measured in links, and, in order to avoid confusion, the total distance is first given in each draft. The first two angles were taken from the magnetic meridian. The figures $\frac{305}{1}$ denote that line No. 3 is from the distance 305, that is, the end of line No. 1.

The angles taken with the circumferenter are reduced to angles from one meridian by applying the following rule:—To the first meridian angle, add the next observed horizontal angle. If the sum exceeds 180°, deduct that amount from it. If the sum is less than 180°, add that amount to it. The result will be the second meridian angle. Thus, the angles taken in the survey given will be reduced to angles from one meridian in the following manner:—

Meridian, . .   0° 00' + 1st angle 340° 00' = 340° 00' = No. 1 mer. angle.
                0° 00' + 2nd angle 343° 45' = 343° 45' = No. 2 mer. angle.
No. 1 mer. angle, 340° 00' + 3rd angle 138° 20' = 478° 20'
                478° 20' − 180° 00' = 298° 20' = No. 3 mer. angle.
No. 3 mer. angle, 298° 20' + 4th angle 131° 15' = 429° 35'
                429° 35' − 180° 00' = 249° 35' = No. 4 mer. angle.

No. 4 mer. angle, 249° 35'+5th angle 273° 21'=522° 56'
522° 56'−180° 00'=342° 56'=**No. 5 mer. angle.**
342° 56'+ 89° 07'=432° 03';
432° 03'−180° 00'=252° 03'=**No. 6.**
252° 03'+ 87° 20'=339° 23';
339° 23'−180° 00'=159° 23'=**No. 7.**
159° 23'+255° 32'=414° 55';
414° 55'−180° 00'=234° 55'=**No. 8.**
234° 55'+ 93° 00'=327° 55';
327° 55'−180° 00'=147° 55'=**No. 9.**
147° 55'+ 94° 15'=242° 10';
242° 10'−180° 00'= 62° 10'=**No. 10.**
62° 10'+251° 16'=313° 26';
313° 26'−180° 00'=133° 26'=**No. 11.**
133° 26'+131° 22'=264° 48';
264° 48'−180° 00'= 84° 48'=**No. 12.**
84° 48'+273° 20'=358° 08';
358° 08'−180° 00'=178° 08'=**No. 13.**
178° 08'+ 95° 53'=274° 01';
274° 01'−180° 00'= 94° 01'=**No. 14.**

2. There is a second method of traversing with the fast-needle, in which the work is continued from the original base-line by first taking for each line a back-observation with the vernier at the angle last read. With the circumferenter at station 2, and lamp tripods at stations 1 and 3, take a back-observation to the lamp at station 1, the pin keeping the vernier at zero, as described in the first method of traversing. Clamp the vertical axis, take out the pin, and take a fore-observation to the lamp at station 3. Clamp the vernier, and instead of now moving it back to zero, let it remain in the position in which it was clamped, and set up the circumferenter at station 3. Take a back-observation to station 2 by unclamping the vertical axis, leaving the vernier clamped. In this way any number of angles may be measured, the survey being always continued from the same meridian. This method, however, is not to be recommended, as any error made in one observation is carried on throughout the survey.

The observed angles may be reduced to meridian angles by adding the meridian angle of the first line in each case. The observed angle and the meridian angle of any station-line being

SURVEYING WITH THE FIXED NEEDLE.   73

known, subtract the former from the latter, the difference is the meridian angle of the first station-line. If the vernier angle exceeds the meridian angle, add 360° to the latter in order to enable the subtraction to be effected. The meridian angle of the first station-line thus obtained is added to each subsequent vernier angle, the sum in each case being the meridian angle of the line in question.

For example, the following angles were taken with the rack dial, the needle being thrown off except where true bearings were taken at E, looking back to D and forward to F:—

No.	Angles.	True Bearings.	Distance.			Remarks.
			Fms.	Ft.	In.	
A	0° 00′	...	10	4	9	{ From ☉ 2 ft. W. of centre shaft.
B	275° 06′	...	7	3	2	...
C	282° 12′	...	8	1	9	...
D	278° 51′	...	7	3	0	...
E	286° 00′	277° 09′	3	5	9	...
F	292° 00′	283° 09′	9	2	9	...
G	296° 00′	...	9	5	10	END.

At station E the angle and bearing are known. Consequently, to obtain the bearing of line A the angle 286° 00′ must be subtracted from the bearing 277° 09′. The latter being smaller than the former, 360° must be added, giving 360° + 277° 09′ = 637° 09′. This result less 286° 00′ is equal to 351° 09′, the bearing of line A. The same result is obtained with line F. Thus, (283° 09′ + 360°) − 292° = 351° 09′. The bearings of the other station-lines may be easily found by adding 351° 09′ to the observed angle in each case.

The work may be plotted, without any preliminary calculation, with the protractor and scale as if the survey had been made with the magnetic-needle. The protractor must, however, be graduated in the contrary direction to that required for a needle survey, if the dial is a left-handed one.

3. When the dial is numbered from the north from left to right, all calculation can be dispensed with; the angles being

read direct from the magnetic meridian. The Davis dial is graduated in this way. The horizontal circle of that instrument being also graduated from left to right, the bearings can be taken simultaneously with the loose needle and with the vernier, the latter acting as an automatic check on the former.

In making a survey in this way, select some disused road, where there is no iron present, and take its magnetic bearing from stations at the beginning and end. If there is no attraction, the two results will be identical. Then with the dial set up at the end station, clamp the vertical axis by tightening the collar attached to the ball and socket, unclamp the vernier-plate by slackening the clamping screw, and turn the sights by means of the rack and pinion screw, until the vernier reads exactly the same angle as the magnetic bearing just taken. This bearing is used as the basis of the subsequent determinations of the angles of the traverse. Clamp the vernier-plate, unclamp the vertical axis, and by means of the loose collar direct the sights to the lamp at the first station. If the readings obtained with the needle and the vernier are identical, the dial is in adjustment, and the whole of the underground workings may be surveyed from this base-line. In taking a fore-observation, the surveyor must turn the south side of the compass face towards himself, whilst in taking a back-observation, his eye must be at the north sight.

The following is an example of a survey made by this system:—

No.	Vernier Angle.	Meridian Angle.	Distance.	Remarks.
A	30° 05′	30° 05′	Links. 550	From end of disused road.
B²	315° 58′	...	708	...
C²	51° 01′	...	597	...
D²	274° 58′	...	722	...
B	115° 12′	...	658	From A again.
C	10° 33′	...	618	...
D	301° 18′	301° 10′	467	...

The survey was commenced in a disused road, the bearing of which was found to be 30° 05′. The vernier reading was made to correspond with that angle. Then with the instrument set up at

A, a back-observation was taken to the lamp at the end of the disused road, the vernier remaining clamped at 30° 05′. The vertical axis of the dial was then clamped, the vernier-plate unclamped, and a forward-observation taken to B². The vernier was found to read 315° 58′. Clamped at this angle, the dial was moved to B², and the survey continued as before. The survey can be checked at any point by liberating the needle. If the vernier and needle readings differ, the amount of magnetic attraction is the difference between the two readings.

The dial being graduated from left to right, 90° indicates West, and 270° East. In plotting the survey a protractor graduated from right to left must consequently be used.

Surveying in Inclined Shafts.—The vernier-dial is of great value for surveying in inclined shafts containing iron pumps. The survey should be commenced in a level free from magnetic attraction. On the basis of the bearing thus determined, the survey is continued to the shaft.

Should the surveyor be called upon to determine the bearing of an inclined shaft, containing iron pumps, with a miner's dial unprovided with a vernier, he may perform the operation with a cross-staff, either a well-made brass instrument or an improvised one made by drawing two lines at right angles on a board, about 6 inches square and 1 inch thick. The lines must be cut half an inch deep with a fine saw. The instrument thus made is fixed on a three-foot stand.

The cross-staff is set up in such a position that a candle in the shaft can be seen through one pair of sights. In the line of sight of the other pair, the dial is set up in the level out of the way of magnetic attraction. In this way, the candle in the shaft and the dial in the level form a right angle with the cross-staff. An assistant must now look through the sights of the dial to a candle held immediately above the cross-staff, and read the bearing indicated by the needle. Being exactly at right angles to this line, the bearing of the shaft may be at once determined. Thus, assuming that the needle reads 282°, if the underlie is northerly, the bearing of the shaft will be 12°; if southerly, 192°.

The Vernier Compass.—The vernier of the circumferenter may be used for reading the magnetic bearing. In this method of surveying, the compass-box is clamped with the needle lying upon the zero or north and south line marked on the dial. The sights being then directed to the object, the bearing is read direct from the vernier to 3 minutes, or by estimation upon a superior instrument to 1 minute. This method is very expeditious, and gives most accurate results. At any point in the traverse, a fast-needle observation may be made without difficulty.

In working with the fast needle, it is advisable to invariably start with a loose magnetic bearing, and, if practicable, to close with one. Intermediate checks by the same means are desirable, but not essential. In this way, the needle lies upon the zero line at every set, except where local attraction prevails, of which the amount and direction are shown by the needle's deviation from that line. The result is that the traverse angles booked are also magnetic bearings.

In order to show grounds for confidence in this method, the details of an actual survey, made by Mr. W. F. Howard,* may be quoted. The survey was made between the Speedwell and

No.	Vernier Bearing.	Horizontal Distance.	Remarks.
1	N. 34° 24' W.	Links. 13¼	From Speedwell north or down-cast shaft.
2	N. 58° 35' E.	639	... ...
3	N. 45° 41' E.	274	... ...
4	N. 37° 29' E.	130	... ...
5	N. 8° 40' W.	127	... ...
6	N. 15° 02' E.	405	... ...
7	N. 17° 57' E.	206	... ...
8	N. 11° 35' E.	158	... ...
9	N. 35° 37' W.	73	... ...
10	N. 18° 20' E.	260	... ...
11	N. 18° 14' E.	470	... ...
12	N. 69° 42' E.	384	... ...
13	S. 27° 45' E.	63	... ...
14	N. 69° 32' E.	73	... ...
15	N. 71° 57' E.	78	To face of main ventilating drift intended to hole into Netherthorpe shaft.

* *Trans. N. Engl. Inst. M.E.*, vol. xx., 1870, p. 31.

Netherthorpe shafts at Staveley, with the intention of effecting a holing into the latter. The straight distance between the shafts, measured direct on the surface, was 31·13 chains, and the distance between the shafts by the underground roads was 35·43 chains, making the total circuit 66·56 chains, and requiring 16 sets underground. The foregoing is a copy of the survey notes.

The survey was made with a 5-inch Davis dial, divided to half-degrees, with a vernier reading to 3 minutes.

In this instance, the magnetic bearing and the horizontal distance sought, from the face of the heading to the intended up-cast shaft, was calculated to be N. 58° 38′ E., 190·5 links. It was then determined to drive direct into the shaft, and the draft was accordingly set out at the above bearing; and the holing proved this bearing and the calculated distance to be absolutely correct.

CHAPTER VII.

The German Dial.

Invention of the German Dial.—The continental method of surveying mines consists in suspending a compass and a clinometer to a stretched cord representing the line of sight. The compass and the clinometer are read, and the length of the line measured. In this way, the length, bearing, and inclination of the station-line are determined. Mine-surveys were conducted in the manner described by Agricola until the invention of the German dial, or hanging compass, by Balthasar Roessler, who died at Altenberg, in Saxony, in 1673.

Measuring Station-Lines.—The cord is 50 fathoms long. It is made of hemp, and wound round a wooden reel provided with a handle (Fig. 23). This cord is stretched from station to station. The length of the portion stretched depends, of course, on the distance of the stations apart. It should, however, not exceed 8 fathoms, so as to prevent the formation of a catenary curve. The screws (Fig. 24) to which the cord is fastened are 4 inches in length. They are firmly fixed into the timbering

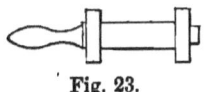

Fig. 23.

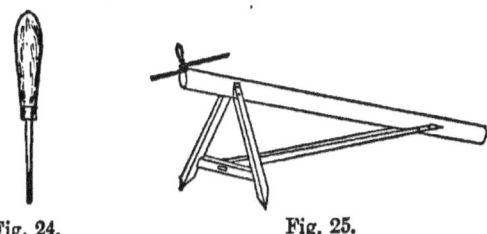

Fig. 24.   Fig. 25.

of the level. When the cord is stretched between the two points, the length of the line is measured. For this purpose, the Hungarian surveyors employ a fathom-rod; the Saxon surveyors use a brass 5-fathom chain.

For surveys at the surface, or in mines where there is no

timbering to hold the screws, a trestle of the form shown in Fig. 25 is employed. It consists of a beam 8 feet in length and 6 inches in diameter, with two short legs. It should be as heavy as possible, and no iron must be used in its construction.

In the Harz mines, instead of the cord, a thin brass chain is used. It is 10 metres in length, and is provided with a hook at one end. Every metre is indicated by a brass tag. The chain is wound on a reel, and used in the same way as the cord. The advantages it offers are: 1, It weighs very little; 2, its length can be read without any delay; 3, the best place for hanging the clinometer can easily be found; 4, no further measurements are required to determine the points where offsets have to be taken. Its disadvantage is that it is liable to stretch, and must therefore be carefully examined and adjusted every time it is used.

The Clinometer is used for determining the inclination of the stretched cord. It consists of a thin brass semicircle

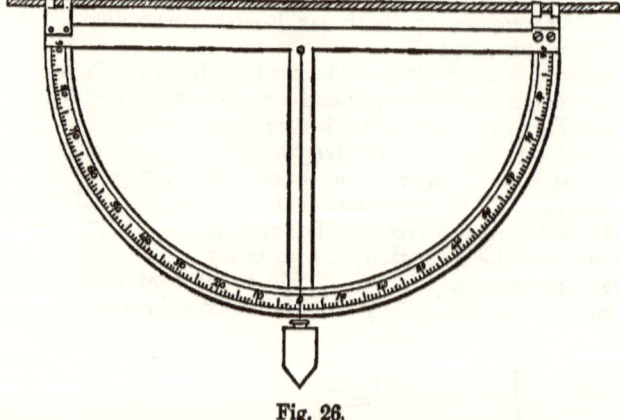

Fig. 26.

(Fig. 26), 9 inches in diameter, provided with hooks for hanging it on to the stretched cord. In the centre of the circle is a hole, through which a black human hair is passed, and fastened on the other side by means of wax. At the other end of the hair, a small brass plumb-bob is fastened. The hair touches the graduation of the semicircle, and enables the angle of inclination to be determined. The hooks open towards opposite sides, and are provided with apertures through which a clamp may be inserted when the clinometer is suspended from a highly inclined cord. The graduation begins at the centre of the semicircle— that is, perpendicularly below the centre from which the plummet hangs. It commences with 0°, and goes to 90° on both sides. Each degree is subdivided into four equal parts, so that an angle can be read direct to 15 minutes. As a rule, the quarter degrees are further divided by the eye into three equal parts, so that angles can be read accurately to 5 minutes. In order to facilitate the reading, the graduated side of the clinometer is usually silver-plated.

Use of the Clinometer.—If a cord, about 10 yards in length, is stretched horizontally, and the clinometer suspended from its centre, the human hair, hanging vertically on account of the weight of the plummet, will coincide with the zero of the graduation, provided that the cord is stretched perfectly tight, and that the clinometer is free from defects of construction. If the cord is inclined at an angle BAC (Fig. 27), the hair will not coincide with zero, but will give the angle DHE, which represents the angle of inclination of the cord. For since

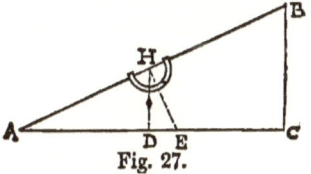

Fig. 27.

$AHD + DHE =$ a right angle, and $AHD + BAC =$ a right angle, $AHD + DHE = AHD + BAC$, therefore $DHE = BAC$. The clinometer thus may be used for determining the inclination of lines.

The cord when stretched forms a catenary curve, and consequently the angle of inclination varies at different points in the curve. There must, however, be a point where the cord is parallel to the line joining the two end points, and there the clinometer must be placed in order to obtain the true inclination. The weight of the clinometer being neglected, the correct point of suspension is slightly below the centre of the cord. But the weight of the clinometer alters the inclination of the cord, as it is not uniformly divided between the two hooks. The place where the clinometer must be suspended, in order to give the correct inclination of the cord, has been found by Professor A. von Miller-Hauenfels. His rule is as follows:—The clinometer must be suspended at a certain distance above the centre of the cord. For cords at an inclination of about 15°, this distance is obtained by multiplying the length of the cord by 0·004 for each degree; for greater angles, the length must be multiplied by 0·003 for each degree. Thus, with a cord 12 metres in length inclined at an angle of 20°, the clinometer must be suspended at a distance of 6·72 metres from the lower end. In practice it is found sufficient to suspend the clinometer at the middle of the cord, when the latter is but slightly inclined. With highly inclined cords, however, it is advisable to suspend the clinometer half a yard from the two ends, and to take the mean of the two readings, as the correct angle of inclination. The error will thus not exceed a few minutes in a cord 10 yards in length.

The Hanging-Compass.—The compass-box is 3 to 4 inches in diameter. It is graduated into 360°, or, more frequently, into twice 12 hours. The numbering commences at the ends of the diameter marked north and south, the 12 o'clock line, and proceeds from right to left. At the 6 o'clock line, the east and west points are transposed as in the ordinary miner's dial. In the larger compasses, each hour is divided into 16 parts; in the smaller ones, into 8 parts. Further sub-divisions may be estimated with the eye. The compass is, as a rule, read in hours, eighths, and sixteenths of eighths. One hour is equal to 15°, one-eighth is 1° 51′ 30″, and one-sixteenth of an eighth is 7′ 2″.

In order that the compass shall assume a horizontal position when suspended to the cord, it is constructed on the plan of a ship's compass. When the compass is fastened in the gimbals of the hanging instrument, and suspended to the cord, the 12 o'clock line is in the same vertical plane as the axis of the cord, and the compass hangs level at all times.

Fig. 28.

The original construction of Rössler's hanging-compass is shown in Fig. 28, copied from Voigtel's *Geometria Subterranea*, the first treatise on mine-surveying ever written. It was published in 1686.

An improved form of hanging-compass, made by Osterland of Freiberg, is shown in Fig. 29. The hanging ring of the old compass is here replaced by two movable arms. In order to keep the centre of gravity as low as possible, the clamping of the magnetic-needle is effected by a large screw underneath the compass-box.

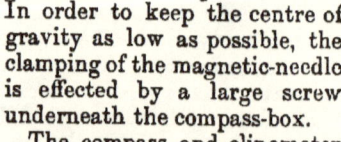

Fig. 29.

The compass and clinometer fit into a leather case fastened to a belt worn round the surveyor's waist. A few hairs, some wax, and a plummet must always be carried in reserve.

Surveying with the German Dial.—In booking a survey made with the German dial, the date, the name of the mine, and a description of the starting-point should first be noted. A fixed point having been selected as a starting-point, intermediate points are so chosen that they can be connected without hindrance by cords 6 to 8 fathoms in length. These points are either in the permanent timbering of the level, or in timbers temporarily inserted for the purpose. At these points, cord-screws are fixed. The loop at the end of the cord is placed over the first screw. The cord is tightly stretched to the next screw, and having been wound round it two or three times, is carried on to the next again. Six to ten station-lines are thus obtained, and the survey is commenced. A plummet is dropped from the first screw to the floor of the level, and the perpendicular distance measured. The length of the stretched cord is measured by placing the measuring rod gently along it. The clinometer is then suspended from the middle of the cord, and the rise or fall read. Lastly, the hanging-compass is suspended to the cord near the end-point of the line, care being taken that the north end of the dial is directed towards the end-point of the line. The bearing of the cord is then read. The mode of procedure is the same with the other lines.

The observations are noted in the dialling-book. In the column for remarks, sketches of portions of the level are inserted, showing the position of the offsets measured from the stretched cord. The bearing and dip of any veins or cross-courses met, should also be noted. As the end-point of the survey, a fixed point should, if possible, be selected, and the distance from the floor of the level measured. When great accuracy is required, a reverse survey is made as a check.

When the survey is complete, the bases and perpendiculars of the inclined lines have to be determined. The cord being the hypothenuse of a right-angled triangle, its length must be multiplied by the cosine of the angle of inclination, in order to obtain the base of the triangle, that is, the plotting length of the line. The perpendicular is obtained by multiplying the inclined length by the sine of the angle of inclination.

The form of dialling-book adopted is given on next page.

In this survey, the distances were measured in metres. The hanging-compass used was divided into half-degrees, which were subdivided by the eye into tenths of degrees. The clinometer was also read to tenths of degrees. The figures obtained by calculation, in the "base" and "perpendicular" columns, are usually entered in red ink. If the survey is to be plotted trigonometrically or by means of the protractor, the observed bearings are first corrected for the magnetic declination. The following is an example of the method of booking recommended at the Freiberg School of Mines:—

CARL MINE, ALSACE.—SURVEY OF ADIT LEVEL WITH THE HANGING-COMPASS.

Begun at + on right Timber, at entrance to Level.

No.	Length.	Inclination.	Bearing.		Base.	Perpendicular.		Remarks.
			Observed.	Corrected.		Rise.	Fall.	
...	1·34	R. 90°·0	...	...	...	1·34	...	To +
A	7·36	0°·0	240°·9	228°·9	7·36	...	...	...
B	5·41	R. 3°·1	210°·3	198°·3	5·40	0·29	...	...
C	6·83	F. 1°·2	210°·2	198°·2	6·82	...	0·14	...
D	4·81	R. 3°·8	186°·6	174°·6	4·80	0·31	...	...
E	6·24	F. 0°·4	202°·8	190°·8	6·24	...	0·04	...
F	4·68	R. 1°·1	173°·1	161°·1	4·68	0·09	...	...
...	1·32	F. 90°·0	...	...	...	...	1·32	To floor of level.

In the Harz, where a thin wire is used instead of a cord, the station-line is, if possible, made 10 metres in length. The trigonometrical calculations are thus greatly facilitated, especially if logarithms are used. The form of dialling-book adopted when the compass is divided into hours, is shown on the next page.

The right-hand page of the survey-book is reserved for sketches, showing the position of the offsets taken.

Plotting the Survey.—The survey may be plotted by means of the compass that was used underground. The plotting instrument (Fig. 30), consists of a truly rectangular plate of brass, 10 inches long and 5 inches wide, with a raised ring in the middle for the reception of the compass-box. The diameter of the ring parallel to the long side of the plate is marked on its surface by means of two fine lines. The compass-box is placed in the ring, and clamped so that the 12-hour line coincides with

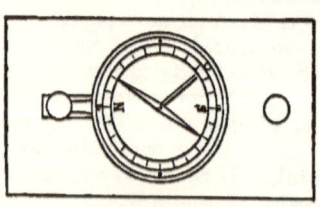

Fig. 30.

DOROTHEA MINE, CLAUSTHAL.—SURVEY OF PART OF THE 19TH FATHOM LEVEL WITH THE HANGING-COMPASS.—Magnetic Declination, 13° 45' W.

No.		Compass.				Base.	Inclination of Cord. Rise or Fall.	Length of Inclined Cord.	Perpendicular.		Remarks.
From	To	E. or W.	Hour.	'	1/16				Rise.	Fall.	
+	A	E	9	5	9	Metres. 6·358	F. 12°00'	Metres. 6·50	Metres. ...	Metres. 1·351	...
A	B	E	9	1	15	11·917	R. 6°42½'	12·00	1·402	...	...
B	C	E	7	0	0	7·430	F. 7°50'	7·50	...	1·022	...
C	D	E	9	0	12	9·868	R. 9°20'	10·00	1·622	...	...
D	E	E	9	1	0	10·913	F. 7°12¼'	11·00	...	1·380	...
E	F	E	10	2	0	9·919	R. 7°17½'	10·00	1·269	...	...
F	G	E	9	7	9	9·911	F. 7°40'	10·00	...	1·334	...
G	H	E	10	0	1	9·868	R. 9°20'	10·00	1·622	...	...
H	J	E	10	4	8	9·872	F. 9°10'	10·00	...	1·593	...
J	K	E	10	5	4	9·907	R. 9°50'	10·00	1·363	...	...
K	L	E	9	7	8	10·481	F. 7°00'	10·56	...	1·287	...
L	M	...	...	...	...	...	R. 90°00'	1·34	1·340	...	...

these two lines. The upper edges of the rectangular plate are bevelled, so as to diminish the shadow on the paper.

The paper, on which the plan is to be drawn, is fastened to a horizontal table. The plotting-instrument is then placed on the paper, and turned until the marked end of the needle points to the north. A line is then drawn along the side of the plate which will represent the north line of the plan. A point for commencing the plotting is selected, and the instrument turned at that point until the needle points to the bearing of the first line. A line is then drawn along the side of the instrument, and the required distance measured with a scale.

This method presents the advantage of plotting the survey with the actual instrument used to make it, and consequently with the same degree of approximation. But the errors due to magnetic influences are not eliminated, as the conditions are not the same as they were in the mine. In a drawing office, too, there are always iron objects that may affect the needle. At the French collieries of Decize in Nièvre, a drawing office has been built in which all the ironwork has been replaced by copper, for the purpose of employing this instrument without inconvenience.

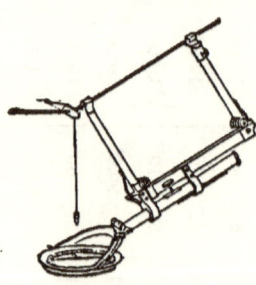

Fig. 31.

Surveying with the Hanging-compass in the Presence of Iron.—Numerous attempts have been made to modify the construction of the hanging-compass in such a way that it can be used for surveying over iron. Perhaps the most successful is the adjustable hanging-compass (Fig. 31), invented by Mr. Penkert* of Beuthen. It is so arranged that it can be centred under the point of junction of two cords, and thus the bearing of the two lines can be taken from the same place. The instrument is manufactured by A. Ott, of Kempten, Bavaria.

Use of the German Dial.—The hanging compass in Germany and France is being replaced by the theodolite; but it is still found useful in narrow workings. It is occasionally used in America. Thus, in surveying the Longdale iron mine in Virginia, Mr. G. R. Johnson has found it a useful auxiliary. The four main adit levels of the mine having been surveyed, and their entrances connected by level and theodolite lines, it remained to survey the stopes and workings in order to make a

* *Berg. H. Ztg.*, vol. xxxix, 1880, p. 9.

complete map, and to test the accuracy of the foregoing work. To do this with the theodolite and level was out of the question, both on account of the roughness of the workings, and also because they were much too small—so small in places that a man could scarcely crawl through them. The hanging compass was consequently used with very satisfactory results, the ends of the survey coinciding with the corresponding points determined in the theodolite survey.

CHAPTER VIII.

THE THEODOLITE.

Historical Sketch.—In mine-surveys, where extreme accuracy is required, the theodolite should be employed. There is, however, no occasion for it to be used exclusively, as the modern vernier-dial is a form of theodolite, which from its simplicity and compactness is better adapted for underground work than the theodolite itself, and proved by severe tests to give highly satisfactory results. For surface-surveying the dial is, however, decidedly inferior to the theodolite.

The employment of improved instruments for measuring angles underground in place of the compass, dates from the end of the last century. In 1798, H. C. W. Breithaupt, of Cassel, invented a mine-surveying instrument, resembling an *astrolabium*. This was essentially a theodolite. It had a graduated horizontal circle with verniers, a vertical arc, a sighting-tube, and a compass. Two sets of legs were used with the instrument. In the same year, Professor Guiliani, of Klagenfurt, invented a mining theodolite, calling it a *catageolabium*. Mine-surveys, too, were made at the end of the last century by the Polish General, Komarzewsk, with a *graphomètre souterrain* which he invented. Since 1832, the theodolite has been used, more or less, in all mine-surveys, where great accuracy is required. Theodolites specially constructed for mining purposes are now made in great numbers by the continental and American instrument-makers. In Great Britain, however, the tendency has been to improve the construction of the circumferenter, making it more and more like the theodolite, so that with it results can be obtained as accurate as those made with a German mining theodolite of the same size.

Description of the Theodolite.—The theodolite is the most important, but at the same time the most complicated, instrument used by the mine-surveyor. In general outline, it may be described as a telescope mounted on a horizontal and a vertical axis, in such a way that the horizontal and vertical rotation of its optical axis may be measured.

There are many forms of theodolite, but there are certain essential parts common to all. The cost of a theodolite being considerable, the mine-surveyor is, as a rule, not in a position to have several of different sizes. In purchasing an instrument, therefore, he must select one which will fulfil all his requirements. It must be sufficiently large to give accurate results in triangulation, and at the same time it must be sufficiently portable to be used in the mine. In its construction, all metal must be avoided that will affect the magnetic-needle. The horizontal circle should be 5 inches in diameter, divided into half-degrees, and provided with verniers reading to single minutes.

The various parts of the theodolite are shown in Fig. 32. The most important part is the *horizontal circle*, G, which has its edge bevelled and graduated, the degrees being numbered continuously round it towards the right up to 360°. At the centre of this circle is another circular plate, the *vernier-plate* F, capable of rotation independently of the horizontal circle. On the vernier-plate is engraved a line, the index line, passing exactly through the centre, the end-points, or indices, extending to the graduation of the horizontal circle. The indices are provided with verniers, read by means of the microscopes g, g, which are sometimes provided with plates of ivory to reflect light on the scale. The horizontal circle and

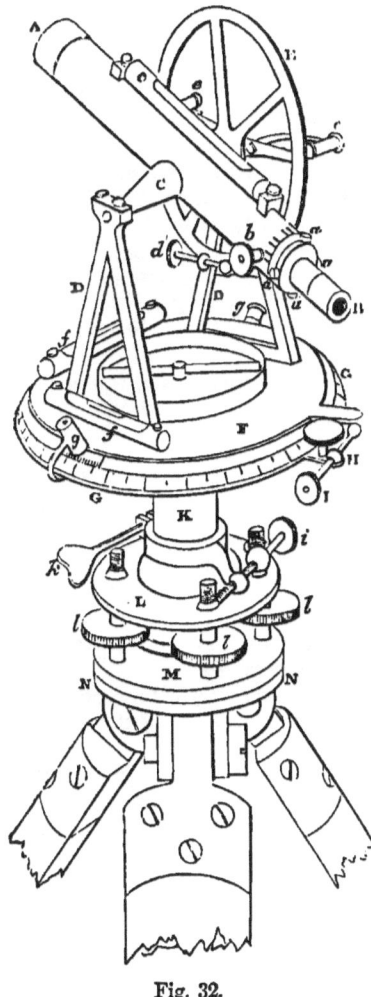

Fig. 32.

the vernier-plate together are sometimes termed the *horizontal limb*, in which case G is called the *lower limb*. The instrument-makers' names are (F) *plate*, and (G) *limb*.

On the vernier-plate are two uprights or supports, D, D, which support the horizontal axis, C, of the *vertical* or *altitude circle*, E. The latter is provided with two indices with verniers at the opposite ends of a horizontal bar, read by the microscopes *e, e*. The telescope A B is fixed directly upon the horizontal axis.

The horizontal circle is screwed by a flange to a brass vertical axis, K, passing through the collar of a clamp, where it may be fixed or loosened by the clamp screw, *k*. Below the collar, the vertical axis works freely on a ball and socket joint at its lower end. The ball and socket is placed between the parallel plates, L, M, which are provided with four levelling screws, *l*. The vernier-plate is provided with two spirit-levels, *f,f*, and a longer spirit-level, *c*, is attached to the telescope. The whole instrument is supported on a strong tripod stand.

The vertical circle is divided into four quadrants, the degrees in each of which are numbered from 0° to 90°, as shown in Fig. 33. In the old-fashioned theodolite the vertical limb is a semicircle. This is surmounted by an oblong flat piece of brass, the *stage*, to the ends of which are screwed the two forked rests called Y's, by which the bell-metal collars of the telescope are supported. Under the telescope is a long spirit-level. A theodolite of this kind is termed a *plane* theodolite, whilst one with a complete circle as vertical limb is termed a *transit* theodolite. The advantages

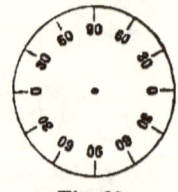

Fig. 33.

presented by the latter form are the greater vertical sweep of the telescope and the greater accuracy of the readings of the vertical limb.

Connected with the horizontal circle and vernier-plate, there are two screws, H, I, one of which, H, is a clamping screw and the other a slow-motion or tangent screw. When H is loose, the two plates, G and F, can be moved independently, but when the screw H is tightened they can only be moved separately by means of the tangent screw I. Beneath the horizontal plates, there are two screws, *k* and *i*, one of which, *k*, is a clamping screw and the other a tangent screw. When the screw *k* is loose, the whole of the upper part of the theodolite above the screw can be rotated in either direction, in which case the horizontal circle moves upon the double conical axis upon which it rests. On tightening the screw *k*, the upper part can be moved only by means of the tangent screw *i*. Two screws refer to the vertical circle, a clamping screw and a tangent screw d. When the clamping screw is loose, the vertical circle can be moved freely; but when it is tightened, the circle can be moved only by means of the tangent screw d.

As an aid to memory, the screws may be divided into three sets, each of which consists of a clamping and a tangent screw. The upper set belongs solely to the vertical circle; the centre set, H, I, belongs to the horizontal circle F; and the lower set, k, i, refers to the entire portion of the instrument above it.

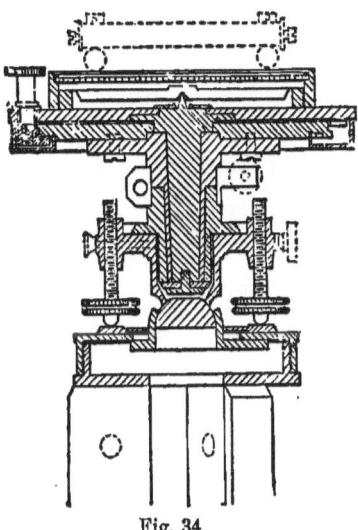

Fig. 34.

The circular plates with their accompanying sockets are shown in section in Fig. 34. The upper plate carrying the compass-box, &c., is screwed fast to the flange of the interior spindle, the lower plate is fastened to the exterior socket, which in its turn is fitted to and turns in the hollow socket of the levelling head.

The **telescope** consists of two tubes, one sliding within the other, with the object glass at the further end, A, of the outer tube, and with an eye-piece at the nearer end, B, of the inner tube. The object glass is achromatic, that is, made of two lenses, one of crown and one of flint-glass, the curvatures of which are suitably combined. The object glass forms between the eye-piece and its principal focus an inverted image of the object sighted, and the eye-piece, consisting of two condensing lenses, acts as a magnifying glass, and gives a virtual and highly magnified image of the inverted image thus obtained. Sometimes, especially in American instruments, the eye-piece is made up of four plano-convex lenses. An erect image is thus obtained. An erecting eye-piece, however, causes a considerable loss of light, and is therefore not to be recommended. It requires but little practice to get accustomed to the use of an inverting eye-piece, and the brilliancy with which objects appear, owing to the amount of light gained by dispensing with two lenses, is very marked in comparison with the results obtained with an erecting eye-piece of the same power. The telescope may be focussed by moving the inner tube by a rack and pinion turned by the milled head, *b* (Fig. 32).

The rays proceeding from the object-glass form a cone of light. In order to get a line from the point of the cone straight through the optical centre of the object-glass, and on, without deviation, to the object examined, recourse must be had to the device of *collimation*. The collimator of a theodolite telescope is a circular brass diaphragm, with a hole about half an inch in diameter in its centre. It has a rim on its edge, and in this are the collimating screws, *a, a*. The hole is crossed by three spider-webs or equally fine platinum wires (see Fig. 35), one horizontal, A B, and the other two, C D, E G, deviating slightly to opposite sides of a vertical plane. The point F where the wires cross each other should be exactly in the axis or line of collimation of the telescope. It is adjusted to that position by the collimating screws.

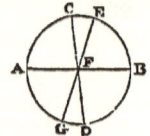

Fig. 35.

Various Forms.—(*a.*) **Hoskold's transit-theodolite** is an instrument of great perfection, specially adapted for mining work. It differs from the ordinary transit-theodolite in the arrangement of the upper plate, which is made to project over the lower plate at the points where the upright supports are attached, so as to enable a larger compass to be employed. Thus, a 5-inch circle will carry a 4½-inch compass; whilst in an ordinary theodolite of the same size a 2½-inch compass would be used. The Hoskold theodolite presents the further advantage that the compass is not obscured by the appendages of the upper plate. In order to enable short sights to be taken, a pair of folding sights, like those of a miner's dial, are fixed to the top of the telescope. The instrument is also provided with a diagonal eye-piece, which enables the telescope to be pointed vertically without any discomfort to the observer.

In this theodolite and some others, a second telescope is sometimes attached below the horizontal circle. This is used like the outer pair of sights of the Henderson dial, to determine whether the circle has been disturbed during the interval between two observations.

(*b.*) **The Everest Theodolite.**—This instrument differs considerably from the ordinary transit-theodolite, though the principles of its construction are exactly the same. It was designed by Captain Everest, and was first made by Messrs. Troughton & Simms in 1838. Instead of the upper parallel plate, this instrument has three diverging arms (Fig. 36) with

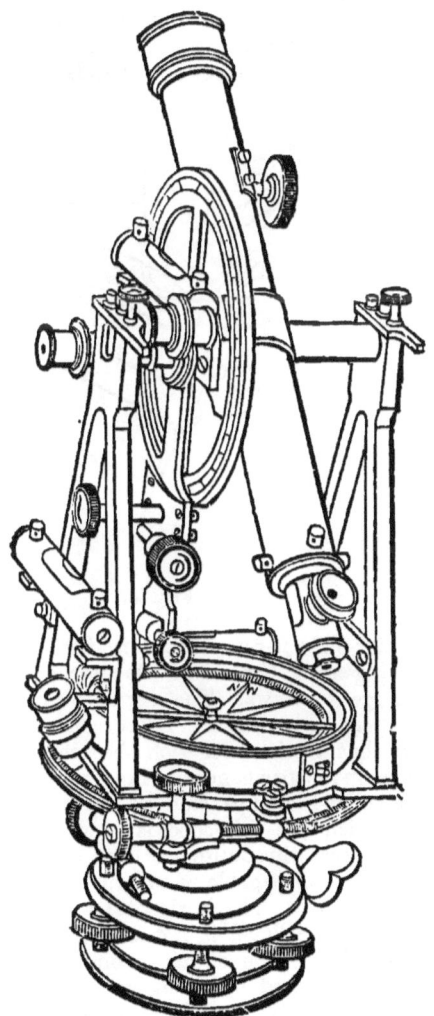

Fig. 35A.—Hoskold's miner's transit theodolite.

a vertical levelling screw supporting the end of each. Each screw has a flange at its lower end, by means of which it is held down to the plate forming the top of the staff head. The chief advantage of this construction is that the three levelling screws can be adjusted with one hand, whilst the adjustment of four levelling screws requires both hands.

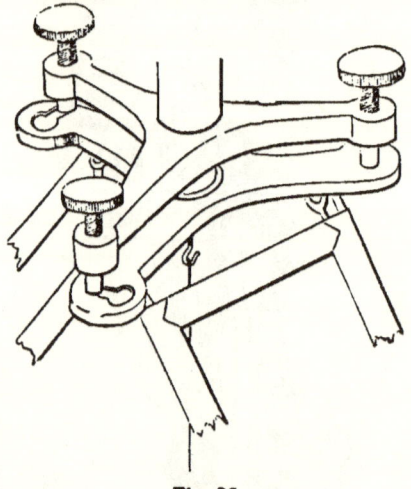

Fig. 36.

The vernier-plate is represented in the Everest theodolite by four radiating arms, three with verniers, the fourth with clamping and tangent screws. The verniers are read with the aid of an independently moving microscope. The mean of three readings is thus obtained for each observation.

The telescope is permanently fixed to the horizontal axis by means of a collar-like expansion at the middle of the bell-metal axis, into which the telescope is fixed. Instead of a vertical circle, the Everest theodolite has two opposite sectors of about 90° each, so as to be capable of measuring elevations and depressions, as far as 45°. The horizontal axis works in a Y-shaped upright. The spirit-level is not attached to the telescope, but to the index bar. The circular compass-box of the ordinary instrument is replaced by a long compass-box placed above the telescope, reading only a few degrees east or west of the magnetic meridian. The spirit-level for the horizontal circle is attached to a stage below the Y's.

(c.) **The Hoffman Tripod Head.**—The theodolites made by

Messrs. J. Davis & Son are provided with the Hoffman tripod head (see p. 64). Ever since the introduction of the theodolite, efforts have been made to give it the same facility of levelling as is possessed by the miner's dial. The ball and socket motion has been frequently tried. The upper part of a theodolite is, however, much heavier than that of the dial, and requires more binding power than can be obtained with an ordinary ball and socket joint.

The great need for a tripod that can be easily manipulated is apparent, as it rarely happens that there is a level surface on which to set the theodolite, and much of the time in surveying is employed in adjusting the levelling screws. It has been pointed out that it is almost impossible to level up a sensitive bubble so that it will remain in position long enough for a satisfactory sight to be taken, and the difficulty of centering a plummet over a station has also been shown. The latter defect has been obviated by the addition of the sliding-head, which permits the entire instrument, with its plummet, to be accurately placed over a fixed point, after the operation has been approximately performed by moving the legs.

The Hoffman tripod head,* as modified by Professor J. H. Harden of the University of Pennsylvania, is shown in Fig 37.

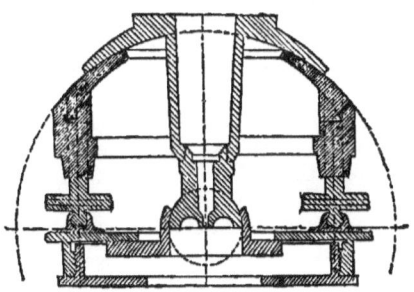

Fig. 37.

On unscrewing the levelling screws, the plate forming part of the socket of the small ball, the centre of which is the axis of the instrument, and the point from which the plummet is suspended, can be moved in any direction within the limits of the inside opening of the screw cap. It will be observed that besides the small ball and socket, there is an extra and larger ball and socket formed by a part of the plate to which the instrument is fastened,

* *Trans. Amer. Inst. Min. Eng.*, vol. vii., p. 308.

and the part to which the levelling screws are attached. The latter part always remains parallel to the screw cap of the tripod head, on which the points of the levelling screws rest, so that whatever position the instrument may assume in relation to the tripod head, the screw will always act directly perpendicular to both plates.

Under all conditions, the instrument moves upon a centre common to the two balls, this being the point to which the plummet is attached. It is therefore impossible for the plummet not to be perpendicular to the axis of the instrument.

The advantages claimed for the Hoffman tripod head are as follows:—1. A saving of one-half to two-thirds of the time usually occupied with screwing and unscrewing as in the old plan. The instrument can be levelled approximately without the use of the screws. Less than half a turn is then necessary to bring the instrument to a perfect level, the operation at the same time clamping it. 2. The levelling screws are at all times perpendicular to the plate to which they are attached, and to the plate and screw cap on which they rest. 3. The levelling screws are reduced in length, and their duty to a minimum, the instrument being no higher nor heavier than before. 4. The shifting head for plumbing over a fixed point—an improvement common to all first-class instruments—is retained, and no extra screws are required to clamp the instrument. 5. The levelling screws are covered from dust, and at the same time are no obstruction to the working of the instrument in any position in which it can be placed.

Numerous other attempts have been made to apply the ball and socket motion for levelling theodolites rapidly, and several American devices of this kind have proved very successful. Thus, Messrs. W. & L. E. Gurley, of Troy, have patented a quick-levelling tripod, somewhat similar in principle to that of Hoffman. The spherical surfaces are, in this case, concave, and the friction of these surfaces may be increased or diminished at will by means of spiral springs. Messrs. Buff & Berger, of Boston, furnish their theodolites with a quick-levelling attachment, which does not form part of the instrument proper, but consists of a coupling, with a ball and socket joint, which can be screwed between the instrument and the tripod.

(*d.*) **American Theodolites.**—In America, the miner's dial is very rarely used for mine-surveys. In all important work, the transit-theodolite is alone used. This instrument is known in America as the *transit*. The name *theodolite* is reserved for the Y-instrument in which the telescope cannot be revolved on its horizontal axis. The transit instrument which has no vertical

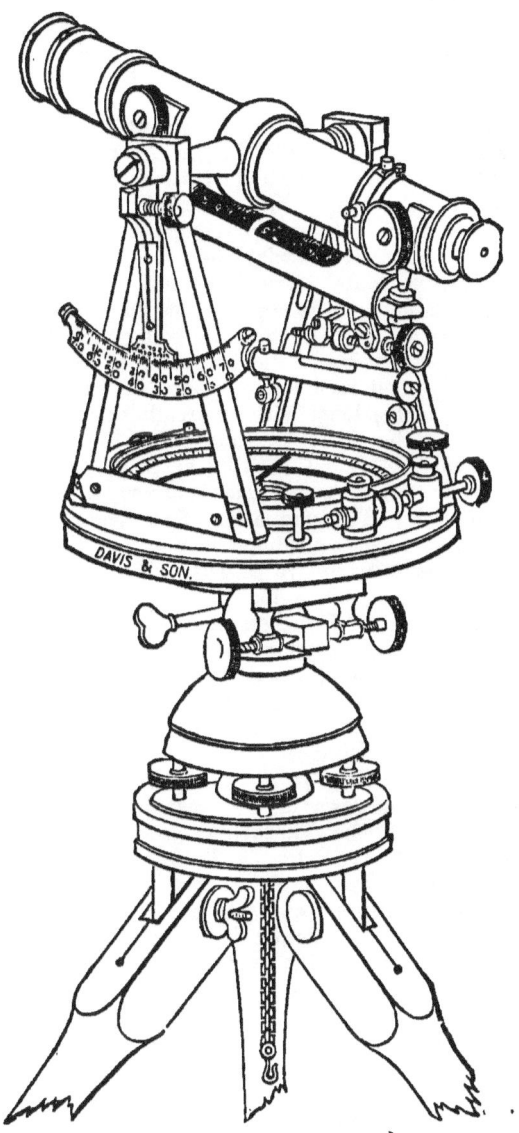

Fig. 37A.—Theodolite of the American type, with Hoffman tripod head.

circle and no spirit-level attached to its telescope is called the *plain transit*.

An excellent transit-theodolite, manufactured by Messrs. Heller & Brightly, of Philadelphia, is described by Dr. R. W. Raymond.* It is a small portable instrument specially adapted for use in mine-surveying. The principal peculiarity is the ribbing and flanging of the parts requiring strength, so as to dispose the minimum amount of material where it will secure the greatest rigidity. The horizontal circle is $4\frac{1}{2}$ inches in diameter, and is read by two double opposite verniers, placed outside the compass-box, the vernier openings in the plate being made very wide so as to allow the easy reading of the graduations. There is a 3-inch magnetic-needle, and its ring is divided to half-degrees. The telescope is $7\frac{1}{4}$ inches long, with an erecting eye-piece. A sensitive level, $4\frac{1}{2}$ inches long, is attached to the telescope. The tripod is furnished with a shifting head for precise centering. Clamps and tangent-screw movements are supplied to the plates and vertical circle. The graduation of the compass ring and of the horizontal circle is continuous from 0° to 360°. The weight of the instrument, exclusive of the tripod, is $5\frac{1}{2}$ lbs. The weight of the tripod is $3\frac{1}{2}$ lbs. The height of the instrument from the tripod legs is 7 inches, the extreme diameter of the plates 5 inches. The instrument and tripod head are packed in a box $7\frac{1}{2}$ inches square, arranged with straps to allow its being carried over the shoulder, while the folded tripod legs serve as a walking-stick. Such compactness and lightness are very important for underground work. This also applies to surface-surveys, especially in a country like America, where the surveyor has often to carry his own instrument.

(*e.*) Traveller's Transit-Theodolite.—A still smaller transit-theodolite is manufactured by Mr. L. Casella, of London, for the use of travellers. It has complete 3-inch circles, both vertical and horizontal, with verniers reading to one minute. It can therefore be used as an altazimuth for determining time, latitude, and azimuth, as well as for ordinary surveying purposes. Its telescope is eccentric. It is provided with a diagonal eye-piece and a reflector for illuminating the cross-wires. It is thus well adapted for shaft-surveying. It is supplied with a dark glass for solar observations, a finely divided level, and a compass. It packs in a mahogany case, $6\frac{3}{4}$ inches by $5\frac{1}{4}$ inches, and 4 inches deep; the whole weighing only $3\frac{1}{2}$ lbs.

A light tripod stand is added. Many important surveys have been made with the instrument with very satisfactory results.

---

* *Trans. Amer. Inst. Min. Eng.*, vol. i., p. 375.

This instrument is also constructed with the telescope in the centre, the supports being raised to allow it to revolve vertically. By this arrangement, whilst the height is increased, the width is reduced in proportion.

Adjustments of the Theodolite.—Every time the instrument is used, the observer must make the following adjustments:—

1. Place the theodolite exactly over the station by means of a plummet hung from a hook directly under the vertical axis. It must next be levelled, that is to say, the vertical axis must be placed truly vertical. The easiest way to do this is to make the vernier-plate truly horizontal, by means of the spirit-levels, f, f (Fig. 32). For this purpose, the vernier-plate is turned into such a position that the two spirit-levels shall be parallel to the two diagonals of the square formed by the four levelling screws. Two opposite screws must then be turned simultaneously and equally, but in opposite directions, until the bubble is brought to the centre of the level. The other screws are then turned in the same way, until the bubble of the second level is brought to the centre of its tube.

A more exact adjustment can be made by means of the larger and more delicate level, c, attached to the telescope. For this purpose, set the instrument approximately level, clamp the axis of the limb by k, leaving the plate free, and move the latter until the telescope is over two of the levelling screws. Then bring the bubble to the middle of its tube by the tangent screw, d. Then turn the vernier-plate, carrying with it the telescope, through half a revolution, and if the bubble is not in the centre of the tube, bring it half way back by the tangent screw, and the other half by the levelling screw. Repeat this until the bubble remains central with the telescope in either position. Then turn the vernier-plate through 90°, so as to place the telescope at right angles to its former position, and repeat the process until at last the bubble remains central during the complete rotation of the telescope. If the instrument is correctly constructed, the vernier of the vertical circle should read 0° 0′.

If the bubbles are not at the centres of the vernier-plate levels, when the bubble remains central in the level attached to the telescope, the vernier-plate levels are not truly perpendicular to the vertical axis, and must be adjusted by means of the screws at their ends. This adjustment is rarely required with a well-made theodolite.

2. When the image of the object viewed, formed by the object glass, either falls short of or beyond the place of the cross-wires, an error arises, which is called *parallax*. Its existence may be detected by moving the head from side to side when looking

through the telescope, observing whether the image appears to move. To correct this error, the eye-piece must first be adjusted by means of the movable eye-piece tube, until the cross-wires are seen clearly defined. Then direct the telescope to some distant object, and by means of the milled-head screw, b (Fig. 32), at the side of the telescope, move the inner tube in or out until the proper focus is obtained. When disregarded, parallax gives rise to serious error.

3. In addition to the temporary adjustments described above, there are certain permanent adjustments which should be tested from time to time, but which in a well-made theodolite seldom require correction.

The adjustment of the line of *collimation* consists in placing that line accurately at right angles to the horizontal axis. To effect this, direct the telescope to a distant object, making the cross-wires bisect the object precisely. Then carefully lift the telescope out of its bearings, and replace with the ends reversed. Revolve vertically, and again direct the telescope to the distant object. If the cross-wires still coincide with the object, the line of collimation is perpendicular to the horizontal axis. If not, move the cross-wires one-half of the deviation by turning the screws holding the diaphragm, and correct the other half by moving the tangent screw of the horizontal circle. Reverse the telescope again, and repeat the operation until the adjustment is perfect.

In the Y-theodolite, the line of collimation is adjusted by bringing the intersection of the cross-wires upon some well-defined distant object. The telescope is turned round on its collars in the Y's until the level is uppermost. Then, if the cross-wires do not continue to coincide with the object, half the difference must be corrected by moving the cross-wires, and the other half by moving the tangent screw of the horizontal circle.

4. The level attached to the telescope must be parallel to the adjusted line of collimation. To effect this adjustment in the transit-theodolite, the elevation or depression of a distant object is taken. The instrument is then reversed, the telescope revolved vertically, and again directed to the same object. The mean of the two readings will be the true elevation or depression of the object. Set the verniers to this mean angle, and again observe the object, making the intersection by means of the screws retaining the index in its horizontal position. Then, correct the level by its own adjusting screws.

To effect the adjustment in the Y-theodolite, the clips for securing the supports that hold the telescope should be thrown open, and the bubble of the spirit-level brought to the centre of the tube by means of the tangent screw attached to the vertical arc. The telescope should then be lifted out of its supports, and reversed. If the bubble does not remain central, correct half the error by the adjusting screws connecting the level with the telescope, and the other half by the tangent screw of the vertical arc.

5. When the telescope level has been adjusted, and the vernier-plate is truly horizontal, it is necessary to note whether the zero of the vertical circle coincides with the zero of its vernier. If it does, there is no *index-error*. If it does not, the amount of error should be noted and applied as a constant correction to all subsequent readings.

6. The adjustment of the horizontal axis exactly perpendicular to the vertical axis is, as a rule, left to the instrument-maker. In some theodolites, however, there are adjusting screws for the supports of the vertical axis. This is usually the case in instruments of American make. In order to determine whether the horizontal axis is perpendicular to the vertical axis, direct the intersection of the cross-wires to an object, the altitude of which is considerable. Then turn the vertical limb, until the cross-wires cut some other well-defined point near the ground. Revolve the telescope on its axis, and turn the vernier-plate 180°. Then if, in raising and lowering the telescope, the line of collimation passes through the two objects, the adjustment is correct. If not, half the deviation is to be corrected by the tangent screw of the horizontal circle, and the other half by the adjusting screws of the supports. The operation must be repeated until the adjustment is correct.

The permanent adjustments described above should be made with great care. Many valuable instruments have been injured by students who were anxious to adjust them, but were unacquainted with the method. It is necessary to be quite certain that an adjustment is required before a screw is touched.

Measuring Horizontal Angles.—The theodolite, having been set up so that the centre of the horizontal circle is perpendicularly above or below the station-point, is carefully levelled. The horizontal vernier-plate is then clamped at zero. The position of the second vernier is noted, in case it does not read 180° exactly. The horizontal circle and vernier-plate clamped together are turned, until the telescope is directed to the left-hand station. The horizontal circle is then clamped, and the cross-wires are made to accurately bisect the point by means of the tangent screw. The vernier-plate is then released, and the telescope carefully moved, the lower supports only being touched, until the right-hand object is bisected. The vernier-plate is then clamped, and the cross-wires are made to accurately coincide with the object by means of the tangent screw attached to the vernier-plate. The two verniers have thus described an arc on the horizontal circle equal to the angle to be measured. This may be read direct from vernier I. With vernier II. it is found by taking the difference of its two readings. The mean of the results obtained with the two verniers is taken as the correct angle.

Another method of measuring horizontal angles is to clamp the horizontal circle in any position. Then, direct the telescope to one of the stations, clamp the vernier-plate, and turn the tangent screw attached until the cross-wires accurately bisect the left-hand object. Read the angles indicated by the two verniers, and note the mean of the two readings. Then release the vernier-plate, and move the telescope until the right-hand object is bisected. Clamp the vernier-plate, and make the cross-wires accurately coincide with the object by means of the tangent screw. Again read the two verniers, and note the mean of the two readings. The difference between the first and second mean readings will be the horizontal angular distance between the two points. Thus, as an example :—

	Vernier I.	Vernier II.	Mean.
The first reading	173° 11′	353° 11′	173° 11′ 00″
The second reading	259° 35′	79° 34′	259° 34′ 30″
Correct angle,			86° 23′ 30″

The reason for reading the two verniers is to correct any error due to eccentricity or incorrect graduation of the plates.

It is advisable to measure the angle a second time with the telescope inverted. The errors occurring during the first measurement also occur during the measurement with the telescope inverted, but on the opposite side, so that the mean of the two measurements gives a result nearly free from error.

Repetition.—In measuring horizontal angles, when great accuracy is required, the errors of graduation may be diminished by the process known as *repeating*, an operation invented by Tobias Mayer, of Göttingen, in 1752.

The mode of procedure is as follows :—Determine the horizontal angle between the points A and B in the usual way, the vernier-plate being clamped at zero. Let the angular distance between A and B be 30° 10′. Now, leaving the vernier-plate clamped to the horizontal circle, unclamp the vertical axis, and turn the instrument back to A. Then clamp the vertical axis, release the vernier-plate, and again direct the telescope to B. In this way the reading will be repeated, beginning at 30° 10′ instead of

0° 0′. Suppose the result now is 60° 25′. Repeat again, starting this time from 60° 25′, and suppose that the third result is 90° 40′. Dividing this result by the number of readings, we obtain, as mean result, 30° 13′ 20″.

The operation may be repeated any number of times, care being always taken to direct the telescope towards A by turning the vertical axis, and towards B by turning the vernier-plate. For each complete revolution of the vernier-plate, 360° must be allowed. It is advisable to perform the operation with the telescope inverted, and to take the mean of the two results obtained with the telescope in its two positions.

The following is an example of repetition :—

The horizontal angular distance between the two points determined in the usual way was 102° 45′. On repeating, the following results were obtained :—

No. of Repetitions.	Reading.	Mean.	Angle.
4	Ver. I. 51° 00′ 45″ Ver. II. 231° 00′ 45″	411° 00′ 45″	102° 45′ 11″
5	Ver. I. 153° 45′ 45″ Ver. II. 333° 45′ 45″	513° 45′ 45″	102° 45′ 09″
6	Ver. I. 256° 31′ 00″ Ver. II. 76° 31′ 00″	616° 31′ 00″	102° 45′ 10″

With the telescope inverted, the following results were obtained :—

No. of Repetitions.	Reading.	Mean.	Angle.
4	Ver. I. 51° 00′ 15″ Ver. II. 231° 00′ 15″	411° 00′ 15″	102° 45′ 04″
5	Ver. I. 153° 45′ 20″ Ver. II. 333° 45′ 30″	513° 45′ 25″	102° 45′ 05″
6	Ver. I. 256° 30′ 40″ Ver. II. 76° 30′ 30″	616° 30′ 35″	102° 45′ 06″

Mean = 102° 45′ 08″.

Measurement of Vertical Angles.—The instrument having been carefully levelled, the telescope is directed to the object, the elevation or depression of which is to be measured. The cross-wires are made to accurately bisect the object by means of the

THE THEODOLITE.

tangent screw attached to the vertical circle. The angle is then read from both verniers, and the mean of the two readings taken as the correct angle. When great accuracy is required, the determination should also be made with the telescope inverted.

The following is an example of the measurement of a vertical angle in this way:—

	Reading.	With Telescope Inverted.	Mean.
Vernier I.	12° 45′	13° 02′	12° 53′ 30″
Vernier II.	13° 06′	12° 40′	12° 53′ 00″
	Mean = 12° 53′ 15″.		

The Solar Attachment is a contrivance that is fastened to the telescope axis of American transit instruments for the purpose of determining the true meridian. The principle was enunciated by W. A. Burt, of Michigan, and applied by him to the compass in 1836. It has since come into general use in the surveys of the United States public lands, the principal lines of which are set-out with reference to the true meridian.

The Burt solar compass consists mainly of three arcs of circles, by which can be set off the latitude of a place, the declination of the sun, and the hour of the day. Through the centre of the hour arc passes a hollow socket, containing the spindle of the declination arc. This is termed the polar axis. When this axis is parallel to the axis of the earth, the vertical plane of the terrestrial line of sight, as defined by the slits in the vertical sights of the compass, coincides with the meridian.

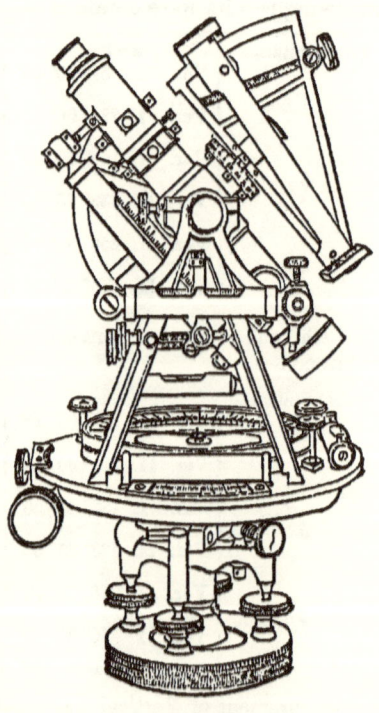

Fig. 38.

Fig. 38 represents the solar apparatus placed upon the cross-bar of the transit-theodolite. The form represented was patented by

Messrs. W. & L. E. Gurley, of Troy. The following is the manufacturers' description of this attachment:—A small circular disc, 1½ inch in diameter, with a short round pivot projecting above its upper surface, is first firmly screwed to the telescope axis. Upon this pivot rests the enlarged base of the polar axis, which is also firmly connected with the disc by four capstan head screws passing from the under side of the disc into the enlarged base. These screws serve to adjust the polar axis.

The hour circle surrounding the base of the polar axis is easily movable about it, and can be fastened at any point desired by two flat-headed screws above. It is divided to 5 minutes of time. It is figured from I. to XII., and is read by a small index fixed to the declination circle moving with it. A hollow socket, fitting closely to the polar axis, moves upon it, and may be clamped at any point desired by a milled-head screw on top. By its two expanded arms below, this furnishes a firm support for the declination arc, which is securely fastened to it by two large screws.

The declination arc is about 5 inches in radius. It is divided to quarter-degrees, and reads by its vernier to single minutes of arc, the divisions of both vernier and limb being in the same plane. At each end of the declination arm is a rectangular block of brass, in which is set a small convex lens, having its focus on the surface of a small silver plate fastened by screws to the inside of the opposite block. On the surface of the plate, two sets of lines are marked intersecting each other at right angles. The two sets are termed the hour lines and the equatorial lines, as having reference respectively to the hour of the day and the position of the sun in relation to the equator. The declination arm is also provided with a clamp and tangent movement.

The latitude is set off by means of a large vertical limb, below the telescope, having a radius of 2½ inches. The arc is divided to 30 minutes, and is figured from the centre each way in two rows, from 0° to 80°, and from 90° to 10°, the former series being intended for reading vertical angles, the latter for setting off the latitude. It is read by its vernier to single minutes. It has a clamp screw inserted near its centre, by which it can be clamped to the telescope axis in any desired position. The vernier of the vertical limb is made movable by the tangent screw, attached so that its zero is readily made to coincide with that of the limb when the arc is clamped to the axis in adjusting the limb to the level of the telescope.

A spirit-level on the under side of the telescope, provided with a scale, is indispensable in the use of the solar attachment.

When the telescope is made horizontal by its spirit-level, the hour-circle will be in the plane of the horizon, the polar axis will point to the zenith, and the zeros of the vertical arc and its vernier will coincide. In this position of the instrument, if the arm of the declination arc is placed at zero, and one lens directed to the sun, its image will be seen between the lines on the silver plate of the opposite block, and will indicate its position in the heavens, on an instrument placed at the North Pole of the earth at the time of the equinoxes, or when the equator is in the plane of the horizon. If the telescope is inclined, as shown in Fig. 37, the polar axis will descend from the direction of the zenith. The angle through which it moves, being laid off on the vertical arc, and shown by its vernier to be (say) 40°, will be the co-latitude of the place where the instrument is supposed to be used. The latitude itself is found by subtracting 40° from 90°, making it 50°. Now, if the declination arm remains at zero, and the lens is again directed to the sun, its image will appear on the opposite plate as before, the instrument being used at the time of the equinoxes at a latitude of 50°. When, however, the sun passes above or below the celestial equator, its declination or angular distance from it, as given in the *Nautical Almanack*, can be allowed for and set off upon the arc, and the image brought into position as before.

In order to do this, it is necessary that the latitude and declination be correctly set off upon their respective arcs, and that the instrument be moved in azimuth until the polar axis points to the pole of the heavens, or, in other words, is placed in the plane of the meridian. Thus the position of the sun's image will not only indicate the latitude of the place, the declination of the sun for the given hour, and the apparent time, but also determine the meridian line passing through the place where the observation is made.

The latitude of a place—that is, its distance north or south of the equator, measured on a meridian—may be found by means of the solar attachment in the following manner:—First carefully level the instrument by means of the spirit-level of the telescope. Next clamp the vertical arc, and, by means of the tangent screw, make its zero and that of the vernier exactly coincide. Then, having the declination of the sun for 12 o'clock of the given day as affected by refraction carefully set out upon the declination arc, note also the equation of time. The sun is sometimes faster and sometimes slower than a clock adjusted to mean time, the difference being termed the equation of time. Fifteen or twenty minutes before noon, the telescope is directed to the north, and the object end lowered until, by moving the instrument on its spindle and the declination arc from side to side, the sun's image is brought nearly into position between the equatorial lines. Then bring the declination arc directly in line with the telescope, clamp the axis firmly, and with the tangent screw bring the image precisely between the lines, and keep it there with the tangent screw, raising it as long as it runs below the equatorial line—that is, as long as the sun continues to rise in the heavens.

When the sun reaches the meridian, the image will remain stationary for an instant. The instant is, of course, apparent noon when the index of the hour-arc should indicate XII. The latitude is determined by reading the vertical arc.

The angle through which the polar axis has moved, being measured from the zenith and not from the horizon, the angle read on the vertical limb is the complement of the latitude. The latitude may, however, be read direct from the inner row of figures on the arc, beginning with 90 at the centre and running to 10 on either side.

A very important addition to the solar attachment, patented by Messrs. W.. & L. E. Gurley, is shown in the figure. It is an arrangement for recovering the latitude of a solar transit-theodolite without referring to the vertical arc, and generally for setting the telescope at any desired angle in setting-out inclines. It consists of a spirit-level, connected by a short conical socket with the end of the telescope axis, to which it is clamped by a milled-head screw, and made adjustable by a screw and spring on opposite sides of the enlarged end of the level-tube. When the milled-head screw at the telescope axis is released, the level turns vertically upon the axis, and can thus be set at any angle with the telescope.

The latitude being set off upon the vertical arc, as usual, the level is clamped, and centred. The telescope may then be released and used in running lines, until it is desired to recover the latitude again. This is accurately done with the spirit-level alone without referring to the vertical arc.

The declination of the sun given in the *Nautical Almanack* from year to year is calculated for apparent noon at Greenwich. To determime it for any other hour at any other place, reference must be made not only to the difference of time arising from the longitude, but also to the change of declination from day to day. Thus, supposing that the observations are being made at a place eight hours west of Greenwich, the declination given in the almanack for Greenwich noon of any day, will correspond to the declination at the place in question at 4 o'clock a.m., of the same date. To this must be added algebraically the hourly change in the declination, also given in the almanack. A table may thus be prepared giving the declination for each hour of the day.

CHAPTER IX.

Traversing Underground.

Use of the Theodolite in the Mine.—In making a surface-survey with the theodolite, one line may be measured, from which all the other distances may be calculated by making them sides of a series of imaginary triangles, the angles of which are determined. This method obviously cannot be employed in the narrow workings of a mine, and consequently recourse must always be had to the method of traversing. A traverse is a series of consecutive drafts, of which the lengths and bearings or azimuths are determined. When the miner's dial is used, the bearing of each course is determined by the needle independently of that of the preceding course. When the theodolite is used, the readings taken are the angles contained by each successive line and the preceding one.

When the station representing the angular point is marked on the roof of the level, the theodolite must be so placed that the centre of its horizontal circle is exactly perpendicular below that point. The accuracy of the survey depends to a very great extent upon the manner in which this operation is performed.

When the angular points are to be permanently marked, brass or iron hooks (Fig. 39) may advantageously be used. The station-point is marked by a hole in the hook, through which a plumb-line may be passed. The hooks are driven into the timbering of the roof, or with hard rock or masonry into wooden pegs driven into holes previously drilled for the purpose. For centering, a plummet is employed, the point of which coincides with the axis of the line. When the plummet is steady, and its point is directly above the centre of the horizontal circle, the instrument is centered. A mark should be made on the spirit-level, or on the telescope, to indicate the position of the centre of the horizontal circle. In order to ascertain whether this mark is accurately in the axis of rotation of the theodolite, the instrument, having been carefully levelled, is rotated under the plummet. If the mark is in

Fig. 39.

the vertical axis of the theodolite, it will retain the same position under the point of the plummet during the rotation. If not, it will describe a circle, the centre of which is the true point to be used for centering.

If the workings of the mine are so low that a tripod-stand cannot be used, recourse must be had to an iron arm screwed into the timbering or into a vertical prop, or to a thick board firmly fixed horizontally across the level, as a support for the instrument. A new theodolite stand, intended to replace the ordinary tripod, was shown at the Budapest Exhibition in 1885. It is the invention of Professor Chrismár of the Schemnitz School of Mines. It consists of a support fixed across the level at such a height that the mine trucks can pass underneath it. A survey can thus be made without interfering with the ordinary work of the mine. The instrument consists of two hollow wrought-iron pipes, one sliding within the other, in such a way that the length may rapidly be increased or decreased. By means of a steel wedge working in a screw, the stand may be forced against the side timbers of the level with a pressure of as much as 800 lbs. without any part of the construction being injured. The stand is prevented from rotating by providing it at one end with three steel points. These stands can be used from 35 inches up to 5 feet, and, with the lengthening bar supplied, up to 6 feet 9 inches in width. The total weight of the apparatus is 16 lbs. The plate for the reception of the theodolite is connected by a spindle with the outer iron pipe. This stand has been adopted in the surveys of several of the Hungarian mines with considerable success.

In using the theodolite underground, care must be taken to avoid, as far as possible, short lines of sight. In the mine, the cross-wires may be made to coincide with the object, and the verniers may be read by artificial light, with the same precision as at the surface. The unfavourable atmospheric conditions, which so often interfere with the accuracy of surveys at the surface, are not encountered underground. It cannot of course be denied that, in subterranean excavations, difficulties have to be overcome which never occur at the surface. For example, great difficulties are met with in surveying with the theodolite in very confined spaces, and particularly in shafts.

For long station-lines, a candle-flame is the best object to sight, care being taken to shield it from draughts. With station-lines less than 30 fathoms in length, it is advisable to sight a plumbline suspended from the angular point. This is distinctly seen as a black line on a white ground, if a sheet of paper dipped in oil is held behind it, and illuminated from behind by the flame of a candle or lamp. A sheet of paper rendered transparent in this way is visible at a much greater distance than a sheet simply illuminated from the front side. When the air of the mine is quite clear, a plumb-line can be sighted in this way at a distance of 180 yards. Care must be taken that the paper is not held in front of the plumb-line and the light behind, as, in this case, the telescope will be directed not to the plumb-line, but to its shadow, which also appears as a black line upon a white ground.

Weissbach advocated the use of a plummet-lamp, the flame of which is accurately centered under the angular point. His lamp has, however, not been adopted to any great extent, as it is found to oscillate even with a moderate air-current. In collieries, a safety-lamp suspended in the same way may be advantageously used. A contrivance for turning the lamp on its longitudinal axis must be provided, in case one of the rods outside the glass cylinder obscures the flame. The flame of a safety-lamp burns very uniformly, and is a very good object to sight. The lamp, too, hangs very steadily on account of its weight.

In the anthracite mines of Pennsylvania, a plummet-lamp is used in underground surveying. It consists of a brass lamp, suspended by two chains, and terminated below in a conical plummet. It is provided with a so-called compensating ring, that is, a gimbal ring, surrounding and supporting the lamp, which swings freely within it upon an axis. The two chains are attached to this ring at the extremities of a diameter perpendicular to the axis. Thus the point of suspension, the centre of the lamp-flame, and the steel point of the plummet always lie in a true vertical line, no matter how much the brass chains may alter in length from the heating of the lamp or the wearing of the links. A shield at the top prevents the flame from burning the string. These lamps are used in pairs for back and forward observations.

The safety-lamp may be supported on a truly horizontal tripod-rest, in which case it is advisable to use three tripods, a central one carrying the theodolite, and two others carrying safety-lamps in brass cups for back- and fore-sight respectively. Mr. W. F. Howard advocates the adoption of coloured glasses, red and green, for the object-lamps. Additional certainty is thus afforded from the impossibility of mistaking other mining lights for the object. For the same reason, H. Huebner[*] employs a plummet-lamp with a red glass.

---

[*] *Preuss. Zeitschr.*, vol. xxxii., p. 309, 1884.

In reading the graduations of the theodolite, a copper or brass lamp should be used. The metal should be tested as to its freedom from magnetic substances. An oil lamp will be found more agreeable to use than a candle. In fiery collieries, a small copper or brass safety-lamp must be used. Unfortunately, all safety-lamps give a poorer light than the open lamp or candle, and their construction will not permit of the flame being brought near the compass graduation and the verniers. A method of increasing the illuminating power of safety-lamps, suggested by Mr. Przyborski,* a Hungarian mine-surveyor, appears, therefore, to merit attention. To one of the rods guarding the gauze externally, a powerful condensing lens is fastened by means of a double-jointed arm. The lens can thus be brought into any position that may be desired. Safety-lamps modified in this way have been used for some time in the surveys of the Resicza collieries in Hungary, with great success. Mr. E. B. Coxe† in Pennsylvania has constructed a plummet-Mueseler safety-lamp for surveys in fiery mines.

An ingenious device recently suggested by Professor Brathuhn, of the Clausthal School of Mines, will probably come into general use. To two of the rods outside the glass cylinder of the safety-lamp (Fig. 39a) a small plate is fastened by two screws. In the

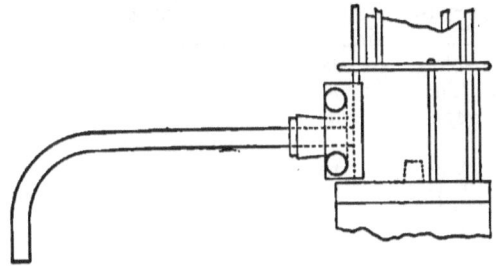

Fig. 39a.

centre of this plate, opposite the flame, a tube is inserted, and into this a bored cork fits. Through the bored cork passes a curved glass rod, with a circular section 0·43 inch in diameter. The light which passes in at the terminal surface is totally reflected by the curved surfaces of the rod, and passes out at

* *Berg. H. Ztg.*, vol. xliii., p. 49, 1884.
† *Trans. Amer. Inst. M.E.*, vol. iii., p. 39.

the lower end in full intensity. The free end of the glass rod, which can easily be moved in its cork-holder, is placed over the vernier, and a steady adequate light is obtained. Even in mines free from gas it appears worth while to use a light safety-lamp for theodolite work, as the flame is so steady and so free from smoke.

A novel method of lighting has been adopted by Mr. Stanley, who has adapted the prismatic compass of the military surveyor for use underground. In this instrument the floating ring attached to the magnetic needle is made of transparent celluloid, and light is thrown under it from a small movable lamp by means of a large prism. The floating ring is divided to half-degrees, and the divisions can be very clearly read.

The electric light has been successfully applied to surveying purposes by Professor Chrismár,* who, in his theodolite-surveys of the Schemnitz mines, uses incandescent lamps as objects to be sighted, and a smaller incandescent lamp for reading the verniers. The electric current is obtained from an accumulator.

When the theodolite is used underground, it is necessary to illuminate the cross-wires. This is best done by reflecting light into the telescope through the object-glass, in such a way that the object can, at the same time, be sighted without hindrance. For this purpose, a ring is fitted on to the object-end of the telescope. To the ring is fixed at an angle of 45° a piece of brass, silver-plated on the under side, with an elliptical hole in the centre. The optical axis of the telescope thus passes approximately through the centre of the hole in the reflector. Two forms of reflector are shown in Fig. 40. In one case there is an elliptical hole, in the other there is a small ellipse of metal. A light held near the reflecting surface illuminates the cross-wires. Satisfactory results can be obtained when the reflector is made of white cardboard. For illuminating the cross-wires very little light is required. The elliptical hole of the one reflector must therefore not be too small, nor the small ellipse of the other too large. In the theodolites made by Messrs. Troughton and Simms, the cross-wires are illuminated by means of a hole drilled in the supports, and a small mirror placed at an angle of 45°, in the axis of the telescope. The light is held near the supports, instead of near the object-glass.

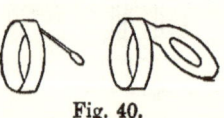

Fig. 40.

* *Oesterr. Ztschr.*, 1886, p. 395.

Shades of white note-paper should be fixed to the vernier-microscopes of the theodolite, and the light should be allowed to fall on the back of them. In this way, the vernier can be read underground with great precision. In some theodolites, ground glass or ivory reflectors are placed above the verniers. They are useful, not only in the mine, but at the surface on a bright day when there is a difficulty in reading the vernier owing to the glare of the silver surface.

The following is an example of the survey of a closed polygon with the theodolite :—

No. of Line.	Horizontal Angles.	Meridian Angles.	Measured Distance.
Mag. mer. . .	0° 00'	0° 00'	Links. ...
1 off mag. mer.	121° 27'	121° 27'	1091
2 off 1 . . .	97° 36'	39° 03'	252
3 off 2 . . .	209° 01'	68° 04'	196
4 off 3 . . .	159° 40'	47° 44'	534
5 off 4 . . .	195° 32'	63° 16'	384
6 off 5 . . .	85° 31'	328° 47'	336
7 off 6 . . .	152° 07'	300° 54'	1055
8 off 7 . . .	103° 34'	224° 28'	771
9 off 8 . . .	104° 03'	148° 31'	154
10 off 9 . . .	262° 58'	231° 29'	605
1 off 10 . . .	69° 58'	121° 27'	proof line.

In traversing underground, the theodolite is set up at a station, B, and after levelling, and clamping the plates, the magnetic meridian is observed. The telescope is then directed to a line suspended down the shaft at A. The vernier-plate is then released, and the telescope directed to the forward station at C. The first angle is entered in the survey-book as 0° 00', with the length of the line A B in the distance column. The angle indicated by the verniers is read, and noted in the column for horizontal angles. The distance, B C, is then measured, and noted with any remarks that may be necessary. Then, remove the instrument to C, level, clamp the vernier-plate at zero, and direct the telescope to the back station, B. Release the vernier-plate, and direct the telescope to station D. Read the angle, and note it, while CD is being measured. After reading the horizontal angles, the vertical angles are read if required, and noted as angles of elevation or depression. Proceeding in this way, the conclusion of the survey is arrived at.

Before this traverse can be laid down upon paper, the horizontal angles must be reduced to angles from the first line (in this case the magnetic meridian) as meridian for the whole. The rule for reducing the horizontal angles to plotting angles from one meridian is as follows:—*Rule:* To the first meridian angle add the next observed horizontal angle. If the sum exceeds 180°, deduct that amount from it. The remainder will be the second meridian angle. To this, add the next observed angle and proceed as before. When the sum of the meridian angle and the next observed angle is less than 180°, it must be increased by 180°. If, after deducting 180°, the remainder exceeds 360°, it must be diminished by that amount, to give the required meridian angle.

In the example given, the angles would be reduced to one meridian in the following manner:—

Meridian 0° 00' + 1st angle 121° 27'   = 121° 27' = No. 1 mer. angle
    No. 1 meridian angle 121° 27' + 2nd angle   97° 36' = 219° 03'
                         219° 03' − 180° 00'   = 39° 03' = No. 2
    (39° 03' + 209° 01') − 180°   = 68° 04' = No. 3
    (68° 04' + 159° 40') − 180°   = 47° 44' = No. 4
    (47° 44' + 195° 32') − 180°   = 63° 16' = No. 5
    (63° 16' + 85° 31') + 180°   = 328° 47' = No. 6
    (328° 47' + 152° 07') − 180°   = 300° 54' = No. 7
    (300° 54' + 103° 34') − 180°   = 224° 28' = No. 8
    (224° 28' + 104° 03') − 180°   = 148° 31' = No. 9
    (148° 31' + 262° 58') − 180°   = 231° 29' = No. 10
    (231° 29' + 69° 58') − 180°   = 121° 27' = Proof

In working a closed traverse, the angles recorded form the angles of the polygon. If the survey has been kept on the left hand these angles will be interior ones, and a means is afforded of testing the accuracy of the survey, as the interior angles of the polygon together with four right angles should be equal to twice as many right angles as the figure has sides.

The interior angles of a traverse may be found from the bearings or courses by the following rules:—

1. When the two lines lie in the first and second quadrants, N.-E. and S.-E., or in the third and fourth quadrants, S.-W. and N.-W., their sum is the interior angle.

2. When the two lines lie in the first and third quadrants, N.-E. and S.-W., or in the second and fourth quadrants, S.-E. and N.-W., their difference is the interior angle.

3. When the two lines lie in the second and third quadrants, S.-E. and S.-W., or in the first and fourth quadrants, N.-E. and N.-W., their sum deducted from 180° is the interior angle.

4. When the two lines lie both in the same quadrant, their difference added to 180° is the interior angle.

For example.—Let line 1 bear N. 63° 16' E., and line 2 bear S. 59° 06' E., then the angle between the two bearings is

$$63° \ 16' + 59° \ 06' = 122° \ 22'.$$

There is another method of measuring angles well adapted for use in mines. It is, however, only practicable with a transit-theodolite. The mode of procedure is as follows:—Clamp the vernier-plate at 0° 00', unclamp the vertical axis; direct the telescope to the back object, and direct the line of collimation exactly towards the object by the tangent screw of the vertical axis. Revolve the telescope vertically. Unclamp the vernier-plate; direct the telescope to the forward object; clamp the vernier-plate, and direct the line of collimation exactly towards the object by the tangent screw of the vernier-plate. Angles where the vernier has moved in the direction of the graduation are minus, or to be subtracted. When the vernier has moved in the opposite direction, the angles are plus, or to be added.

This is the method of surveying adopted in the anthracite mines of Pennsylvania. Mr. E. B. Coxe* works with the transit-theodolite and plummet-lamps, with a single assistant, in the following manner:—He first selects the stations, marking the places where spuds, or nails with a hole in the head, are to be driven into the timbers. This is done before any instrumental work is begun, as much labour can be spared, and very short sights can often be avoided. When the stations have been marked out, he goes to station 2 with the transit-theodolite, and by means of the plumb-bob belonging to the instrument centres his instrument exactly under the spud. His assistant in the meantime takes the two plummet-lamps, suspends one from spud No. 1, and the other from spud No. 3, and then comes back to hold the light while the final adjustments are made and the readings taken. Mr. Coxe sets the vernier at zero, and sights back to lamp No. 1. He then reads the compass-needle, inverts

* *Trans. Amer. Inst. Min. Eng.*, vol. i., p. 375; vol. ii., p. 219.

TRAVERSING UNDERGROUND. 115

the telescope, and sights the lamp at station 3. Having read the two verniers and the needle, he turns the telescope back, sights No. 1, and turns the vernier-plate round nearly 180° until he sights No. 3, when he again reads the two verniers. Thus he obtains four readings of the deflection from the verniers, and a compass reading as a check. If the readings are concordant, he is sure that there is no mistake, and proceeds with the instrument to No. 3. In the meantime the assistant brings the plummet-lamp from No. 1 to No. 2, and then takes the lamp from No. 3 to No. 4. The distances are measured with a 500-foot steel band.

A survey made by Mr. Coxe, in the anthracite coal region of Pennsylvania, of a closed polygon with a periphery of 6660·19 feet gave the following results:—

| Station. | Angle. | | Reduced Angle. | Distance. |
	Right.	Left.		
1	0° 04′	...	+ 0° 04′	Feet. 664·97
2	0° 47′	...	+ 0° 51′	711·55
3	...	0° 52′	− 0° 01′	408·60
4	0° 33′	...	+ 0° 32′	567·25
5	...	179° 32′	− 179° 00′	186·05
B	...	31° 12′	− 210° 12′	88·42
B_1	...	19° 39′	− 229° 51′	389·50
B_2	...	9° 36′	− 239° 27′	631·00
B_3	4° 06′	...	− 235° 21′	381·25
B_4	35° 55′	...	− 199° 26′	752·50
B_5	62° 39′	...	− 136° 47′	294·80
5	...	9° 01′	− 145° 48′	527·20
4	86° 27′	...	− 59° 21′	464·85
3	...	44° 17′	− 103° 38′	210·05
2	...	5° 51′	− 109° 29′	382·20

The mode of procedure in the surveys of the anthracite mines of Pennsylvania varies considerably in the different districts. The excellent method adopted in the mines of the Pennsylvania Railroad has been fully described by Mr. R. van A. Norris.* The surveying party consists of a theodolite-man, station-man, backsight, foresight, and chain-man, with a fireman to attend to the safety of the party. Three tripods are used, but the wicks of the tripod lamps, which were found too large for accurate sighting, are replaced by steel wire one-sixteenth of an inch in diameter and three-eighths of an inch in height. The sights are taken to the bottom of this wire, and measurements are taken along the line of sight with a 300-foot steel tape, marked at every 5 feet. The station-man keeps ahead of the party and fixes the stations by drilling a small conical hole in the roof and suspending a plumb-line from an iron rod with a notched end fitting the hole. The point is then transferred to the floor. A better method is to put a horse-shoe nail, with a hole punched in the end, into a plug of wood driven into a hole in the roof, and then to suspend the plumb-line from the ring and to set up the theodolite underneath. A still better method is to put a shoe-peg holding a small loop of cooper wire in the hole.

Continuous azimuth angles are run, and the entries in the note-book consist of the vernier reading on a continuous gradation from 0° to 360°, and the quadrant reading or course. A needle reading is taken roughly with a view to detect serious errors. At the commencement of the survey, the vernier is set to the course of the first line taken from the notes of a previous survey. The error in a closed survey of fifteen or more lines is rarely found to exceed three minutes. For levelling purposes, the vertical angles are read very carefully, the sight-wire being so arranged that it is just 0·5 foot below the centre of the instrument. The method of booking adopted is shown on the next page. The error on closing this survey is one minute. The horizontal distances, elevations, and vertical distances are calculated in the office; and the column headed "staff" gives the distance from the centre of the instrument to the station in the roof. With this method of surveying, it is possible to attain great speed, from forty to fifty stations being considered a fair night's work. All main stations are plotted from calculated latitudes and departures (see Chapter XI.), and the stations in the workings are filled in with the aid of the protractor.

* *School of Mines Quarterly*, vol. xi., 1890, p. 328.

EXAMPLE OF MR. NORRIS'S METHOD OF BOOKING COLLIERY-SURVEYS.
May 1, 1889. Continuation of Survey of No. 3 Plane.

Stations.	Courses.			Distances.			Elevations.			Remarks.
	Needle.	Angle.	Course.	Vertical angle.	Hor. dist.	Tape.	Ht Inst.	Staff.	Elevation.	Vertical distance.
1-2	...	...	...	...	...	...	−1·54	...	+233·89	...
2-3	S. 4° E.	173·46	S. 6° 14′ E.	−6° 00′	57·60	57·28	...	+1·90	+228·32	−6·02
3-x	N. 82° W.	...	N. 83° 50′ W.	...	68·00	...	...	...	...	Face.
3-4	N. 85¼° E.	84·21	N. 84° 21′ E.	−2° 56′	22·76	22·73	...	+2·25	+228·01	−1·16
4-5	S. 8° E.	170·45	S. 9° 15′ E.	−5° 46′	52·10	51·83	...	+2·05	+223·08	−5·23
5-6	S. 88° E.	91·24	S. 88° 36′ E.	−3° 07′	27·64	27·60	...	+1·85	+221·88	−1·50
6-x	N. 87° E.	...	N. 85° 30′ E.	−2° 15′	106·00	105·92	...	...	...	...
6-7	S. 4¼° E.	174·20	S. 5° 40′ E.	−5° 56′	52·58	52·30	...	+1·85	+216·95	−5·43
7-x	N. 85° W.	...	N. 86° 50′ W.	+1° 30′	86·00	...	...	...	...	Face.
7-8	N. 86° E.	84·59	N. 84° 59′ E.	−3° 42′	25·19	25·13	...	+2·10	+216·08	−1·62
8-9	S. 1° E.	177·33	S. 2° 27′ E.	−4° 00′	34·37	34·28	...	+0·90	+212·99	−2·39
9-10	S. 73° E.	107·50	S. 72° 10′ E.	−5° 29′	99·36	99·50	...	+1·90	+204·94	−9·55
10-8	N. 81° E.	80·12	N. 80° 12′ E.	−4° 01′	50·00	49·87	...	+1·10	+201·14	−3·50
8-7	...	...	N. 78° 55′ E.	...	...	...	...	...	...	...

Comparison of the Theodolite and Compass.—On account of the great cost of mining works, the surveys for determining the direction, in which levels or tunnels are to be set out, are of such importance that the greatest possible accuracy is demanded. For this reason, the mine-surveyor ought to employ the instruments and methods that will give the most accurate results, and to use less perfect instruments only for unimportant or preliminary surveys. The compass is an imperfect instrument of this kind. It is of great value in certain cases, especially for filling in details. When, however, it is used for large and important surveys, there is always a danger of meeting with great inaccuracies. The daily variation of the declination of the needle is nearly 10 minutes. Disregarding the occasional irregular perturbations of the needle, it is obvious that errors of 10 minutes or more may occur in the period between 8 a.m. and 1 p.m., when the declination of the needle passes from its minimum to its maximum. With a radius of 100, the chord of 10' is 0·29. Therefore, from the change in the direction of the needle, there will be in a length of 100 fathoms a lateral displacement of nearly three-tenths of a fathom.

The uncertainty of the readings of the compass is also a disadvantage. With compasses of the ordinary size, the needle cannot be read more accurately than to one-fifth of a degree. Thus, errors of one-tenth of a degree, or 6 minutes, are unavoidable. In a length of 100 fathoms, this error in the bearing gives a lateral error of 0·174 fathom.

Magnetic storms and the influence of ferriferous rock masses[*] in the neighbourhood may give rise to considerable error, often difficult to detect while the survey is in progress.

With the theodolite very different results are obtained. With a 6-inch instrument, the horizontal angle, even without repeating, may be determined accurately to 30 seconds. The chord of this angle being 0·000145, in a length of 100 fathoms, the lateral error will not exceed 0·0145 fathom. The accuracy of the theodolite is thus 30 times as great as that of the compass.

The repetition of the angles not only ensures great accuracy, but is also a valuable check on the results. If, for example, an angle has been repeated four times, and if the second, third, and fourth observations give results closely approaching the result of the first observation multiplied by two, three, and four respectively, it is evident there can have been no serious error. With the compass, on the other hand, when a bearing is read repeatedly, the conditions remain the same, and it is quite possible to have exactly the same error each time.

In reading a bearing with the compass, the instrument must

---

[*] See paper by Prof. A. W. Rücker on "Regional Magnetic Disturbances." *Proc. Royal Soc.*, vol. xlviii., p. 505, 1890.

remain unmoved. The surveyor is therefore compelled to put his eye, his head, and sometimes his whole body into a particular position with reference to the instrument. With the theodolite, however, there is no necessity for such inconvenience, as the horizontal circle may be turned to any required position, without changing the angle indicated by the vernier. The results are therefore read with far greater precision.

The disadvantages of the compass pointed out in this comparison are not presented by the vernier form of that instrument. The modern vernier-compass or circumferenter is practically a theodolite, from its compactness and simplicity specially adapted to underground surveying.

The theodolite of the usual size has the disadvantage of want of portability, its weight being a great drawback to its use underground. The telescope, too, cannot be used in mines when the air is bad from powder-smoke.

CHAPTER X.

SURFACE-SURVEYS WITH THE THEODOLITE.

Triangulation.—The surface-survey of a mine royalty may be made with almost any degree of accuracy that may be required by having recourse to a system of triangulation. A base-line is measured with great accuracy, and, from its ends, angles are taken to distant stations. The instrument is placed at each of these new stations, and angles taken to other stations. In this way, the ground is covered with a network of imaginary triangles, all the angles of which have been measured. The length of the base-line being known, the lengths of the sides of the triangles may be calculated trigonometrically.

The first operation is the measurement of the base-line, a proceeding requiring careful attention, as any errors will be multiplied in proportion to the extent of the survey. The base-line should be measured upon a level piece of ground, and from both of its ends the principal objects in the surrounding country should be visible. The length of the base-line should be in proportion to the extent of the survey. For mine-surveying purposes, a base-line need never be longer than 300 fathoms.

The last triangle of the system should be selected in such a way that one of its sides may be measured. This line is called the *base of verification*. One base-line can then be calculated from the other, and the calculated and measured results compared. In this way the accuracy of the survey may be tested.

The ends of the base-line should be marked by means of some permanent object, such as a large stone sunk in the ground, or a pile driven deep and concealed from casual observation. In the level surface of the stone, a hole about 3 inches in depth should be bored to mark the exact end of the line, and to serve for the reception of a signal pole. Permanently marked in this way, stations could be readily found at a future period.

The triangles should be as nearly equilateral as possible. Special care must be taken to avoid *ill-conditioned* triangles, that is, triangles with any angle less than 30° or more than 150°, as a point is not definitely defined if the lines fixing it meet at a

SURFACE-SURVEYS WITH THE THEODOLITE. 121

very obtuse or very acute angle. The triangular points may be marked by means of wooden pickets, 1 foot long and 4 inches thick, driven into the ground. In these, holes should be bored to a depth of 4 inches for the reception of the signal poles.

In measuring the angles, the telescope is first directed to the left-hand object and then to the right-hand one, so that the verniers move in the direction in which the horizontal circle is graduated. If the telescope is directed to the right-hand object first, the angle read must be subtracted from 360° in order to give the interior angle required.

The three angles of each triangle should be measured, so that the accuracy of the operations may be checked, by adding them together; when they should amount to 180°. In the case of the great triangles occurring in geodetic-surveys, the total exceeds 180°. The so-called *spherical excess* is due to the fact that the triangle is spherical on account of the curvature of the earth. Small errors made in measuring the angles may be corrected by adding to, or subtracting from, each angle one-third of the total error.

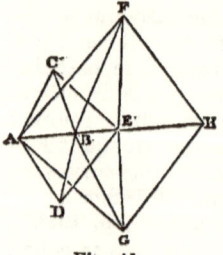

Fig. 41.

It sometimes happens that the level ground is of limited extent, and not suited for the measurement of the whole of a base-line. In such a case the base-line is prolonged by ranging lines in continuation of it, at one or both ends, until a suitable length is obtained. The lengths of the additional lines are calculated from angular measurements, as follows:—

When the measured base, A B (Fig. 41), can be conveniently extended in one direction only, towards H, select a lateral station point, C, so that the resulting triangles, A B C and B C E, shall be well-conditioned, and if possible nearly equilateral. Measure all the angles of these two triangles, and calculate the length of the side B C. Then choose a point E in the line ranged in continuation of A B, and by means of the side B C and the angles C E B, B C E, calculate the length of B E. Check the result by selecting another lateral station, D, on the opposite side of the base-line, and by solving the triangles, A B D, D B E. The length of the line B E is thus calculated from independent data. E H represents a farther prolongation of the base-line, and F and G the lateral stations, which form the triangles, by means of which its length is calculated.

A comparatively short base-line may be connected with the sides of large triangles, without prolonging it and without introducing ill-conditioned triangles, by continually increasing the sides of the triangle, as shown in Fig. 42. A B is the measured base-line, and C and D are the nearest stations. In the triangles A B C, A B D, all the angles and the side A B being known, the other sides can be readily calculated. Then in each of the triangles D A C and D B C, two sides and the included angle being known, the length D C may be calculated in a variety of different ways which will check each other. Taking D C as a base-line, choose a pair of stations, E and F, at opposite sides of the base, and as far from each other as is consistent with making C D F and C D E well-conditioned triangles. Proceed as before to calculate the distance E F. This will probably be sufficiently long to serve as the side of a pair of triangles. If not, continue the process until a distance sufficiently long is obtained.

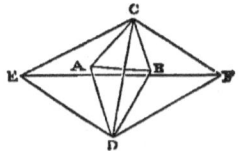

Fig. 42.

The triangulation-survey of a mine royalty is based on the same principles, operations, and methods as are adopted on the trigonometrical surveys of countries. In such surveys, the spheroidal form of the earth's surface has to be taken into account, and the amount of accuracy required is much greater than that required for any ordinary topographical survey. Thus, on the Ordnance Survey of the United Kingdom, the average length of the sides of the Primary Triangulation was 35 miles; the longest side was 111 miles. The angles were measured with four large theodolites, two 3 feet in diameter, one 2 feet, and one 18 inches. With the exception of the theodolite 2 feet in diameter, these instruments were constructed by Ramsden at the commencement of the trigonometrical operations in England in 1798. They are now exhibited in the South Kensington Museum, and are still in perfect condition.

In order to show how accurately the main triangulation was conducted, it may be mentioned that in 1826, a base-line was measured at Lough Foyle, in the north of Ireland, by means of General Colby's compensated bars, and in 1849 the old base-line on Salisbury Plain was remeasured with the same apparatus. The length of the Salisbury Plain base was 6·97 miles, and that of the Lough Foyle base 7·89 miles. The length of the latter base was calculated by a triangulation carried from the Salisbury Plain base, and the difference between the calculated and measured length of the Lough Foyle base was only 5 inches.

By means of secondary triangulation, the long sides of the principal triangulation were reduced to lengths of 5 miles. The angles were measured with a 12-inch theodolite. The stations selected were, as far as possible, permanent objects such as church towers.

The 5-mile sides of the secondary triangulation were reduced by means of the Parish triangulation to lengths of 1 mile, or less. In towns, the points were sometimes within as short a distance as 10 chains. The angles were measured with a 7-inch theodolite. Finally, the details were filled in by means of ordinary chain-surveying.

Computing the Sides of the Triangles.—For the solution of the triangles when the base and the three angles are given, the ordinary sine ratio is employed—

$$\frac{\sin A}{a} = \frac{\sin B}{b} = \frac{\sin C}{c},$$

when, if c represents the base,

$$a = \frac{c \sin A}{\sin C};$$

or, using logarithms,

$$\log a = \log c + \text{L. sin } A - \text{L. sin } C.$$

The sine of an angle A is equal to $1 \div \text{cosec } A$. Instead, therefore, of subtracting L. sin C, L. cosec C may be added; the formula then is—

$$\log a = \log c + \text{L. sin } A + \text{L. cosec } C - 20.$$

In the survey of the triangles shown in Fig. 43, the base-line af was found on measuring to be 4009·5 links. The angles were as follows:—

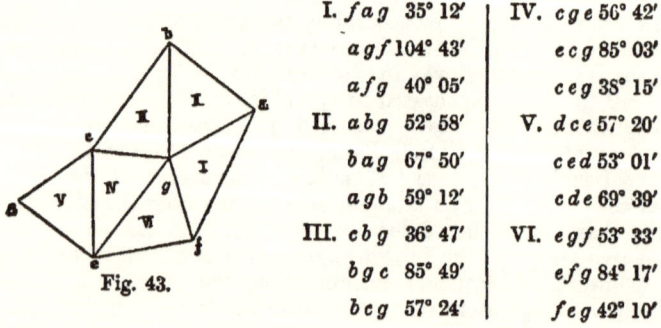

Fig. 43.

I.	fag	35° 12′	IV.	cge	56° 42′
	agf	104° 43′		ecg	85° 03′
	afg	40° 05′		ceg	38° 15′
II.	abg	52° 58′	V.	dce	57° 20′
	bag	67° 50′		ced	53° 01′
	agb	59° 12′		cde	69° 39′
III.	cbg	36° 47′	VI.	egf	53° 33′
	bgc	85° 49′		efg	84° 17′
	bcg	57° 24′		feg	42° 10′

The sides are calculated in the following manner:—

To find side ag in Triangle I.

$$af : ag = \sin agf : \sin afg$$

$$\log ag = \log af + \text{L. sin } afg - \text{L. sin } agf.$$

log 4009·5	=	3·6030902
+ L. sin 40° 05′	=	9·8088192
− L. sin 104° 43′	=	9·9855135
log ag	=	3·4263959
ag	=	2669·3 links.

If instead of subtracting the sine of the angle opposite to the given side, its cosecant is added, the result will be as follows:—

log 4009·5	=	3·6030902
+ L. sin 40° 05′	=	9·8088192
+ L. cosec 104° 43′	=	10·0144865
log ag	=	3·4263959

To find side fg in Triangle I.

$$af : fg = \sin agf : \sin fag.$$

log 4009·5	=	3·6030902
+ L. sin 35° 12′	=	9·7607483
+ L. cosec 104° 43′	=	10·0144865
log fg	=	3·3783250
fg	=	2389·6

To find side ab in Triangle II.

log ag	=	3·4263959
+ L. sin 59° 12′	=	9·9339729
+ L. cosec 52° 58′	=	10·0978419
log ab	=	3·4582107
ab	=	2872·2

To find side bg in Triangle II.

$\log ag$	=	3·4263959
+ L. sin 67° 50′	=	9·9666533
+ L. cosec 52° 58′	=	10·0978419
$\log bg$	=	3·4908911
bg	=	3096·7

In the same way, the lengths of the other sides will be found to be as follows:—

Triangle III.

$\log bc = \log bg$ + L. sin 85° 49′ + L. cosec 57° 24′ − 20
bc = 3666·0 links.
$\log cg = \log bg$ + L. sin 36° 47′ + L. cosec 57° 24′ − 20
cg = 2201·0 links.

Triangle IV.

$\log ce = \log cg$ + L. sin 56° 42′ + L. cosec 38° 15′ − 20
ce = 2971·5 links.
$\log eg = \log cg$ + L. sin 85° 03′ + L. cosec 38° 15′ − 20
eg = 3541·9 links.

Triangle V.

$\log cd = \log ce$ + L. sin 53° 01′ + L. cosec 69° 39′ − 20
cd = 2531·7 links.
$\log de = \log ce$ + L. sin 57° 20′ + L. cosec 69° 39′ − 20
de = 2668·0 links.

Triangle VI.

$\log ef = \log eg$ + L. sin 53° 33′ + L. cosec 84° 17′ − 20
ef = 2863·3 links.
$\log fg = \log eg$ + L. sin 42° 10′ + L. cosec 84° 17′ − 20

$\log eg$	=	3·5492413
L. sin 42° 10′	=	9·8269098
L. cosec 84° 17′	=	10·0021653
$\log fg$	=	3·3783164
fg	=	2389·55 links.

a result practically the same as that obtained in the solution of triangle I.

In some cases the two sides of a triangle and the angle contained between them may be known, and it is required to find the two other angles, and the third side. In this case, the sum of the two sides is to their difference, as the tangent of half the sum of the two unknown angles is to the tangent of half their difference. Half their difference thus found, added to half their sum will be the greater of the two angles required—that is, the angle opposite to the greater side.

Interior Detail of the Triangulation.—The triangulation for a survey being completed, the filling-in of the interior detail presents no difficulty. Roads, rivers, woods, &c., may be surveyed by traversing with the theodolite or with the dial. For filling in details, the *prismatic compass* is of great use. It is a hand instrument consisting of a glass-covered circular brass box, $2\frac{1}{2}$ inches in diameter, containing a graduated card or aluminium ring, under or across which a magnetic-needle is fixed. The card or ring is divided to half or one-third of a degree. The needle and card are accurately balanced. Sights are attached to the rim of the box. The farther sight has a fine thread stretched along its opening in the direction of its length. The near sight has a small slit below which is a reflecting magnifying triangular prism, so placed that on looking through the slit the eye sees at the same time the vertical wire of the farther sight and the needle-reading, the divisions on the card appearing as a continuation of the wire. The graduation of the ring begins at the south end of the needle, and proceeds towards the right, round to 360°. In this way bearings are shown to the east of north. With this instrument, when held in the hand, bearings may be read to within 30 minutes to 2 degrees. The instrument is thus suitable only for preliminary and unimportant work. Mounted on a stand, the instrument gives more satisfactory results.

The *plane table** is an instrument which may be advantageously used for filling in details where minute accuracy is not required. It consists of a drawing-board mounted on a portable tripod capable of being levelled, like the graduated limb of the theodolite. It must also have a free horizontal angular movement, and be provided with a clamp and tangent screw. The index on the board consists of a flat straight-edge, either with upright sights at its ends or with a telescope for determining the line of sight. The use of the plane table is similar to that of the theodolite. Instead, however, of reading off horizontal angles and afterwards plotting them on paper, the angles are at once laid down in the field on a sheet of paper strained on the top of the table.

* Consult J. Pierce's paper on the economic use of the plane table, *Min. Proc. Inst. C.E.*, vol. xcii., 1888, p. 187.

Before the introduction of the theodolite, the plane table was largely used for mine-surveying in Sweden, where the magnetic nature of the iron ore deposits renders the compass useless for surveying purposes.

American Mining Claims.—Prospectors are usually without suitable instruments to lay off their claims on the surface with any degree of accuracy, and consequently the methods they employ are generally very crude. Before the patent or title from the United States can be obtained, a very accurate survey of the claim must be made with the theodolite by a deputy of the United States Surveyor-General of Public Lands. These officers are known as the United States Deputy Mineral Surveyors, and are required to pass an examination.

Mining claims are of different dimensions according to the local laws. The length is limited by the United States laws to 1,500 feet in the direction, or along the strike, of the vein. The width varies in the different States; it is usually 300 feet on each side of the middle of the vein at the surface. The end lines of the claims must be parallel, but the side lines need not be so. This prevents more than 1,500 feet of a vein being included in one claim.

When mineral discoveries are made on surveyed land, the surveys must be so connected with the public survey that there will be no difficulty in finding some fixed point or corner of that survey. When discoveries are made on unsurveyed land, the survey must be connected with permanent natural objects, such as mountain peaks or rocks.

It is frequently found that two or more claims conflict or overlap. In such cases, priority of location determines the ownership of the area in dispute. In making the plan, the United States Deputy-Surveyors must deduct the area in conflict from the subsequent claim. When the survey for patent is completed, the claim must be marked by at least four stakes, one in each corner.

According to the instructions issued to the United States Deputy Mineral Surveyors, all mineral surveys must be made with a transit-theodolite with solar attachment, or with some other instrument acting independently of the magnetic meridian. All courses must be referred to the true meridian. The magnetic declination must be noted at each corner of the survey.

In case the claim is situated in a district where there are no corners of the public survey within 2 miles, the surveyor must establish a permanent mineral location monument. This should consist of a post 8 feet long and 6 inches square, set 3 feet in the ground, and protected by a well-built conical mound of stone, 3 feet high and 6 feet in diameter at the base. All corners of the claim must be established in a permanent manner, and the corner and survey number must be neatly chiselled on the sides facing the claim. In case the point for the corner is inaccessible, a witness-corner must be established as near as practicable to the true corner, with which it must be connected by course and distance.

The claimant is required by law to show that 500 dollars' worth of labour has been expended upon the claim by himself. The surveyor must, therefore, give full details of all improvements made upon the claim. A preliminary plan on a scale of 200 feet to an inch must be filed with the field-notes. With the notes, too, a report must be submitted stating in detail the observations and calculation for the establishment of the meridian from which the courses were deflected, in cases where the solar attachment was not used. If any of the lines of the survey were determined by triangulation or traverse, full details must be given of the calculations whereby the results reported in the field-notes were obtained.

The field-notes must be prepared in conformity with the accompanying specimen :—

FIELD-NOTES*

OF THE SURVEY OF THE CLAIM OF THE "ARGENTUM MINING COMPANY" UPON THE SILVER KING AND GOLD QUEEN LODES, AND SILVER KING MILL SITE, IN ALPINE MINING DISTRICT, LAKE COUNTY, COLORADO. Surveyed by G. LIGHTFOOT, April 22 to 24, 1886.

Survey No. 4225 A—*Silver King Lode.*—Beginning at corner No. 1, identical with corner No. 1 of the location. A spruce post, 5 feet long 4 inches square, set 2 feet in the ground, with a mound of stone marked (1) 4225 A, whence the W. ¼ corner Section 22, Township 11 S., Range 81 W. of the 6th principal meridian, bears S. 79° 34' W., 1378·2 feet. Corner No. 1, Gottenburg lode (unsurveyed), bears S. 40° 29' W., 187·67 feet. A pine, 12 inches in diameter, blazed and marked B. T. (bearing-tree) (1) 4225 A, bears S. 7° 25' E., 22 feet. Mount Ouray bears N. 11° E. Hiawatha Peak bears N. 47° 45' W.

Thence S. 24° 45' W. (variation 15° 12' E.), 1242 feet to trail coursing N.-W. and S.-E., 1365·28 feet to corner No. 2. A granite stone, 25 by 9 by 6 inches, set 18 inches in the ground, chiselled (2) 4225 A, whence corner No. 2 of the location bears S. 24° 45' W., 134·72 feet. Corner No. 1, survey No 2560, Carnarvon lode, bears S. 3° 28' E., 116·6 feet. North end of bridge, over Columbine Creek, bears S. 65° 15' E., 650 feet.

Thence N. 65° 15' W. (variation 15° 20' E.), 152 feet intersect line 4-1, survey No. 2560, at N. 38° 52' W., 231·2 feet from corner No. 1. 300 feet to corner No. 3. A cross at corner point, and (3) 4225 A chiselled on a granite rock in place, 20 by 14 by 6 feet above the general level, whence

* For a copy of these notes, I am indebted to the kindness of Mr. O. Carstarphen, U.S. Surveyor-General, Colorado.

corner No. 3 of the location bears S. 24° 45' W., 134·72 feet. A spruce 16 inches in diameter, blazed and marked B. T. (3) 4225 A, bears S. 58° W., 18 feet.

Thence N. 24° 45' E. (variation 15° 20' E.), 73·4 feet intersect line 4-1, survey No. 2560, at N. 38° 52' W., 396·4 feet from corner No. 1. 150 feet intersect line 6-7 of this survey. 237 feet to trail, coursing N.-W. and S.-E. 1000·9 feet intersect line 2-3, Gottenburg lode, at N. 25° 56' W, 76·26 feet from corner No. 2. 1365·28 feet to corner No. 4, identical with corner No. 4 of the location. A pine post, 4·5 feet long, 5 inches square, set 1 foot in the ground, with a mound of earth and stone, marked (4) 4225 A, whence a cross, chiselled on rock in place, marked B. R. (bearing rock) (4) 4225 A, bears N. 28° 10' E., 58·9 feet.

Thence S. 65° 15' E. (variation 15° 12' E.), 28·5 feet intersect line 1-4, Gottenburg lode, at N. 25° 56' W., 285·13 feet from corner No. 1. 65 feet intersect line 5-6 of this survey. 300 feet to corner No. 1, the place of beginning.

Gold Queen Lode.—Beginning at corner No. 5, a pine post, 5 feet long, 5 inches square, set 2 feet in the ground, with mound of earth and stone, marked (5) 4225 A, whence corner No. 1, of this survey, bears S. 14° 54' E., 370·16 feet. A pine, 18 inches in diameter, bears S. 33° 15' W., 51 feet, and a silver spruce, 13 inches in diameter, bears N. 60° W., 23 feet. Both are blazed and marked B. T. (5) 4225 A.

Thence S. 24° 30' W. (variation 15° 14' E.), 285 feet intersect line 4-1 of this survey. 315 feet intersect line 4-1, Gottenburg lode, at N. 25° 56' W., 237·78 feet from corner No. 1. 688·3 feet intersect line 1-2, Gottenburg lode, at N. 64° 04' E., 12·23 feet from corner No. 2. 1438 feet to trail, coursing N.-W. and S.-E. 1500 feet to corner No. 6, a granite stone, 34 by 14 by 6 inches, set 1 foot in the ground to bed-rock, with mound of stone, chiselled (6) 4225 A, whence a cross, chiselled on ledge of rock, marked B. R. (6) 4225 A, bears due north 12 feet.

Thence N. 65° 30' W (variation 15° 20' E.), 70·3 feet intersect line 3-4 of this survey. 223·37 feet intersect line 4-1, survey No. 2560, at N. 38° 52' W., 567·28 feet from corner No. 1. 300 feet to corner No. 7, a cross at corner point, and (7) 4225 A chiselled on a granite boulder, 12 by 6 by 3 feet above ground, whence a cross chiselled on vertical face of cliff, marked B. R. (7) 4225 A, bears N. 72° W., 56·2 feet. A pine, 14 inches in diameter, blazed and marked B. T. (7) 4225 A, bears N. 10° E., 39 feet.

Thence N. 24° 30' E. (variation not determined on account of local attraction), 38·43 feet intersect line 4-1, survey No. 2560, at N. 38° 52' W., 653 feet from corner No. 1. 165 feet to trail, coursing N.-W. and S.-E. 1043·73 feet intersect line 2-3, Gottenburg lode, at N. 25° 56' W., 379·06 feet from corner No. 2. 1432·90 feet intersect line 4-1, Gottenburg lode, at N. 25° 56' W., 626·94 feet from corner No. 1. 1500 feet to corner No. 8, a spruce post 6 feet long, 5 inches square, set 2·5 feet in the ground, with mound of stone, marked (8) 4225 A, whence a cross chiselled on rock in place, marked B. R. (8) 4225 A, bears S. 9° 12' E., 15·8 feet. A pine, 20 inches in diameter, blazed and marked B. T. (8) 4225 A, bears N. 83° E., 28·5 feet.

Thence S. 65° 30' E. (variation 15° 16' E.), 300 feet to corner No. 5, the place of beginning.

Area.—Total area of Silver King lode, 9·403 acres. Less area in conflict with survey No. 2560, 0·124 acre, and in conflict with Gottenburg lode, 1·363 acre; total 1·487 acres. Net area of Silver King lode, 7·916 acres.

Total area of Gold Queen lode, 10·331 acres. Area in conflict with other surveys, 4·022 acres, thus, with survey No. 2560, 0·034 acre, with Gottenburg lode, 2·679 acres, with Silver King lode (exclusive of conflict of said Silver King lode with the Gottenburg lode), 1·309 acres. Net area of Gold Queen lode, 6·309 acres.

The net area of the lode claim, including the Gold Queen lode and Silver King lode, is 14·225 acres.

Survey No. 4225 B—*Silver King Mill Site.*—Beginning at corner No. 1, a gneiss stone, 32 by 8 by 6 inches, set 2 feet in the ground, chiselled (1) 4225 B, whence W. ¼ corner section 22, Township 11 S., Range 81 W. of the 6th principal meridian, bears N. 80° W., 1880 feet. Corner No. 1,

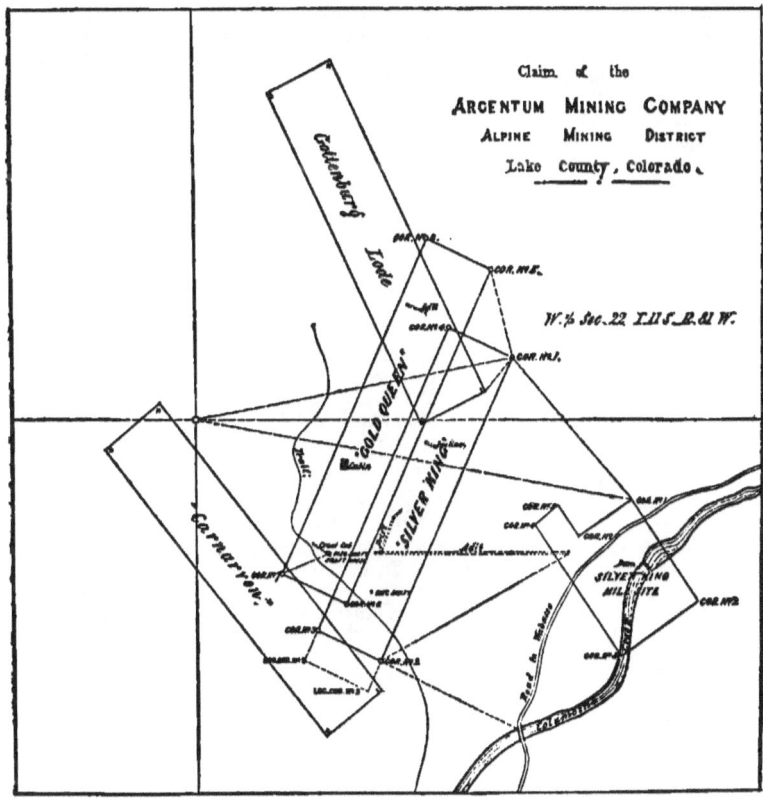

Fig. 44.

survey No. 4225 A, bears N. 40° 44′ W., 760·2 feet. A cotton-wood, 18 inches in diameter, blazed and marked (1) 4225 B, bears S. 5° 30′ E., 17 feet.

Thence S. 34° E., 90 feet road to Wabasso, coursing N.-E. and S.-W. 208 feet right bank of Columbine Creek, 75 feet wide, flowing S.-W. 504·8 feet to corner No. 2, an iron bolt, 18 inches long, 1 inch in diameter, set 1 foot in rock in place, chiselled (2) 4225 B, whence a cotton-wood, blazed and marked B. T. (2) 4225 B, bears due east, 182 feet.

Thence S. 56° W., 351 feet left bank of Columbine Creek. 394·4 feet to corner No. 3, a point in bed of creek, unsuitable for the establishment of a permanent corner.

Thence N. 34° W., 15 feet right bank of Columbine Creek. 40 feet to witness corner No. 3, a pine post, 4·5 feet long, 5 inches in diameter, set 1 foot in ground, with mound of stone, marked W. C. (3) 4552 B, whence a cotton-wood, 15 inches in diameter, bears N. 11° E., 16·5 feet, and a cotton-wood, 19 inches in diameter, bears N. 83° W., 23 feet; both blazed and marked B. T. W. C. (3) 4225 B. 370 feet road to Wabasso, coursing N.-E. and S.-W. 647·2 feet to corner No. 4, a gneiss stone, 24 by 10 by 4 inches, set 18 inches in the ground, chiselled (4) 4225 B, whence a cross, chiselled on ledge of rock, marked B. R. (4) 4225 B, bears N. 85° 10′ E., 26·4 feet.

Thence N. 48° 43′ E., 125·5 feet to corner No. 5, a gneiss stone, 30 by 8 by 5 inches, set 2 feet in the ground, chiselled (5) 4225 B.

Thence S. 34° E., 158·3 feet to corner No. 6, a pine post, 5 feet long, 5 inches square, set 2 feet in the ground, with mound of earth and stone, marked (6) 4225 B, whence a pine, 12 inches in diameter, blazed and marked B. T. (6) 4225 B, bears S. 33° E., 63·5 feet.

Thence N. 56° E., 270 feet to corner No. 1, the place of beginning. The variation at all the corners is 15° 20′ E. The area of the mill site is 5 acres.

Expenditure of Five Hundred Dollars.—The value of the labour and improvements upon this claim is not less than 500 dollars. The said improvements consist of:—

The discovery shaft of the Silver King lode, 6 by 3 feet, 10 feet deep in earth and rock, which bears from corner No. 2, N. 6° 42′ W., 237·5 feet. Value 80 dollars. An incline, 7 by 5 feet, 45 feet deep in coarse gravel and rock, timbered, course N. 58° 15′ W., dip 62°, the mouth of which bears from corner No. 2, N. 15° 37′ E., 908 feet. Value 550 dollars. The discovery shaft of the Gold Queen lode, 5 by 5 feet, 18 feet deep in rock, which bears from corner No. 7, N. 67° 39′ E., 219·3 feet, at the bottom of which is a cross-cut, 6·5 by 4 feet, running N. 59° 26′ W., 75 feet. Value of shaft and cross-cut 1000 dollars. A log shaft-house, 14 feet square, over the last-mentioned shaft, value 100 dollars. Two-thirds interest in an adit, 6·5 by 5 feet, running due west 835 feet, timbered, the mouth of which bears from corner No. 2, N. 61° 15′ E., 920 feet. This adit is in course of construction for the development of the Silver King and Gold Queen lodes of this claim, and survey No. 2560, Carnarvon lode. The remaining one-third interest has already been included in the estimate of 500 dollars expenditure upon the latter claim. Total value of adit, 13,000 dollars. A drift, 6·5 by 4 feet, on the Silver King lode, beginning at a point in the adit 800 feet from the mouth, and running N. 20° 20′ E., 195 feet; thence N. 54° 15′ E, 40 feet to breast. Value 2,800 dollars.

Other improvements consist of:—

A log cabin, 35 by 28 feet, the S.-W. corner of which bears from corner No. 7, N. 30° 44′ E., 496 feet. A dam, 4 feet high, 50 feet long, across Columbine Creek, the south end of which bears, from corner No. 2 of the mill-site, N. 58° 20′ W., 240 feet. An adit, 6 by 4 feet, running N. 70° 50′ W., 100 feet, the mouth of which bears, from corner No. 5, S. 58° 12′ W., 323 feet.

Instrument.—The survey was made with a Young & Sons' mountain transit-theodolite with solar attachment. The courses were deflected from the true meridian as determined by solar observations. The distances were measured with a 50-foot steel tape.

The first corner of the survey must be connected by course and distance with some corner of the survey of public lands of the United States, if the claim lies within 2 miles of such corner. The United States public lands include all the territory north of the Ohio River and west of the Mississippi River, not owned by individuals previous to the date of cession to the United States Government. All this territory has been laid out in rectangular tracts bounded by north and south, and east and west lines, each tract having a particular name. The reference lines consist of principal meridians and standard parallels. The former may be more than 100 miles apart. The standard parallels are 24 or 30 miles apart. In setting-out these lines, each mile is marked by a stone, tree, or mound, and is called a *section corner*. Every sixth mile has a different mark, and is called a *township corner*. From each of these, auxiliary meridians are set-out north to the next standard parallel. The territory is thus divided into *ranges*, which are 6 miles wide and 24 miles long. Each range is numbered east and west from the principal meridian. The ranges, being cut by east and west lines joining the corresponding township corners on the meridian, are thus divided into *townships* each 6 miles square. Each township is divided into 36 squares called *sections*, by meridians 1 mile apart, and by east and west lines at the same distance from each other. The sections are divided into half-sections and quarter-sections. The law requires that all excesses or deficiencies, either from erroneous measurement or from the convergence of the meridians, shall, so far as possible, be thrown on the extreme tier of sections and half-sections contiguous to the north and west boundaries of townships.

Surveying in South Africa.—In the colony of the Cape of Good Hope the legal unit of land measure is the *Cape rood*. The Cape measures are as follows:—

Measures of Length.				Measures of Surface.			
Mile.	Roods.	Feet.	Inches.	Morgen.	Sq. roods.	Sq. feet.	Sq. inches.
1	425·94	...	...	1	600	...	...
...	1	12	...	...	1	144	...
...	...	1	12	...	...	1	144

In order to convert British feet into Cape roods, multiply by 0·08067, and acres into morgen, multiply by 0·47246. In order to convert Cape roods into feet, multiply by 12·396, and morgen into acres, multiply by 2·11654.

In ordinary survey work in South Africa, measurements of distances by chain or steel tape are less frequently resorted to than in Europe. The use of the chain is limited to the measurement of base lines, from which the longer distances are derived by triangulation. Base lines should be measured at least twice, and the results should agree within an inch in 100 roods. The triangulation is commenced from the base line, and the size of the triangles increased as rapidly as possible without making them ill-conditioned until their sides have an average length sufficient to enable the surveyor to cover the area to be surveyed with a set of comparatively large triangles. With this main triangulation, all other points of the survey are connected by minor triangulation. The vertices of the triangles are shown by flags, the staves of which should be perpendicularly fixed in the ground. The theodolite is invariably used for measuring the angles.

In the gold law of the Transvaal, as set forth in Act No. 14 of 1894, the drawing and maintaining of accurate detailed plans of the surface and of underground works is enjoined on all mining companies. The plans must be drawn to the true meridian, and must be posted every six months. All benchmarks, fixed survey points, the strike and dip of reefs, faults and dykes must be shown. All general plans must be drawn to a scale of 1 to 5,000. Mine plans may be on a scale of 1 to 500, or of 1 to 1,000. All underground workings about to be abandoned must be surveyed before they become inaccessible. Misrepresentation in plans is subject to a penalty of £500, or one year's imprisonment.

CHAPTER XI.

Plotting the Survey.

Scales.—Plotting a survey consists in representing on paper, to a smaller scale, the lines and angles determined on the ground. The operation of drawing lines, the length of which shall be some fraction of that of the lines measured on the ground, is called *drawing to scale*.

A scale may be defined as an artificial means of representing any given dimensions. Thus, a fathom may be represented by a straight line 1 inch long; then 2 fathoms would be represented by a line of 2 inches, $3\frac{1}{3}$ fathoms by $3\frac{1}{3}$ inches, and so on. Three kinds of scales of equal parts may be distinguished—1, simply divided scales; 2, diagonal scales; and 3, vernier scales.

1. **Simply divided scales** consist of any extent of equal divisions, numbered 1, 2, 3, &c., beginning at the second division on the left hand. The first of these primary divisions is sub-divided into 10 equal parts, and from these sub-divisions the scale is named. Thus it is a scale of 30, when 30 of these secondary divisions are equal to 1 inch. If the primary divisions are taken as units, the secondary divisions will represent tenths.

As an illustration of the method of constructing scales, let it be required to construct a scale of 3 chains to the inch, to exhibit 18 chains. Draw a line 6 inches long, and divide it into 18 equal parts. These are the primary divisions, each of which represents one chain. Divide the first primary division into 10 equal parts; each of these secondary divisions will represent 10 links. Next draw a thicker line at a short distance below the first line, and draw vertical lines between them to indicate the divisions of the first lines. Place the zero at the line between the first and second primary divisions, and then, from left to right, place in succession the numbers 1, 2, 3, &c., at each primary division. Number the secondary divisions from the zero from right to left, 0·1, 0·2, 0·3, &c. With this system of numbering, lengths are taken from the scale with greater facility. Thus, to take off 3 chains 25 links from the scale described, one point of the dividers must be placed at the figure 3 on the scale, and the other point extended back to a place midway between the second and third secondary divisions.

In cases where fathoms and feet are required to be shown, the first primary division is divided into 6 divisions representing feet. If the scale is to show feet and inches, the first primary division must be divided into 12 equal divisions, representing inches.

A scale constructed in this way should be drawn upon every mine plan. Paper, when exposed to atmospheric influences, is found to expand or contract to a considerable extent. This is especially the case with new paper, or newly-mounted paper. The serious errors apt to arise from this cause are, to a large extent, obviated by making a scale on the paper as an accurate standard of measurement. This will expand and contract with the paper, and thus afford a valuable indication of the state of the paper.

The scales usually employed for the plans of metalliferous mines are 4 or 8 fathoms to the inch, sometimes 5 or 10 fathoms. For colliery plans, scales of 2 or 3 chains to the inch, or of 25·34 inches to the mile, are the most usual.

In order to assist in giving a clearer idea of the relative proportions of the scales used, it is desirable that they should be expressed fractionally—that is to say, that they should be so named as to indicate the ratio the line drawn on the paper bears to the line measured on the ground. Thus, a scale of 2 fathoms to the inch is a scale of $\frac{1}{144}$, or, as it may also be written, 1 : 144, since 1 inch represents 2 fathoms, or 144 inches of real length. A scale of this kind is called a *natural* scale.

In the construction of the maps of the Ordnance Survey of Great Britain, the following scales are used:—

Towns,	1 : 500, or 126·72	inches to the mile.
Parishes,	1 : 2500, or 25·34	,, ,,
Counties,	1 : 10560, or 6	,, ,,
The Kingdom,	1 : 63360, or 1	,, ,,

In the scale adopted for the parish maps, largely used for colliery plans, 1 square inch represents an acre.

2. **Diagonal Scales.**—A diagonal scale of equal parts is constructed in the following manner:—Draw eleven straight lines parallel to each other and $\frac{1}{10}$ inch apart. Divide the top line into equal parts, these primary divisions being of any required length. Through the points marking these primary divisions, draw perpendiculars cutting all the parallels. Number the primary

divisions from the left, 1, 0, 1, 2, 3, &c., as in the case of the simply divided scale. Then sub-divide the top and bottom lines of the first primary division into 10 equal parts. Number the alternate divisions, 2, 4, 6, 8, from right to left along the bottom line, and number the alternate parallel lines, 2, 4, 6, 8, from the bottom upwards. Then draw lines, as in Fig. 45, from the zero of the bottom line to the first division of the top line, from the first of the bottom to the second of the top, and so on until the scale is complete.

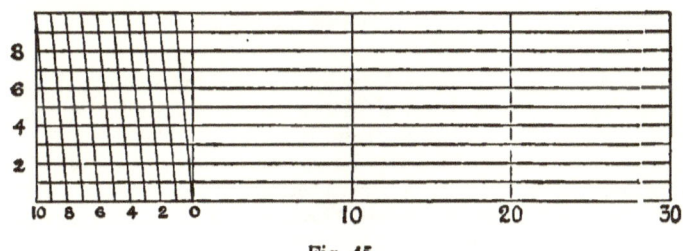

Fig. 45.

The diagonal lines are all parallel. Consequently the distance between any two successive lines, measured up any of the eleven parallel lines which they intersect, is the same as the distance measured upon the highest and lowest of those lines. The distance between the perpendicular which passes through the zero point, and the diagonal at the same point, is 0 on the top line, and equal to one sub-division on the bottom line. It is therefore equal (*Euclid*, vi. 4) to one-tenth of a sub-division on the second line, two-tenths of a sub-division on the third, and so on. In this way, each of the diagonal lines, as it reaches each successive parallel, separates farther from the perpendicular through the zero point by one-tenth of the extent of a sub-division, or one-hundredth of the extent of a primary division. Thus, by means of a diagonal scale a distance can be taken off to two places of decimals.

The general rule for taking off any number consisting of three figures from a diagonal scale is as follows:—On the parallel line indicated by the third figure, measure from the diagonal indicated by the second to the vertical indicated by the first.

3. **Vernier Scales.**—The construction of the vernier scale is similar to that of the vernier of circumferenters and theodolites (see p. 58). In order to show how the principle of the vernier is applied to the construction of scales, let it be required to

construct a scale of 6 feet to the inch to show feet and decimals of a foot. Construct a scale of feet in the ordinary way, subdivided throughout its entire length. Above the first primary division draw a line parallel to the scale and ending at the zero point. From this point set off towards the left along the line parallel to the scale a distance equal to 11 sub-divisions, and divide this distance into 10 equal parts as shown in Fig. 46.

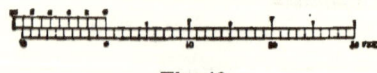

Fig. 46.

Eleven divisions of the scale being divided into 10 equal parts on the vernier, each division of the latter represents $\frac{11}{10}$ or $1\frac{1}{10}$ foot. Thus, the distances from the zero of the scale to the successive divisions of the vernier represent 1 foot 1-tenth, 2 feet 2-tenths, 3 feet 3-tenths, 4 feet 4-tenths, 5 feet 5-tenths, 6 feet 6-tenths, 7 feet 7-tenths, 8 feet 8-tenths, 9 feet 9-tenths, 10 feet 10-tenths, and 11 feet.

The manner of using the scale is as follows:—To take off a distance of 16 feet 7-tenths, one point of the dividers must be placed on the 7th division of the vernier, and the other on the 9th division of the scale. From 0 to the 7th division of the vernier represents 7 feet 7-tenths, and that distance subtracted from 16 feet 7-tenths leaves 9 feet.

Plotting Scales.—The most convenient scales of equal parts for plotting are those of ivory or box-wood, which have a feather edge along which they are divided, so that distances can be at once marked off without the application of the dividers. In the same way, the length of a given line can be at once read off. Dividers should never be used to measure distances when an edge scale is available for the purpose. An ivory scale is soon spoilt by being dug into by the dividers.

Each plotting scale should be provided with a shorter scale for the purpose of plotting offsets. The offset scale should be edge-divided like the plotting scale. In plotting a survey, the plotting scale is placed along the station-line with its zero point at the beginning of the line. The offset scale is placed at right angles to the plotting scale, and slid along the latter, until its edge comes to the distance at which an offset was taken. The length of this is then marked off from the offset scale by means of a needle. The offset scale is slid along to the next distance, and the operation repeated. The points thus obtained are joined by straight lines.

Plotting with a Protractor.—A semicircular protractor may be used to lay down or protract angles. It consists of a semicircle of horn, brass, or German-silver, divided to half-degrees. The degrees are numbered from 0 to 180 both ways. To lay off an angle at any point of a straight line, the protractor must be placed so that its straight side, that is, the diameter of the semicircle, is on the given line, with the middle of the diameter, which is indicated by a small notch, at the given point. With a sharp pencil or a needle, a mark is made on the paper at the required number of degrees, and a line is drawn from that mark to the given point.

In using this instrument for plotting a survey, the straight side must be applied to an assumed meridian line drawn on the paper, the centre of the protractor coinciding with the point in the meridian line selected for the commencement of the survey. A line must then be drawn from the centre of the protractor passing through the degree required. The length of this line is marked off by means of a scale. Then at the end point of the line a second meridian line is drawn parallel to the first, and the protractor applied to this in the same way as before. The meridians at each station may be drawn by means of a T-square, the north and south lines on the paper being made parallel to one of the sides of the drawing-board.

Fitted with a movable arm and a vernier, the semicircular protractor may be read with great precision. Supposing it is required to plot a line through a given point at a certain angle with the meridian of a plan, a semicircular protractor fitted with a vernier may be used, in conjunction with a 60° set-square and a straight-edge. The arm of the protractor is set by the vernier at the required angle, and at the same time the arm-line is laid on the meridian of the plan. The set-square is then placed against the protractor by the straight-edge, and slid along the latter until its edge passes through the given point, when the line drawn through that point will form the required angle with the meridian. According to T. Welizki,* this method of plotting is preferred by almost all Russian surveyors.

More accurate results are obtained with a full-circle protractor of brass or of vulcanite. With this instrument, not only the bearing itself but the corresponding bearing on the other side should also be marked off. Then, if the line drawn from one point to the other passes through the centre previously marked on the meridian line, it is evident that the bearing is accurately plotted.

* *Zeit. f. Vermessungswesen*, vol. xii., p. 252, 1883.

PLOTTING THE SURVEY. 139

Drawing meridian lines at each station is apt to give rise to error, and always presents the inconvenience of having a number of lines on the plan which have to be rubbed out. With a circular protractor this unnecessary labour is avoided by placing the instrument along a meridian line drawn near the centre of the paper, and marking off in rotation the various bearings of the survey. Confusion may be avoided by figuring on the paper by the edge of the protractor the bearing, not the number or letter of the draft, as is often done. The bearings having been thus marked, the protractor is removed, and the lines are transferred to their proper positions on the plan by means of a rolling parallel ruler. This instrument necessitates the use of a perfectly true drawing-board. It is provided with two rollers of exactly the same circumference, firmly attached to the same axis. It is made of ebony or of brass.

Elaborate circular protractors are made with a movable arm provided with a vernier. Such instruments are usually made with a glass centre, with two fine lines intersecting at the centre point. The most perfect instrument for accurate plotting is the folding arm protractor. This is provided with two opposite arms, each with a vernier, and a clamp and tangent motion for setting the angles. The extreme end of each arm carries a point, which by a gentle pressure may be caused to puncture a fine hole in the plan. These instruments are usually 6 inches in diameter, and divided on silver.

The most rapid method of plotting a survey is by means of a cardboard protractor, as with this instrument there is no occasion to figure the various bearings on the paper. The cardboard protractor, as used in the Ordnance Survey Office, is 12 inches in diameter. The centre portion is cut out, and the north and south line made to coincide with the meridian on the paper. The parallel ruler is then placed at once on the required bearing, and on the bearing directly opposite. The survey line is then drawn in the vacant space inside the circumference. Much time is thus saved, and the plan is kept clean, and not covered with pencilled bearings. The results are very accurate, on account of the large diameter of the protractor.

Plotting by Means of Chords.—A traverse may be plotted from one meridian, without a protractor, by means of a table of chords and a parallel ruler. For this method, all that is required is a table of sines, or, better still, of chords, and a good rolling 2-foot parallel roller. Since the chord of an angle is twice the sine of half the angle to a radius of unity, a ready means is afforded of protracting to any radius required. The meridian angles, if they have been taken with the theodolite or from the

outer circle of the dial, must first be reduced to bearings; the rule for performing this reduction being as follows :—
For angles between—

0° and 90°, enter in bearing column as N.E.
90° and 180°, subtract from 180°, and enter result as S.E.
180° and 270°, deduct 180°, and enter result as S.W.
270° and 360°, subtract from 360°, and enter result as N.W.

Having tabulated the chords of the bearings, describe a circle with a radius of 1000 units (say 10 inches). This avoids the necessity of multiplying the chord by the radius; the decimal point merely having to be moved 3 places to the right. Angles can be laid down by this method as easily as with a 20-inch protractor.

The circle is drawn in a convenient part of the plan, and the meridian line drawn through it; the north and south ends being marked. If the bearing is N.E., the chord is measured off from the north point, eastwards. Thus, for a bearing of N. 64° 14' E., the point at which the scale reading 1063·2 intersects the circumference of the circle is noted, and the number of the station is affixed. The north and south points on the circle are the zero points to measure from, and from these points the chords are measured off to the east or west as the case may be.

The following sample page illustrates the method of reducing the survey notes.

Plotting by Rectangular Co-ordinates.—This is the most accurate method of plotting a survey, because the position of each station is plotted without being affected by any errors committed in plotting previous stations.

It consists in assuming two fixed axes, O X and O Y, crossing at right angles at a fixed point or *origin*, O, and in calculating the perpendicular distances, or *co-ordinates*, of each station from those axes. When the direction of the true meridian has been ascertained, it is advisable to make one of the axes represent it.

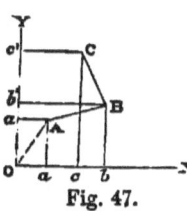

Fig. 47.

Thus, in Fig. 47, let A O represent a horizontal line surveyed. Through the starting point O, draw a north and south line, O Y, and at right angles to this, through the same point, an east and west line, O X, then the angle Y O A will represent the bearing of the line O A. The line O Y is taken as abscissa axis, and the line O X as ordinate axis. From the end point of the given line, O A, the two perpendiculars A a and A a' are let fall to those

SURVEY OF LONG-WALL WORKINGS AT A SCOTTISH COLLIERY.

No. 10 Pit. From centre of shaft, 12 ft. × 6 ft.; long side bearing S. 18° E.

No.	Meridian Angle.	Bearing.	Chords $r = 1000$.	Distance.	Remarks.
				Links.	
A	298° 00′	N. 62° 00′ W.	1030·0	116	... ...
B	299° 30′	N. 60° 30′ W.	1007·5	47	... ...
C	320° 00′	N. 40° 00′ W.	684·0	71	... ...
D²	315° 00′	N. 45° 00′ W.	765·3	...	bearing only, into air course.
D	227° 30′	S. 47° 30′ W.	805·4	151	into stone drift.
E	228° 00′	S. 48° 00′ W.	813·4	59	... ...
F	301° 00′	N. 59° 00′ W.	984·8	86	... ...
G	297° 30′	N. 62° 30′ W.	1037·5	45	... ...
H²	20° 00′	N. 20° 00′ E.	347·2	100	... ...
J²	14° 30′	N. 14° 30′ E.	252·3	45	... ...
K²	42° 30′	N. 42° 30′ E.	724·8	66	to face lying N. 68° W.
H	319° 00′	N. 41° 00′ W.	700·4	103	... ...
J²	16° 00′	N. 16° 00′ E.	278·3	58	... ...
K²	10° 30′	N. 10° 30′ E.	183·0	45	... ...
L²	10° 15′	N. 10° 15′ E.	178·6	97	... ...
M²	40° 00′	N. 40° 00′ E.	684·0	43	... ...
N²	55° 30′	N. 55° 30′ E.	931·2	23	to face lying S. 30° E.
J	313° 00′	N. 47° 00′ W.	797·4	95	... ...
K²	20° 00′	N. 20° 00′ E.	347·2	68	... ...
L²	9° 30′	N. 9° 30′ E.	165·6	117	... ...
M²	8° 00′	N. 8° 00′ E.	139·5	44	... ...
N²	20° 30′	N. 20° 30′ E.	355·8	35	10 links to face, lying N. 58° W.
K	304° 00′	N. 56° 00′ W.	938·9	101	... ...
L²	13° 30′	N. 13° 30′ E.	235·0	100	... ...
M²	355° 00′	N. 5° 00′ W.	87·2	99	to face running E. and W.
L	290° 00′	N. 70° 00′ W.	1147·1	87	... ...
M²	1° 00′	N. 1° 00′ E.	17·4	64	... ...
N²	348° 00′	N. 12° 00′ W.	209·0	70	to face lying S. 65° W.
M	278° 00′	N. 82° 00′ W.	1312·1	49	... ...
N	266° 00′	S. 86° 00′ W.	1363·9	29	... ...
O²	349° 00′	N. 11° 00′ W.	191·6	52	... ...
P²	332° 00′	N. 28° 00′ W.	483·8	28	to face lying N. 60° E.
O	261° 00′	S. 81° 00′ W.	1298·8	94	... ...
P²	2° 00′	N. 2° 00′ E.	34·9	50	to face lying S. 89° E.
P	261° 30′	S. 81° 30′ W.	1305·5	38	to end of level.

axes. A a is termed the *latitude* and A a' the *departure* of the line O A. The latitude of a point may be defined as its distance north or south of some parallel of latitude. The distance that one end of a line is due north or south of the other end, is called the difference of latitude of the ends of the line, or, briefly, the latitude of the line, or its *northing* or *southing*. Similarly the distance which one end of a line is due east or west of the other end is called the difference of longitude of the ends of the line, or the *departure* of the line, or its *easting* or *westing*.

On regarding the right-angled triangles O A a and O A a' in Fig. 47, it will at once be seen that the latitude and departure may be calculated from the length O A and the bearing A O a' or β. Now a' A is equal to O a, and a' O is equal to A a; it is therefore evident that $\dfrac{A\ a'}{A\ O}$ = sin β, and consequently A a' = O A sin β, and O a = O A sin β. Similarly O a' = O A cos β, and A a = O A cos β. In other words, to find the latitude of any line, multiply its length by the cosine of its bearing, and to find its departure, multiply its length by the sine of its bearing. If the foreward bearing of the line is northward, its latitude is north and is regarded as positive. If the foreward bearing of the line is eastward, its departure is east, and is regarded as positive. West departures and south latitudes are regarded as negative magnitudes.

In Fig. 47, let O Y represent the meridian, and let O A B C represent a mine road, the survey of which with the circumferenter gave the following results :—

No.	Angle.	Bearing.	Distance.
			Links.
A	0° 00'	32° 15'	176
B	220° 17'	72° 32'	180
C	79° 13'	331° 45'	155

The vernier-angles must first be reduced to meridian angles with the result given above. The reduced bearings must then be calculated. They will be found to be as follows :—A, N. 32° 15' E.; B, N. 72° 32' E.; C, N. 28° 15' W. The latitudes and departures may then be obtained from the formulæ—

Latitude = Distance × cos bearing,
Departure = Distance × sin bearing.

PLOTTING THE SURVEY.

The troublesome and tedious multiplication by natural sines and cosines may be avoided by using logarithms. The calculations will then be as follows:—

	Departures.			Latitudes.
A. log 176 =	2·245512	log 176 =	2·245512
L. sin 32° 15′ =	9·727227	L. cos 32° 15′ =	9·927230
	1·972739		2·172742
Easting =	93·91	Northing =	148·85
B. log 180 =	2·255272	log 180 =	2·255272
L. sin 72° 32′ =	9·979499	L. cos 72° 32′ =	9·477339
	2·234771		1·732611
Easting =	171·70	Northing =	54·02
C. log 155 =	2·190331	log 155 =	2·190331
L. sin 28° 15′ =	9·675154	L. cos 28° 15′ =	9·944922
	1·865485		2·135253
Westing =	73·36	Northing =	136·54

In making calculations with logarithms, it must be remembered that in tables of logarithmic sines and cosines, the logarithm of the assumed radius is 10·000000. Consequently in the preceding calculations, the log. radius 10 is deducted in order to give the log. of the natural number sought.

The results of the calculation should be entered in four columns, for northing, southing, easting, and westing respectively.

No.	Reduced Bearing.	Distance.	Latitude.		Departure.	
			N.	S.	E.	W.
A	N. 32° 15′ E.	Links. 176	148·85	...	93·91	...
B	N. 72° 32′ E.	180	54·02	...	171·70	...
C	N. 28° 15′ W.	155	136·54	...	...	73·36
...	...	...	339·41	...	265·61	73·36

144   MINE-SURVEYING.

Regarding the northing as positive and the southing as negative, the algebraical sum of the latitudes is 339·41 links. The easting being positive, and the westing negative, the algebraical sum of the departures is 265·61 − 73·36 = 192·25 links.

Before the calculated co-ordinates can be used for plotting purposes, the total latitudes and the total departures must be calculated. This is done by taking the algebraical sum at each station, as follows :—

No.	Total Latitudes from Station O.	Total Departures from Station O.
O	0·00	0·00
A	+ 148·85	+ 93·91
B	+ 202·87	+ 265·61
C	+ 339·41	+ 192·25

Having prepared this table, draw a meridian line through the first station O, Fig. 47. Along the meridian, north latitudes are set off upwards, and south latitudes downwards. East departures are set off perpendicularly to the right, and west departures perpendicularly to the left. Set off, therefore, along the meridian in a northerly distance the latitude 148·85 links to the scale required. This gives the point a'. From that point, set off perpendicularly to the right the departure 93·91 links. The station A is thus fixed on the plan. Join the points O and A. From O again set off upwards 202·87 links to b', and from that point set off 265·61 links perpendicularly to the right. This gives the point B. Join the points A and B. From O again set off upwards the latitude 339·41 links to c', and from that point set off the departure 192·25 links. The last point C is thus fixed.

In this way any survey may be plotted with great ease and rapidity, and with greater accuracy than is possible by any other method.

The calculated co-ordinates are of great value for testing the accuracy of a closed traverse. Obviously, when a surveyor makes a circuitous survey returning to the starting point, he has gone exactly as far to the north as he has to the south, and as far to the east as to the west. Consequently, if his survey is correct, the sum of the northings should be equal to that of the southings, and the sum of the eastings equal to that of the westings.

An illustration of this is afforded by the survey of a closed

PLOTTING THE SURVEY.

polygon with a theodolite, the notes of which are given on p. 107. On calculating the co-ordinates, the following results are obtained:—

No.	Reduced Bearings.	Distance.	Latitudes.		Departures.	
			North +	South −	East +	West −
1	S. 58° 33′ E.	Links. 1,091	...	569·5	931·3	...
2	N. 39° 03′ E.	252	195·5	...	158·8	...
3	N. 68° 04′ E.	196	73·1	...	182·0	...
4	N. 47° 44′ E.	534	358·9	...	395·3	...
5	N. 63° 16′ E.	384	172·5	...	343·1	...
6	N. 31° 13′ W.	336	287·1	...	...	174·0
7	N. 59° 06′ W.	1,055	541·3	...	...	904·5
8	S. 44° 28′ W.	771	...	550·5	...	539·5
9	S. 31° 29′ E.	154	...	131·4	80·5	...
10	S. 51° 29′ W.	605	...	377·0	...	473·0
...	...	...	1628·4	1628·4	2091·0	2091·0

If there should be a slight error, the latitudes and departures must be corrected, before plotting, so that their sums shall be equal in each case. This is done by distributing the error among the lines in proportion to their length, the *balancing* being effected by the following proportion:—As the sum of all the lengths is to each particular length, so is the total error in latitude (or departure) to the correction of the corresponding latitude (or departure). The correction has been made in the above example. It may frequently be made by determining the error per chain, without making the exact proportion.

The error of closure is the ratio of the length of the line joining the first and last points of the survey of a closed polygon, to the whole perimeter. Being the hypothenuse of a right-angled triangle, of which the errors in latitude and in departure are the other sides, the length of this line is equal to the square root of the sum of the squares of those two errors. This divided by the whole perimeter gives the error of closure. In mine-surveys, it should not be more than 1 in 1,600, or 5 links per mile. In ordinary surface-surveys it will average 1 in 300 or 27 links per mile.

A co-ordinate protractor, called a *trigonometer* by the makers, Messrs. Keuffel and Esser of New York, has recently been introduced in America. It consists of a plate 15 inches square (Fig. 48), divided into 100 equal squares by horizontal and vertical lines. It is provided with an arm fastened with its zero upon the zero at one corner of the plate. It is graduated, with the same division as the plate, to read distances from the centre outwards. On the sides, the plate has angular graduations, the zero joint being the centre of the quadrant. By moving the arm to the given angle, the latitude is at once read off on the vertical scale and the departure on the horizontal scale, for the given length as read on the arm. If, for instance, B A C is the given angle, and A D the given distance, D E and D F are the co-ordinates. The readings are exact to within 0·1 per cent. The instrument is also of use for calculating the bases and perpendiculars of inclined station-lines in mine-surveys.

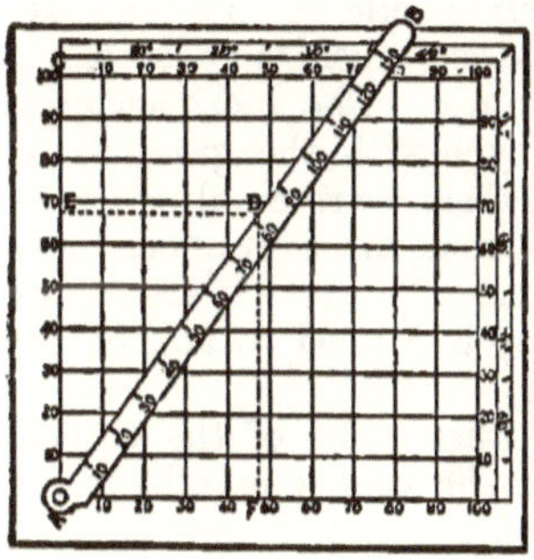

Fig. 48.

Though described in 1886 by Mr. E. G. Gaertner * as a new invention, this instrument was known two hundred years previously. It is, I find, described on p. 127, and figured on plate 7 of Nicolaus Voigtel's *Geometria Subterranea*, published at Eisleben in 1686.

Calculating Scales.—For ordinary practical work the co-ordinates may be determined with great rapidity by means of the slide rule. On this rule, logarithms of numbers, sines, and cosines are represented graphically in the form of scales. The instrument consists of a rule, having on its face a groove cut throughout its entire length, in which a second rule slides smoothly. The bearing and length of a given line being known, its departure is found by setting 1 on the slide to the length on the rule, and against the sine on the slide will be found the required departure on the rule. Latitudes are found in a similar way, the cosines being read off by reading the sines backwards. To avoid this operation, complementary figures may be pencilled along the line of sines.

* *Trans. Amer. Inst. M.E.*, vol. xiv., p. 180, 1886.

PLOTTING THE SURVEY.

No slide rules of English make can compare in accuracy and portability with those made by Gravét, of Paris. One 26 centimetres long is accurate to one part in 500. Co-ordinates of the lines occurring in mine-surveys may thus be determined accurately to the first place of decimals. The back of the slide is divided for sines, tangents, and logarithms, all of which can be read at the back through special openings without removing the slide, or the slide may be reversed. A sliding index, or *cursor*, is provided, which adds materially to the power of the instrument. For important theodolite surveys, the slide rule is not accurate enough. For this work, however, it saves much time in calculating differences of logarithmic sines, &c. The most accurate slide rule available is of the Gravét type with the graduations not on wood, but on celluloid, a white substance resembling ivory. Careful tests of this instrument show that the average error in calculating co-ordinates is 0·12 per cent. The errors are consequently inappreciable when the survey is plotted to any of the scales usually employed for mine-plans.

With the celluloid slide rule, and other rules of the Gravét type, the departure of a given line in the survey may be found by placing the given angle, as shown on the line of sines against the index at the back of the rule, and by reading off the number, on the scale on the face of the slide, corresponding with the given distance, as shown on the upper scale. The latitude is found in a similar way, the cosine being used in place of the sine. In this way results may easily be found without calculation, accurate to the first place of decimals.*

In the Government Mining Offices on the Continent, calculating machines are extensively used for computing the co-ordinates of mine-surveys. The type of instrument generally used is that invented by M. Thomas, of Colmar, in Alsace. This instrument has recently been improved by Mr. Edmondson and by Mr. Tate. Full descriptions of the three instruments are given by Mr. C. V. Boys.†

Traverse Tables.—Tables which show by inspection the amount of the latitude and departure for any bearing and distance are termed traverse tables, because by their aid the resolution of traverses is effected without calculation.

In order to be of any use to the mine-surveyor, such tables must be calculated for every minute of bearing and to four places of decimals. These conditions are fulfilled by the tables calculated by J. T. Boileau, by W. Crellin, and by R. L. Gurden. There are several other tables published, which, though well arranged, are not sufficiently in detail for mine-surveying pur-

---

* *Colliery Guardian*, p. 587, 1889.
† *Journ. Soc. Arts*, vol. xxxiv., p. 384, 1886.

poses. For example, the traverse tables given in Chambers's Mathematical Tables are calculated only for every degree of bearing to one place of decimals. Though valuable for problems in navigation, they are useless for mining purposes.

The following example will illustrate the method of using Boileau's tables, which are calculated for every minute of bearing and to 5 decimal places for distances of 1 to 10:—Given the bearing of a line, N. 32° 15′ E., and its length 1 chain 76 links, required its latitude and departure. Seek the table headed 32°, and from the section 15′, take out the latitudes and departures separately for the hundreds, tens, and units, removing the decimal point in each case as many places to the right as the figures in each separated portion of the distance exceed those in the corresponding numbers in the tabular distance columns. The distance 1 chain 76 links will be separated into 100, 70, and 6 links, and the traverses for each will be taken out separately, thus:—

Reduced Bearing.	Distance.	Latitude.	Departure.
N. 32° 15′ W.	100	84·5727	53·3614
	70	59·2009	37·3530
	6	5·0743	3·2016
	176	148·8479	93·9160

The most accurate traverse tables published are those computed by Mr. R. L. Gurden, Authorised Surveyor for the Governments of New South Wales and Victoria. These tables are calculated to four places of decimals for every minute of angle up to 100 of distance, so that the sines and cosines for a distance of 12 miles may be ascertained correctly to within half an inch.

In the example given above, the latitude and departure are found with Gurden's tables, thus—

Reduced Bearing.	Distance.	Latitude.	Departure.
N. 32° 15′ W.	100	84·5728	53·3615
	76	64·2753	40·5547
	176	148·8481	93·9162

Only one opening of the traverse tables is required. With logarithms, on the other hand, the book has to be opened in four places, two separate additions have to be made, and in taking out natural numbers proportional parts have to be resorted to, in order to find figures of the second place of decimals. The advantage of these traverse tables over logarithms, both as regards simplicity and economy of labour in calculation, is thus apparent.

In important undertakings it will be found advisable to calculate the co-ordinates by logarithms, and repeat the calculation by the traverse tables, so as to obtain an independent check and verification.

PLOTTING THE SURVEY.

Combined Surveying and Plotting Instrument.—Henderson's rapid traverser is based on what is known as the plane-table system of surveying. By its aid, underground or surface surveys can be made, and the results laid down on paper with very great rapidity. Unlike the plane-table, however, it is not intended that the rapid traverser should be used for plotting the survey in the field, this being done in the drawing-office, with the aid of a parallel rolling ruler and scale.

The instrument consists of a circular metal table of about 10 inches diameter, mounted on an ordinary tripod stand, with the usual adjusting screws. It is provided with a brass alidade, with an ordinary sight at each end, revolving round a fixed centre pin. Upon the face of the table a disc of celluloid is screwed, and over this the alidade, by means of a groove, can travel freely. The disc is divided into five or more concentric rings marked on the celluloid, and the feather-edge of the alidade is also divided by means of a rectangular notch at each ring, for the purpose of pencilling on the disc the line observed. By means of clamping screws, similar to those of the circumferentor, the disc can be clamped to the stand, and the alidade, with sights attached, to the table when required.

In traversing, the instrument is levelled and the alidade is sighted back to the starting point of the survey. Both the alidade and the table are then secured clamped. The direction of this first line of the survey is marked with a finely pointed H H pencil on the selected ring of the disc, at two points equidistant from the centre, and duly lettered or figured within the notch cut in the feather-edge of the alidade. Three tripods are used. Each of the two spare ones carries a candle-holder with levels attached, a white card replacing the candle in surface surveys. The alidade is next unclamped, sighted to the forward tripod, and clamped, the direction of the second line being marked on the celluloid as before. The instrument is then removed from its tripod and fixed, with the alidade still clamped on the forward stand, and sighted back to the position it previously occupied and clamped. This having been done, the alidade is unclamped, sighted to the next forward station, again clamped, and the direction marked as before, the process being repeated for the remainder of the traverse. The magnetic meridian is taken at any convenient spot in the course of the traverse by means of a trough compass placed temporarily against the back edge of the alidade. The line thus given, pencilled on the disc, establishes the orientation of the whole of the survey.

The sights of the alidade are graduated to give angles of depression or elevation up to 25°. Thus, the instrument suffices for the majority of collieries, for the levels of metalliferous mines, and for all ordinary surface surveys. Where greater accuracy in vertical angles is required, as in inclined shafts, a vertical semicircle is attached to the alidade, and the angles read as with the theodolite.

In plotting the survey, the celluloid disc is unscrewed from its circular table and placed with the north line, that has been marked on it, in its proper position on the meridian line drawn on the intended plan. A rolling parallel ruler is then applied to each line of the survey in succession as shown on the disc, and marked off on the plan. In a large survey, the disc may be moved to any meridian line as required. For future reference, the disc itself may be preserved with the name and date of the survey recorded on it, or, if necessary, the magnetic bearings may be read off with the aid of a protractor and booked, when the celluloid disc may be cleaned for future use.

This instrument has been successfully used by the inventor, Mr. James Henderson, in numerous surveys of Cornish mines, notably at West Wheal Frances, at Redruth. In November, 1892, it was decided to put out a cross-cut south from the 174-fathom level so as to come under the perpendicular portion of Bailey's shaft, which was perpendicular only as far as the 60-fathom level, and then went off to the south following the underlie of the lode. After the cross-cut, which was 20 fathoms in length, had been driven, a rise had to be carried up through some 55 fathoms of ground to the bottom of the perpendicular portion of Bailey's shaft. In order to do this, the relative position of the two points was determined by surveying down 80 fathoms of the inclined portion of the shaft to the winze to the 174-fathom level, the total distance of levels surveyed amounting to 300 fathoms, and the number of stations required being fifty-three. The perfect holing on October 17, 1893, affords a guarantee of the adaptability of this instrument to complicated underground surveys.

Plotting Colliery Surveys in Scotland.—In the West of Scotland, a method of plotting colliery surveys, which differs from that in vogue in other districts, is frequently employed. The protractor used consists of a circular brass plate, 2 feet in diameter, pivoted at the centre, so that it can rotate in a horizontal plane. It is supported in a square mahogany frame, the surfaces of the frame and of the protractor being flush. A brass or steel straight-edge is attached to one side of this square frame. The drawing-paper is used in circular sheets, which are fastened on the face of the protractor inside the graduated circle. A sheet of paper is permanently glued on, and sheets may be attached to this by means of wafers as required. A T-square replaces the parallel ruler used in other methods of plotting with the protractor. It is brought to the diameter of the protractor, and then the required bearing is brought under the edge of the T-square by rotating the protractor. The protractor is then held steady, while the T-square is moved along the straight edge attached to the mahogany frame, in order that a line may be drawn through a station point. A day's survey having been plotted, a tracing is made and transferred to the main plan of the colliery.

Calculating the Co-ordinates of a Triangulation.—In South Africa, where triangulation is exclusively used for surveys of mine concessions, it is usual to plot by co-ordinates. For the calculations necessary, C. L. H. Max Jurisch's "Tables of natural sines and cosines to seven decimal figures of all angles between 0° and 90° to every 10 seconds with proportional parts for single seconds" (Cape Town, 1884), are chiefly used. The problem occurring is as follows:—Given the co-ordinates of two points, P and Q, the angles of direction $x\,P\,Q$ or $x\,Q\,P$, the distance $P\,Q$ and by observation, the angles of the triangle $P\,Q\,R$; required the co-ordinates of R. From the given data the distance $P\,R$ and $Q\,R$ and their angles of direction $x\,P\,R$ and $x\,Q\,R$ may be calculated.

Consequently—

$P R \sin x P R = y -$ distance of R from $P = \Delta y$

$P R \cos x P R = x -$ distance of R from $P = \Delta x$

$Q R \sin x Q R = y -$ distance of R from $Q = \Delta' x$

$Q R \cos x Q R = x -$ distance of R from $Q = \Delta' x$

y of $P + \Delta y = y$ of R; x of $P + \Delta x = x$ of R

y of $Q + \Delta' y = y$ of R; x of $Q + \Delta' x = x$ of R

It is usual to calculate the co-ordinates of R from both equations, in order to have a check on the calculations. In these equations, the co-ordinate drawn from any point parallel to the vertical or y axis is briefly called the y of that point, and the other co-ordinate is called the x of that point.

The following example, given by Leopold Marquard ("Co-ordinate Geometry," Cape Town, 1882), will illustrate the manner in which the calculations are made:—

152 MINE-SURVEYING.

Given

Lines. Cape Roods.	Angles.
A B = 41·26	A B C = + 69° 54'
B C = 37·98	B C D = + 134° 44'
C D = 66·46	C D E = − 47° 12'
D E = 118·30	D E F = − 87° 03'
E F = 167·75	E F G = + 277° 13'
F G = 148·55	

Required the co-ordinates of A, B, C, D, E, F, G.

The line A B having been selected as x axis and B as the origin, we have—

y of A = 0; x of A = + B A = + 41·26
y of B = 0; x of B = 0

Angle X B C = 69° 54', to this is added B C D = + 134° 44', and from the sum 180° is subtracted. When the angle of intersection of two lines and the angle of direction of *one* of them is known, the angle of direction of the other is found thus:—When the two angles have the same vertex, their algebraical sum is the required angle of direction, and when they have different vertices, their algebraical sum, either diminished or increased by 180°, as may be most convenient, will be the required angle of direction. Consequently—

Angle X C D =   24° 38'
Add   C D E = − 47° 12' and add 180°.
─────────────────────────
Then X D E =   157° 26'
Add   D E F = − 87° 03' and add 180°.
─────────────────────────
Then X E F =   250° 23'
Add   E F G = + 277° 13' and subtract 180°.
─────────────────────────
Then X F G =   347° 36'.

To determine the co-ordinates of C:—

log B C (37·98) = 1·5795550   log B C = 1·5795550
log sin X B C (69° 54') = 9·9727092 log cos X B C = 9·5361286
─────────────────   ─────────────────
            1·5522642   1·1156836

y of C = + 35·67 x of C = + 13·05

Similarly the co-ordinates of the other points will be found to be as follows:—

	y	x
D	+ 63·37	+ 73·46
E	+ 108·77	− 35·78
F	− 49·24	− 92·10
G	− 81·14	+ 52·98

CHAPTER XII.

CALCULATION OF AREAS.

Measures of Area.—The area of mine-royalties and of coal wrought is usually expressed in acres. The *statute acre* is equal to 10 square chains or 100,000 square links. It is sub-divided either decimally or into 4 *roods* of 1,210 square yards, and 160 *perches* of $30\frac{1}{4}$ square yards. One square mile is equal to 640 acres.

In order to reduce square links to acres, roods, and perches, divide by 100,000 by cutting off five figures to the right hand. The figures remaining to the left will be *acres*. Multiply the remainder by 4; the whole-number remaining will represent *roods*. Multiply the remaining fraction by 40; the figures beyond the decimal point will be *perches*. The nearest round number is usually taken; fractions less than half a perch being disregarded.

The metric unit of land measure is the *hectare* of 10,000 square metres. This is equal to 2·4711 acres.

Three methods of measuring areas are employed: the method of triangles, the method of ordinates, and the mechanical method.

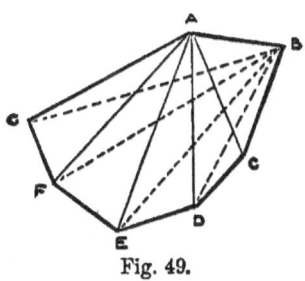

Fig. 49.

1. Method of Triangles.—The survey of the ground having been plotted, lines are drawn on the plan so as to divide it into a number of triangles, the area of each of which is calculated. Thus, in order to calculate the area of the polygon A B C D E F G (Fig. 49), measure all the sides of the figure, and the diagonals A C, A D, A E, and A F. Then if the lengths of the three sides of the triangle A B C are denoted by a, b, and c, the area of the triangle is given by the formula—

$$\text{Area} = \sqrt{s\,(s-a)\,(s-b)\,(s-c)},$$

in which s represents the half sum of the lengths of the sides of the triangle.

Assuming that the side B C is 120 links in length, A C 135 links, and A B 90 links, the area of the triangle is—

$$\sqrt{172{\cdot}5 \times 52{\cdot}5 \times 37{\cdot}5 \times 82{\cdot}5},$$

or 5293·18 square links.

If logarithms are employed, the formula is—

log. area $= \tfrac{1}{2}$ {log s + log $(s - a)$ + log $(s - b)$ + log $(s - c)$}.

In the same way, the area of the remaining four triangles in Fig. 49 are calculated. By taking the sum of the areas of the five triangles, the area of the whole polygon is obtained. As a check on the calculations, the lengths of the diagonals B D, B E, B F, and B G may be determined. Five new triangles would thus be obtained. The sum of these five areas should be the same as the result of the first calculation. If there is a small difference, the mean of the two results is taken as the correct area. If the difference is considerable, the measurement must be repeated.

Another useful formula for calculating the area of triangles is the following:—

$$\text{Area} = \frac{a\,p}{2}$$

in which a is any one of the sides of the triangle, and p a perpendicular let fall upon that side from the opposite angle.

When two sides and the included angle are known, the area is given by the formula—

$$\text{Area} = \frac{a\,b\,\sin C}{2};$$

a and b representing the two sides, and C the included angle.

When one side of a triangle and the adjacent angles are given, its area is equal to $\dfrac{a^2 \sin B \sin C}{2 \sin (B + C)}$.

The areas of figures with curved outlines may be found by the method of triangles preceded by a process termed *equalising* or *giving and taking*. This consists in drawing through the boundary a straight line, leaving as much space outside the straight line as there is inside it, as nearly as the eye can estimate.

It is sometimes advisable to reduce a polygon to a single triangle equivalent in area, as in the following example:—In the polygon A B C D E in Fig. 50, draw a line from A to C, and with a parallel ruler draw a line B F parallel to A C cutting C D produced in F. Join A F. Then the area of the quadrilateral figure A F D E is equal to that of the original figure. The

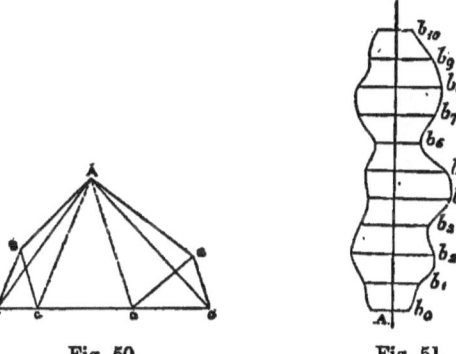

Fig. 50.   Fig. 51.

triangles A B F, C B F being on the same base, B F, and between the same parallels, are equal. Take away from each the common triangle B H F, H being the point at which the lines A F and B C intersect; the remaining triangles A B H, C F H are equal. But in the alteration of the figure, C F H has been substituted for A B H; therefore, the area of the quadrilateral is equal to that of the original figure. Similarly, by drawing E G parallel to A D, intersecting C D produced in G, and by joining A G, the area of the triangle A F G may be made equal to that of the quadrilateral figure A F D E, and consequently to the original figure. Whatever may be the number of sides of the polygon, a similar process will reduce it to a triangle having the same area.

2. **Method of Ordinates.**—An axis A X is measured along the greatest length of the track to be measured (Fig. 51). Offsets are measured at right angles to that axis, sufficiently close together to make the spaces between them approximate to trapezoids. Let d be the distance along the axis between two adjacent offsets or ordinates, and b, b', the breadths of the figure at those ordinates. The area of the trapezoid is then $\frac{(b + b') d}{2}$, and the area of the whole figure is the sum of the areas of the trapezoids into which it is divided.

For example.—Let A X in Fig. 51 represent the chain from which offsets were taken to a curved fence. The lengths of the

CALCULATION OF AREAS. 157

offsets measured in links, were as follows:—$b = 30$, $b_1 = 38$, $b_2 = 61$, $b_3 = 50$, $b_4 = 85$, $b_5 = 80$, $b_6 = 40$, $b_7 = 60$, $b_8 = 69$, $b_9 = 48$, and $b_{10} = 19$. The area included between the chain and the fence is—

$$
\begin{aligned}
50 \times (30 + 38) &= 3{,}400 \\
50 \times (38 + 61) &= 4{,}950 \\
50 \times (61 + 50) &= 5{,}550 \\
50 \times (50 + 85) &= 6{,}750 \\
50 \times (85 + 80) &= 8{,}250 \\
50 \times (80 + 40) &= 6{,}000 \\
50 \times (40 + 60) &= 5{,}000 \\
50 \times (60 + 69) &= 6{,}450 \\
50 \times (69 + 48) &= 5{,}850 \\
50 \times (48 + 19) &= 3{,}350 \\
\hline
\text{Total} \quad . \quad . \quad &= 55{,}550
\end{aligned}
$$

Half this total, that is, 27,775, is the area in square links.

When the intervals between the offsets are all equal, as in the above example, the calculation may be considerably simplified. All the values of d being equal, the formula becomes

$$\text{Area} = \left(\frac{b}{2} + b_1 + b_2 + b_3 + \&c. + \frac{b_n}{2} \right) d;$$

that is to say, the area is equal to the sum of all the intermediate offsets, and of one half the end offsets multiplied by the constant interval between them. Applying this formula to the above example—

Area = $(15 + 531 + 9\tfrac{1}{2}) \times 50 = 27{,}775$ square links.

When the line determined by the offsets is curved, the area may be calculated with greater accuracy by Simpson's formula. This assumes that the lateral boundaries of the figure consist of short parabolic arcs. An even number of equal distances must be measured along the axis, when the formula is

$$\text{Area} = \left\{ b_0 + b_n + 2(b_2 + b_4 + \&c.) + 4(b_1 + b_3 + \&c.) \right\} \frac{d}{3};$$

that is, the area is equal to one-third of the constant interval between the offsets multiplied by the sum of the first and last offsets, twice the sum of the even offsets, and four times the sum of the odd offsets. Applying this formula to the example given,

$$\text{Area} = (30 + 19 + 510 \times 1104)\frac{50}{3}$$
$$= 27716\tfrac{2}{3} \text{ square links.}$$

In calculating the area of a surveyed piece of land, it is advisable to use exclusively the dimensions given in the field-book. The process is, however, very laborious, and may frequently be dispensed with by equalising boundaries and taking measurements on the plan.

By means of rectangular co-ordinates, the area of a piece of land may be accurately calculated without necessitating the preparation of a plan. The general rule for finding areas by this method is as follows:—Multiply the total latitude of each station by the sum of the departures of the two adjacent courses. The algebraical half sum of these products is the area.

The total latitude of each station is found by adding the latitude of the preceding course to the total latitude of the preceding station. To find the adjacent departures, add the departures of the two courses, one on each side of the station. The following is an example of this method of calculation :—

No.	Bearing.	Distance	Latitude.		Departure.		Total Latitude.	Adjacent Departures.	Double Areas.
			N. +	S. −	E. +	W. −			
A	N. 51° 33′ E.	Chains. 29·18	18·14	...	22·85	...	...	...	...
B	S. 73° 07′ E.	12·30	...	3·57	11·77	...	+18·14	+34·62	+628·00
C	S. 20° 37′ W.	18·32	...	17·15	...	6·45	+14·57	+ 5·32	+ 77·51
D	S. 78° 45′ W.	25·40	...	4·95	...	24·91	− 2·58	−31·36	+ 80·90
E	N. 23° 26′ W.	8·21	7·53	...	...	3·26	− 7·53	−28·17	+212·12
...	...	...	25·67	25·67	34·62	34·62	...	...	998·53

The double area of the polygon is thus 998·53 square chains. The area, therefore, is 499·26 square chains, or 49·926 acres.

3. **Mechanical Method.**—Instruments for measuring areas on plans are termed *planimeters*. The form most generally used

CALCULATION OF AREAS. 159

is the polar planimeter of Amsler, of which the general principle is shown in Fig. 52. This is an instrument for measuring the

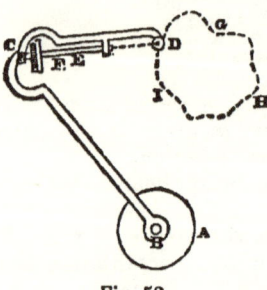

Fig. 52.

area of any figure, however irregular, by the mere passage of a tracer round about its perimeter. It consists essentially of three parts, the adjustable arm C D, the polar arm B C of fixed length, and the rolling wheel F, which rests upon the plan. The wheel is graduated and provided with a vernier. The two arms of the instrument are hinged together by a hardened steel axis C, and permit of an angular motion of nearly 180°. The rolling wheel is mounted on a steel axis parallel to the adjustable arm C D, that is, parallel to the imaginary line joining the tracing point at D and the axis C of the polar arm. The number of complete revolutions of the rolling wheel are shown by a record disc driven by an endless screw on the shaft E. At the end of the arm B is a loaded disc which rests upon the table, and serves as a fixed support for the instrument. In its centre at B is an upright pin forming the turning point or pole of the whole instrument. At the end of the adjustable arm, at the same distance from it as the axis E, the tracing point D is screwed in vertically.

When the tracing point D is carried round the outline of any figure, such as G H I, so as to return to the point from which it started, it can be proved[*] that the distance rolled by the edge of the wheel F is equal to the area of the figure divided by C D, and consequently that the area of the figure is equal to C D multiplied by the distance rolled by the wheel F. In Great Britain and the United States, the graduations on the circle usually represent square inches of area on the plan.

This planimeter gives results sufficiently accurate for mining purposes, and its cheapness and simplicity render it of great value. When, however, a very high degree of accuracy is required, it is found that the planimeter is seriously affected by the paper on which the measuring-wheel revolves. This is particularly noticeable with old plans that have been folded up for a length of time. It is also noticeable when the operation takes place near the edge of the paper, necessitating the wheel passing over that edge.

In cases where the use of the polar planimeter appears imprac-

[*] For proof, consult the report on this instrument by Sir Frederick Bramwell in *Rep. of Forty-second Meeting of the Brit. Assoc.*, p. 401. 1872.

11

ticable, recourse must be had to the precision planimeters made by G. Coradi, of Zurich. In these instruments, the so-called *suspended planimeters* and *linear rolling planimeters*, the measuring wheel does not travel on the plan itself but on a disc, which is an integral part of the instrument.

The suspended planimeter is essentially a polar planimeter; it gives, however, results ten times more accurate than those given by Amsler's instrument. The linear rolling planimeter is the most accurate instrument of its kind yet invented. Instead of revolving round about a pole, the rolling planimeter moves in a straight line, on either side of which the area is determined.

The following table showing the mean error in planimeter readings has been drawn up from the results of a series of experiments made by Professor Lorber* of the School of Mines of Leoben, in Austria :—

Area.		The Mean Error in a Passage of the Tracer amounts to the following fraction of the Area:—			
In Square Centimetres.	In Square Inches.	With the Polar Planimeter. Unit of Vernier 10 sq. mm. (0·015 sq. in.)	With the Suspended Planimeter. Unit of Vernier 1 sq. mm. (0·001 sq. in.)	With the Rolling Planimeter. Unit of Vernier 1 sq. mm. (0·001 sq. in.)	With the Rolling Planimeter. Unit of Vernier 0·5 sq. mm. (0·0005 sq. in.)
10	1·55	1 in 75	1 in 625	1 in 625	1 in 1,000
20	3·10	1 in 148	1 in 1,111	1 in 1,000	1 in 2,000
50	7·75	1 in 355	1 in 2,500	1 in 2,000	1 in 3,000
100	15·50	1 in 682	1 in 4,167	1 in 3,333	1 in 5,000
200	31·00	1 in 1,274	1 in 7,143	1 in 5,128	1 in 7,693
300	46·50	...	1 in 9,375	1 in 8,000	1 in 10,000

The simplest of all area-measurers is the hatchet-planimeter.† This is merely a trammel of fixed length, with at one end, a tracing pointer, and at the other end, in the same plane, a curved knife-edge called the hatchet. The boundary of the figure, whose area is to be ascertained, is traced continuously in one direction, while the hatchet describes a path from which the area of the figure can be directly measured.

Produce of Coal-seams.—The area of coal wrought in any particular seam may be estimated by dividing the plan into squares of 10 acres each. It will be found useful to have a sheet of tracing cloth, divided into 1-acre squares, drawn to the same scale as the plan with which it is to be used. The side of a square, of which the area is 1 acre, measures 316·228 links. The squares should be drawn in black lines, and sub-divided into quarter-acres by means of faint red lines. The area of coal

---

* *Zeit. des oesterr. Ingenieur- und Architektenvereins*, part iv. 1884.

† *Engineering*, vol. lvii., 1894, p. 687. See also O. Henrici's monograph, *Rep. Brit. Assoc.*, 1894, pp. 496-522.

wrought can be estimated with considerable accuracy by merely placing the sheet of tracing cloth over the plan, and by counting the squares covering the space on the plan representing that area.

The area of the coal wrought and the thickness of the seam being known, the tonnage may easily be calculated, as the specific gravity of the coal (1,250 to 1,500), with that of water taken as 1,000 for standard, is equal to the number of ounces in a cubic foot.

The produce of coal-seams depends not only upon the specific gravity of the coal (1·25 to 1·50), but also upon the system of working, and the number of faults. According to Professor J. H. Merivale, at a Durham colliery working the Harvey seam 3 feet 6 inches in thickness, 5,185 tons per acre were obtained when working by the long wall system, and 5,052 tons when working by the bord and pillar system. The yield per acre per foot thick of the South Staffordshire thick coal by the various methods of working is calculated by Mr. H. W. Hughes[*] to be as follows :—Square work, 1243 tons; longwall (two divisions), 1398 tons; longwall (one division), 1155 tons.

A rough rule is to calculate the produce at 100 tons per inch per acre, which leaves an ample allowance of some 25 per cent. for loss of every kind. Another rule frequently used is to calculate the produce at 18 cwt. to the cubic yard. This gives $120\frac{5}{8}$ tons per inch per acre or 1,450 tons per foot per acre.

The Calculation of Ore-Reserves.—Having finished the survey of a metalliferous mine, the surveyor is sometimes called upon to calculate the quantity of ore-reserves in that mine. Various methods are employed for this purpose. Indeed different surveyors will not agree within wide limits as to the amount of ore-reserves in the same mine. Sometimes the amount of ore in sight will be considered to be a rectangular block limited by the outcrop of the vein, the depth of the shaft, and the extreme points of the levels, diminished by the amount extracted. Other surveyors would avoid so excessive an estimate and take but one-third of that amount.

The following method is recommended by Mr. J. G. Murphy, an experienced American mining-engineer, as the fairest and most trustworthy :—Let it be required to calculate the ore-reserves in a mine opened up on a vein with a mean cross-section of 6 feet; a cubic foot of the vein matter in place weighing 150 lbs. The ore stopes are generally very irregular. In this case, however, it may be supposed that the stope faces are 11 feet apart and 8 feet high. There is an inclined shaft, 10 feet by

---

[*] *The Thick Coal of South Staffordshire*, Sheffield, 1885, p. 17.

6 feet, following the dip of the vein, and 6 levels, each 7 feet by 6 feet, 100 feet apart. The lengths of the levels are—

I.	200 feet west	;	150 feet east.	
II.	160	,,	100	,,
III.	120	,,	400	,,
IV.	100	,,	140	,,
V.	165	,,	180	,,
VI.	350	,,	150	,,

The longest level west is 350 feet and the shortest 100 feet. Assume the bounding line of the area of available ore to be at a distance west of the shaft,

$$100 + \frac{350 - 100}{2} = 225 \text{ ft.}$$

The longest level east is 400 feet, and the shortest 100 feet. The bounding line in this direction calculated in a similar way will be at a distance of 250 feet from the shaft.

The inclined shaft has opened up the vein for 670 feet. Deducting say 15 feet for the irregularity of the surface, the quantity of ore in sight will be a rectangular block 655 feet deep, 225 + 250 or 475 feet long, and 6 feet wide, that is, 1,866,750 cubic feet.

From this quantity, however, must be deducted the quantity of ore extracted, namely—

							Cubic Feet.
Inclined shaft,	655	×	10	×	6	=	39,300
Level I.,	350	×	7	×	6	=	14,700
Level II.,	260	×	7	×	6	=	10,920
Level III.,	520	×	7	×	6	=	21,840
Level IV.,	240	×	7	×	6	=	10,080
Level V.,	345	×	7	×	6	=	14,490
Level VI.,	500	×	7	×	6	=	21,000
Level I., stoped east (rough estimate),							3,400
Level I., stoped west,			.	.	.		6,500
Level II., stoped west,			.	.	.		7,000
Level III., stoped east,			.	.	.		20,000
Level VI., stoped west,			.	.	.		12,000
Total,	.	.	.	.			181,230
Or in round numbers,			.	.			182,000

CALCULATION OF AREAS. 163

This quantity, deducted from 1,866,750 cubic feet, leaves 1,684,750 cubic feet. Divided by $13\frac{1}{2}$, the number of cubic feet required for a ton, this gives 124,797 tons of ore in sight.

The quantity of ore discovered in a mine may be estimated from its specific gravity and the average size of the vein. The specific gravity of the ore, with that of water taken at 1,000 for standard, is equal to the number of ounces in a cubic foot. Great caution is necessary to determine the proportion of the vein which may be considered solid ore.

A vein 6 feet square and 1 inch thick contains 3 cubic feet; therefore, in order to find the number of cubic feet per square fathom of a vein, it is merely necessary to multiply the thickness in inches by three.

The following example illustrates the method of finding the weight of any ore per square fathom in a vein:—What quantity of galena will be produced per square fathom from a mineral vein 6 inches in width? One quarter of the vein consists of galena, the remainder of zinc-blende. One-twentieth must be allowed for cavities in the vein.

The specific gravity of galena is 7·5, and a cubic foot of water weighs 1,000 ounces; therefore, a cubic foot of galena weighs 7,500 ounces. The vein being 6 inches thick, there are 18 cubic feet in a square fathom. One quarter of that amount, or 4·5 cubic feet, consists of galena. The weight of galena in ounces is therefore

$$7,500 \times 4·5 = 33,750 = 2109·375 \text{ lbs.}$$

From this, one-twentieth, or 105·468 lbs., must be deducted, leaving 2003·907 lbs., or 17 cwt. 3 qrs. 15 lbs., as the weight of lead ore per square fathom.

CHAPTER XIII.

LEVELLING.

Definitions and Principles.—Levelling is the art of determining the relative distances of points from the centre of the earth. One point is said to be above another when it is farther from the centre of the earth, and the difference of distance from that centre is called the difference of level between the two points. The operation of finding how much one point is higher or lower than another may be trigonometrical, geometrical, or physical.

Trigonometrical levelling necessitates the measurement of lengths and angles. As an illustration, the simplest case may

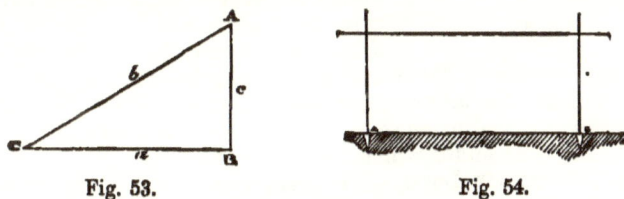

Fig. 53. Fig. 54.

be taken. In order to determine the difference of level between A and C (Fig. 53), or in other words the line A B, the angle A C B, and one of the two lines A C and C B must be measured. The height required is then found by trigonometrical calculation from the two magnitudes measured.

In geometrical levelling, a horizontal line or plane is constructed, and the distance of the two points A and B (Fig. 54) from this is measured directly by setting-up vertical staves. The difference of the two readings on the staves is the difference in level between the two points.

Physical levelling is based on the change of atmospheric pressure at different altitudes. The most important instrument for this method of levelling is the barometer.

The Mason's Level and Boning-staves.—For geometrical levelling, there may be employed the mason's level, boning-staves, or the spirit-level.

The mason's level is based on the principle of the plumb-line. It is only used for levelling, when no other instrument can be obtained. To use the instrument, two pickets are driven into the ground and adjusted until the plumb-line of the mason's level shows that their heads are truly level.

The same operation is more rapidly performed by means of boning-staves, which are simply 3-foot staves having a T-head. Both these methods are very rough and inaccurate, and only suitable for very short distances.

The Spirit-level is the instrument commonly used. The spirit-level proper is a glass tube B C, Fig. 55, hermetically sealed at both ends, partially filled with liquid. By giving the tube a slight arched curvature, the bubble may be made to rest firmly in the middle, and by regulating the curvature, the travelling of the bubble may measure small angular deviations from the horizontal line. The tubes are ground on the inside so as to give a similar curvature to the part of the tube under which the bubble travels.

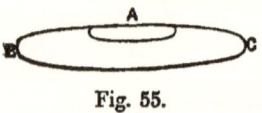

Fig. 55.

(*a.*) **The Dumpy Level.**—The term spirit-level is also applied to the levelling instrument, of which the spirit-level proper is the essential part. The instrument most generally used in Great Britain is the *dumpy level*, invented by W. Gravatt. It is represented in Fig. 56. A is the spirit-level attached by screws at *a, a,* to the telescope B C. The small circle near the object end B of the telescope represents a small transverse spirit-level used to show whether the cross-wire of the telescope is truly horizontal. D D is a flat bar or oblong plate fixed on the top of the vertical axis E. To this bar the telescope is attached by adjusting screws *d, d*. The hollow vertical axis turns upon a spindle fixed to the upper parallel plate F, the spindle being continued downwards and being attached to the lower parallel plate G by a ball and socket joint. There are four levelling-screws *f*, by which the vertical axis is set truly vertical.

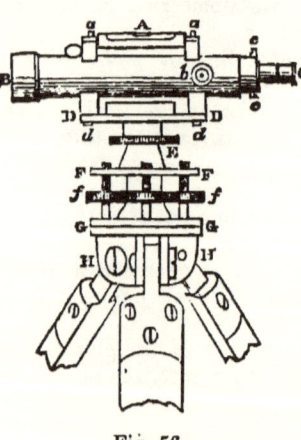

Fig. 56.

The lower plate is screwed on the tripod head H. The tripod consists of three wooden legs like those of the theodolite. In some instruments, a compass is carried on the top of the plate *d, d* for taking the bearings of lines of trial sections.

The telescope of the level is similar to that of the theodolite, except that the diaphragm contains one horizontal wire and two parallel vertical cross-wires, as shown in Fig. 57. This levelling instrument derives its name from its dumpy appearance, due to the large aperture and short focal length of the telescope. The latter is usually 9 to 14 inches in length.

Fig. 57.

(*b*.) **The Y-Level.**—Of the different varieties of levelling instrument, that termed the Y-level is preferred by American engineers. In this instrument the telescope is mounted on Y's, like those of the Y-theodolite.

A recent form of American Y-level, made by Messrs. Heller & Brightly, of Philadelphia, is shown in Fig. 58. The telescope rests on Y's, and is confined in them by clips fastened by binding-pins. The telescope is 17 to 20 inches long. It has at each end

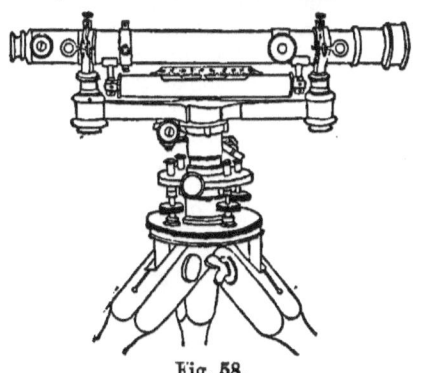

Fig. 58.

a ring of bell-metal; by these it revolves in the agate bearings of the Y's, and can be clamped in any position. The spirit-level is attached to the under side of the telescope, and is provided at its ends with screws for horizontal and vertical adjustment. The level scale extends over the whole length, and is graduated into tenths of an inch. A clamp and tangent screw are connected with the axis for moving the bar and telescope.

(*c*.) **The Troughton Level.**—In the Troughton and Simms' pattern of fixed telescope level, the brass case of the spirit-level is embedded in the top of the outer telescope tube. There are no adjusting screws. These levels are made with telescopes of 10 to 26 inches in length.

The Adjustments of the Level are the same as those of the theodolite. They are as follows:—*Temporary Adjustments*: 1. For parallax. 2. To place the vertical axis truly vertical by means of the levelling-screws. *Permanent Adjustments:* 3. For collimation. 4. To make the spirit-level parallel to the line of collimation. 5. To place the telescope and spirit-level perpendicular to the vertical axis.

The adjustment of the line of collimation in the Y-level is obtained by rotating the telescope on its collars. The parallelism of the level to the line of collimation is obtained by reversing the telescope end for end on its Y's.

The adjustments of the levelling-instruments with fixed telescopes are not so simple, but they are much more permanent. In the dumpy level, the adjustment for collimation is made by the instrument-maker before soldering the telescope tube to the two blocks that support it. In this case, the adjusting-screws of the diaphragm should never afterwards be disturbed. To make the level and line of collimation parallel, a level piece of ground is selected, and after levelling the instrument by means of the levelling-screws, it is directed to a staff held by an assistant at a distance of about 10 chains. The difference between the height read and that of the centre of the telescope above the ground is noted. The instrument and the staff are then made to change places, and the observation repeated. If the results agree, the level and the line of collimation are parallel. If they do not, the inclination of the telescope must be altered by means of the levelling-screws, and the bubble then brought to the middle of its tube by means of the adjusting-screws a, a (Fig. 56).

(*d.*) **Cushing's Reversible Level.**—On account of the inconvenience attending the adjustment for collimation in levelling-instruments where the telescope is fixed, it occurred to Mr. Cushing,[*] Inspector of Scientific Instruments to the India Office, to make the eye-end and object-end of the telescope interchangeable. For this purpose he fixes to the internal tube of the telescope a gun-metal socket, which is turned and ground with a short conical fitting and wide flange to receive the eye-end, with its eye-piece and diaphragm. On the opposite end of the outer tube, a precisely similar fitting receives the cell containing the object-glass. Both ends are identical as regards the fitting, though the object-end is necessarily rather longer than the eye-end on account of its having to carry on the outside the cover or dew-cap. The line of collimation is adjusted by reversing the collimation stop, which in this level is a glass disc with lines engraved upon it by a fine diamond, instead of the ordinary cross-wires.

The **Levelling-staff** serves to measure the vertical distance from the horizontal line formed by the axis of the telescope down

[*] *Min. Proc. Inst. C.E.*, vol. lix., 1880, p. 278.

to the station on the ground. Formerly the levelling-staff consisted of a wooden rod, furnished with a sliding vane or target, which was raised or lowered by the staff-holder in response to signals from the observer. Such staves are now rarely used. The principal objection to which they are liable is that the observer must depend on the staff-holder to read the height observed, or if the latter is not sufficiently intelligent to perform so important a duty, must himself go and read off the height of the vane. In this way great loss of time is caused, and there is uncertainty in the results, as the vane may possibly have shifted in the meantime.

A very perfect staff of this kind, known as the New York target rod, is largely used in the United States. It is graduated to hundredths of a foot. To indicate where the horizontal line cuts the staff, a target is used, the face of which is divided into quadrants painted with two alternate colours. In the face, there is an opening a tenth of a foot long, through which the figures can be seen on the face of the rod. The right edge of the opening is provided with a vernier, by means of which the staff can be read to thousandths of a foot.

In order to avoid entrusting the reading of the staff to an attendant, Mr. W. Gravatt invented a staff, the face of which was graduated distinctly enough for the observer himself to read off the figures through the telescope of his instrument. The sliding vane is thus dispensed with, and the staff-holder has nothing to do but to hold the staff vertical.

The levelling-staff usually consists of three parts, sliding one within the other, and, when opened out for use, forms a staff 14 to 16 feet in length. It is made of mahogany soaked in boiled oil, and painted with several coats of oil paint. The whole length is divided into hundredths of a foot, coloured alternately black and white, and occupying half the breadth of the staff. The patterns of levelling-staves are very various. The form shown in Fig. 59, invented by T. Sopwith, F.R.S., is that most frequently used. In this the feet are represented by large red figures, the tenths are shown by odd black figures, and the hundredths are coloured alternately black and white. Between the odd figures representing tenths, a black diamond is painted to indicate the alternate five-hundredths. The top of every figure represents its value. Of the black and white divisions, the bottom of each black space represents odd hundredths, the top even hundredths. The staff is usually 14 feet in length, and divided into 3 parts, which, when drawn out, are held in position by a spring clip

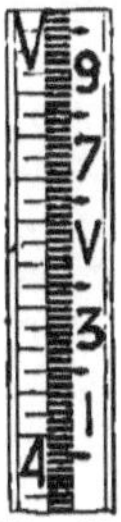

Fig. 59.

at the back. When closed, they form a staff about 5 feet 3 inches in length, 3 inches wide, and 1½ inch deep.

An important modification has been introduced in the graduation by Mr. A. G. Thornton, of Manchester. It consists in the repetition at each 3 inches of the number of feet in small red figures on the left of the staff. This improvement will be found very advantageous, especially with short lines of sight, as an exact reading can be taken on any part of the staff where the cross-wire falls, without the necessity of raising or lowering the staff. It is important that the staff be held truly vertical while it is being read. To help the staff-holder in this, a small plummet is suspended in a groove cut in the side of the staff, by means of which its verticality can be determined in one direction. The observer himself can detect by means of the two vertical wires of the telescope whether it inclines in the other direction. The plummet may be replaced by a round spirit-level, the tangential plane of which is perpendicular to the back of the staff.

The error caused by the staff being inclined is considerable. Let h be the reading on the staff when it is held vertical, and h' the reading when the staff is inclined at an angle of δ from the vertical. Then $\frac{h}{h'} = \cos \delta$, and $h' = \frac{h}{\cos \delta}$. Thus, if $\delta = 2°$, and $h = 4$ feet, then $h' = 4 \cdot 002$ feet.

If necessity should compel the staff to be used without a plummet or round spirit-level, it should be moved backwards and forwards by the staff-holder; the lowest reading will be the most correct one.

A triangular piece of sheet iron, about one-tenth of an inch in thickness, having the corners turned down, is used to rest the staff on. The corners are pressed into the ground. By means of this iron plate, the staff is kept on the same spot, and at the same height from the ground, while the observer is reading the back- and fore-sight. A chain and ring are attached to the plate for the convenience of the staff-holder in lifting it from the ground, and in carrying it from station to station.

Mine Levelling-Staves.—For levelling underground, staves may be employed similar in construction to those used at the surface. They must, of course, be shorter. The best sizes are a 9-foot Sopwith staff to close down to 3 feet 6 inches, or a 6-foot Sopwith staff to close down to 2 feet 6 inches. The staff is illuminated by means of a miner's candle or a safety-lamp. Mr. Stanley has designed a staff, made in lengths of 18 inches, like a folding rule.

Mr. G. J. Jee* has designed a useful staff for colliery work. It consists of three lengths, sliding one into the other. The bottom length is graduated upwards in the ordinary way, and is 3 feet in length. At the top of the first division of the staff is attached a 2-inch band, which is graduated upwards, and forms an accurate continuation of the scale on the lower division of the staff. The band passes over a brass roller attached to the top division of the staff, and thence is carried down and wound round a brass drum, fixed just below the roller, to the top of the same length of the staff, the band being kept in tension by means of a box-spring attached on one side to the axis of the cylinder. It is thus evident that when the second length of the staff is drawn out, the band unwinds and gives a continuous reading up to 5 feet 8 inches, or to any intermediate distance that the height of the roof will allow. In the same way when the third length is drawn out, a continuous reading may be obtained up to 9 feet, or to any intermediate distance required. The weight of the staff is 5 lbs. It is manufactured by Messrs. J. Davis & Son, of Derby.

The clumsy contrivances used in the St. Gothard tunnel induced Professor M. Schmidt,† of the Freiberg School of Mines, to devise a staff specially adapted for levelling in mines. It consists of two staves, each 5 feet in length. The front one is graduated, whilst the second acts as a pedestal. The two are joined together by two clamps and screws, in such a way that the graduated staff may slide along the pedestal for a distance of 4 feet. The graduated staff is backed with an iron plate drilled with small holes, corresponding to its graduation. Into these a steel pin on the pedestal works automatically with a spring, whenever the graduated staff is drawn in or out. A pointer is attached to the pedestal at a given height (*e.g.*, 4 feet), when the graduated staff is pushed home. When the latter is drawn out, the reading, less the difference between the foot and the pointer, added to the constant height, denotes the height of the line of sight above the foot of the staff.

Attached to the side of the staff, is a portable reflector lamp for illuminating the scale. It can be raised or lowered at will, and its reflector is so placed that as much light as possible falls upon the scale, whilst the flame itself is kept out of sight. In mines where the ground is stony or soft, a cast-iron shoe with a hemispherical steel head is placed under the staff.

For rough levelling in metalliferous mines, a levelling instru-

---

*Colliery Guardian, vol xxxviii., p. 576, 1879.
† *Oesterr. Zeitschr*, vol. xxix., p. 295, 1881.

ment may be made out of an ordinary carpenter's level, fitted with sights, and made to fit on the dial tripod. The staff used in conjunction with this instrument may be made out of a piece of planed deal, 3 inches in width, marked into lines representing feet and inches by means of a piece of red-hot hoop iron. The numbers of the feet may also be burnt-in in bold Roman figures, every half foot being indicated by a longer line. The level having no telescope, the reading of the staff has to be entrusted to the staff-holder.

For very accurate levelling, Borchers' vane-rod is generally used in the Continental mines. To enable this contrivance to be used, all the station-points must be marked by small hooks fixed into the roof of the underground road. The contrivance consists of a steel rod, rectangular in section, 5 feet 5 inches in length, provided at its upper end with a movable hook. The rod is graduated into inches, the graduation proceeding from the inside of the hook to the lower end of the rod. Up and down the rod slides a sheet-iron circular vane or target, 8 inches in diameter, which may be clamped at any height. At right angles to the longitudinal axis of the rod, a line is scratched through the centre of the vane. With their centres truly on this line, three circular apertures are cut, two 0·4 inch in diameter, and one 0·07 inch in diameter. In front of one of the larger openings a piece of ground glass is fastened. To the back of the vane a vernier is fastened with its zero coinciding with the horizontal line scratched on the vane.

In levelling, the rod is hung from a hook in the roof of the mine-road, and the vane placed at right angles to the line of sight. For very short station-lines, the flame of a miner's lamp is held behind the small hole, and the vane moved up or down until the horizontal cross-wire of the telescope coincides with the point of light sighted. For greater distances of 60 to 200 yards, the aperture covered with ground glass is used if the air is clear; with still greater distances the uncovered aperture is used. Very long station-lines are not to be recommended, on account of the difficulty of communicating with the assistant.

This levelling-rod is exceedingly simple. It hangs perpendicularly by its own weight, and, unlike wooden staves, it is not affected by the water and dirt in the mine. At the same time it presents the advantages of fine adjustment, exact reading, and great rapidity.

Practice of Levelling.—If it is required to determine the difference of level between two points not very far apart, this may be done by *simple levelling*. For this purpose, the levelling-instrument is set up midway between the two stations A and B, Fig.

60. With the bubble remaining unmoved in the middle of its tube, the telescope is directed towards a staff held vertically at A, and the reading h noted. The staff is then held vertically at B, and the telescope directed towards it, the reading h' being noted. The difference of level between the two points A and B is then $h - h'$, and B is higher than A when h is greater than h'. The difference of level is thus

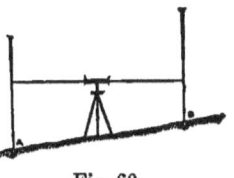

Fig. 60.

determined by two readings on the staff, one with the telescope directed backwards towards the staff at A, and the other with the telescope directed forewards to the staff at B, or, in other words, by means of a *back-sight* and a *fore-sight*.

In order to obtain the greatest accuracy, the instrument is set up as nearly as possible midway between the two stations A and B. The advantage of thus placing the instrument is that the instrumental errors and the errors due to the curvature of the earth and to refraction are neutralised.

Let the instrument be set up at m, Fig. 61, so that $ma = mb$, and let ab be a horizontal line. Then if all the sources of error act in such a way that the optic axis of the telescope directed towards the staff at A gives an angle, amd, with the horizontal line, the cross-wires of the telescope will not coincide with the point a, but with the point d, and on directing the telescope to the staff at B, the cross-wires will coincide not with point b, but with c.

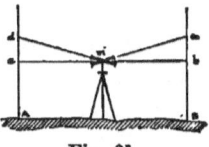

Fig. 61.

The same causes being at work in both positions of the telescope, the angles amd and bmc must be equal. Because $ma = mb$, $ad = bc$. The difference in level is equal to $h - h'$, that is $(Aa + ad) - (Bb + bc)$. It is here assumed that the condition of the atmosphere is the same with the fore-sight as with the back-sight, and thus the refraction is the same in both cases.

The influence of the curvature of the earth's surface is dependent on the radius of the earth, r, and on the length of the station-line l. Imagine an arc of a circle to be described passing through the telescope axis A, Fig. 62, and with the centre of the earth as centre. The arc will intersect the staff set up at B in the point C. The curvature in the figure is of course very much exaggerated. The horizontal line passing through A, inter

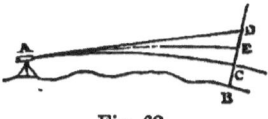

Fig. 62.

sects the staff at the point D. Thus, A C is the true horizontal line, A D the apparent horizontal line, and C D the depression of the true below the apparent horizontal line. Then the correction for curvature is − C D, a third proportional to the earth's diameter and distance between the level and the staff. C D is thus equal to $\frac{l^2}{2r}$. For a distance of 1 mile this correction is 8 inches, or two-thirds of a foot. Two-thirds of the square of the distance in miles will be the amount of the correction in feet.

The error C D is diminished by the refracting action of the air, as the real line of sight is a curved line, in which light proceeds. The curve being concave downwards, the point D is not seen at the cross-wires of the telescope, but the point E. With a calm clear atmosphere, D E is equal to 0·1348 C D, or $0·1348 \frac{l^2}{2r}$. The coefficient 0·1348 is the mean of the determinations of several physicists.

The total error due to the curvature of the earth and to refraction is thus $\frac{l^2}{2r} - 0·1348 \frac{l^2}{2r} = \frac{0·4326\, l^2}{r}$. The earth's diameter being equal to 41,778,000 feet, the correction for curvature and refraction per mile would be

$$0·4326 \times 5280^2 \div 20{,}889{,}000 = 0·577 \text{ foot} = 6·92 \text{ inches.}$$

At distances up to 10 chains, the errors produced by curvature and refraction are so small that they may be neglected.

In crossing over a deep valley it is sometimes advisable to set up the level at one of the points A and the staff at the other point B, in which case the height of the centre of the instrument above the ground must be measured. The difference of level d will then be equal to the height of the instrument i above the ground, less the reading on the staff h—that is, $d = i - h$. If the correction c for curvature and refraction has to be taken into account the formula becomes

$$d = i - (h - c) = i - h + c.$$

If the instrument is placed at B, and the staff at A, the difference of level is

$$d = h' - c - i'.$$

The mean of these two values gives the difference of level independently of all correction—

$$d = \frac{h' - h}{2} + \frac{i - i'}{2}.$$

When the distance is too great or the ground too much inclined for the difference of level to be determined by one operation, recourse must be had to *compound levelling*, a process consisting of several simple levelling operations. The difference of level of each two successive points is determined in the way described. Fig. 63 gives an example of compound levelling.

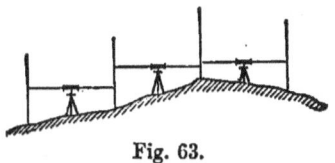

Fig. 63.

By setting up the levelling-instrument at the three stations, the following values were obtained:—

	Back-Sight. Feet.		Fore-Sight. Feet.		Feet.
I.	A D = 6·71	B E =	3·92	Rise from A to B =	2·79
II.	C F = 7·86	C G =	2·41	Rise from B to C =	5·45
III.	H C = 2·84	D I =	6·39	Fall from C to D =	3·55
	17·41		12·72	Rise =	4·69

If the back-sight is greater than the fore-sight, the ground rises. If the fore-sight is greater than the back-sight, the ground falls. The rises being regarded as positive, and the falls as negative, the algebraical sum gives as the result of the levelling that D is 4·69 feet higher than A. The same result is obtained when the sums of the back-sights and of the fore-sights are taken, and the smaller sum subtracted from the larger. Thus 17·41 - 12·72 = 4·69. The difference obtained is difference in level between the end points. It indicates a rise when the sum of the back-sights is the greater, and a fall when that of the fore-sights is the greater.

This is the method of conducting a *flying-level*—that is, a levelling operation merely to determine how much one point is above or below another. If, for example, it is required to determine what thickness of strata there is, at a certain point A at the surface, above the present workings in the mine below it, the depth of the shaft is measured, and levelling commenced at the bottom of the shaft and continued to the point underground directly below A. A flying-level is then made at the surface from the shaft to A. The depth of the shaft being known, the thickness of the strata at A can be calculated from the rise or fall determined at the surface and underground. Thus, if the shaft is 300 feet deep, and the point underground is found to be 5 feet lower than the bottom of the shaft, whilst the point

LEVELLING. 175

A at the surface is found to be 40 feet higher than the top of the shaft, the thickness of the strata at A will be 300 + 5 + 40 = 345 feet.

Section-levelling.—When a section of the ground is to be drawn, the distances between the several stations must be carefully measured. The levelling-instrument should be placed as near as possible midway between the two stations, and the levelling is then conducted in the manner described. To facilitate the plotting of the section, the vertical distances of the points are calculated above an assumed level-line called the *datum-line*.

The observations are recorded in the levelling-book in the following manner:—

FORM OF RECORD L

No.	Back-Sight.	Fore-Sight.	Rise.	Fall.	Height above Datum 50·00.	Distance.	Remarks.
A	5·49	0·06	5·43	...	55·43	Chains. 1·50	
B	4·32	2·24	2·08	...	57·51	4·70	
C	8·40	1·52	6·88	...	64·39	9·12	
D	3·21	7·42	...	4·21	60·18	10·36	
E	1·41	6·50	...	5·09	55·09	13·96	
F	1·68	4·53	...	2·85	52·24	16·38	
G	7·20	0·22	6·98	...	59·22	19·98	
H	12·60	9·51	3·09	...	62·31	24·98	
J	9·51	0·33	9·18	...	71·49	29·18	
K	5·02	4·18	0·84	...	72·33	32·78	
L	5·08	4·02	1·06	...	73·39	36·36	
M	6·01	3·07	2·94	...	76·33	40·68	
N	6·82	4·00	2·82	...	79·15	45·73	
...	76·75	47·60	41·30	12·15	−50·00	...	
...	...	29·15	...	29·15	29·15	...	

The starting-point is 50 feet above the datum-line, which in this case was the level of the high-water mark at London Bridge. The column headed "Height above Datum" contains the absolute height of each forward station above the horizontal line passing through the high-water mark. The numbers are obtained by taking the algebraical sum of the rises and falls, the former being considered positive, and the latter negative.

As a test of the accuracy of the arithmetical work, the columns of back- and fore-sights should be added up, and the smaller sum subtracted from the larger. The result should agree with the calculated height above datum. Another test is afforded by adding up the rise and fall columns, when if, upon subtracting the smaller sum from the greater, the remainder is the same as that obtained by the two other operations, there can be no doubt that the levels have been correctly calculated. Thus, in the example given, the height of N above the starting-point is $79 \cdot 15 - 50 \cdot 00 = 29 \cdot 15$ feet. The sum of the back-sights being 76·75, and that of the fore-sights 47·60, the difference also gives 29·15 feet as the height of N above the starting-point. Lastly, the sum of the rises is 41·30, and that of the falls 12·15, the difference being 29·15 feet as before.

In order to make a correct section of a continuous surface, the levels of a series of points may be determined with the instrument at one station. The first and last observations are then the principal back- and fore-sights respectively. Thus, in Fig. 64,

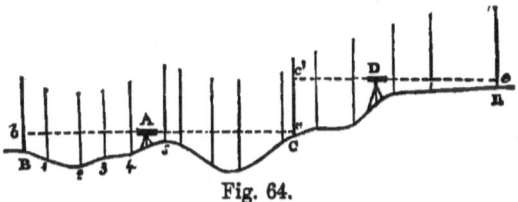

Fig. 64.

A is a station where the instrument is set up, and bAc is the line of sight. The first back-sight is taken with the staff at the starting-point B, of which the height above the datum-line is known. The reading on the staff is Bb, or 2·95 feet. The first fore-sight is taken with the staff at C, giving the reading Cc, or 0·58 foot. Between the points B and C, several intermediate sights are taken. The first intermediate-sight, taken with the staff at the point marked 1, is at the same time a fore-sight to B, and a back-sight to the point marked 2; 3 is a fore-sight to 2 and a back-sight to 4, and so on with the other points. When the level is carried on to a new station D, the assistant holds the

LEVELLING. 177

staff steadily at C, at exactly the same point as it was for the fore-sight from A. The first back-sight C*c* is taken, and the process repeated until the fore-sight E*e*, or 1·01 foot, is taken. The staff is then held stationary until the levelling-instrument is moved on to the next station.

The readings are recorded and reduced in the manner shown in the following example:—

FORM OF RECORD II.

No.	Back-Sight.	Fore-Sight.	Rise.	Fall.	Height above datum 100·00.	Distance.	Remarks.
1	2·95	3·99	...	1·04	98·96	Links. 35	
2	3·99	4·90	...	0·91	98·05	90	
3	4·90	3·99	0·91	...	98·96	125	
4	3·99	3·08	0·91	...	99·87	165	
5	3·08	1·07	2·01	...	101·88	220	
6	1·07	1·88	...	0·81	101·07	245	
7	1·88	5·00	...	3·12	97·95	295	
8	5·00	5·52	...	0·52	97·43	335	
9	5·52	1·23	4·29	...	101·72	400	
10	1·23	0·58	0·65	...	102·37	420	
11	8·20	7·30	0·90	...	103·27	455	
12	7·30	6·50	0·80	...	104·07	515	
13	6·50	2·08	4·42	...	108·49	580	
14	2·08	1·81	0·27	...	108·76	635	
15	1·81	1·01	0·80	...	109·56	740	
...	59·50	49·94	15·96	6·40	−100·00	...	
...	...	9·56	...	9·56	9·56	...	

The first back-sight and last fore-sight of each line of sight are the most important in point of accuracy. Any error made in taking an intermediate sight affects that line only, whilst any error in the back-sight or fore-sight is carried on throughout the section. In order to correct for curvature and refraction, the first back-sight and last fore-sight of each line should be at points as nearly as practicable equidistant from the instrument.

In recording the readings in the levelling-book, a separate column may be used for the intermediate sights. The readings are reduced, and the computations checked in the manner shown in the following example :—

FORM OF RECORD III.

No.	Back-Sight.	Intermediate.	Fore-Sight.	Rise.	Fall.	Height above datum 100·00.	Total Distance.
1	2·95	3·99	...	...	1·04	98·96	Links. 35
2	...	4·90	...	...	0·91	98·05	90
3	...	3·99	...	0·91	...	98·96	125
4	...	3·08	...	0·91	...	99·87	165
5	...	1·07	...	2·01	...	101·88	220
6	...	1·88	...	...	0·81	101·07	245
7	...	5·00	...	...	3·12	97·95	295
8	...	5·52	...	...	0·52	97·43	335
9	...	1·23	...	4·29	...	101·72	400
10	...	...	0·58	0·65	...	102·37	420
11	8·20	7·30	...	0·90	...	103·27	455
12	...	6·50	...	0·80	...	104·07	515
13	...	2·08	...	4·42	...	108·49	580
14	...	1·81	...	0·27	...	108·76	635
15	...	...	1·01	0·80	...	109·56	740
...	11·15	...	1·59	15·96	6·40	−100·00	...
...	...	...	9·56	...	9·56	9·56	...

In this way a large amount of unnecessary addition is avoided. There is a third method, known as the collimation method, of reducing levels. It saves one column of figures, and is easier to work out, as the distinction between rises and falls is not considered. The following is the form of record:—

FORM OF RECORD IV.

Back-Sights.	Intermediate.	Fore-Sights.	Height of Line of Collimation above Datum.	Height of Surface above Datum.	Distances.	Total Distances.
					Chains.	Chains.
0·15	...	...	206·04	205·89	0·00	38·00
...	4·80	...	...	201·24	1·00	39·00
...	3·80	...	...	202·24	1·00	40·00
5·49	...	8·00	203·53	198·04	1·00	41·00
...	5·44	...	...	198·09	1·00	42·00
...	9·25	...	...	194·28	1·00	43·00
...	...	9·64	...	193·89	1·00	44·00
5·64	...	17·64	...	−12·00	...	...
12·00	...	...	...	...	...	...

A modification of this form of booking will be found advantageous for levelling in mines. Only two columns are used for entering the heights observed on the staff. The intermediate and fore-sights are placed in one column, the latter being distinguished by being underlined. The reduced levels for the "height above datum" column are obtained in the following way:—Add the back-sight to the reduced height for collimation and subtract intermediate and fore-sights. On reaching a fore-sight, the next back-sight is added to the reduced height at that point, when the intermediate and fore-sights are subtracted as before.

Should it be required to work out the levels backwards, the rule is:—Add the fore-sight to the reduced height for collimation and subtract intermediate and back-sights.

On reaching the bottom of a page in the levelling-book, if there is no necessity to move the instrument, the last intermediate sight is booked as a fore-sight at the bottom of the page, and again as a back-sight at the top of the following page. By so doing, the same number is added to, and subtracted from the collimation height, and consequently the reduced heights are not affected. The accuracy of the calculations is ascertained in the ordinary way, by adding all the back-sights and all the fore-sights, and subtracting the smaller total from the larger one.

The advantages of this method, especially for underground levelling, are apparent, as it necessitates the writing of fewer figures. The form of record for this system, recommended by Mr. H. W. Hughes, is shown by the extract from his levelling-book of a South Staffordshire colliery given on p. 181.

Bench Marks.—When a section has been completed, it is generally necessary to check its accuracy by repetition. To do this, it is advisable in levelling to follow the shortest route, and to level at intervals to some known points on the exact line of section. The points thus selected are usually *bench marks*. These are fixed points of reference, the levels of which are known. In the Ordnance Survey of Great Britain, the bench marks are generally chiselled on some permanent stone slab, pillar, or wall.

The form of mark for them is the broad arrow ⋏. In levelling on long lines of section, a bench mark is generally made at every quarter of a mile, so that any error in the operation may not involve re-levelling the whole line. By referring to the maps of the Ordnance Survey, the heights may be found of the bench marks above the datum-line (the level of mean tide at Liverpool).

In collieries it is the general practice to record the levels of the works from some fixed datum near the shaft, as, for example, the flat sheets at the top or bottom of the shaft, the delivery of water from the high set of pumps, or some other fixed point. Mr. J. A. Ramsay * proposes to take or continue the Ordnance levels into the workings. In the Ordnance bench mark the broad arrow points upwards to a horizontal line. To make a distinction, it is suggested that as soon as the levels become lower than the datum line or sea-level, the broad arrow should be reversed. The levels obtained in this way may be written upon the plan in plain figures at particular points on the main roads, and, when necessary, may be continued into the face of the off-workings.

Mr. Ramsay gives the accompanying extract from his levelling-book to illustrate the method he proposes of continuing the Ordnance levels into the workings of a colliery. (See p. 182.)

---

* *Trans. N. Eng. Inst. M.E.*, vol. xx., 1870, p. 73.

FORM OF RECORD V.

Back-Sight.	Fore and Intermediate Sights.	Reduced Heights.	Distance.	Remarks.
			Feet.	
0·70	...	102·72	5,466	Datum 100 feet below inset, distance measured from pit shaft. Section of coal.—Coal, 3' 9"; dirt, 0' 5"; coal, 3' 2"; floor composed of clay.
	2·98	100·44	5,500	floor of coal.
	5·74	97·68	5,544	3" up coal.
0·13	5·08	92·73	5,600	floor of coal.
0·13				
	6·37	86·49	5,671	,, ,,
0·88				
	2·94	84·43	5,700	,, ,,
	5 35	82·02	5,761	3" up coal.
4·55				
	4·96	81·61	5,800	5" below coal.
	3·75	82·82	5,823	floor of coal.
4·00				foot of fault, rise about 9 yards, fault hades 15°.
	4·30	82·52	5,900	
	0·18	86·64	5,966	
5·18				
	0·30	91·52	6,015	
4·50				
	0·16	95·86	6,048	
5·29				crossing measures below coal.
	0·05	101·10	6,078	
3·80				
	0·01	104·89	6,111	
6·58	0·01	111·46	6,136	
4·15				
	4·50	111·11	6,251	floor of seam.
	2·35	113·26	6,348	1' 0" above bottom of coal.
	2·75	112·86	6,402	0' 6" ,, ,,
4·48				
	4·46	112·89	6,517	floor of seam, road to left.
	3·64	113·70	6,623	2" above bottom of coal.
3·93				
	3·11	114·52	6,781	floor of coal.
	4·08	113·55	6,803	,, ,,
	5·15	112·48	6,921	,, ,,
	5·30	112·33	7,017	3" below coal.

Proof.—Total fore-sights = 38·69; total back-sights = 48·30. Difference (viz., rise) = 9·61, which, added to 102·72, the reduced height at 5,466, gives 112·33, the reduced height at 7,017.

FORM OF RECORD VI.

No.	Back-Sight.	Fore-Sight.	Rise.	Fall.	Datum.	Dist.	Remarks.
					85·90	...	Ordnance B.M. on north-east corner of watch house
1	3·31	5·08	...	1·77	84·13	...	...
2	4·02	11·00	...	6·98	77·15	...	...
3	2·60	4·40	...	1·80	75·35	...	The flat sheets on lip of pit.
	...	...	...	518·91	443·56	...	Take Depth of the Pit with 100 feet Chain. Depth, 518 ft. 11 in.=518·91. Less surface height above datum. Flat sheets at bottom of pit; reversed Ordnance B.M. cut into stone walling, side of pit.
							Level down Cross-cut to make Section for Engine Plane.
1	6·85	5·94	0·91	...	442·65	90	7·9 ft. high—Hard post cover.
2	5·94	5·19	0·75	...	441·90	129	7·5 do. do.
3	5·19	5·04	0·15	...	441·75	165	8·0 do. do.
4	5·04	3·29	1·75	...	440·00	210	6·0 do. Blue metal cover.
5	3·75	5·05	...	1·30	441·30	276	5·3 do. do. timbered
6	2·53	5·54	...	3·01	444·31	354	On the brow of large down-throw trouble, measure down, with straight edge and plumb-line— Dist.—6 ft.+5½ ft.+3½ ft.+6 ft.+6 ft.=27 ft.
7	0·00	20·69	...	20·69	465·00	381	Down,4·33+4·45+3·39+3·32+5·20=20·69.
8	3·45	2·11	1·34	...	463·66	425	4 ft. high—Roof very jointy and bad—top coal left on.
9	3·97	2·34	1·63	...	462·03	462	4·3 full height of seam, bad roof, closely timbered.
10	2·89	3·86	...	0·97	463·00	507	4·6 do. do. do.
11	2·06	4·49	...	2·43	465·43	555	5·0 better roof, timbered in places only.
12	1·95	4·82	...	2·87	468·30	600	5·0 ordinary height of seam—good roof.
13	3·15	4·15	...	1·00	469·30	657	5·0 do. do.
14	4·00	3·37	0·63	...	468·67	705	5·0 do. do.
15	4·73	3·03	1·70	...	466·97	780	5·0 do. do.
16	3·26	3·84	...	0·58	467·55	840	5·0 do. do.
17	2·76	4·71	...	1·95	469·50	885	5·0 do. do.
...	61·52	87·46	8·86	34·80	...	...	
...	25·94	...	25·94	...	...	...	

(e.) **The Reflecting Level.**—For rough surface levelling, the reflecting level may be used. It consists of a small sighting-tube, with a bubble-tube set above it. It is so arranged that the bubble is seen through the bottom of its tube, and reflected by a mirror into the sighting-tube. An instrument of this kind, invented by Abney, is also useful as a clinometer. In this instrument, the bubble-tube is fastened to an arc 2½ inches in diameter. In taking a level, the vernier, fastened to a bar at right angles to the spirit-level, is set to the zero of the vertical arc. On looking through the tube, the object observed will be level with the eye when it is intersected by the bubble. The results obtained are very satisfactory. Like all reflecting instruments, this level is useless in the bad light of a mine.

Sources of Error in Spirit-Levelling.—There are four sources of error in levelling—1, Errors of observation; 2, instrumental errors; 3, errors from unstable supports; 4, atmospheric errors.

Errors of observation are mostly unavoidable, and arise chiefly from the bubble not being carefully centred. Instrumental errors are due to the instrument not being in adjustment, and to the staff not being vertical. Errors from unstable supports can only be eliminated by duplicating the levelling in the opposite direction, and by taking the mean of the results. Atmospheric errors arise from wind, tremulousness of the air in clear sunny weather, and variable refraction due to sudden bursts of sunshine on the line.

A waterproof cloth should be thrown over the level in case of rain. Staves should be wiped dry after being exposed to the rain, placed horizontally to prevent warping, and occasionally compared with a standard length.

Accuracy Attainable in Spirit-levelling.—Mr. W. Seibt arrives at some interesting results, calculated from observations made under ordinary conditions. His telescope of 18-inch focal length had a magnifying power of 42, and an object glass of 1⅝-inch aperture, besides a very sensitive spirit-level. The instrument was always set up between the back and forward staves, and the observations taken by one central cross-wire; both ends of the spirit-level being read at each observation. Observations were only made in still clear weather; the back- and fore-sights being taken as soon as possible after one another. Each complete observation occupied 6 minutes, and 24 pairs of observations were taken at each station. Although the mine-surveyor is rarely in a position to use an instrument as delicate as that described, the results arrived at are of interest for the sake of comparison.

The mean error m, in an observation consisting of a back- and fore-reading, was found to be as follows:—

At 50 metres (164 feet) ± 0·28 millimetre (0·011 inch).
„ 100 „ (328 „) ± 0·62 „ (0·024 „).
„ 150 „ (492 „) ± 0·71 „ (0·028 „).
„ 200 „ (656 „) ± 0·91 „ (0·035 „).

The distance for observing should be limited by the capacity of the observer and of his instrument. It will always be rightly chosen when it is extended as far as the nature of the ground to be levelled will allow, and on the other hand, when it is so short that no trace of air movement is noticeable through the telescope, and the graduation of the staff is presented as a perfectly stationary and sharply-defined image. If this principle is acted on, it is asserted that the mean error per kilometre should not exceed 0·64 millimetre, as in extensive levelling operations the line of sight does not usually exceed 100 metres.

At the second International Geodetic Conference it was decided that the probable error in the difference of level between two points, 1 kilometre apart, must not, as a rule, exceed 3 millimetres, and in no case exceed 5 millimetres. According to the report of the United States Coast and Geodetic Survey, on the line from Sandy Hook to St. Louis, 1009 miles in length, the probable error per kilometre was 1·2 millimetre.

Plotting Sections.—In order to plot a section from the reduced levels as entered in the levelling-book, it is first necessary to rule a straight line to represent the datum-line from which the heights are calculated. Along this line the horizontal distances between the points are marked off, and at each point a line is drawn at right angles to the datum-line. Along the lines thus obtained, the vertical heights are marked off, the figures given in the "height above datum" column being used for this purpose. In marking off on the datum-line each distance separately, any error made is carried forwards. To remove this source of error, it will be found advisable to add the measured lengths together so as to obtain the absolute distance of each station from the starting point.

As a rule, in plotting a section two scales are used, one for the horizontal distances, and the other for the vertical heights and depths. An exaggerated representation of the section is thus obtained. By making the vertical scale much greater than the horizontal one, the depths of cutting and embankment required are shown with greater clearness than if both scales are the same. The section shown in Fig. 64 is plotted on a horizontal scale of 3 chains to the inch, and a vertical scale of 30 feet to the inch.

Sections of the main ways in collieries are usually plotted on a horizontal scale of 2 chains to the inch, and a vertical scale of 20 feet to the inch. As a rule, the scale for the horizontal distances should be the same as that of the plan with which it corresponds.

Sections may be plotted with great rapidity by means of Marquois scales. These consist of a right-angled triangle, the hypothenuse of which is three times the length of the shorter side, and two rectangular scales of equal parts, each with two scales, a so-called artificial scale placed close to the edge, and a natural scale immediately within this. The divisions on the artificial scale are three times the size of those on the natural scale. The latter is a simply divided scale of equal parts, with the divisions numbered from left to right. In the artificial scale the zero is placed in the middle of the edge of the rule, and the divisions are numbered both ways from that point to the two ends of the rule. A pair of Marquois scales usually has scales of 30, 60, 25, 50, 35, 45, 20, and 40. The triangle has a short line drawn perpendicular to the hypothenuse near the middle to serve as an index.

To draw a line parallel to another, one of the rulers is laid on the paper, and the short side of the triangle placed against it, when parallel lines may be drawn by sliding the triangle up or down.

To draw a line perpendicular to a given line from a given point in it, the shortest side of the triangle is made to coincide with the given line, and the ruler placed against the hypothenuse. The triangle is then slid along the rule, until a line drawn along the longest side of the triangle passes through the given point.

With these scales the sight is assisted by the divisions on the artificial scale being so much larger than those of the natural scale to which the section is drawn, and any error on the setting of the index produces an error of but one-third the amount in the section.

For the purpose of receiving the plotting of sections, a special kind of paper is prepared, on which faint lines are printed, dividing it horizontally and vertically into one-twentieths of an inch. By the use of this section-paper, much time is saved, as no scale is required.

(*f.*) The Water-Level is a very simple instrument which, when necessary, may take the place of a more elaborate levelling-instrument. It requires no adjustment; it may be made by any intelligent workman at very slight expense; and in short distances no serious error can be made when using it. It consists of a horizontal tube made of tin-plate or brass, terminated at each end by a vertical glass tube in which the surface of a liquid gives a horizontal line. By means of this line, the vane of a levelling-staff is adjusted to the right height. The tube is made so as to revolve on a light portable stand.

A water-level (*chorobates*) is described by Vitruvius (*de Architectura*, viii. 6), as used in the construction of the Roman aqueducts. It consisted, not of a tube, but of an open trench 5 feet long, 1 inch wide, and 1½ inch deep, cut in a plank 20 feet in length. It was adjusted until the water was at the same height from the top at each end. The plank was provided with legs accurately at right angles to it. They were of equal length, and rested on the line to be levelled.

The water-level was in common use in the Derbyshire lead-mines in the 17th century. The method of levelling then employed is described by Thomas Houghton, writing in 1681, as follows:—

"The Instrument for this purpose may be like the following— viz., a Water Stand, with one or more Channels, which the Miner may make himself, upon an old season'd Joyce, cutting a Mortess therein, a yard long, or more, as his own Discretion directs, plaining the same very well and even."

The observer sights through a hole above the water channel, at a staff 6 yards long; the staff being moved until the top of it can be seen. The instrument is then moved to the place occupied by the staff, and the operation repeated, "till you have finished the whole, and come to the Place where you intend to begin your Sough [adit level]: then reducing your Poles into Fathoms, compare them with the depth of your Mine, and thus you may know whether it will lay it dry or no."

A modification of the water-level has recently been employed with success by Dr. Luigi Aita, of Padua. His instrument consists of two levelling-staves, in front of each of which a glass tube, 7·87 inches long and 0·79 inch in diameter, slides up and down. The two glass tubes are connected by an india-rubber pipe, 30 yards in length. At one end of the india-rubber tube is a stopcock, by means of which the connection between the two glass tubes may be interrupted. When in use, one glass tube and the india-rubber pipe are filled with a coloured liquid, the staves are set up at the two stations, and the glass tubes raised approximately to the same height at both staves. The stopcock is then carefully opened, the fluid will stand at the same level in both glass tubes, and its position can be read at both staves. With this instrument a mile may be levelled in 6 hours. For levelling in narrow, crooked, and partially fallen-in workings, this instrument offers great advantages.

In mines where the seams are thin and inclined, the use of the telescope-level is attended with great inconvenience. For this work, Mr. T. L. Galloway and Mr. C. Z. Bunning* have introduced a modification of Aita's water-level. The apparatus consists of two glass tubes connected by an india-rubber pipe, which may be of any convenient length from 10 yards upwards. Each glass tube is attached to a scale graduated into feet, tenths and hundredths in the same way as the ordinary levelling-staff. The tubes are filled up to the centre of each scale with coloured water. The scales being held vertically upon any sloping surface and at any distance apart that the length of pipe will admit, the difference of level between the stations at which the scales are held will be represented by the difference of the readings denoting the position of the coloured liquid in each tube.

In order to remove the source of error arising from the presence of air-bubbles in the liquid, a stopcock is fitted at each end of the india-rubber pipe. These stopcocks being closed under water prevent all oscillation while the apparatus is being carried from station to station, so that there can be no possibility of the intrusion of air-bubbles. Falls of stone, sudden bends in the road, or timbering, obstacles so frequently interrupting the line of sight in levelling underground, present no difficulty with this apparatus, as it is obviously as easy to proceed over or around any obstacle as to advance in a straight line. The instrument has been used in mines under the most difficult circumstances, and has been found to answer in all cases exceedingly well, the saving in time being very considerable.

Trigonometrical Levelling.—The trigonometrical method of levelling is based on the solution of a right-angled triangle A B C (Fig. 53), of which the base B C and the angle B C A are known. The difference of level B A of the points A and C will be equal to the base B C multiplied by the tangent of the angle B C A. This method is less exact than spirit-levelling, because a small error in the angle may give rise to a considerable error in the difference of level.

Any instrument with a vertical limb may be employed for levelling trigonometrically. A series of angles of depression and

---

* *Trans. N. Engl. Inst. M.E.*, vol. xxvii., p. 3.

elevation are taken along the line of section, the instrument being sighted to a staff with a vane or a cross-piece fixed to it at exactly the same height from the ground as the centre of the axis of the telescope is. The staff must be held vertically while the observer measures the vertical angle which the line of sight makes with the horizon. The instrument and staff are then made to change places, and the vertical angle determined. The mean of the two readings is taken as the correct result. The distance must then be measured. As the distance is the hypothenuse of a right-angled triangle of which the perpendicular is the difference of level, the latter is obtained by multiplying the measured distance by the sine of the angle observed.

The following is an example of the field record:—

LEVELLING BY VERTICAL ANGLES WITH THE THEODOLITE—1.

From	To	Inclined lengths in feet.	Vertical angles.	Rise.	Fall.	Height above datum 50·00.	Horizontal lengths.	Total distances.
2	1	471·0	7° 21′ R	60·24	...	110·24	467·09	467·09
2	3	192·5	3° 11′ R	10·68	...	120·92	192·19	659·28
4	3	313·5	5° 15′ F	...	28·68	92·24	312·18	971·46
4	5	340·0	1° 47′ F	...	10·57	81·67	339·83	1311·29
6	5	368·0	2° 18′ F	...	14·75	66·92	367·66	1678·95
...	...	...	...	70·92	54·00	− 50·00	...	...
...	...	...	...	...	16·92	16·92	...	...

When the line to be levelled is marked out on the ground by stakes set at a horizontal distance apart of 100 feet, the height will be found by multiplying the horizontal distance by the tangent of the angle of inclination. The form of record in this case will be seen on next page.

In this section, in six stations a height of 145 feet has been ascended in equal distances of 100 feet. With a spirit-level and a 12-foot staff, the number of stations would have been doubled. In order to simplify the calculations with this method of levelling, Mr. A. Faul, of Baltimore, has computed a table of

LEVELLING BY VERTICAL ANGLES WITH THE THEODOLITE—2.

From	To	Horizontal Lengths measured in feet.	Vertical Angles.	Rise.	Fall.	Height above Datum 100·00.	Remarks.
1	0	100	9° 45′ R	17·18	...	117·18	
1	2	100	7° 15′ R	12·72	...	129·90	
3	2	100	9° 30′ R	16·73	...	146·63	
3	4	100	10° 15′ R	18·08	...	164·71	
5	4	100	3° 30′ F	...	6·12	158·59	
5	6	100	8° 45′ R	15·39	...	173·98	
7	6	100	8° 30′ R	14·95	...	188·93	
7	8	100	10° 00′ R	17·63	...	206·56	
9	8	100	11° 15′ R	19·89	...	226·45	
9	10	100	12° 30′ R	22·17	...	248·62	
11	10	100	1° 45′ F	...	3·06	245·56	
...	...	...	...	154·74	9·18	− 100·00	
...	...	...	...	...	145·56	145·56	

heights* for all angles from 0° to 22¼°, in minutes, for any distance required. His object is to bring levelling by vertical angles into more general use, and save the many stations required in spirit-levelling. The latter method is very tedious in hilly countries where extreme accuracy is immaterial, especially so in all preliminary surveys. The method of levelling by vertical angles gives approximate results in the shortest possible time.

Levelling may be performed by the theodolite by setting up the instrument at the foot of a steep incline, with the line of

* *A Short Treatise on Levelling by Vertical Angles with Tables of Heights.* New York, 1886.

collimation set at a known angle of inclination. Sights are then taken, as if with a spirit-level. Thus, suppose that the theodolite is placed at A, Fig. 65, and that $b\,A\,C$ represents the inclined line of sight. Then B b, C c, and the other vertical lines will represent the heights read off the staff. The requisite data for drawing the section are thus obtained. This method saves time in taking the levels of steeply inclined ground.

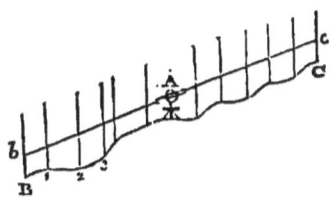

Fig. 65.

When a proper levelling-instrument is not available, the line of collimation may be placed horizontal, and the theodolite used in the same way as the spirit-level.

The Clinometer.—For exploratory work, where great accuracy is not required, the clinometer is of great value, on account of its portability. It resembles a jointed foot-rule, with an inlaid spirit-level and sights on one arm, and a divided arc at the hinge to indicate the angular degree of opening. It is set level on a stand, and the hinge is opened until the object is seen through the sights. The angle of inclination is then read.

Fig. 65A.

The best instruments of this kind are provided with a 2-inch

LEVELLING.

compass attached on pivots to the lower arm. The clinometer should have a spirit-level attached to each arm, and folding sights, and should screw on to a portable tripod, provided with a ball-and-socket joint. In this form, the instrument is practically a miner's dial, on account of its portability well adapted for prospecting purposes.

In the clinometer, manufactured by Messrs. J. Davis & Son, several improvements have been introduced by Mr. H. Louis.

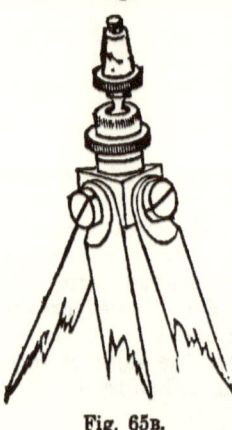

Fig. 65B.

The compass pivots are carried on a brass arc capable of revolving in the lower portion of the clinometer frame, so that the compass can be placed horizontally and read without regard to the position of the lower limb. In this way, the dip and strike of strata may be read simultaneously. The compass, too, may be reversed so that the same end of the needle may be used for all dial readings in running lines up and down hill. A further improvement consists in mounting the spirit-level of the lower limb on a swivel, so that the instrument may be levelled both ways without being reversed. The clinometer (Fig. 65A) is $6\frac{1}{4}$ inches in length, $\frac{1}{2}$ inch in width, and 3 inches in depth. It weighs 1 lb. 2 oz., and is mounted on a tripod (Fig. 65B), which is provided with a ball-and-socket joint, and which is 3 feet 10 inches in length and 1 lb. 8 oz. in weight.

Physical Levelling.—The application of the barometer to the measurement of heights is based on the fact that for a constant temperature, the density of the air is proportional to the pressure which it sustains. Since the atmospheric pressure decreases as we ascend, it is obvious that the barometer will keep on falling as it is taken to a greater and greater height.

The *mountain barometer* is an ordinary barometer tube, made as portable as possible, and protected against external injury. When in use, it is mounted on a portable tripod, and when not in use, it is packed in a leather case. The mercury is contained in a wooden cistern at the lower part of the instrument. A screw compresses the mercury and forces it, when required, up to the upper portion of the graduated tube. By means of a vernier, the height of the column of mercury may be read to the one-thousandth part of an inch. Attached to the barometer is a thermometer, enabling a correction to be made for temperature. This correction is necessary because the air and the mercury are unequally expanded by heat.

The simplest barometric rule is as follows:—Observe the height of the barometer in inches at two stations. Then, as the sum of the two readings is to their difference, so is 55,000 to the difference between the height of the stations stated in feet.

For example.—What is the difference in level between two points at which the barometers read 30·014 inches, and 29·870 inches respectively ? The thermometers read the same at both stations.

$$\text{Difference in level} = 55,000 \times \frac{0\cdot 144}{59\cdot 884} = 132\cdot 3 \text{ feet.}$$

To correct for temperature, add $\frac{1}{440}$ of the result for each degree, that the mean temperature of the air at the two stations exceeds 55°. Subtract the same amount if the mean temperature is below 55°. When the upper thermometer reads higher than the lower, $\frac{1}{440}$ of the result must be subtracted when the mean temperature of the air exceeds 55°, and added when it is below 55°.

On the United States Geological Survey, a simple and direct method of hypsometry is in use. In this method, proposed by Mr. G. K. Gilbert,[*] three barometers are used instead of two. Two of these are placed at points whose heights are known, the third being read at the point to be determined. From the reading of the two barometers at the points of known height, the weight of the intervening air column is deduced, and, both the weight and height of the column being known, its density is computable. The density thus derived is then used in the computation of the height of a second column of air between one of the known points and the point to be determined.

Levelling by the barometer may be occasionally used for taking flying levels in exploring a district. An approximation, however, is all that can be obtained, even if the most elaborate formulæ are employed. The mountain barometer is a cumbrous instrument. It must be more than 30 inches long, exclusive of the cistern, and the mercury is always troublesome to transport.

On account of these disadvantages, for engineering purposes the mercurial barometer has been to a great extent replaced by the *aneroid barometer* invented by Vidi, and patented in Great Britain in 1844. It consists of a circular box, the face of which

---

[*] *Second Annual Report of the U.S. Geol. Surv.*, 1882, p. 405. In this valuable monograph all the principal methods that have hitherto been employed are fully described.

is made of thin metal, rendered more elastic by being stamped into concentric circular wave-like corrugations. The box is nearly exhausted of air, and its elastic face supports the pressure of the atmosphere, yielding to it with elastic resistance in proportion to the amount of pressure. The movement is communicated to an index, and registered upon the dial. Aneroid barometers are made of pocket-size, carefully compensated so as not to be affected by changes of temperature, and with double scales, one a barometrical scale of inches, the other a scale of altitudes; that is to say, a scale of differences of altitudes for one given pressure.

When specially constructed for mining use, the instrument is graduated to represent 6 inches of the mercurial column, from 27 inches to 33 inches. This scale enables observations to be made from 2,000 feet below sea-level to 4,000 feet above. The finest divisions of the altitude scale represent 10 feet measurement, which can be divided by a vernier, moved by rackwork adjustment, to single feet. A lens, which rotates on the outer circumference, enables the vernier to be read with facility. The instrument is $4\frac{1}{2}$ inches in diameter, and is provided with a leather sling case. In order to retain the sensitiveness of action of the aneroid, it should be cleaned and adjusted every two or three years by an instrument-maker.

The principle that the boiling-point of water varies with the atmospheric pressure is sometimes applied for the measurement of heights. The instrument used for this purpose, the *hypsometer*, consists of a thermometer, surrounded by a double-telescopic chamber, and suspended so that its bulb is above the surface of some water in a metal boiler, heated by a spirit-lamp. It is thus enveloped in steam when the water boils. This cheap and portable instrument for measuring heights is to be preferred, for its simplicity and certainty, to the mountain barometer. Tables are published by the maker, Mr. L. Casella, of London, giving instructions for using the hypsometer.

Determination of the Depths of Shafts.—In connection with levelling operations underground, it is frequently necessary to measure the depths of shafts. For this purpose, a wire with weights at the end, or the winding-rope with the cage or the kibble, is let down, and the length of the wire or rope measured by means of rods. Or the depth of the shaft may be measured direct by applying rods, chains, or steel bands to the timbering of the shaft. Good results have been obtained by both methods. It is, however, evident that the direct measurement is more trustworthy, though more difficult and tedious, than the indirect method. The measurement must be so contrived that the starting- and end-points can be easily connected with the surface and underground levellings.

The measurement by means of a wire is usually effected by changing the vertical into horizontal measurement in the following manner:—From a small windlass (Fig. 66) erected at a suitable distance from the shaft, the steel wire (piano wire) is unwound, and passed over a pulley, which is placed over the mouth of the shaft in such a way that the wire weighted with 10 to 30 lbs. can without hindrance sink to the bottom of the shaft. The starting- and end-points are distinguished by threads tied on. The depth is measured on letting down and hauling up the wire, and is done most conveniently with the horizontal portion between the pulley and the windlass. The wire is kept in sufficient tension by the weight. The elongation of the wire, caused by its own weight and the attached weight, does not interfere with the accuracy of the result, as the wire is measured in its stretched condition. The method is very rapid; at Firminy, near St. Etienne, a depth of 280 yards has been measured in half an hour.

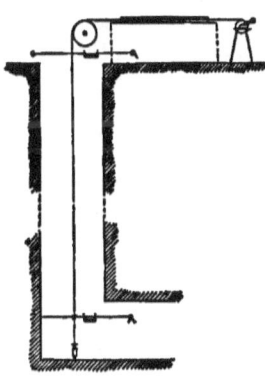

Fig. 66.

Experiments made at Firminy show that the error with this method does not exceed one-fifth of an inch per hundred yards of depth. Accurate results have also been obtained at Schemnitz, in Hungary, by Professor Chrismár, who measured in an hour a depth of 210 yards accurately to within $\frac{1}{4500}$ of the measured length.

Local conditions may render it necessary to apply the measure to the vertical part of the wire, in which case the operation is somewhat more inconvenient, but in other respects similar to the preceding.

Instead of the wire, the winding-rope may be used. In this case, the measure is applied to the rope direct above the mouth of the shaft. The results thus obtained are very similar to those obtained with the wire. Thus, Borchers measured one and the same shaft once with the wire and once with the winding-rope; the results being 129 fathoms 3 feet $3\frac{1}{2}$ inches and 129 fathoms 3 feet 3·54 inches respectively.

For the direct measurement of shafts, iron surveying-chains, steel bands, or specially constructed measuring-rods are employed.

The chain employed for measuring the depths of shafts must

first be carefully tested. It is then let down the shaft at a suitable point, and suspended by the upper handle to a nail. A second nail is driven within the lower handle, and touching it. The chain is then removed, the lower handle being hung to the second nail, and the process repeated as before. The depth thus obtained must be diminished by the thickness of the nails included in the measurement. It is therefore desirable to employ round nails of uniform diameter. The chain, of course, must be allowed to hang perpendicularly, and all obstacles, such as platforms, in the shaft must be removed or bored through. Sometimes it is impossible to measure the shaft in one straight line; a suitable point must then be found in a line at right angles to the chain, and the measurement continued.

With the steel band, shafts are measured in a similar manner. This method has been employed with success by Mr. Graefe[*] in the Stassfurt salt-mines for measuring shafts of considerable depth. For this purpose, at a measured distance above the roof of the cage, a seat is fastened to the winding-rope in such a way that a miner can sit in it without danger, and apply the upper end of the steel band to the guides. The mine-surveyor stands on the roof of the cage, and carries the lower end of the band. Beside him stands a second workman, whose duty it is to give the signal for raising or lowering the cage. In this way, after all the preparations had been made, the Leopoldshall shaft was measured three times in six hours with the following results:—

First measurement,	.	.	.	1,095 feet 5·80 inches.
Second ,,			.	1,095 ,, 5·84 ,,
Third ,,			.	1,095 ,, 5·84 ,,

In this case, the heights of 8 levels entering the shaft had also to be determined.

In almost as short a time the Von der Heydt shaft, at Stassfurt, was measured four times; the heights of 7 levels entering the shaft being determined at the same time. The results were—

First measurement,	.	.	.	1,152 feet 2·15 inches.
Second ,,			.	1,152 ,, 2·07 ,,
Third ,,			.	1,152 ,, 2·23 ,,
Fourth ,,			.	1,152 ,, 2·11 ,,

The most accurate means of measuring the depths of shafts is afforded by the measuring-rods constructed for this purpose by Borchers, which are frequently employed in the continental mines. The rods consist of a number of round steel bars 0·16 to 0·24 inch in diameter, and 1 to 4 yards in length. The ends are

[*] Berg. H. Ztg., vol. xlii., 1883, p. 4.

screwed, and may be connected by brass double screws, so that a measuring-rod of any required length may be constructed. The true end surfaces of the separate rods must be exactly at right angles to the longitudinal axis, and the brass caps are provided with an opening on both sides, so that the contact of the end planes of two rods can be seen. The first rod is provided with a hook, from the inner surface of which the counting commences. On using these rods, the influence of temperature has to be taken into account.

The measurement of the depths of inclined shafts presents the greatest difficulties. In such shafts, Fig. 67, a plumb-line is used, the points of suspension being found by means of a spirit-level.

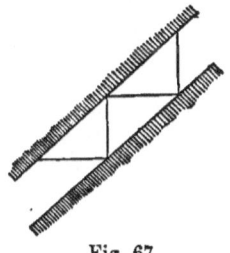

Fig. 67.

Such shafts are frequently tortuous in inclination and in direction, in which case they must be surveyed in the same way as levels, the vertical arc of the dial being employed in conjunction with a plumb-line. It is an operation of great difficulty, and one which in former times has given rise to serious errors in the surveys of the mines of Cornwall, Derbyshire, and the Harz.

In surveying and levelling in the shafts of the Lehigh Valley Coal Company, in the United States, a new form of plummet has recently been adopted. It consists of a vertical core 12 inches long, with eight radiating flanges 9 inches high by 3 inches wide of $\frac{1}{4}$-inch metal. At the bottom there is a circular disc acting as a web. This plumb-bob weighs 20 lbs., and has a surface area of about 630 square inches. An ordinary bob of equal weight would have a surface of 90 square inches. In a dry shaft, 500 feet deep, this form of plumb-bob will settle, under ordinary conditions, in about one hour instead of in five or six hours, as is the case with the older form.

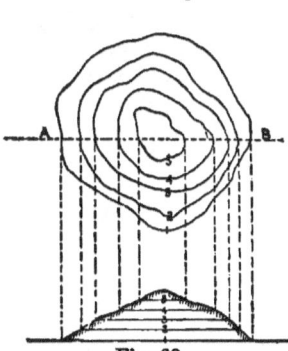

Fig. 68.

Contour Lines on the earth's surface are lines traversing all the points on the ground which are at a given constant height above the datum level. A contour line may also be described as a horizontal section of the earth's surface, or as the line where the earth's surface is cut by a given horizontal surface, or as the outline of an imaginary sheet of water covering the ground up to a certain height. Fig. 68 represents the contours of a hill.

Tracing contour lines consists in determining equidistant series of points satisfying these conditions. The vertical distance between successive contour lines on a plan depends on the figure of the ground, and on the scale of the plan. Two methods of tracing contour lines are employed—(1) The regular method, consisting in tracing the lines on the ground, and then surveying them; (2) the irregular method, which consists in collecting, on the ground, data to enable the lines to be constructed on the plan.

On the Ordnance maps of Great Britain, on the scale of 6 inches to the mile, contour lines are drawn at each 25 feet of height, with principal contour lines, determined with greater precision, at every 50 feet in the flatter parts of the country, and at every 100 feet in the hilly parts.

Mr. W. F. Howard advocates that colliery plans should exhibit contour lines at regular and frequent intervals. In this way the vertical throw of each fault, excluding the mere bending up or down of the adjacent strata, which has often a tendency to mislead, would be continuously shown though the fault should be rarely penetrated. Contour lines are generally shown on the plans of the anthracite mines of Pennsylvania.

Applications of Levelling.—A branch of engineering, in which the application of levelling is of great importance, is the setting out of aerial wire ropeways. The importance of this mode of transport in the development of mineral resources is known to every mining engineer. As a case in point, the rich iron ores of the Sierra de Bedar, in southern Spain, would probably have remained untouched to this day but for an aerial wire ropeway, $9\frac{3}{4}$ miles in length, which connects the mines with the shore of the Mediterranean, near the town of Garrucha, and which affords cheap transport to the point of shipment. An ordinary railway would have cost £100,000, whilst an aerial ropeway could be built for about one-quarter of that sum, an outlay which left a satisfactory margin for profits on the sale of ore.

In the older systems of ropeways, one endless rope is employed, serving both as carrying rope and hauling rope for the buckets. Many examples of lines of this class can be seen in the Bilbao iron ore district. The characteristic of the modern or Otto system consists in the employment of two ropes—a heavy fixed carrying rope and a light travelling hauling rope, the buckets being fitted with special devices for gripping the latter. With ropeways of this class loads of 20 cwt. can be carried, so that as much as 800 tons may be transported in a day of ten hours.

The most important Otto ropeway yet constructed is that for the transport of iron ore at Garrucha. The line is divided into four independent sections, the two first being driven by a 30 horse-power engine, and the two last by a 70 horse-power engine. The greatest span of the line is 918 feet, the height above the valley being 164 to 196 feet. The steepest gradient is 1 in $2\frac{1}{2}$, and the tallest standard is 118 feet. The guaranteed capacity of the line is 400 tons per day of ten hours. Since the commencement of 1890, the line has been worked in two shifts of eight hours, and no less than 900 tons per day have been transported to the coast. Despite many difficulties, the line was surveyed, erected, and ready for work within ten months.

Another important Otto wire ropeway is that constructed for the Sheba gold mine in the Transvaal. This is $2\frac{3}{4}$ miles in length, and has a capacity of 150 tons per day of ten hours. The maximum incline is 1 in 1·6, and the greatest span 1,480 feet.

In making the preliminary survey for an Otto wire ropeway, there are several points to which attention should be paid. The terminal points of the line should, whenever possible, be so placed that the ropeway joining them shall be in a straight line, as each turn increases not only the amount of construction necessary, but also the cost of working, as it necessitates the erection of a complete station. For lines of more than $3\frac{1}{2}$ miles in length, one or more intermediate stations must be erected, as greater lengths than this cannot be worked with one hauling rope. At the stations the line can form any desired angle. The points selected for the supports for the bearing-rope should be marked on the ground by wooden pegs distinctly numbered, and should be shown in the section drawn. The supports should be 50 yards apart, when 50 to 100 tons are transported in 10 hours, 40 yards apart for 100 to 600 tons, and 35 yards apart for amounts above 600 tons in 10 hours. This rule may be neglected in crossing roads, in which case one support should be at the side of the road, and it may be neglected when this rule would necessitate the support being placed in a narrow valley or hollow, in which case, in order to avoid unnecessary height, the post may be moved. For crossing valleys and rivers, spans of 350 yards may exceptionally be employed, when supports are impossible or would exceed 35 yards in height. In crossing roads, cross-sections must be made in order to give the requisite data for the erection of a protecting bridge, and cross-sections must be taken at every point selected for a station.

Marshy sites must be avoided as far as possible; but in cases where this is out of the question, the surveyor must determine the depth to the solid ground.

The hydraulic mining ditches of California afford some interesting examples of levelling successfully conducted in the face of great difficulties. Hydraulic mining consists in the disintegration of auriferous gravel deposits by propelling a heavy jet of water under pressure upon the bank, and in washing off the gravel in sluices in which mercury is distributed. The gold forms an amalgam, and remains caught. This method of mining was introduced in California in 1856, although Pliny describes a system of hydraulic mining in Spain, which resembled in many respects the modern method. Hydraulic mining has given rise to an extensive system of artificial reservoirs in the Sierra Nevada for the storage of water, and to the construction of artificial water-courses to convey the water thus stored to the scene of mining operations. The setting out of these canals at a grade of from 4 to 20 feet per mile, over deep gorges and along precipitous cliffs, presents problems of great difficulty to the mine surveyor. In many places it is impossible to find room along the sides of the great cañons for miles, to excavate a canal or to rest a conduit or "flume," as it is locally termed. The bracket flume of the Miocene mine is a marvellous example of engineering skill. Here, in order to obviate the erection of a trestle 180 feet in height, the water is conveyed in a wooden flume—4 feet wide and 3 feet deep—round a cliff 350 feet in height. The flume is suspended upon brackets made of T-rails, fixed into holes previously drilled in the vertical cliff. In another place, in the line of this ditch, is a piece of breastwork 1,088 feet long and 80 feet high. Again, the Blue Tent Mine has a ditch running for a distance of six miles along the face of a cliff, over which the surveyors had to be suspended by ropes 1,000 feet above the bottom of the gorge, in order to establish the line of the flume.

In other places deep gorges are crossed by means of inverted siphons. The Cherokee ditch crosses a deep cañon in this way, the pipe sustaining a columnar pressure equal to 800 feet in perpendicular height. In making the crossing, 12,000 feet of 38-inch pipes, $\frac{3}{8}$-inch in thickness, were used. A few years ago there were in California 6,000 miles of mining ditches, their estimated total cost being £3,000,000. Some of them have been built at a cost of £5,000 per mile. The cost, too, of keeping them in repair is very considerable, as the hydraulic miner has constantly to contend with the elements—frost and flood, ice and snow, wind and rain.

In the preliminary survey, to determine the best situation for a long ditch, comparative observations should be made with aneroid barometers, care being taken to determine the elevations, not only of the end points, but also of intermediate points, from which different surveying parties can start on the subsequent setting out of the line. The necessary points being established, the line is staked out, all stations being properly numbered and pegs driven in to indicate the gradient. According to Mr. Bowie, the author of the standard work on this subject, stations may be from 50 to 100 feet apart on ordinary ground; but very irregular country obviously demands shorter intervals. Bench-marks should be placed every $\frac{1}{4}$ or $\frac{1}{2}$ mile for convenient reference. All details of tunnels, cuttings, and depressions, which require pipes or flumes, should be worked out in full, a work in which the hand-level can often be advantageously employed. Complete notes should be made of the character of the ground along the whole line.

In laying out mining ditches in California it is usual to employ a light frame shaped like the letter A, made of $\frac{1}{2}$ by $1\frac{1}{2}$ inch wood, and provided with a heavy plummet hanging on a fine wire from a notch at the apex. The height of the frame is usually 6 feet, and the base 10 feet. To commence, one end is placed on a level piece of ground, and the other end is raised or lowered until both ends are level, and the plumb-line marks the same position on the cross-bar, if turned completely round. The grade for the proposed mining ditch being decided upon, say $\frac{1}{2}$ inch in 10 feet, a $\frac{1}{2}$ inch piece of wood is placed under the rear end of the frame, and the point indicated by the plumb-line is marked on the cross-piece. One man then holds the frame, while another lifts the front end until the plummet coincides with the mark, he then drives in a peg in front. The rear end of the frame is then placed exactly where the front end was, and the process is repeated. In this way the ditch can be set out with great rapidity. The only danger lies in getting the wrong end foremost.

On the survey of the Manmad-Dhuha Railway in India, F. R. Johnson (*Min. Proc. Inst. C.E.*, vol. cxv., 1894, p. 343) found that theodolite levelling by angles of inclination proved accurate under very unfavourable conditions, and he is convinced that the theodolite is the best instrument for rapidly exploring rough ground, and for taking a section by angles of inclination. This method gives all the information required in the shortest possible time.

CHAPTER XIV.

CONNECTION OF THE UNDERGROUND- AND SURFACE-SURVEYS.

Methods Employed.—A correct survey of the underground workings of a mine, and of the surface or royalty having been made, it is necessary to determine accurately the bearing of a line underground with a view to connect the two surveys. For this purpose the following methods have been employed :—
(1) By means of an adit-level or inclined shaft; (2) by means of two shafts; (3) by means of one shaft with two suspended plumb-lines; (4) by means of the transit-instrument; (5) by means of the transit-theodolite; (6) by means of the magnetic-needle.

1. **By Means of an Adit-level.**—When the mine is connected with the surface by means of an adit-level, the connection of the surveys is easily effected by continuing the underground traverse through the adit-level to the nearest side of the triangle of the surface-survey.

2. **By Means of two Shafts.**—If both the shafts are vertical, the connection of the underground- and surface-surveys is made by means of two plumb-lines, one suspended in each shaft. The points of suspension are joined to the surface-triangulation by means of careful measurements. In this way the length and bearing of the line joining the two plumb-lines may be calculated by means of rectangular co-ordinates. A traverse is then made underground from one plumb-line to the other, and from the data thus obtained the length and bearing of the line joining the two plumb-lines is again calculated by means of co-ordinates.

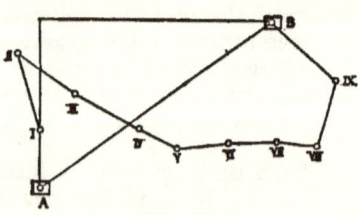

Fig. 69.

Example.—In two perpendicular shafts, plumb-lines are hung at the points A and B (Fig. 69). From the surface-triangulation it is found that the length of the line A B is 56·29 chains, and its bearing 118° 36′. In the mine, a traverse was made with the following results:—

MINE-SURVEYING.

From	To	Length, Chains.	Measured Angles.	Angles Reduced to one Meridian.	LATITUDE.		DEPARTURE.	
					N.	S.	E.	W.
A.	I.	1·76	0° 00′	0° 00′	1·76	...	...	...
I.	II.	4·24	177° 33′	357° 33′	4·23	...	...	0·18
II.	III.	13·00	284° 57′	102° 30′	...	2·81	12·69	...
III.	IV.	16·75	177° 56′	100° 26′	...	3·03	16·47	...
IV.	V.	9·30	180° 52′	101° 18′	...	1·82	9·11	...
V.	VI.	8·28	158° 33′	79° 51′	1·45	...	8·15	...
VI.	VII.	3·74	184° 53′	84° 44′	0·34	...	3·72	...
VII.	VIII.	6·32	184° 26′	89° 10′	0·09	...	6·31	...
VIII.	IX.	6·12	93° 53′	3° 03′	6·11	...	0·32	...
IX.	B.	1·18	135° 11′	318° 14′	0·88	...	...	0·78
...	...	...	...	...	14·86	7·66	56·77	0·96
...	...	...	...	...	7·66	...	0·96	...
...	...	...	...	...	7·20	...	55·81	...

With the co-ordinates 7·20 chains N., and 55·81 chains E., the length and direction of the hypothenuse may be calculated from the formula: base^2 + perpendicular^2 = hypothenuse^2, or tangent of angle of bearing = $\dfrac{\text{departure}}{\text{latitude}}$, and the distance = latitude × secant of angle of bearing. The hypothenuse in the above traverse will then be found as follows:—

$$
\begin{aligned}
\log 55\cdot 81 &= 1\cdot 7467120 \\
\log 7\cdot 20 &= 0\cdot 8573325 \\
\hline
L.\tan BAC &= 10\cdot 8893795 \quad BAC = 82° 39′ \\
\log 7\cdot 20 &= 0\cdot 8573325 \\
L.\sec 82° 39′ &= 10\cdot 8930271 \\
\hline
& 11\cdot 7503596 \quad \text{distance} = 56\cdot 28 \text{ chains}
\end{aligned}
$$

From this angle—that is, the angle formed by the hypothenuse A B and the first line of the underground-survey A I, and from the bearing of the line A B determined at the surface (118° 36'), the bearing of the first station-line underground may be determined. In the above example, this is done by subtraction, 118° 36' − 82° 38' = 35° 58'. From this may be deduced the bearing of the other lines of the traverse. In the example, this is done by increasing the reduced meridian angles by 35° 58' in each case. With the aid of these bearings, the co-ordinates of the underground-traverse should be recalculated, and the results balanced.

For suspending the plummet, a thin wire of iron or brass is used. Hemp cords are useless for the purpose; because of their torsion and contracting when wet. They present a greater surface to the action of air-currents and water than thin wire, and do not admit of such precise sighting. The plummet weighs 5 to 8 lbs. It should not be hung on when the wire is let down the shaft in case of accident from the wire breaking. A smaller weight may be used when the wire is being let down, and at the bottom of the shaft it can easily be changed for the required weight. The plumb-line must, of course, hang perfectly free, without coming in contact with the sides of the shaft. To ensure this being the case, a lamp is slowly passed round the wire at the bottom of the shaft. If, in whatever position it is placed, the light can be seen from the top, the wire is clear.

The plumb-lines may be sighted without any difficulty in the surface-survey, as the upper part of each wire does not move. In the mine, however, the plumb-line has to be sighted at its lower end, which continues to vibrate like a pendulum. The motion may be reduced by allowing the plummet to dip into a bucket of water, and by shielding the wire from air-currents and falling water as far as possible. It is, however, impossible to stop the vibrations altogether.

To lessen the motion of the plumb-lines, Mr. H. D. Hoskold proposes the adoption of iron chains made from wire three-sixteenths of an inch in diameter. The method would, however, be inapplicable in a shaft of considerable depth.

In sighting a plumb-line with the theodolite, it is best to follow it by means of the tangent-screw to the end of its vibration. There is then sufficient time to read the vernier before it reaches the other end of its course, as well as to intersect it in that position with the cross-wires. This operation is repeated several times, and the mean taken of all the results. When the arc is very small, the mean may be estimated, and the cross-wires set at that angle direct. The plumb-lines are rendered visible by holding behind them a sheet of oiled paper illuminated by a lamp from behind. This method of sighting a plumb-line is very fatiguing, and necessitates great skill to read the vernier and direct the telescope to the next extremity of the course, in the comparatively short time in which the plummet completes its swing.

These difficulties have been overcome by Professor Schmidt,* of the Freiberg School of Mines. The plummets he uses are hung to thick wire (0·04 inch in diameter), and their weight is considerable, being as much as 50 lbs. They do not dip into water, but are allowed to swing freely. At a short distance above the bottom of the shaft, a horizontal finely-divided scale is placed perpendicular to the line of sight of the telescope. The swinging plumb-line is then observed with the telescope, and the successive extreme positions are read and noted, the plumb-line being purposely made to swing parallel to the plane of the scale. The latter is illuminated by means of an ordinary miner's lamp or candle.

From one or more series of double observations, the mean position of rest of the plummet on the scale is calculated, and for the subsequent survey the cross-wires of the telescope are made to coincide with that calculated point. The calculation of the position of rest is a very exact one. From two trials, one made at a depth of 557 feet under favourable conditions, the other at a depth of 1,722 feet under unfavourable conditions, Professor Schmidt found that the mean error of one series of observations was ± 0·12 inch, and the mean error of the result of a double series was ± 0·08 inch. Under unfavourable conditions the errors were 0·17 inch and 0·12 inch respectively.

In cases where it is required to connect the surface-survey with the underground survey at several levels at different heights in the shaft, it is desirable to fix the plumb-line. For this purpose, Professor Schmidt† has invented a simple centering apparatus. On a perforated cast-iron plate, a prismatic centre-piece may be slid in two directions at right angles to one another by means of four centering screws. Above the latter are two scales at right angles. The iron plate is placed so that one pair of centering screws is in the line of sight of the theodolite-telescope, the other pair being in the line of sight of a second small telescope of low power. With this small telescope and with that of the theodolite, the swingings of the plumb-line are observed, and the position of rest calculated. The weight is then removed

---

* *Saechs. Jahrbuch.*, 1882, p. 145.
† *Berg. H. Ztg.*, vol. xliii., 1884, p. 217.

from the plumb-line, and a cap-screw placed on the wire. The weight is then replaced, and screwed into the centre-piece of the apparatus. With the aid of the two telescopes, and the centering screws, the centre-piece can be brought into such a position that the plumb-line is in its calculated position of rest.

If either of the shafts used for connecting the underground- and surface-surveys, is inclined, or if both are, the method is the same, except that the shaft is surveyed by traversing instead of by suspending a plumb-line.

3. By Means of one Shaft.—When there is only one perpendicular shaft, the underground- and surface-surveys may be connected by transferring a short line from the surface to the mine by means of two plumb-lines suspended in the shaft. The bearing and length of this short line may be determined with sufficient accuracy by connecting it with the surface-triangulation. Then, if the underground-survey also includes the line formed at the bottom of the shaft by the two plumb-lines hanging vertically, the connection can be made from the known bearing of that line. Thus, the survey is made at the surface and in the mine in the same way, by constructing a triangle of which the line joining the plumb-lines is a side.

The following details of the connection of the underground- and surface-surveys effected in this way may serve as an example:—Fig. 70 is a plan of a portion of a mine, in which D G represents a line at the surface, connected with the triangulation, and E F a line of the traverse of the 135-fathom level of the mine. In order to connect these two lines, two plumb-lines A and B were suspended in the perpendicular shaft, as far apart as circumstances would allow. The distance in this case was 0·9315 fathom. The two wires were sighted from the point G in the doorway of the mine-house, and the angles B G D and A G D and the distances G B and G A accurately measured. The triangle G A B was in this way completely solved, and the position of the line A B formed by the two plumb-lines was determined with reference to G D. The theodolite was then set up at C in the cross-cut at the 135-fathom level, and with it were carefully measured the angles B C A = 32° 08′, A C E = 159° 21′, and C E F = 269° 31′ 33″, and the horizontal distances C B = 1·6373,

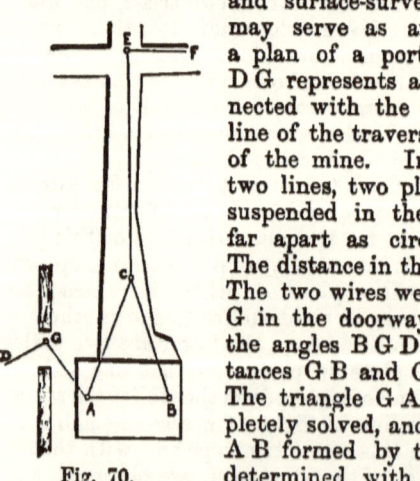

Fig. 70.

C A = 1·7169, and C E = 15·6563 fathoms. Since in the triangle C B A the three sides were determined, it was unnecessary to measure the angle B C A. This was, however, done as a check. On calculation, the angle B C A was found to be 32° 8′ 10″, C A B = 69° 13′ 15″, and C B A = 78° 38′ 37″. Of the measured and calculated values of the angle B C A, the mean 32° 8′ 5″ was taken. The two other angles of the triangle C A B were balanced so as to make the sum of the three angles equal to 180°. In this way the point G at the surface and the point E in the mine are connected by known horizontal distances. The angle which the line D G at the surface makes with the line E F in the mine may then be easily determined.

The line D G being taken as the meridian, the line A B was found from the surface-survey to form an angle of 23° 12′ 10″ with that meridian. Underground the angles formed by the meridian and the various lines were—

$$A C \quad 69° 13′ 15″ - 23° 12′ 10″ = 46° 01′ 05″$$
$$C E \quad 159° 21′ 00″ - 46° 01′ 05″ = 113° 19′ 55″$$
$$E F \quad 113° 19′ 55″ - 90° 28′ 27″ = 22° 51′ 28″$$

In some cases the theodolite may be set up and centred at the points A and B at the surface, but underground this cannot be done with sufficient accuracy.

The accuracy of the connection depends on the correct determination of the angles A and B in the triangle A B C. These angles usually have to be calculated from the known length A B and from the sides A C and C B measured underground, as well as from the angle C. This may be done by the ordinary sine rule—

$$\text{Sin A} = \frac{a \sin C}{c}, \quad \sin B = \frac{b \sin C}{c}.$$

In this formula, sin A is dependent upon the three magnitudes C, c, and a. The length c and the angle C may be measured underground with great accuracy, if Schmidt's method is employed.

The influence of an error in the length a on the angle A varies considerably according to the form of the triangle. It is great when the sides a and b are of equal length—that is, when the triangle A B C is an isosceles one. It is least when the triangle has a very acute-angled form. The sines of angles near 0° and 180° do not increase or decrease in proportion to a slight increase or decrease of the angle. Conversely a small change in the sine has an inappreciable influence on the corresponding angle. Consequently a small error in the length a has no effect on the determination of the angle A, when the triangle is an acute-angled one. If possible, then, the ordinary well-conditioned triangle must in this case be avoided, and the theodolite placed as nearly as possible in the continuation of the base-line.

By means of two plumb-lines, the connection between the underground- and surface-surveys has been effected with considerable success by Mr. E. Clark* in the brown hæmatite mines belonging to the Glendon Iron Co. of Pennsylvania. The shafts are usually 4 feet square, but, where an extensive plant of pumping machinery is required, the size is increased to 8 feet by 6 feet. The depth of the shafts varies from 75 to 200 feet. The principal difficulty in the survey of these mines has always been the trouble experienced in connecting the underground-survey with the surface-survey, on account of the small size of the shafts, and the gradual movement of the ground pushing the shaft out of the perpendicular.

The method adopted by Mr. Clark has been to establish a line at the surface, and, by means of a straight-edge, wire, and plumb-bob, to project that line to the bottom of the shaft, and there use it as a base-line for the underground-survey. The line across the shaft is marked in the timbers by nails, which may be permanent and used in future surveys, if the earth about the shaft is sufficiently firm. A straight-edge is placed against the nails, and the assistant above lowers the plumb-bob by means of a reel and annealed-iron wire of sufficient strength to hold the plumb-bob, which is of cast-iron, and weighs 10 lbs. The two plumb-bobs are each received into a bucket filled with water at the bottom of the shaft. Vibration may be lessened by mud thrown into the bucket. When the plummets have become nearly stationary, a theodolite is set up in line with the wires. This is done by moving the instrument until the nearer wire coincides with the vertical hair, and the second wire is concealed by the first; or the transit will be in line when the extent of the vibration of the second wire to one side of the first is equal to the extent of the vibration to the other side. The greater the distance between the wires, and the farther the theodolite is from them, the more accurately can it be placed in line. The average distance in 15 shafts surveyed in this way was 18 to 6 inches, this distance being the base-line upon which the mine-survey was based. In the coal-mines of Pennsylvania very good results have been obtained by this method, with a base-line of 9 feet in length.

* *Trans. Amer. Inst. M.E.*, vol. vii., 1879, p. 139.

4. By Means of a Transit-instrument.—The most accurate method of effecting the connection between the underground- and surface-surveys is by means of the transit-instrument.

The transit-instrument is the standard instrument in every astronomical observatory. It consists of a telescope formed of two parts connected by a spherical centre-piece, into which are fitted the larger ends of two cones, the common axis of which is placed at right angles to the axis of the telescope, to serve as the horizontal axis of the instrument. The two small ends of the cones are ground into two equal cylinders or pivots, which rest upon angular bearings or Y's, supported upon standards. One of the pivots is pierced, and allows the light from a lamp to fall upon a plane mirror, fixed in the spherical centre-piece, on the axis of the telescope, and inclined to that axis at an angle of 45°. Light is thus thrown directly down the telescope, and illuminates the cross-wires.

The transit-instrument was first used to obtain the connection between the underground- and surface-surveys by Mr. A. Beanlands,* in 1856. The first method he proposed was a purely astronomical one. Having set up the transit-instrument with its plane considerably out of the meridian and its telescope pointed upwards, he observed the passage of several known stars across the wires of the diaphragm in the usual manner. It was found that at the surface the deviation of the plane of the instrument from the meridian could thus be approximately determined. Underground, however, with the telescope pointed up a vertical shaft, it was found that the operation was attended with such difficulty that it had to be abandoned. Instead of observing stars, recourse was had to lights fixed at the top of the shaft. The experiments were perfectly successful, and led to the method identified with Mr. Beanlands' name.

As a matter of convenience is has been found advisable to fix the transit-instrument at the top of the shaft, and to place illuminated marks at the bottom as nearly as possible in the same vertical plane as the instrument. The marks are illuminated by the light of a lamp reflected upwards. They are placed in such a position that they can also be sighted by a theodolite placed in a line with them at the bottom of the shaft. If now the cross-wires of the transit-telescope coincide with each of these two points, it is evident that the horizontal line represented by the marks coincides with the vertical plane of the instrument, and is therefore parallel to the position of the telescope when directed horizontally. In this way two lines are obtained, one,

* *Trans. N. Engl. Inst. M.E.*, vol. iv., p. 267; vol. xx., p. 85.

at the top of the shaft represented by the optical axis of the telescope pointed horizontally, the other at the bottom of the shaft represented by the line joining the centres of the marks.

If the two marks cannot be brought exactly to the centre of the telescope, the apparent distance of each mark from the cross-wires is measured by a micrometer, and the angular deviation of the base-line from the plane of the transit calculated. The bearing of the base-line is then deduced from that of the instrument, and the connection between the underground- and surface-surveys effected as in the previous case. By this method the bearing of a line underground may be determined with a degree of accuracy that has never been obtained with any other method.

As illustrations of the severe practical tests to which this method has been subjected, the following examples may be given:—

In 1857, Mr. Beanlands made a survey at Etherley Colliery for the purpose of setting out a drift between the workings of the George Pit, and a new sinking, the Dean Pit, half a mile to the east. There was no connection underground between the shafts, and it was therefore necessary to make a surface-survey, and to connect it with the workings at both shafts. At the George Pit, the connection was made by means of a very steep and narrow day-drift, whilst at the Dean Pit, the transit-instrument was employed, marks being left in each case for the purpose of setting out the drift. The latter was worked from both ends; the length being 700 yards. At the end of six months a very accurate holing was effected, the deviation between the two ends being 6 inches. If this deviation had been due solely to the bearing, it would imply an error of $1\frac{1}{2}$ minute. It is, however, evident that it represents not only the error of the bearing above and underground, but also of setting out and working the drift. A more convincing proof of the accuracy of this method of connecting the underground- and surface-surveys could hardly be given.

The Pelton Colliery, near Chester-le-Street was worked, in 1864, by two adjacent shafts, 50 fathoms in depth. At a distance of 50 yards from the bottom of these shafts, an underground sinking had been made to explore a lower coal-seam. It was afterwards thought desirable that a shaft should be sunk from the surface immediately above that already existing underground. Mr. Beanlands made a survey for setting out the centre of this shaft. The measurements were made with great care with a levelling-staff, and the connection between the underground- and surface-surveys was effected with the transit-instrument. The shaft was set out from Beanlands' plan, and was found to correspond with the lower shaft within 2 inches.

In shafts of very great depth the method has been employed invariably with successful results. For example, in the Ryhope Colliery, where the shaft is 253 fathoms deep, the bearing was determined twice in different months, the difference between the two results being only 1' 10".

As the method requires only one shaft with a clear view from top to bottom, it can obviously be adopted in nearly every colliery. Though a considerable time is necessarily spent in erecting a platform for the transit, a bearing sufficiently accurate for practical purposes may be obtained in a few hours.

4a. **The Severn Tunnel Method.**—On account of the length of the heading, the incessant jar of the pumping engines, and the extreme wetness of the shaft, a plumb-line method was not applicable in driving the Severn Tunnel. The length of the proposed heading was 2 miles, and that of the available base-line 12 feet. Consequently an error of $\frac{1}{20}$ of an inch would become 45 inches at the end of the two miles. To overcome the difficulty, Mr. Richardson,* the engineer, devised the following method :—A large transit-instrument was firmly set up over the shaft, and accurately in the vertical line passing through the centre of the tunnel. This line was determined by two staves, one on each side of the river. The heading having been driven a short distance, a horizontal wire, 100 yards long, was stretched at the bottom of the shaft. One end, A, was attached to the side of the shaft furthest from the heading, the other, B, at a point 100 yards along the heading. A length of 14 feet of wire was visible from the top of the shaft when illuminated by an electric light. The ends of the wire were passed over the V-threads of horizontal screws, and stretched by means of weights suspended from the ends. Thus, by turning either screw, a very slight lateral motion could be imparted to the corresponding end. The transit having been carefully levelled, the end A was first sighted, and the corresponding screw turned until this end was brought truly into the centre line. The telescope was then directed towards the farthest point of the wire visible on the other side of the shaft, and this point also brought into the centre line by turning the screw at the end B, 100 yards distant. The whole length of the wire thus was accurately directed into the line of the tunnel. A base-line 100 yards in length, and practically free from error, was thus obtained. Proof of the accuracy of the method was afforded by the results obtained in driving the tunnel. The headings were found to meet exactly.

5. **By means of the Transit-Theodolite.**—In cases where the shaft is of limited depth, and where a large and powerful transit-

* *Engineering*, vol. xxxiii., 1882, p. 48.

instrument it not available, the connection between the underground- and surface-surveys may conveniently be effected by means of the transit-theodolite.

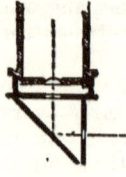

Fig. 71.

The instrument is set up at the bottom of the shaft. To enable its telescope to be pointed vertically upwards, a diagonal eye piece must be employed. This consists of a small right-angled glass prism (Fig. 71), placed at the eye-end of the telescope, in which the line of sight is reflected from the plane of the hypothenuse vertically upwards.

The mode of procedure is as follows:—Having set up the transit-theodolite at the centre of the shaft A (Fig. 72), it is levelled, and the telescope directed to a small bright light placed on the peg at B. Great care must be taken to ensure the instrument being in perfect adjustment so that the telescope shall revolve in a vertical plane. The vertical circle is then unclamped, and the telescope pointed up the shaft in the same vertical plane in the direction of the point a', where a lamp-flame or a white peg is brought exactly into the line of sight. A permanent mark is placed at a'. The telescope is then directed towards the other side of the shaft, and a mark placed at b'. In this way two points are obtained at the surface in the same vertical plane as the line AB underground. The latter is carefully measured, and the distance thus found is measured off from A' to C by stretching a cord through the centres of the marks a and b. An iron peg should be driven into the ground at C, with a hole made in its centre for future reference. This hole is directly over the centre of the peg previously driven into the floor of the level at B.

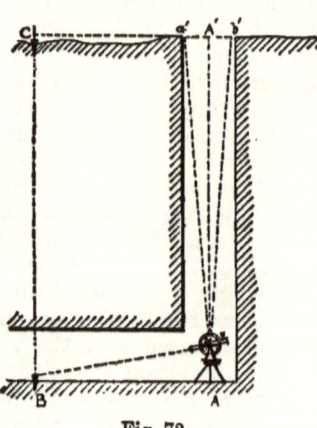

Fig. 72.

With this method, Mr. H. D. Hoskold has obtained, with his miner's transit-theodolite, very satisfactory results in the Dean Forest mines. The method is well adapted for use in mines where the shaft is of limited depth, and the workings not very extensive. The shaft must obviously be of average width, and not subject to any considerable dropping of water.

For connecting the underground- and surface-surveys, mining transit-theodolites with eccentric telescopes are frequently employed in America and on the Continent. In these instruments an auxiliary telescope is attached outside the standards to the

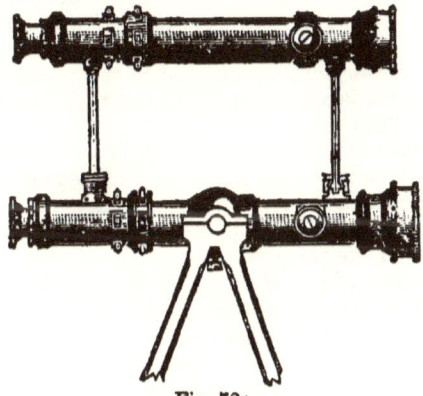

Fig. 72A.

prolongation of the horizontal axis of the principal telescope, or that telescope itself is permanently mounted in a similar posi-

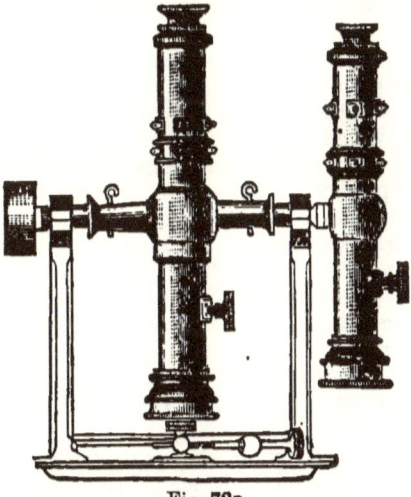

Fig. 72B.

tion. Sometimes the theodolite is made with an extra telescope attached to the top of the central telescope, by means of coupling nuts, which fasten it directly over the centre of the instrument, and allow its ready removal without disturbing the adjustments.

This method of arranging the supplementary telescope is shown in fig. 72A. This form is that generally used in conjunction with the American theodolite, shown in fig. 37A. The auxiliary telescope is attached to the main telescope by two pillars, which project beyond the edge of the horizontal plate when the telescope is placed vertically. The method of placing the auxiliary telescope eccentrically is shown in fig. 72B. In this case, a counterpoise is fastened to the prolongation of the axis. In both these attachments, the extra telescope is parallel to the principal telescope.

The objection to the side-telescope is that a correction must be applied to each reading of a horizontal angle equal to the tangent of the angle, which is formed by the distance from the side-telescope to the centre of the instrument, and the horizontal distance between the stations.

In place of the diagonal eye-piece for sighting vertically upwards, an artificial horizon may be used. No special construction of the telescope is then required, as it is merely necessary to sight the image of the flame (Fig. 73). The image and the flame itself are in the same vertical plane, and the image is seen at an angle of depression α equal to the angle of elevation β that would have been observed had the diagonal eye-piece been employed.

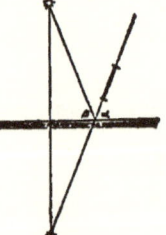

Fig. 73.

The artificial horizon may be made of oil mixed with lamp-black. The fluid is filtered through linen, and carried into the mine in a small bottle. When required for use, it is poured into a cylindrical brass vessel, care being taken to protect the surface of the liquid from air-currents.

The artificial horizon will be found more convenient than the diagonal eye-piece for surveying in highly-inclined shafts.

6. **By Means of the Magnetic-Needle.**—When the mine has only one shaft, the underground- and surface-surveys may be connected by means of the magnetic-needle, provided that the shaft is not sunk in magnetic strata. If the shaft is vertical, a plumb-line is suspended in the shaft, and from this the underground-survey starts. If the shaft is inclined, a traverse is made down the shaft.

The method of employing the magnetic-needle consists in determining the angle made by one of the sides of a triangle of the surface-survey, as well as that made by one of the lines of the underground traverse, with the magnetic meridian. The lines are then connected by a survey made with the theodolite.

The accuracy of the method is increased by observing the magnetic bearings of two or more lines at the surface and underground.

As the whole of the underground-survey depends on the accuracy of the determination of the magnetic bearing of two lines, it is advisable to use the theodolite for that operation. The theodolite is provided with a magnetic-needle, which serves to bring the telescope into the direction of the magnetic meridian. As a rule, in theodolites, the diameter 0°–180° is in the direction of the telescope. It is, however, not absolutely necessary that the optical axis of the telescope should accurately coincide with that diameter, nor is a compass with a complete graduated circle necessary. A long narrow box, provided with an index-line, Fig. 74, suffices; indeed, it has the advantage of being less in the way. The needle should be as light as possible with thin points, and its centre of gravity must not be too low down below the point on which it rests. A magnifying-glass is used to see when the needle exactly coincides with the index-line.

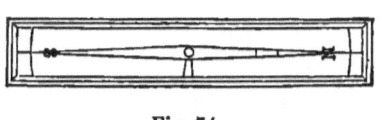

Fig. 74.

The *tubular compass* is very convenient for mine-surveying purposes. It consists of a tubular case, the north end of which is closed with ground glass, on which a fine scale is marked. By means of a lens at the south end of the tube, this scale appears slightly magnified. In front of the scale, swings the north-seeking point of the needle, which is bent upwards, so that it can easily be read with precision in the mine. This compass can easily be adapted to any form of theodolite, as it is not necessary to read it from above, but by looking through it in the same way as a telescope.

With this compass, only one end of the needle is seen. To obviate this disadvantage, Mr. Hildebrand* has devised a new form of tubular compass (Fig. 75). In this, both ends of the

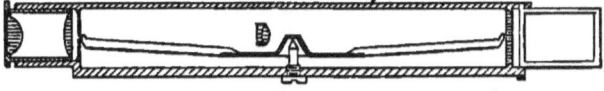

Fig. 75.

needle are seen at once, magnified ten times, the graduation also appearing magnified to the same degree. The compass can easily

* *Min. Proc. Inst. C.E.*, vol. xxxvi., 1886, p. 459.

be read to a single minute in the mine, the light of a candle at a distance of a yard being sufficient. The tube is rectangular, and in it a magnetic-needle, 4·32 inches long, swings on a steel point. Close by the south end of the needle is a glass micrometer, and in front of that is a micrometer eye-piece magnifying ten times. Between the south end and the centre of the needle is a small telescope object-glass. By means of the eye-piece, the glass micrometer and the south end of the needle are seen magnified ten times, the magnified inverted optical image of the north end, formed by the object-glass, being also visible. In other words, by means of the eye-piece both the north and south ends of the needle are seen passing before the glass micrometer. The latter is divided into tenths of a millimetre, one division as seen through the eye-piece consequently appearing equal to one millimetre. The middle line of the scale, the zero line, is lengthened in both directions. When the needle is properly adjusted, the images of the south end and of the inverted north end will appear on that line. But if the needle gets out of adjustment, its centre and its north and south points are no longer in the same plane, and the two ends will not coincide with the zero line. The compass must then be so placed that the two ends of the needle appear at the same distance from the zero line. The north end of the compass case is protected from dust by a glass-plate, in front of which is hinged a plate of ground glass, by means of which the artificial illumination is assisted.

As the magnetic meridian is continually changing, it is advisable that the observations at the surface and underground should be made as nearly as practicable at the same time. The best results are obtained when the bearings at the surface are observed before and after those of the underground-lines.

If a considerable interval elapses between the observations, the magnitude of the changes in the magnetic meridian must be observed, and the error thus arising eliminated by calculation. A knowledge of the absolute declination of the needle is not indispensable. The most important point is to determine the diurnal variation. This can only be done with sufficient accuracy by means of a magnet suspended by a long thin silk fibre, provided with a contrivance for observing the vibrations by means of a telescope. Magnetic-needles supported on pivots, as in the miner's dial, do not admit of sufficient accuracy.

Two contrivances are used for observing the vibrations of the magnetic-needle—(1.) Attached to a cylindrical magnet, suspended by a silk fibre, at the north end is a glass plate with a small photographic scale, and at the south end is a small achromatic lens. The centre of the glass-plate is in the principal focus of the lens, so that the line joining the middle division of the scale is nearly parallel to the axis of the magnet. The scale is viewed through the lens by means of a fixed telescope. The motion of the magnet can thus be followed by observing the apparent motion of the scale across the cross-wires of the telescope.

(2.) Another arrangement is to rigidly attach a mirror to the magnet, so that the perpendicular to its surface is nearly parallel to the magnetic axis. In this mirror, the image of a fixed horizontal scale is observed by means of a fixed telescope, and the angular motion of the magnet deduced from the motion of the scale divisions over the cross-wires of the telescope. This is called the mirror-method, and was first employed by C. F. Gauss in the magnetometer constructed by him in 1830. The magnetic observatory belonging to the Clausthal mines in the Harz is arranged in accordance with this method. A Gauss magnetometer is undoubtedly the best means of observing the variation of the declination. The cost, however, puts it out of the reach of most mine-surveyors.

A small magnetometer may easily be constructed of ordinary surveying instruments. With a second theodolite or a levelling instrument, the readings can be effected, and a scale can be easily prepared. There is then only necessary a magnet with a mirror. It is not absolutely necessary that the mirror shall be perpendicular to the axis of the magnet. It may be attached at any point of the magnet, suited to the station at which the telescope is placed.

A portable magnetometer, on the collimation principle, invented by Professor Borchers, has been used with great success in the German mines. It consists of a magnet suspended by a silk fibre, provided with a lens and scale, and enclosed in a glass case. It is attached by a brass arm to the tripod head of the theodolite.

The use of a somewhat similar instrument has been advocated by Mr. R. S. Newall.* In this, however, the needle is mounted on a pivot instead of being suspended by a silk fibre. Attached to the centre of the needle at right angles to its axis is a small mirror, whilst a minutely graduated scale, consisting of a short length, about 4 inches, of a circle 3 feet in diameter, is fixed at the eye-end of a theodolite telescope, and so adjusted that the degrees are reflected back to the eye by the mirror fixed on the needle. In this way, the scale is magnified twice, and may be easily read to a small fraction of a degree. The arm carrying the telescope is attached to a circle graduated into 360°, and provided with sights, so that bearings may be taken in the same way as with the ordinary miner's-dial.

* *Trans. N. Engl. Inst. M.E.*, vol. xx., 1871, p. 108.

CHAPTER XV.

MEASURING DISTANCES BY TELESCOPE.

Theory of Telescopic Measurements.—The indirect measurement of distances by means of the telescope is based on the solution of a triangle (Fig. 76). Suppose the instrument to be at A and a graduated staff at B C; then the length A D will be known, if the angle D A C and the height D C are known. Two classes of instruments are employed. In one, the angle D A C is constant, and the height of the staff D C varies with the distance. In the other, the height of the staff is constant, and the angle D A C variable.

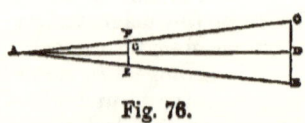

Fig. 76.

The typical instrument of the latter class is that of Stampfer. This consists of a telescope that may be moved 8° in a vertical direction. Two divisions on a staff, held at a distance, are sighted successively. These embrace a constant height s. By means of a micrometer screw it is easy to determine the angle, through which the telescope has moved in passing from one division to the other. Let a represent this angle, which is equal to the number of turns n of the screw multiplied by a constant c. The angle being small, it may be assumed that $\tan a = c n$. The distance required will then be equal to $\dfrac{s}{\tan a}$ or $\dfrac{s}{c n}$. The constant c is determined by observations along a known distance, and tables are constructed giving the distance for any number of turns given to the screw.

The same principle is applied in Eckhold's omnimeter,[*] an instrument used in revenue surveys in India and in railway surveys in America.

In American transit-theodolites, a so-called *gradienter* screw is frequently attached to the horizontal axis of the telescope. It consists of a tangent screw with a micrometer head, graduated into 50 equal parts. As the screw is turned, the head passes over a small silvered scale, so graduated that one revolution of the screw corresponds to one space on the scale. Thus, the number of whole revolutions made by the screw in turning the

[*] Valuable information regarding the use of this instrument is given by E. W. Young, *Min. Proc. Inst. C.E.*, vol. cxvii., 1894, p. 296.

telescope through a vertical arc can be ascertained from the scale. When unclamped, the telescope may be revolved; but when clamped, it can only be moved by the gradienter screw, which thus takes the place of the ordinary vertical tangent screw. The micrometer head is so graduated that one revolution causes the horizontal cross-line of the telescope to move over a space of half a foot at a distance of 100 feet. The micrometer head being divided into 50 parts, each division is equivalent to one-hundredth of a foot in 100 feet. It is evident that, with this screw, slopes can be established with great rapidity.

It is also useful for obtaining approximate distances, since for any horizontal distance, the space on an ordinary levelling-staff expressed in hundredths of feet, included in two revolutions of the screw, will be the number of feet the staff is distant from the instrument. Thus, if the difference between two readings of the staff is 2·854 feet when the telescope is moved vertically through two revolutions of the screw, the staff is distant 285·4 feet.

On sloping ground, the staff is still held vertical, and the distance read is too great. If a is the angle of elevation, the true horizontal distance may be found by multiplying the space on the vertical staff included in two revolutions of the gradienter screw by $\frac{d}{nh} \cos^2 a - \frac{1}{2} \sin 2a$, in which h is the height above a horizontal line subtended by one revolution of the gradienter screw at a distance d, and n is the number of revolutions made in any given case. The gradienter screw is usually so cut and placed that when $d = 100$, $n = 2$, and $h = \frac{1}{2}$, the factor then becomes

$$100 \cos^2 a - \frac{1}{2} \sin 2a.$$

With the object of reducing the computation to a simple multiplication, Messrs. Buff & Berger, of Boston, U.S., supply with their transits a table of factors calculated for vertical angles of 0° to 15°.

Instruments in which the angle is constant, and the height of the staff variable, are more important and more numerous. The original instrument of this class is the stadia, invented by Wm. Green in 1778. An early form of the instrument used in conjunction with the stadia or staff consisted of a tube provided with three parallel wires. In Fig. 76, let G, E, and F represent these wires; G being the axial wire, and E and F the end wires; then the constant angle a will be determined by the height G F, or i, and the distance A G, or r, from the eye-piece to the wires. If A D, the distance to be measured, is represented by d, and if s represents the height of the staff D C, intercepted by the wires G and F, the equation obtained is $d = \frac{r}{i}s$.

The stadia is no longer employed in this primitive form. In Austria, however, a similar instrument is occasionally used in levelling for railway sections. In this the tube is replaced by a pair of sight-vanes, one of which has two parallel wires 0·03 metre apart, stretched across the aperture. The distance from one sight to the other being 0·3 metre, the ratio $\frac{r}{i}$ is equal to 10, so that, in order to measure distances in metres with this instrument, it is merely necessary to use a staff divided into decimetres.

As a rule, the distances to be measured are so great that a telescope has to be employed; in which case the formula is $d = \frac{r}{i}s$, as with the stadia tube; r, however, is not constant, but varies according to the proportion $\frac{1}{r} + \frac{1}{d} = \frac{1}{f}$; f being the focal length of the objective lens.

In the telescopes used in surveying, f is equal to 12 to 15 inches, and r varies as much as 0·24 inch for distances of 20 to 700 yards. Thus, for distances of 100 yards, the variation of r in proportion to the focal length is very slight. It must, however, be taken into account, because r is used as a multiplier.

Various methods are employed for remedying the variability of r. The telescope may be employed like the old stadia tube; the staff being graduated for a single distance, and no corrections applied when the distance is greater or less than this. This method can be used only when great accuracy is not required.

Early in this century, Reichenbach, a Bavarian engineer, proposed a method that is still in frequent use. He eliminated r in the equations $\frac{1}{r} + \frac{1}{d} = \frac{1}{f}$ and $d = \frac{r}{i}s$, obtaining $d = \frac{f}{i}s + f$. The value d, it is seen, is composed of two terms, one being proportional to s and the other being the focal length f. The distance measured from a point as far in front of the object-glass as the focal length of that lens, is thus proportional to s. Then, if the distance is to be reckoned from the centre of the instrument, a constant, c, the distance from the centre of the instrument to the object-glass, must be added. This may be made by the instrument-maker equal to 0·5f. The formula is then

$$d = \frac{f}{i}s + f + c.$$

All distances will thus be reckoned from the centre of the instrument, if the sum of the focal length and the distance from the object-glass to the centre of the axis of the telescope is added to the reading at every sight. For example, if the object-glass has a focal length of 6 inches, and the micrometer wires are 6 inches from the object-glass, 1 foot is the constant to be added to each reading.

A staff may be graduated to read the distance direct. It is, however, useful only for measuring distances, and not for levelling at the same time. It is preferable to use an ordinary levelling-staff and a telescope, in which the instrument-maker has selected for $\frac{f}{i}$ some multiple of 100. Suppose, for example, that $\frac{f}{i} = 100$. The distance from the centre of the instrument would then be $100 s +$ the constant. The calculation of distances is thus greatly facilitated.

When the line of sight is inclined towards the staff, the space intercepted is increased in the ratio of 1 to the cosine of the angle with the horizon. Thus, the space s' for the staff perpendicular to the horizon becomes s for the staff when vertical, and, by approximation, $s' = s \cos \alpha$. The inclined distance is then equal to $100 s \cos \alpha + (f + c)$, and the horizontal distance is equal to $100 s \cos^2 \alpha + (f + c) \cos \alpha$. But since $(f + c)$ is, at most, equal to 2 feet, and the angle α is so very small, c may be taken as equal to its horizontal projection. The horizontal distance will then be equal to $100 s \cos^2 \alpha + (f + c)$.

In Germany it is usual to hold the staff perpendicular to the line of sight. The inclined distance is then equal to $100 s + (f + c)$, and its horizontal projection is equal to $\{100 s + (f + c)\} \cos \alpha$, or, approximately, $100 s \cos \alpha + (f + c)$.

The most effectual method of remedying the variability of r is that proposed by Porro, a Piedmontese officer, afterwards professor at Milan, who in 1823 modified the construction of the telescope in such a way as to remove all necessity for adding constants, and the distances measured from the centre of the instrument are then directly proportional to s. He introduced between the object-glass and eye-piece a third lens, the focus of which coincided with that of the object-glass. Consequently the rays after passing through this third lens become parallel, whilst the sizes of objects subtending the same angle at the centre of "anallatism," or unchangeableness, are proportional to their distance from that point. This point being placed in the vertical axis of the instrument, the telescope is rendered anallatic. In other words, in consequence of the interposition of the anallatic lens, the rays coming from the end-wires to the staff, form an angle ω with its vertex at O, the centre of the telescope. The angle ω is termed the diastimometric angle, and O the anallatic point. The angle ω varies with the distance of the anallatic lens from the object-glass. If this distance increases, ω decreases, and conversely, whilst the distance remains constant, ω is invariable. It can easily be seen that the distance from O, the centre of the telescope, can be deduced

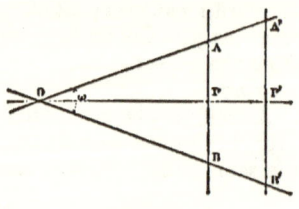

Fig. 77.

from the length A B intercepted by the wires. In fact the sides of the diastimometric angle form with the staff virtual triangles, O A B, O A' B'. These triangles being similar give—

$$\frac{OP}{AB} = \frac{OP'}{A'B'} = k.$$

It is thus merely necessary to determine a simple constant, the diastimometric ratio, and then to move the anallatic lens until ω coresponds to it. As a rule, k is taken as $\frac{1}{200}$, in which case ω is equal to 0·32 centesimal degree. It follows that at 200 yards, for example, the length of staff intercepted should be 1 yard. The diastimometric ratio is represented by the expression 2 tan $\frac{\omega}{2}$. The distance is then $s \div 2 \tan \frac{\omega}{2}$.

The original instruments, tacheometers, made by Porro were very favourably reported on by the Paris Academy of Sciences and by a French Government Commission. Their extremely delicate nature, however, prevented them from coming into general use.

In 1856, M. Moinot, engineer to the Paris, Lyons, and Mediterranean Railway, gave the tacheometer a form resembling that of the larger modern theodolites. His instrument is based on the same principle as that of Porro, but is much less delicate and less expensive, while giving results of great accuracy. Like Porro's original instrument, Moinot's tacheometer permits distances to be measured at the same time as angles and differences in level. Its use has led to a new method of surveying for railway purposes, termed tacheometry, which is quite as accurate as the older method of longitudinal- and cross-sections. By the advantages it presents of greater rapidity, and the small number of assistants required, this method has undoubtedly contributed to the development of railways, notably in mountainous districts. The aim of tacheometry is to survey and level simultaneously a tract of ground with the greatest possible accuracy in the least possible time. In mountainous districts, it is a method of the greatest value, since it dispenses with the chain and spirit level, and thus the laborious, slow, and expensive processes of chaining over bad ground and of levelling up and down hill, are avoided. By means of a single observation, the distance, azimuth and height are determined of every point visible and accessible from a given station point. In this way, surveys are made in one-third to one-fifth of the time that is required for the older methods. Since its first application by Moinot in 1856, on the line from Nice to Genoa, it has been employed in most of the continental countries, excepting perhaps North Germany. There Reichenbach's method is still used; instruments being constructed under the name of tacheometers, more or less similar to Moinot's tacheometer, but without the anallatic telescope.

The tacheometer is so constructed that $2 \tan \frac{\omega}{2}$ is equal to $\frac{1}{200}$. The distance being equal to $200\ s$ may be read direct from the staff, if the latter is graduated in half-centimetres. Thus, if the lower wire coincides with the division marked 100, and the upper one with the division 110, the height s will be equal to $110 - 100 = 10$ half centimetres, and the distance will be 10 metres.

In order to reduce the measured distance to the horizontal, the work is always carried on with the staff held vertical, and the angle of inclination of the optic axis is determined.

Calculations.—For calculating the results of a tacheometer-survey, the slide-rule may advantageously be used. The rule contains scales of numbers, sines, and tangents. To these Moinot has added a scale giving the values of $\sin^2$, the origin of which is so placed that a single setting of the slide gives simultaneously the horizontal distance ($s \sin^2 \varphi$), and the difference of level. By means of these scales, the co-ordinates of points observed from a single station with the tacheometer are rapidly computed, without any direct measurements being made.

The Protractor designed by Moinot for plotting tacheometer-surveys differs from the ordinary protractor, in that it gives at the same time the direction and the distance of the point to be determined on the plan. It is a semicircular protractor, of transparent horn, or of thick paper, provided with a needle-pointed pivot at its centre. Its straight-edge is graduated so that distances can be measured off each way from the centre.

MEASURING DISTANCES BY TELESCOPE. 223

Angles are obtained from the graduated semicircle, reading from a point marked on the plan.

The Tacheometer is nothing more than a theodolite with a concentric distance-measuring telescope. It differs from the theodolite in being furnished with an anallatic lens, and usually in being graduated according to the centesimal method, the circle being divided into 400 parts or degrees. Though not indispensable for a tacheometer, this division is very convenient. The angles are read more rapidly, on account of the simplicity of the division into tens and hundreds, and since they are read from two verniers, one at each end of a diameter of the circle, errors are at once evident, the readings differing by 200°. Lastly, with the centesimal division, the slide-rule computations are greatly facilitated. Tables of logarithms for the centesimal method have been prepared by Callet, Borda, Plausolles, Laland, and others, and have been in use for many years. The best forms of tacheometer are those made by Messrs. Troughton & Simms, Mr. W. F. Stanley, and Mr. L. Casella.

The Staves used in tacheometry are always graduated with sufficient distinctness to be read by the observers. Porro's staff is triangular in section, and has three graduations with different subdivisions according to requirements. For short distances, the divisions are extremely fine; for greater distances only whole metres are marked in bold figures. Moinot's staff is graduated in such a way that it can be used for short or for long distances.

The staff should not exceed 12 to 16 feet in length, and should be made of light wood. During the observation it must be held perfectly vertical. It should therefore be provided with a plumb-line, or, better, with a round spirit-level, the tangential plane of which is perpendicular to the graduation of the staff.

The Field-Work.—Tacheometric-surveys are usually conducted by a party of three, (1) the engineer to direct the work; (2) the observer at the instrument; and (3) the recorder to book the results. On level ground two staff-holders are employed, and on irregular ground one or two more are necessary, in order to prevent loss of time to the observer. For less important surveys one observer and one staff-holder suffice.

When the instrument has been set up at a suitable point, staff-holders are sent to all the points to be surveyed. To each point a number is assigned, and noted in the field-book, and on a sketch made at the same time. The telescope is directed towards the staff, and the micrometer wires are read and noted in the proper column of the field-book. The horizontal and

15

vertical angles are then read and noted. This operation is repeated for all the points that can be seen from this station.

In this way, for every point three figures are obtained—the distance, and the horizontal and vertical angles. The point is thus fixed by means of polar co-ordinates.

If the survey has to be connected with one previously made, some data from the former work are necessary in order to make the connection. Two points, if accurately determined, are sufficient.

The instrument having been set up and levelled, the engineer makes a reconnaissance of the ground to be surveyed, and gives instructions to the staff-holder, who goes successively to all the points selected by the engineer, and at each one holds the staff steadily vertical until he receives a signal to pass on. The observer at the instrument now makes the necessary observations, which are noted in the field-book by the recorder.

When the ground to be surveyed is so extensive that two stations are necessary, the engineer selects two points visible from both stations. When the observation at the first station is finished, the instrument is moved to the second, and the two points are observed. The connection could, of course, be made by means of one point only. It is, however, advisable to employ two as a check on the accuracy of the work. When a number of stations are required the method is similar. The method described is that used by Porro.

Moinot employs the tacheometer in preliminary surveys for railway lines in the following manner:—Before the belt of ground is surveyed, an extensive reconnaissance is undertaken, and the main direction of the railway determined, so that the survey may be limited to a comparatively narrow strip. On account of the rapidity of the method there is no occasion to be too anxious about limiting the width. A strip should always be selected of sufficient width to allow if necessary a lateral displacement of the line. A width of 400 yards is quite sufficient. Marks are fixed 200 to 300 yards apart, and numbers are assigned to them. For filling in details, points are chosen wherever the ground presents any decided change of level. The instrument is set up at a point so selected that connection can be made with any existing survey or railway. The assistant then gives a signal with a whistle or horn to announce that he is ready. In the meantime the recorder has measured and noted the height of the instrument, and the engineer has made a sketch roughly to the scale of the plan to be prepared, showing all the roads, rivers, boundaries, fields, and the station of the instrument. As soon as he hears the signal, the engineer indicates to each staff-holder his place, care being taken that only one staff is ready at a time. The other staff-holder is still on the road, or, if already at his post, he turns the narrow side of the staff towards the instrument, and remains in this position until it is signalled to him that the preceding reading is finished. He then turns the graduation of the staff towards the instrument, and by means of a signal directs attention to his position. He then awaits the signal that he can pass on.

The assistant at the instrument has to read the upper and the lower wires with each staff, and then the vertical and horizontal angles, and to call them out in this order to the recorder, who notes them in the field-book. The recorder enters the points in order, as 1, 2, 3, &c. At every fifth or tenth point the assistant gives a double signal, whereby the engineer, although at a distance from the instrument, has a check on the accuracy of the booking, seeing that he has entered the points in his sketch in the same order.

In order to economise time, the engineer selects the points in such a way that he comes finally in proximity to the point he regarded as being most suitable for the next station. Here he places a mark and sets up a staff, at the same time giving a special signal to the assistant.

When the readings for this next station are finished, the observations at the first station are complete, and the instrument is carried on. In the meantime, the man who was holding the staff at the new station returns to the preceding one just left by the instrument. The recorder begins a new station in the field-book, and at once enters the height of the instrument in its proper column. A back-observation is now taken, and the distance, height, and azimuth should coincide with the results previously obtained.

By the aid of this method, Moinot has surveyed about 1,000 miles for railway purposes. The distances, when measured on the ground with extreme care, have never differed from those shown on the plan by more than one per thousand, and the longitudinal section obtained by accurate spirit-levelling has never presented any appreciable difference when compared with the results afforded by the heights given on the plan.

The Topographical Stadia differs from the tacheometer in that the micrometer is not applied to the telescope of a theodolite, but to the alidade of a plane-table. The points are observed from one station, the distances from this being reduced to the horizontal, and the heights calculated on the spot by means of a special slide-rule. The data thus obtained are at once plotted to the scale required on a sheet of paper stretched on the plane-table, the height of each point being accurately noted. When the height of a sufficient number of points is determined, contour lines are traced with the ground in view. In fact, the ground is practically sketched from nature.

On the United States Coast and Geodetic Survey, the plane-table has been exclusively used for making topographical surveys; the stadia, or *telemeter* as it is called on that service, being used in connection with it. The stadia is graduated experimentally for the particular instrument, and for the eye of the observer who has it in use. It is simply a scale of equal parts painted upon a wooden staff, about 10 feet long, 5 inches wide, and $1\frac{1}{4}$ inch thick, so graduated that the number of divisions, as seen between the horizontal wires of the telescope, is equal to the number of metres in the distance between the observer's eye and the staff held perpendicular to the line of sight.

American experience tends to show that the plane-table is adapted to open country and long distances, where no contour lines are to be determined, and where the stations are comparatively few, as well as where a multiplicity of detail is required. Against the advantage of plotting the work in the field may be placed the disadvantages of having no record but the field-sheet, which is liable to be spoiled in a storm.

The Theodolite and Stadia.—The method of surveying with the plane-table and stadia is being superseded in America by the use of the transit-theodolite and stadia, a method introduced in 1864, when it was officially adopted on the United States Lake Survey. All that can be done with the plane-table may also be done with the transit-theodolite. The plane-table can be used only for topographical work, and requires special practice, whilst the theodolite for the stadia survey can be adopted in all cases where a theodolite is required, and but little special training is required in order to use it with the stadia.

The best instrument to employ is a theodolite reading to 30″. The micrometer wires should be fixed; when adjustable, they are not sufficiently stable to be trustworthy. The stadia is usually a staff, 1 inch thick, 5 inches wide, and 14 feet long. In order to graduate the staff, it is necessary to know what space on it corresponds to 100 feet (or yards, or metres) in distance. To determine this, it is best to measure off $c + f$ in front of the plumb-line, and set a point. From this point, accurately measure a base-line of (say) 200 yards, on level ground, and hold the blank staff at the end of this line. Have a fixed mark on the upper portion of the staff, and set the upper wire on this. Then let an assistant at the staff record the position of the lower wire, as he is directed by the observer at the instrument. Repeat the operation until the mean gives a satisfactory result. If the base was 200 yards long, divide the space intercepted by the two wires into two equal parts, then each of these parts into ten smaller parts, and finally each small space into five equal parts. Each of these last divisions will represent 2 yards. Diagrams are then to be constructed on this scale, in such a way that the number of symbols can be readily estimated at the greatest distance at which the staff is to be held. If, when tested by re-measuring the base-line, the wire interval is found to have changed, the staff must be re-graduated, or a correction must be made to all the readings.

If the wires are adjustable, any unit scale may be selected, and the wires adjusted to this. By this method, distances may be obtained from levelling-staffs, where it is desirable that each foot on the staff should correspond to 100 feet in distance.

In making a survey for the purpose of preparing a contoured plan, a series of points should be determined with reference to each other, both in geographical position and in elevation. These points should not be more than 3 miles apart. The points of elevation, or bench-marks, need not be identical with the points fixed in geographical position. The latter are best determined by triangulation.

A system of triangulation points being established, the angles are observed and the stations plotted on the plan. For small areas the plotting is best done by means of rectangular co-ordinates. The survey may, however, be plotted directly from the polar co-ordinates (azimuth and distance). For this purpose the plan should have printed upon it a protractor circle, 12 inches in diameter, by means of which the lines can be plotted accurately to 5'.

A line of levels is next run, bench-marks being left at convenient points. The topographical survey is then made, and referred to this system of triangulation points and bench-marks. The surveying party should consist of the observer, a recorder, three staff-holders, and, if necessary, two axe-men.

The record in the field-book consists of (1) a description of the point; (2) the reading of the vernier; (3) the distance; (4) the vertical angle. Two columns are left for reduction; (5) the difference of height corresponding to the given vertical angle and distance; (6) the true height of each point above the datum-line. The right-hand page of the field-book is reserved for sketching.

The only calculations necessary are to find the height of all the points taken, with reference to the datum-line, and sometimes to correct the distance read on the staff for inclined sights. These calculations may be performed by means of tables computed by Mr. A. Winslow, of the State Geological Survey of Pennsylvania, or by means of a diagram prepared by Professor J. B. Johnson, of Washington University.

The only available information as to the accuracy of this method of surveying is given in the report of the United States Lake Survey for 1875. The entire stadia work of that year was co-ordinated, and compared with the corresponding distances obtained by triangulation. In this way 141 lines, on an average $1\frac{1}{3}$ mile in length, were tested, the average error being 1 in 650. The length of sight between the stations averaged 800 to 1,000 feet. The limit of error allowable in closing on a triangulation was 1 in 300. No special pains were taken to make these lines more accurate than others, since it was not known at the time that the results were to be tested. The readings were taken to the nearest metre; the staves were graduated for a single distance; and no corrections were applied when the distance read was greater or less than this. The accuracy thus attained was sufficient for the object of the survey. Had more care been exercised in the work, the readings limited to 1,000 feet, and all corrections applied, it would have been easy to bring the error within 1 in 1,200.

This method was employed by Mr. W. B. Dawson,* for the preparation of a map of the gold-field on the Atlantic Coast of Nova Scotia, on a scale of 2 inches to the mile. The traverse lines ran along the roads and principal streams, forming a network of quadrilaterals, and were plotted by co-ordinates. The instruments used in the survey were a Sopwith levelling-staff, and a 6-inch transit-theodolite with a $4\frac{1}{2}$-inch compass-needle. The telescope was fitted with three horizontal spider lines, unequally spaced, the larger interval corresponding to 100 feet of distance for each foot intercepted by the staff. The smaller one was only used for longer sight, and when the view was obstructed. In five months of field work an area of 180 square miles was surveyed, including nearly one hundred lakes from 7 miles long, downwards, all the work being done by Mr. Dawson with one assistant, and one or two men according to circumstances. Wet days were devoted to the reduction of the observations. The total cost of the survey was 16·75 dollars per square mile.

Telescope Measurements in Mine-Surveys.—In mine-surveys very accurate readings may be obtained on account of the steadiness of the air. A transit-theodolite magnifying ten times, with adjustable micrometer wires, was used in 1865 with great

---

* *Trans. Amer. Soc. C.E.*, 1882, p. 397.

success by Mr. B. S. Lyman,* for surveying in an American colliery. It saved much disagreeable groping in the mud to count the links of a chain, and levels were taken at the same time. The wires were placed so far apart that 1 foot of space intercepted on the staff indicated a distance of 100 feet. The figures on the staff were painted with red ink upon thin paper that had been fastened to strips of common window glass by transparent varnish. Then over the paper another coat of varnish was poured, and upon this was placed another strip of glass. The glasses, with the paper between them, were then put into a narrow wooden frame, which formed one side of a long box. This had neither top nor bottom, and its sides were so hinged together that they folded over upon each other when not in use. The back of the box had holes through it to supply air to the lights, and either safety-lamps or candles were fixed to the wood of the back. The box was made 5 feet in length; but for low mines one might be made much shorter. This staff lighted inside makes telescopic measuring and levelling easy underground, where chaining is particularly disagreeable.

To remedy the difficulty of getting sufficient light to read the ordinary staff, Professor Johnson proposes to use two strips, one-quarter of an inch wide, one of which is fastened with its top even with the zero of the stadia scale, whilst the other is moved to suit the position of the other wire. The reading of the top edge of the upper strip then gives the distance, which is read off by the staff-holder.

Tacheometry is specially adapted for geological-surveys, which have frequently to be made in mountainous districts where chaining is laborious and inaccurate, and where levelling up and down the sides of the mountains is not to be thought of. The Geological Survey of Pennsylvania has surveyed some 3,000 square miles by means of the transit-theodolite and stadia. In the vicinity of mines and where land is valuable the work is done with extreme accuracy, the length of the lines being limited to 400 feet.†

* *Journ. Franklin Inst.*, vol. lv., 1868, p. 385.
† For further information on this method of surveying, the student is referred to Prof. J. B. Johnson's *Manual of the Theory and Practice of Topographical Surveying by Means of the Transit and Stadia*, New York, 1885; and to B. H. Brough's paper on "Tacheometry, or Rapid Surveying," *Min. Proc. Inst. C.E.*, vol. xci., 1888, p. 282, in which a bibliography of the subject is given. Papers on this subject have also been written by N. Kennedy, *Min. Proc. Inst., C.E.*, vol. xcix., 1890, p. 308, by W. Airy, *ibid.*, vol. ci., 1890, p. 222, and by R. E. Middleton, *ibid.*, vol. cxvi., 1894, p. 311.

CHAPTER XVI.

Setting-out.

Ranging Straight Lines.—Setting-out, or the location of predetermined points, is defined as that branch of geodetic operations which is the converse of surveying and levelling, the latter consisting in discovering the position of a series of actually-existing points.

In ranging and setting-out a base-line for a surface-survey, ranging rods, 5 to 7 feet in length, are used. They are usually circular in section, and painted in lengths of 1 foot or 1 link, black, white, and red alternately. When one colour cannot be clearly seen, one of the other coloured portions can generally be distinguished.

The rods are planted vertically in the ground, the verticality being judged by the eye. When great accuracy is required, a plumb-bob must be used. Its string is turned over the first and second fingers of the hand, so that when it hangs vertically, the rod may be placed parallel to it. The distance apart of the rods varies from 66 feet to 300 feet.

For ranging straight lines of moderate length, the most convenient instrument is the transit-theodolite, because the telescope may be turned completely over about its horizontal axis, so as to range one straight line in two opposite directions from one station. The error with this instrument should not exceed 10 seconds in angular direction—that is, about 3 inches in a distance of a mile.

For straight lines of very great length, the theodolite is not sufficiently exact. It is then advisable to use a transit-instrument. In order that a vertical circle may be correctly described by that instrument, it is necessary that the line of collimation shall be precisely at right angles to the horizontal axis about which it revolves, and that the pivots of that axis shall be precisely level with each other when they rest in their Y's on the iron stand.

Plotting the Underground Traverse on the Surface.—If it is required to plot the traverse on the surface of the earth, a process which in former times was in general use for determining the position of the boundary of the mine, the first course, from which azimuths were measured, must first be laid down in horizontal length and direction, and its ends marked with stakes. The position of the first station being thus determined, the second station may be found by laying off from the first station, at the proper angle, a horizontal distance equal to the length of the course. In the same way, all the successive underground stations may be marked out on the surface.

This process is tedious, and liable to error, and should consequently only be employed when absolutely necessary. Instead of repeating the traverse on the surface, the required distance and its bearing should be calculated trigonometrically, and marked out on the surface.

Setting-Out Railways to Mines.—Railways to mines may easily be set-out when the ground presents no great irregularities, the best line for the railway being determined by levelling from the starting-point to the mine. The line, of which a trial section shows the fewest difficulties of construction, having been selected, it is roughly marked out on the ground by strong pegs. The entire line is then carefully levelled and an accurate section drawn. From this the amount of cutting and embankment necessary may be determined. The entire line is then set out on the ground.

Two stakes are driven into the ground with their heads at the intended formation level, at distances of about 50 feet apart, near the commencement of a proposed cutting. The excavators are then able to carry on the cutting at the proper rate of inclination by a process called *boning*. This consists in ranging a line, of uniform inclination, from two points in it with T-shaped instruments, called *boning rods*. Boning rods of the same height are held vertically upon the two stakes driven into the ground, and a third rod is held at some point along the intended slope; then, if the inclination is correct, the tops of the three rods will be in line. If the third rod is too low or too high, it must be raised or lowered until it is in line with the tops of the other rods.

Ranging Curves.—Railway curves are of frequent occurrence, and even branch railways to mines, which are usually not of great length, can rarely be made without them.

A common method of setting-out a railway curve of a given radius on the ground is by means of offsets. In Fig. 78, A and G are the ends of the straight portions of the line to be connected by a curve, being the two points at which the curve falls into the straight lines. Let A C, C E, E G be the distances which it is desired that the points found in the curve shall be apart. Then measure, upon the straight line A C produced to D, the distance C D equal to C E, and join D E. This distance D E is called the *offset*, and gives a point E in the curve. Range a straight line through the points C E, and upon it lay off the distance E F equal to E G, and join F G. The point G will be the next point in the curve. Proceed in the same way until the whole extent of the curve has been set out. Let r be the radius of the curve, and d the distance A C, C E, or E G, which it is desired that the points found in the curve shall be apart, then the value of the offset is

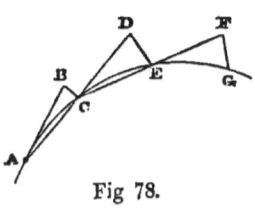

Fig 78.

$$D E = \frac{C E \cdot A D}{2 r}$$

If C E and E G are two equal chords, the offset is

$$F G = \frac{C E \cdot C D}{r} = \frac{C E^2}{r}$$

A B being a tangent to the curve at A, the value of the offset from the tangent is

$$B C = \frac{A C^2}{2 r}$$

The values of C D and E F will be found from the following equations:—

$$\sqrt{C E^2 - D E^2} = C D, \text{ and}$$

$$\frac{C E (r - D E)}{r} = E F.$$

For example.—Let r = 15 chains or 990 feet, and the distance d = 1 chain or 66 feet, the length of the first offset is $\frac{66^2}{2 \times 990}$

= 2·2 feet. The distance to be laid off upon the line A C produced to give the place for this offset is $\sqrt{66^2 - 2\cdot2^2}$ = 65·963 feet. Again the length of the second offset is $\frac{66 \times 65\cdot963}{990}$ = 4·397 feet, and the distance to be laid off upon the chord produced to give the place for this offset is $\frac{66 \times (990 - 2\cdot2)}{990}$ = 65·85 feet.

A rough method of setting out curves is to extend a line from the tangential portion of the railway and measure an offset at the end of each chain. The length of the offset is found from the formula—

$$\text{Length in inches} = \frac{792}{\text{radius of curve in chains}},$$

in which 792 represents the number of inches in a chain.

For example.—If the curve has the radius of 40 chains, the length, in inches, of the offset at the end of the first chain is $\frac{792}{40}$ = 19·8.

A more rapid and more accurate method of setting-out circular curves is by means of angles at the circumference, a method first described by Rankine in 1843. It is based on the theorem (*Euclid*, III., 20) that the angle subtended by any arc of a circle at the centre of the circle is double the angle subtended by the same arc at any point in the circumference of the circle. In Fig. 79, A B is an arc of a circle, C is a point in its circumference lying beyond the arc. The angle A C B is half the angle subtended by A B at the centre of the circle. When the point at which the angle is measured lies upon the arc, as at E, it is the angle B E F = A E G

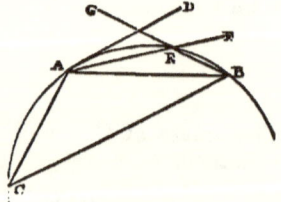

Fig. 79.

that is equal to half the angle at the centre of the circle. When the point at which the angle is measured is one of the ends of the arc, as at A, it is the angle D A B that is equal to half the angle at the centre of the circle, expressed by a formula, the angle at the circumference in minutes = A C B = F E B = D A B = half the angle at the centre

$$= 1718'\cdot 873 \, \frac{\text{length of arc}}{\text{radius of circle}}$$

in which formula, the coefficient is the value in minutes of one half of the arc that is equal to the radius.

The English practice of designating curves by their radii in chains has but few advantages, as there are no acreage calculations involved. It is preferable to express the radii in hundreds of feet, or chains of 100 feet. This method is now coming into general use. The American practice is to designate curves by the number of degrees in the angle subtended at the centre by an arc 100 feet in length. Thus, curves are named one-degree curves, two-degree curves, &c., when the central angle subtended by 100 feet is one degree, two degrees, &c. In this method, which is one of great convenience, confusion is created by terming the centre angle "the angle of deflection." The value of this angle in degrees is 5729·6 divided by the radius in feet.

In setting out curves by means of angles at the circumference, a 6-inch transit-theodolite is set and adjusted at a tangent point, as A, and directed along the tangent to D. An angle equal to half the degree of curvature is deflected from A D towards the side on which the curve is to run. Of the two chainmen, the follower holds his end of the chain at A, and the leader, keeping the chain stretched, is directed by the observer at the instrument into line with the axis of the telescope. In this way, the position of the point E on the curve is fixed. From the line A E, the same angle is set off, the instrument remaining at the tangent point. The chainmen move forward; the follower stopping at E, and the leader moving the stretched chain around that point as centre until the other end comes into line with the axis of the telescope. A second point B on the curve is thus obtained. By continuing the process of setting off angles equal to half the degree of curvature, and causing them to subtend distances of 100 feet each, the entire curve is set-out. It is necessary that the angle formed by producing the straight portions of the line, should be known, in order to find the place on the ground from which the curve is to start. As a rule, this may be taken at once with the theodolite. If an obstacle x intervenes, a point y is selected on one tangent, from which the distance $y z$ to the other tangent may be measured. The lengths $x y$ and $x z$ are then found by solving the triangle $x y z$.

When obstacles prevent all the points from being set-out from one tangent point, the theodolite must be moved to the last point set-out, having the last angle clamped on its upper plate.

SETTING-OUT. 235

The original tangent point being sighted with the vernier clamped at that angle, by setting it off a new tangential direction is obtained. By revolving the telescope, the tangent is produced in the other direction, from which tangential angles may be set-off to fix more points on the curve.

For example.—If the radius of the circle is 19 chains or 1254 feet, and the distance required between the points in the curve 100 feet, the tangent angle to be set-off will be

$$1718 \cdot 873 \times \frac{100}{1254} = 137 \cdot 07 \text{ minutes} = 2° \, 17' \, 4''.$$

The method of setting-out curves assumes that the chord of an arc is equal to the arc itself. The difference does not, however, give rise to sensible error.*

Cross-sections.—When each curve has been ranged, stakes, branded with the distance from the beginning of the line, should be driven in.

To ascertain the amount of excavation or embankment required to form the railway, cross-sections must be taken at each chain length at right angles to the longitudinal-section. The slope at which it is desirable to form a cutting or embankment depends on the nature of the ground. The usual slope is 1 foot fall in 1½ foot horizontal, or expressed by the *ratio of slope* 1½ to 1. Experience shows that fine dry sand will stand at an angle of 35°, dry loose shingle at 39°, and compact damp earth at 54°.

Driving Levels Underground.—In driving levels, it is usually necessary that a certain inclination shall be maintained. The miner must consequently be provided with suitable appliances in order to enable him to fulfil the required conditions.

In metal mines, if the level has to be driven horizontal, the easiest method is to conduct water into it. A dam is erected just before the working end, and the level is so driven that the water always maintains the same height. This method can, however, only be applied when no water is given off from the rock in the level, as with the slightest influx of water, the surface is disturbed and ceases to be horizontal.

The inclination of the level may be checked by means of a

---

* For accounts of the methods of setting-out curves in cases where extreme accuracy is required, the student may consult L. D. Jackson's *Aid to Survey Practice*, London, 1880, pp. 208-288; J. C. Trautwine's *Field Practice of Laying out Circular Curves for Railroads*, New York, twelfth edition, 1886; W. J. M. Rankine's *Civil Engineering*, London, sixteenth edition, 1887.

plumb-bob. The instrument usually employed (Fig. 80) is made of deal boards, 1¼ inch thick. The foot-piece is 6 feet in length and 4½ inches broad. The vertical piece is 3 feet in length, and 6 inches broad at the lower end, tapering upwards until, at the top, it is 4 inches broad. In addition to the plummet, there is a small spirit-level fixed to the foot-piece to serve as a check. The instrument is placed on the floor of the level, and if the latter is being driven truly horizontal, the plummet will hang in the hole made in the vertical piece for its reception, and at the same time the bubble will be in the middle of its tube.

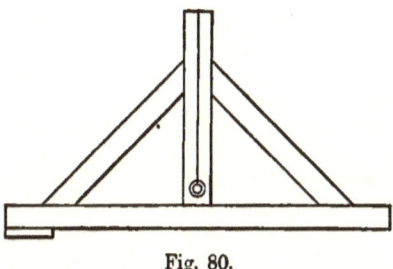

Fig. 80.

The main horse-roads in collieries should be driven with a slight inclination towards the shaft, so that water may flow from the workings to the sump. Experience has shown that an inclination of 1 in 130, or a little more than ¼ inch in the yard, gives the most advantageous effect in drawing by horse-power the loaded waggons towards the shaft, and the empty ones back.

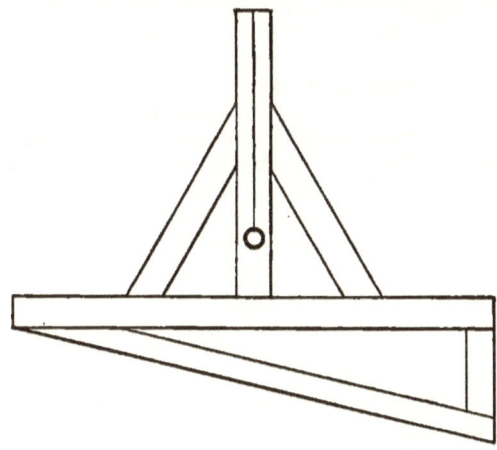

Fig. 81.

Care must be taken that this inclination is not exceeded, as, in driving levels, there is always a tendency to rise too fast. For maintaining the required inclination, a piece of board, ½ inch thick, should be screwed to the foot at the end of the instrument, which is nearer the shaft.

In order to test the inclination of an underground roadway with an inclination of 1 in 5, Mr. W. Wardle uses the instrument shown in Fig. 81. It is provided with two sole-pieces, the bottom of the lower one being at a distance of 1 foot from that of the upper one at one end, whilst at the other end it is brought to a feather edge.

An ingenious clinometer, invented by Colonel G. P. Evelyn (patent 1885, No. 1964), may be advantageously used for setting out levels at any inclination. It consists of a curved tube filled with water or dilute spirit, on which floats a small bubble of compressed air. Adjacent to the tube, and concentric with its outer periphery, is the graduated arc of a circle. When the air-bubble is at the zero point of that arc, the base of the stand, in which the tube is mounted, is horizontal, and any inclination from the horizontal is shown in degrees by the position of the bubble on the graduated arc. The tube is easily filled and emptied, and the size of the bubble is regulated by a screw-cap fitting over the cork.

To drive a level straight at a given bearing, plumb-lines are suspended from points in the roof previously fixed by the dial or theodolite. These lines indicate the direction in which the level has to be driven, and should be placed 30 to 60 feet apart.

Curves for Engine Planes.—Curves may be set out underground by means of a theodolite on a short tripod, and candles or lamps instead of ranging poles.

The direction in which curves for engine planes should be set out is sometimes roughly ascertained by making a careful survey and plan of the pillars and headings, through which it is required to drive the curve. The survey is plotted on a large scale—*e.g.*, 16 feet to an inch. The curve drawn on the plan is divided into equal distances marked by points. The latter are then connected by dotted lines. By means of a protractor, the bearing of each of these lines is determined. For greater accuracy, offsets are measured at every 6 feet on each side of the lines to the sides of the curve. In this way data are obtained from which the curve may be set out.

Setting-out Tunnels.—The centre-line of the tunnel having been ranged on the surface of the ground, a series of shafts are sunk from 100 to 200 yards apart along that line. In order to transfer the ranging of the line from above to below the surface of the ground, it is necessary to have two marks, consisting of nails driven in the cross-timbers in the centre-line at the bottom of each shaft as far apart as possible, to enable the line to be prolonged from the bottom of the shaft in both directions. To determine the positions of the marks underground, a ranging-frame is erected over the shaft. It consists of three half-timbers framed as a triangle and supported at the angular point by stout props. From the frame are suspended two plumb-lines, which are ranged by a transit-instrument.

As this process cannot be satisfactorily used except in calm weather, Mr. F. W. Simms introduced the following modification:—By means of the transit-instrument, the engineer ranges two stakes in the centre-line at the surface, each being about 16 feet from the centre of the shaft, so as to be safe from disturbance while the work is in progress. To mark the exact position of the centre-line a spike (Fig. 82) is driven into the top of each stake. The hole of each spike is carefully ranged in the centre-line, a piece of white paper being held at a short distance behind it, so as to render it visible to the observer at the telescope. A string is stretched centrally across the mouth of the shaft, and its ends are passed through the holes in the spikes. It is then drawn tight and made fast. At each side of the shaft a plank is fixed at right angles to the string, and so placed that one side hangs over the shaft about 3 inches, so that a plumb-line may hang from it without coming in contact with the side of the shaft. A plumb-line being hung from each plank directly under the cord marking the centre-line, the lower ends of these plumb-lines represent two points in the centre-line at the bottom of the shaft.

Fig. 82.

The approximate ranging of the heading connecting the lower ends of the shafts is effected by means of candles, each hung from the timbering in a sort of stirrup. The upper portion of the candle-holder (Fig. 83) employed by Mr. Simms is made of thin sheet-iron with a number of holes in it. The lower portion is of iron wire, carrying a socket for the candle. By means of the rack, the latter can be raised or lowered to the proper level, and being hung by a flat plate, it is prevented from rotating.

The accurate ranging of the centre-line, when the heading has been made, is effected by stretching a string between the marks already ranged at the bottom of the shaft, and fixing, at intervals of about 40 feet, either small perforated blocks of wood carried by cross-bars, or stakes with eyed-spikes driven into their heads, so that the holes may be ranged by the string exactly in the straight line.

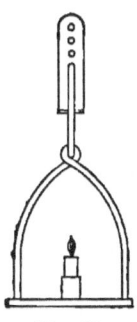

Fig. 83.

This method was employed by Mr. Simms for setting-out the Blechingley and Saltwood tunnels on the South-Eastern Railway. Both these tunnels were straight from end to end, as is generally the case. Their centre-lines were ranged with a transit-instrument of 30 inches focal length with an object-glass of $2\frac{3}{4}$ inches aperture. In order to command a view of every shaft, the instrument, mounted on a cast-iron stand, was set up on the highest point of ground as near the middle of the tunnel as possible, and raised above the surface by the erection of a temporary observatory. This consisted of a building of larch poles, in the centre of which was a brick pier 30 feet in height for the support of the instrument.

When the length of the tunnel is not very great, the transit-instrument and temporary observatory may be dispensed with, and the 6-inch or 5-inch transit-theodolite used with advantage. This was done in setting-out the Clifton tunnel in 1871 to 1874. This tunnel is straight, on an incline of 1 in 64. It is $1737\frac{1}{2}$ yards in length. At a distance of 276 yards from the lower end of the tunnel, where it approaches to within 140 feet of the Blackrock Cliff, a side drift was opened from the face of that cliff to the line of the tunnel. The tunnel was driven from this drift, and from two shafts sunk $998\frac{1}{2}$ yards and 4·63 yards farther on.

When the tunnels are of great length, and can only be driven from the ends, the setting out is much more difficult than when shafts can be sunk along the line. The direction of the axis of the tunnel is determined by a traverse or a triangulation connecting the two ends. In very long tunnels, such as those of the Alps, traversing is not sufficiently accurate, and recourse must be had to triangulation, as was the case at St. Gothard. The St. Gothard tunnel, the longest railway tunnel yet made, is nine miles in length. Its construction lasted from September, 1872, to February, 1880. The holing was effected on February 28, 1880, the length being 25 feet less than was expected. The error in level was 1·97 inch, and the error in alignment was 12·99 inches. (Fig. 83a.)

The Mont Cenis tunnel was set out in the years 1857 to 1858, without triangulation, with the aid of a high observatory. The length of the tunnel was determined by triangulation, and the line of levels was carried over the mountain. The tunnel is upwards of six miles in length, and the junction was effected without any error horizontally, and with only a foot of divergence vertically.

Remarkably accurate results in tunnel alignment were obtained

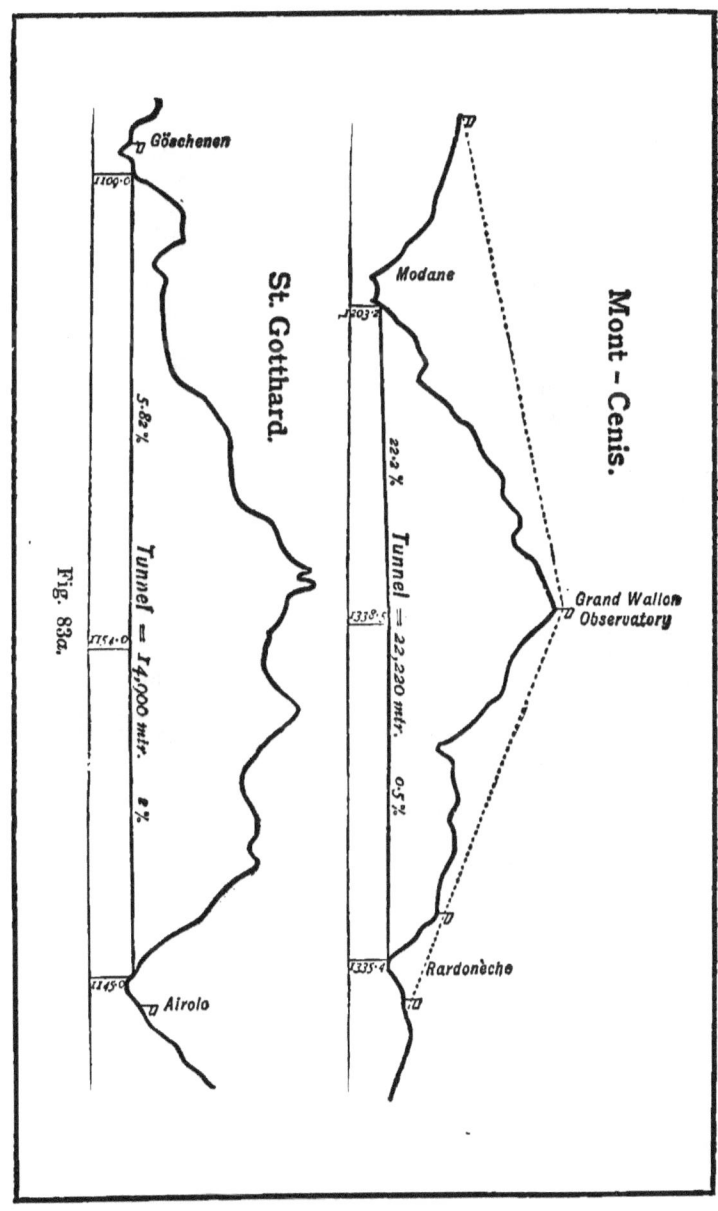

Fig. 83a.

in 1888 in the Croton aqueduct at New York. The points of commencement of two headings were 6,400 feet apart, the one being 270 feet and the other 353 feet below the surface. The diameter of the heading was 16·5 feet. The direction was obtained by means of two plumb-lines, 16·5 feet apart, let down each shaft. When the two headings approached each other, the final connection was made by two drills meeting in the same hole from opposite sides of the rock, and after the blast had been fired, it was found that the error in grade was 0·014 foot, and in alignment 0·09 foot.

In the construction of Division No. 6 of this aqueduct, Mr. F. W. Watkins, the engineer in charge, found that the centre-line wires were very difficult to distinguish, as the cross-hair of the telescope and the two plummet lines appear so nearly alike. He was, therefore, induced to devise an illuminated slit apparatus to replace the wires at the bottom of the tunnel. This instrument consists of two vertical strips of brass (3 inches in height) attached to separate horizontal bars moving in guides, and provided with a tangent-screw motion, by which one or both could be moved right or left and the vertical aperture between them made as small as desired. One of these instruments was screwed to a plank-bracket, close behind each plummet wire, and so placed that the farther one could be seen through the telescope in line just above the other. When these slits were adjusted so as to be directly behind the plummet wires, the latter were removed, and lights placed behind the slits. In this way two fixed and illuminated points were substituted for the wires. The results of tests of the alignment effected in this way show that the accuracy of the surveys was very remarkable.

Taking cross sections for measuring the areas and quantities of excavation in tunnel work is best done by measuring the irregularities of the contour of the section by angles and distances from some point in the vertical plane through the axis of the tunnel. For the Croton aqueduct tunnel, where sections had to be made every 10 feet for over 30 miles of tunnel, a convenient instrument was designed by Mr. A. Craven. This instrument, known from its yellow disc of varnished wood as the sunflower instrument, consists of a light wooden tripod with extensible legs, a shifting top, ball and socket joint, and levelling screws. A vertical brass tube slides through the socket, and carries at its top a wooden graduated disc, 18 inches in diameter. An arm revolving on a central socket traverses the face of the disc, and a wooden measuring rod, 14 feet in length, is placed on this arm, and slid out to touch the surface of the tunnel, the end of the arm at the same time indicating the angle from the vertical. The measuring rod tapers from 2 inches to $\frac{1}{8}$ inch in width, and is graduated in feet and tenths from the smaller end. In order to ensure the cross-section being taken at right angles to the axis of the tunnel, the disc is provided with a small sighting tube perpendicular to its face. The measurements are recorded in the field-book, and the areas of the cross-sections are determined by calculation, or by the planimeter.

When the difficulties of the task are duly considered, it is probable that the accuracy of the work at the Hoosac tunnel has never been equalled. This tunnel passes through the Hoosac Mountain range in Massachusetts, and is 25,031 feet in length. The tunnel was driven from the two ends, and also from a shaft 1,028 feet deep, sunk in the valley between two mountains in the line of the tunnel. On the east side, the headings met at a distance of 1,563 feet from the shaft, and 11,274 feet from the eastern end, the lateral error being 0·025 foot and the vertical error being 0·23 foot at the point of junction. Proceeding westward, the tunnel extended 2,056 feet from the shaft before meeting the excavation on the western side, which was 10,138 feet from the west entrance. The holing showed that the error of alignment was 0·045 foot. The alignment in the central shaft was obtained by two plumb-bobs 25 feet apart.

Curiously enough, the oldest piece of tunnelling of which there is any written record was begun at the two ends, its construction being recorded in the oldest example of Hebrew writing known. The inscription, now known as the Siloam inscription, was discovered by some boys bathing in the Pool of Siloam, in Jerusalem, in 1880. It is cut on a tablet 27 inches square at the mouth of the tunnel, and, according to the translation of Professor Sayce, reads as follows :—

"[Behold] the excavation! Now this is the story of the tunnel: While the miners were still lifting up the pick towards each other, and while there were yet 3 cubits [to be broken], the voice of one called to his neighbour, for there was an excess in the rock on the right. They rose up—they struck on the west of the tunnel; the miners struck each to meet the other pick to pick. And there flowed the waters from their outlet to the Pool for 1,200 cubits, and [three-quarters] of a cubit was the height of the rock over the heads of the miners."

From this inscription, it is evident that the tunnel was begun from the two ends. And this view is confirmed by the results of recent explorations. The Pool of Siloam is supplied with water from the so-called Spring of the Virgin, the only natural spring near Jerusalem, by this tunnel driven in the rock. According to Major Conder's survey, the tunnel is 1,708 feet long, or about 1,200 cubits of 18 inches. It does not, however, run in a straight line, and towards the centre there are two *culs-de-sac*, of which the inscription offers an explanation. We thus see that the engineering skill of the day was by no means despicable. Like the Mont Cenis tunnel, this aqueduct was begun simultaneously at the two ends, and in spite of its windings the workmen almost succeeded in meeting at the middle. They approached, indeed, so nearly to one another that the noise made by the picks of one party of miners was heard by the other, and the parting of rock was accordingly holed. This accounts for the two false cuttings now found at the centre of the tunnel, these representing the extreme points reached by the two parties before they had discovered that instead of meeting they were passing one another.

Though the inscription contains no indication of date, Professor Sayce is of opinion that the tunnel was made in the reign of Hezekiah, or possibly even in the time of Solomon.

With regard to the interpretation of the last line of the inscription that "three-quarters of a cubit was the height of the rock over the heads of the miners," it is remarkable that the difference of height of the two channels at the point of junction is just 13 inches, or close upon three-quarters of a cubit. Unfortunately, however, the text is deficient just in the place where the number occurs, and it may possibly indicate that the miners knew the thickness of the rock above them. In this case, the correct interpretation is probably 100 cubits, the average thickness of rock above the aqueduct. Several marks, evidently artificial, were discovered by Major Conder in the tunnel—square or triangular notches, measuring $1\frac{1}{2}$ inches in width. These appear to have been used, like the peg and nail of the Cornish miner, to mark the end of a periodical survey, or else to serve as a guide in setting the contracts to the miner.

It is certainly remarkable that there should have been so slight a difference in level between the two portions of the tunnel. It would have been easy, by means of a plumb-line or a rude water-level, to preserve the level of the channel floor; but it is extraordinary that the two ends should differ by only a foot in level, considering that they were started independently.

In New South Wales, a very successful alignment was effected by Mr. T. W. Keele* in the construction of the Nepean tunnel, a conduit for supplying Sydney with water. The tunnel is 23,507 feet long, the bases at the east and west ends being 254 feet and 212 feet respectively, situated at the bottoms of precipitous limestone gorges. There were six shafts, admitting of only 12-foot bases, the depths varying from 210·5 feet to 324 feet. The length between shafts Nos. 2 and 3 was 4,341 feet, the headings meeting at a point 3,018 feet from shaft No. 2. The error in alignment was $\frac{5}{8}$ inch, and in grade $\frac{1}{4}$ inch. The tunnel is $7\frac{1}{2}$ feet high and $9\frac{1}{2}$ feet wide, and is inclined at the rate of $2\frac{1}{2}$ feet per mile.

The line was transferred from the surface to the bottom of the shafts by plumbing. At the shafts brick pedestals were erected, one on each side, on the centre line, and about 50 feet apart, the tops being a foot above the shaft platform. Points were then accurately established on each, and a steel wire, 0·02 inch in diameter strained, at its utmost tension, from point to point across the shaft. The process of plumbing down the shaft was then proceeded with. An 8-inch transit theodolite on its centering legs was then set up in one of the headings, and the intersection of its cross-wires brought into coincidence with the line as given by the plummets. After the instrument had been adjusted to prolong the line into the heading, a hole was drilled in the roof and a wooden plug inserted; and on this the point was obtained by sighting on to a plummet lamp, of the type used in Pennsylvania, suspended from it. In order to give the levels in the tunnel, the value of a bench-mark at the bottom of a shaft was ascertained by measuring the calculated distance from the surface with a steel tape; and the levels were run into the headings. At intervals of 100 feet, hooks in pegs in the sides of the tunnel, and opposite to each other at right angles to the line, were so adjusted that strings stretched through them were exactly $2\frac{3}{4}$ feet above the grade. The plummet lamps, hanging from the centre-pegs in the roof, being then lowered until their lights were even with the horizontal strings, the axis of the tunnel was determined, and the miners were provided with both line and grade. All that they required to do was to place a candle at the face in line with the lights from the plummet lamps, and measure down 2 feet 9 inches to find the grade of the invert. Bench-marks were established at intervals of 500 feet, and were frequently checked.

The lengths of the headings and the results of the alignment, when the junctions were effected, were as follows:—

* *Min. Proc. Inst. C.E.*, vol. xcii., 1888, p. 259.

Name of Heading.	Length in Feet.	Error in Inches.	
		In Line.	In Grade.
Inlet.	2054·0 }	3	$\frac{3}{16}$
No. 5, West.	1513·2 }		
No. 5, East.	935·0 }	3	Nil.
No. 4, West.	1970·0 }		
No. 4, East.	2468·0 }	$\frac{7}{8}$	$\frac{3}{16}$
A, West.	425·0 }		
A, East.	496·0 }	$\frac{7}{8}$	$\frac{1}{8}$
No. 3, West.	1359·0 }		
No. 3, East.	1323·4 }	$\frac{7}{8}$	$\frac{1}{8}$
No. 2, West.	3018·0 }		
No. 2, East.	2385·0 }	$\frac{7}{8}$	$\frac{1}{8}$
No. 1, West.	2286·0 }		
No. 1, East.	1126·5 }	$2\frac{7}{8}$	$\frac{3}{16}$
Outlet.	2148·0 }		

After the tunnel had been pierced through, daylight at one end was distinctly seen, without the aid of a telescope, from the other, $4\frac{1}{2}$ miles away.*

* On tunnelling, consult F. W. Simms' *Practical Tunnelling*, 3rd ed., revised by D. K. Clark, London, 1877; H. S. Drinker, *Tunnelling*, New York, 1878, F. Rziha, *Lehrbuch der gesammten Tunnelbaukunst*, 2 vols., Berlin, 1867–72, with the authorities there cited, and F. W. Watkins, on "Tunnel Surveying on the New Croton Aqueduct," *Trans. Amer. Soc. C.E.*, vol. xxiii., 1890, p. 17. Valuable information on the setting-out of tunnels on the Dore and Chinley Railway is given by P. Rickard, *Min. Proc. Inst. C.E.*, vol. cxvi., 1894, p. 115.

CHAPTER XVII.

MINE-SURVEYING PROBLEMS.

Determination of the Direction and Inclination of a Mineral Deposit.—Problems relating to the working of mines may be solved graphically or numerically. Graphic solutions are the most simple, but they require the plans on which they are based to be of undoubted accuracy. Most problems are therefore more conveniently solved by the ordinary methods of descriptive geometry.

To determine the strike and dip of a vein that has been opened by a level driven along it, two points are selected in the axis of the level, either on the floor or on the roof. At these two points two vertical props are set up, when the bearing of a horizontal string connecting the two props will be the strike of the vein. Instead of the stretched string, a rod may be held horizontally.

The strike being determined, the direction of the dip may be determined by setting off a line at right angles to the strike. The dip may be measured with a clinometer.

A convenient instrument for determining the dip of mineral deposits is the so-called *gradometer*, invented by Mr. W. Fairley. It consists essentially of a 9-inch or 4-inch scale made to move up and down a vertical bar. When the lower edge of the scale is placed on the plane of which the dip is to be determined, and is shown to be level by the spirit-level on the upper edge, the plane is horizontal. When the plane is inclined, a slide, like that of the slide-rule, marked on one side in degrees and on the other in inches per yard, is taken out and passed through a slit at right angles to the longitudinal axis of the scale. For measuring dips above 45°, a second slide is provided. The gradometer is of less weight than a clinometer of the same length, and can be read with greater facility.

If the strike of a deposit is known, its dip may be calculated

Thus if a line A E, Fig. 84, is drawn on the plane of the deposit A B C D, and if through the point A, a horizontal plane A F passes, then A B, the line of intersection of the two planes, is the line of strike of the deposit. From any point G on the inclined line A E, let fall a perpendicular G H to the horizontal plane A F, and in the latter draw a horizontal line A J, which is the line of strike of the inclined line A E. The

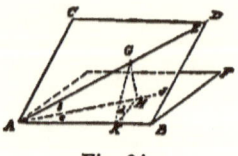

Fig. 84.

horizontal angle B A J is the difference in bearing between the line of strike of the deposit and that of the inclined line; whilst the angle G A H in the vertical plane E A J represents the dip of the inclined line A E. Let fall in the horizontal plane A F from the point H a perpendicular line H K to the line of strike A B, and join G K. Then G K is the line of dip of the deposit A B C D, and the angle G K H in the vertical plane G H K represents the angle of the dip of the deposit.

If the strike A B of the deposit is expressed by c, and the angle B A J = e, and the strike of the inclined line = a, then $e = c - a$. In the right-angled plane triangles A G H and A H K,

$$GH = AG \sin b, \text{ and}$$
$$HK = AG \cos b \sin e.$$

Then from the triangle G H K, the value of the required angle of dip may be found from the formula—

$$\tan GKH = \frac{GH}{HK} = \frac{AG \sin b}{AG \cos b . \sin e}$$

$$= \frac{\tan b}{\sin e}$$

Conversely if the angle of dip d is known, the strike may be found from the formula $\sin e = \tan b . \cotan d$.

For example.—1. What is the dip of a seam coursing 127° 30′, if a diagonal heading driven in the seam has a dip of 4°, and courses 90° or due east and west? The angle e is = 127° 30′ − 90° 00′ = 37° 30′. The dip d is then found from the equation

$$\tan d = \frac{\tan 4°}{\sin 37° 30'}.$$

Employing logarithms, this gives

$$L \tan 4° = 8\cdot 8446437$$
$$L \sin 37° 30' = 9\cdot 7844471$$
$$L \tan d = 9\cdot 0601966$$

Thus $d = 6° 33' 10''$.

2. *Example.*—Determine the strike of a seam dipping 8°, in which a diagonal heading is driven, dipping 5° and coursing 60°. In this case

$$\sin e = \frac{\tan 5°}{\tan 8°}.$$

Employing logarithms, this gives

$$L \tan 5° = 8\cdot 9419518$$
$$L \tan 8° = 9\cdot 1478025$$
$$L \sin e = 9\cdot 7941493$$

Therefore $e = 38° 30'$.

The strike c required is found from the equation $c = e + a$, thus

$$c = 38° 30' + 60° 00' = 98° 30'.$$

The strike and dip of a seam may be determined if three points in it are given. Thus if three bore-holes, not in a straight line, have been sunk to the floor of a seam, as shown in the plan, Fig. 85, H M T, the problem is solved as follows:—Measure the depths of the three bore-holes from the same assumed horizontal plane at the surface. In this case, T represents the deepest, and H the highest point of the deposit. Imagine perpendiculars to be erected to H M at the points H and M, and on them laid off the heights H H' and M M', representing the heights that the floor of the seam at the bore-holes H and M is above the floor at the bore-hole T. In this way, H' M' represents the line of inclination of the seam between H and M. That line is produced until it cuts the line H M produced at N. Thus a point in the seam is determined, which is situated at the same level as the bottom of the bore-hole T, and T N is the line of strike of the seam.

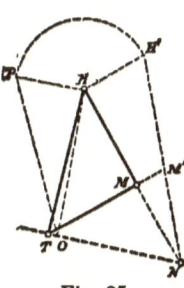

Fig. 85.

The line H N is found, from the similar right-angled triangles H H' N and M M' N, to be equal to

$$HN = \frac{HH' \cdot HM}{HH' - MM'} \qquad . \quad . \quad (1.)$$

From the bore-holes, the strike of H T and the angle N H T are known, and as H N is found from equation 1, in the triangle H N T there are two sides and the included angle known, consequently

$$HN + HT : HN - HT = \tan \tfrac{1}{2}(T + N) : \tan \tfrac{1}{2}(T - N) \quad (2.)$$

From this, the angles T and N are found, as half their sum is known. From the given strike H T and the angle T, the strike of the line T N may be deduced.

In order to determine the dip of the deposit, imagine a line H O drawn from H perpendicular to the line of strike T N, then in the right-angled triangle H O T, $\frac{HO}{HT} = \sin T$, whence it follows that H O = H T sin T.

At the point H erect a line perpendicular to H O, and along it lay off the height H P, being the height which the floor of the seam in the bore-hole H is above that in the bore-hole T. Then the line obtained O P is the true line of dip, and the angle H O P represents the angle of dip of the deposit. Thus tan H O P $= \frac{HP}{HO}$, or, by substitution, tan H O P $= \frac{HP}{HT \sin T}$.

Expressed by general formulæ,

$$\tan S = \frac{d'}{a \sin V}, \text{ and}$$

$$\tan V = \frac{\dfrac{d a'}{d'} \sin W}{a - \dfrac{d a'}{d'} \cos W}$$

in which S is the angle of dip of the bed, V the angle between the strike of the bed and M H, a the distance from M to H, a' the distance from M to T, W the angle in a horizontal plane between

M H and M T, d the difference of the depths of the bore-holes M and H, and d' the difference of the depths of M and T.

For example.—In Fig. 85, H T = 150 yards, H M = 112 yards, and M T = 100 yards, measured horizontally. The angle M H T = 41° 48′ 37″. T is the deepest bore-hole, and the floor of the seam in the bore-hole M is 32 yards, and in the bore-hole H 73 yards higher than in the bore-hole T. It is required to determine the strike and dip of the seam, when T H courses 172° 30′.

From the first equation given,

$$H N = \frac{73 \times 112}{73 - 32} = 199 \cdot 41 \text{ yards.}$$

Now, T + N = 180° − 41° 48′ 37″ = 138° 11′ 23″, and half T + N = 69° 5′ 41·5″. From the second equation

$$\tan \frac{T - N}{2} = \frac{199 \cdot 41 - 150}{199 \cdot 41 + 150} \cdot \tan 69° 5' 41 \cdot 5''$$

$$= \frac{49 \cdot 41}{349 \cdot 41} \cdot \tan 69° 5' 41 \cdot 5''$$

From this, half T − N is found by logarithms to be 20° 18′ 55″. Half T + N being 69° 5′ 41·5″, T is equal to 89° 24′ 36·5″, and N is equal to 48° 46′ 46·5″.

As the strike of T H is 172° 30′, and as T N lies to the right of T H, the strike of the latter is

$$(172° 30' + 89° 24' 36 \cdot 5'') - 180° = 81° 54' 36 \cdot 5''.$$

The angle of dip H O P is found from the equation

$$\tan H O P = \frac{73}{150 \cdot \sin 89° 24' 36 \cdot 5''}$$

By the aid of logarithms, the angle H O P is found to be 25° 57′ 7″.

The strike of the seam, as found above, can be set out at the surface in the usual way.

Determination of a Point at the Surface directly above one Underground.—If it is required to determine the position of the

MINE-SURVEYING PROBLEMS. 251

end of a level, it will be found advisable to calculate it trigonometrically instead of by plotting the traverse at the surface.

The rectangular co-ordinates of the underground-survey are calculated, and the distance and bearing of the end from the shaft found from the formulæ:

$$\tan \text{ of bearing} = \frac{\text{departure}}{\text{latitude}}, \text{ and}$$

$$\text{distance} = \text{latitude} \times \sec \text{ of bearing}.$$

For example.—In order to calculate the bearing and distance of the end of the level from the centre of the shaft in the survey of the Work and Rest mine, the record of which is given on p. 34, the latitudes and departures must first be calculated, with the following results:—

WORK AND REST MINE. REDUCED SURVEY NOTES.

No.	Distance.	Bearing.	Latitude.		Departure.	
			N.	S.	E.	W.
A	Feet. 74·50	N. 0° 15' W.	74·49	...	...	0·32
B	82·83	N. 14° 00' W.	80·37	...	...	20·03
C	63·00	N. 27° 39' W.	55·80	...	...	29·23
D	30·16	N. 84° 57' W.	2·65	...	...	30·04
E	23·75	S. 74° 06' W.	...	6·50	...	22·84
F	192·00	N. 67° 45' W.	72·70	...	...	177·70
G	96·50	N. 88° 00' W.	3·36	...	...	96·44
H	34·00	S. 84° 06' W.	...	3·49	...	33·82
J	23·75	S. 52° 00' W.	...	14·62	...	18·71
...	...	...	289·37	24·61	...	429·13

The total latitude is 289·37 − 24·61 = 264·76 feet, and the total departure is 429·13 feet. The distance from the shaft to the station-point J at the end of the level is found from the formulæ:

$$\tan \text{ of bearing} = \frac{429 \cdot 13}{264 \cdot 76}, \text{ and}$$

distance = 264·76 sec. of bearing.

The calculations are performed most quickly by means of logarithms, thus—

log 429·13	=	2·632588
log 264·76	=	2·422852
	10 +	0·209736 = L. tan 58° 20'
L. sec 58° 20'	=	10·2798601
log 264·76	=	2·422852
		12·7027121 − 10 = log 504·32

To determine the position of the point at the surface corresponding to the end underground, it is merely necessary to set-out from the shaft a horizontal distance of 504·32 feet at a bearing of 58° 20' or N. 58° 20' E.

This problem is of great importance for the determination of the position of the underground workings in reference to the boundaries of the concession or royalty.

Holing from one Excavation to another.—The usual problem relative to holing consists in determining the length and direction of the axis of a gallery joining two given points. The problem may be solved graphically or numerically. In the former case the plans employed must be rigorously exact. In the numerical method, the length and bearing are deduced from the co-ordinates of the end points.

For example.—In the survey between the Speedwell and Netherthorpe shafts at Staveley, of which the record is given on p. 75, the latitudes and departures of the 15 drafts underground from the Speedwell downcast shaft to the face of the main ventilating drift, intended to hole into Netherthorpe shaft, were calculated with the following results:—

REDUCED SURVEY NOTES.

No.	Bearing.	Distance.	Latitude.		Departure.	
			N.	S.	E.	W.
A	N. 34° 24' W.	Links. 13½	11·14	...	...	7·63
B	N. 58° 35' E.	639	333·08	...	545·32	...
C	N. 45° 41' E.	274	191·42	...	196·04	...
D	N. 37° 29' E.	130	103·16	...	79·11	...
E	N. 8° 40' W.	127	125·55	...	...	19·13
F	N. 15° 02' E.	405	391·14	...	105·05	...
G	N. 17° 57' E.	206	195·97	...	63·48	...
H	N. 11° 35' E.	158	154·78	...	31·72	...
J	N. 35° 37' W.	73	59·34	...	...	42·51
K	N. 18° 20' E.	260	246·80	...	81·78	...
L	N. 18° 14' E.	470	446·40	...	147·05	...
M	N. 69° 42' E.	384	133·22	...	360·15	...
N	S. 27° 45' E.	63	...	55·75	29·33	...
O	N. 69° 32' E.	73	25·52	...	68·39	...
P	N. 71° 57' E.	78	24·17	...	74·16	...
...	...	...	2441·69	55·75	1781·58	69·27

The total latitude amounts to 2441·69 − 55·75 = 2385·94 links, and the total departure 1781·58 − 69·27 = 1712·31 links.

The direct bearing and distance measured at the surface from the Speedwell downcast shaft to centre of Netherthorpe shaft, intended upcast, were N. 37° 02' E., 3113 links, representing 2485·06 links north latitude, and 1874·89 links east departure.

The positions from Speedwell shaft, in terms of latitude and departure, were consequently as follows:—

254   MINE-SURVEYING.

	N. Latitude.	E. Departure.
Netherthorpe shaft,	2485·06	1874·90
Face of heading,	2385·94	1712·31
	99·12	162·59

Now, tan of bearing = departure ÷ latitude, and distance = latitude × sec of bearing, therefore the distance to be holed is found as follows:—

log departure = log 162·59	=	2·211093
log latitude = log 99·12	=	1·996161
L tan of bearing	= 10 +	0·214932

The bearing is therefore N. 58° 38' E.

log latitude = log 99·12	=	1·996161
L sec 58° 38'	=	10·283568
log distance	=	12·279729 − 10

The distance is therefore 190·43 links.

Having thus calculated the bearing and horizontal distance from the face of the heading to the intended upcast shaft, Mr. Howard determined to drive direct into the shaft, and the drift was accordingly set-out at the calculated bearing and distance. His survey and calculations were proved by the holing to be absolutely correct.

If it is required to determine the inclination and distance of the axis of the heading uniting the two given points, and the co-ordinates of those two points referred to three axes of rectangular co-ordinates are $x\ y\ z$ and $x'\ y'\ z'$ respectively, the distance d, the bearing β, and the inclination α, may be found from the formulæ—

$$d = \sqrt{(x - x')^2 + (y - y')^2 + (z - z')^2}$$

$$\tan \beta = -\frac{x - x'}{y - y'},$$

$$\sin \alpha = \frac{z - z'}{\sqrt{(x - x')^2 + (y - y')^2 + (z - z')^2}}$$

Attention must be paid to the signs of the co-ordinates, which always indicate the position in space of the axis considered.

A remarkable example of successful holing is afforded by the Ernst-August adit level in the Harz. This great adit, one of the longest in the world, was commenced in 1850 and completed on

22nd July, 1864; it has a total length of 25,956 metres. It was driven from the bearings and distances calculated from the results of a survey made with extreme accuracy by means of the theodolite and spirit-level from a number of points. The results of the holings were as follows :—

ERNST-AUGUST ADIT LEVEL.

	Length Surveyed.	Error on Holing.	
		In Direction.	In Level.
	Fathoms.	Inches.	Inches.
1. Holing in Regenbogen mine,	310	0·2	0·15
2. Holing between the mouth of the adit at Gittelde, and the Fahlenberg shaft,	880	0·3	0·40
3. Holing between the Meding shaft and the George shaft,	2,700	1·5	0·40
4. Holing between the Hülfe Gottes shaft and the mouth,	2,760	1·0	0·23
5. Holing between the George shaft and the Knesebeck shaft,	1,580	1·5	0·60
6. Holing between the Knesebeck shaft and the Hülfe Gottes shaft,	1,430	1·1	0·14
7. Holing between the Schreibfeld shaft and the Haus Sachsen shaft,	1,890	1·5	0·37
8. Holing between the Meding shaft and the Ernst-August shaft,	3,960	1·2	0·09
9. Holing between the Ernst-August shaft and the Haus Sachsen shaft,	1,190	0·7	0·06

To drive a tunnel through a hill, the line of the tunnel is set out over the hill, and carefully levelled from the commencement at the foot of the hill. When it is thought that the level of the starting-point has been reached, or, in other words, when the rises are equal to the falls, an assumed mark is placed, and the levels accurately calculated. The assumed mark is then moved up or down the height by which the rises and falls differ, to give the exact position of the floor of the tunnel on the farther side of the hill.

If the levelling is effected by the theodolite instead of by the spirit-level, the total of the calculated bases of the various drafts gives the length of the tunnel.

Sinking Shafts from Several Levels.—Similar problems to those relating to galleries are presented by shafts which have to be sunk from several levels. If the shaft to be sunk is near an existing shaft, the problem is comparatively simple, as it is then merely necessary to drive headings from that shaft at different levels until their ends reach the axis of the shaft to be sunk.

The conditions are not always so favourable; the shaft to be sunk may be at a considerable distance from any existing shaft. In such a case, points are selected at each level of the mine-workings, as near as possible to the shaft to be sunk. From these points headings are driven to the axis of the shaft. The length and direction of these headings may be calculated from surveys made at the various levels of the mine. It is, of course, necessary that the surveys shall be made with extreme accuracy with the theodolite.

This method was employed in the Harz for sinking the Königin Marie shaft, the first perpendicular shaft sunk in that district. In 1851 it was decided by the Government authorities to drive a deep water-level at a depth of $120\frac{1}{4}$ fathoms under the Ernst-August deep adit, by which the mines of the Upper Harz were then drained. The new deep water-level was intended to serve as a great common water-reservoir for the mines of the district. From this level, which is 324 fathoms below the surface, and 116 feet below sea-level, the water is raised to the Ernst-August adit. For the reception of the engine for raising the water, it was decided to sink a new perpendicular shaft, the Königin Marie shaft, which should also be utilized for raising the ore from several mines.

In order to expedite as far as possible this important work, the shaft had to be sunk from several levels. It was sunk from the surface to the deep George adit, a depth of 146 fathoms, and at the same time commenced at a level 202 fathoms below the surface, and at another 270 fathoms below the surface.

Careful surveys having been made at each level, the shaft was set-out from the points obtained from the calculated co-ordinates. The different holings were successfully effected in 1866.

The accuracy of the work was then tested by suspending a plumb-line in the shaft, and determining the position of the shaft at the three levels. The plumb-line at the surface was exactly in the centre of the hoisting compartment of the shaft, at a distance of 40 inches from each of the long sides, and 70 inches from each of the short sides.

Designating the shaft as A B C D, the distance of the plumb-line from the sides at the different levels was as follows:—

	AB Inches.	CD Inches.	AC Inches.	BD Inches.
At the surface,	40·0	40·0	70·0	70·0
At the 146-fathom level,	41·5	38·5	71·0	69·0
At the 202-fathom level,	42·6	37·4	70·0	70·0
At the 270-fathom level,	40·8	39·2	68·6	71·4

From these results it follows that the deviation of the shaft from the vertical was as follows:—

	Short Sides. Inches.	Long Sides. Inches.
At the 146-fathom level,	1·0	1·5
At the 202-fathom level,	0·0	2·6
At the 270-fathom level,	1·4	0·8

Thus, the Königin-Marie shaft presents a brilliant illustration of accurate mine-surveying.

The Cubical Content of a Mine-Reservoir may easily be determined by the aid of a levelling-instrument. The cubical content must be calculated so as to ascertain the quantity of water which the proposed reservoir will hold. In shape, a mine-reservoir resembles most closely a truncated pyramid. It is therefore supposed to be cut, at given vertical distances, parallel to the surface of the water. The cubical content of the reservoir is then determined from the area of these horizontal sections and their vertical distance apart.

When a suitable site for the reservoir has been selected, and the height of the dam fixed, the highest level (1, Fig. 86) of the water is marked by a stake fixed into the dam. The water-line of the reservoir is then determined by finding with the spirit-level a number of points lying in the level of 1. All these points are then marked by numbered stakes. Some 2 to 3 yards vertically below the first stake, a second stake is fixed into the dam. The contour of the reservoir at this level is then determined by the spirit-level, and marked

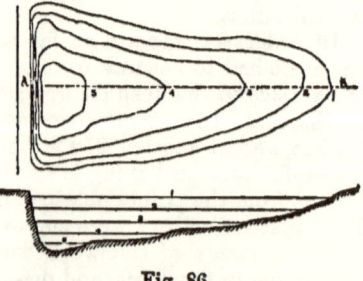

Fig. 86.

by numbered stakes. In a similar way, contours of the reservoir at lower water-levels are determined and marked out. The contours marked out by the numbered stakes are then surveyed by means of the dial, the prismatic compass, or the plane-table, and laid down on a plan to a large scale. From this plan, the areas, the cubical content of the reservoir is calculated by means of the formula $V = \frac{1}{3} h (B + \sqrt{Bb} + b)$, where h is the vertical height and B, b the area of the ends.

For example.—In the mine-reservoir, shown in Fig. 86, five horizontal sections were determined at vertical distances of 1·000, 1·050, 1·000, and 0·875 fathoms apart. The vertical distance from the fifth and last section to the bottom of the reservoir was 0·375 fathom. Each of the five water-levels were distinguished by numbered stakes, so marked that all belonging to one section had the same number. The five horizontal sections were then surveyed with the compass, and plotted on a suitable scale (1 : 1,000). The cubical content was then found to be 41814·13 cubic fathoms as shown in the following table:—

CUBICAL CONTENT OF A MINE-RESERVOIR.

Level.	Area.	Vertical Distance of Levels Apart.	Cubical Content.
1	Square Fathoms. 21843·31	Fathoms. 1·000	Cubic Fathoms. 18931·11
2	16161·29	1·050	13362·90
3	9577·30	1·000	6825·46
4	4404·34	0·875	2500·50
5	1553·25	0·375	194·16
Bottom.	0·00	...	...
...	...	...	41814·13

The cubical content of a dump-heap is found in a similar manner.

Determination of the Strike and Dip of the Line of Intersection of Two Veins.—It is important to determine the position of this line, as it is frequently found to be a line near or along which a run of rich deposit is likely to be met with. It is also of value in solving problems relating to the dislocations of veins. Rules for determining by means of spherical trigonometry the strike of the line of intersection are given in the treatises on mine-surveying by Von Oppel (1749), Kaestner (1775), and Lempe (1782). The simplest trigonometrical solution to the problem is that given by A. Rhodius.*

The problem may be solved by construction. Let $a\,b'$ and $b''\,c$ (Fig. 87) be the lines of strike, at a given level, of the two lodes dipping at angles of α and α'.
In order to determine the line of intersection, the perpendiculars $i\,k$ and $l\,m$ are let fall in the direction of the dip of the lodes, and made the bases of right-angled triangles, the hypothenuses of which are inclined at angles of α and α' respectively, the perpendicular being the same (h) in both cases. The lines $k\,n$ and $m\,o$ are

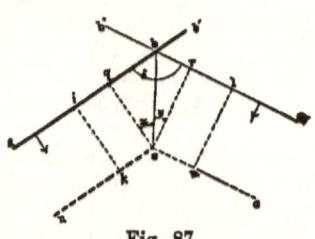

Fig. 87.

then drawn parallel to $a\,b'$ and $b''\,c$, and continued until they intersect in the point e. Then e is a point of intersection of the two lodes at a level which is deeper than the point of intersection b, by a distance h, and consequently $b\,e$ is the line of intersection of the two lodes. The strike of this line can be measured with the protractor.

By constructing a right-angled triangle with its base equal to the line of intersection, $b\,e$, and its perpendicular equal to h, then the angle at e represents the angle of inclination or dip of the line of intersection. This angle may be measured with the protractor.

The preceding construction is generally to be recommended. The problem may, however, be solved by means of plane trigonometry. The following is the solution given by Rhodius:—If $b\,e$, as in the first solution, represents the line of intersection of the two veins $a\,b'$ and $b''\,c$, then $e\,q$ and $e\,r$, lines parallel to $i\,k$ and $l\,m$, are lines at right angles to the strike of the veins. The angles which $e\,q$ and $e\,r$ form with the line of strike $b\,e$ of the line of intersection being indicated by x and y respectively, the following equations are obtained:—

$$eq = h \cot \alpha\,;\ er = h \cot \alpha',\quad . \quad (1.)$$

$$eq = be \cdot \cos x\,;\ er = be \cdot \cos y,\quad . \quad (2.)$$

---

* *Preuss. Ztschr.*, vol. xiv., 1866, p. 119.

$$\therefore \frac{eq}{er} = \frac{\cotan \alpha}{\cotan \alpha'} = \frac{\cos x}{\cos y}, \quad . \quad . \quad . \quad (3 \text{ and } 4.)$$

and
$$\frac{\cotan \alpha + \cotan \alpha'}{\cotan \alpha'} = \frac{\cos x + \cos y}{\cos y}, \quad . \quad . \quad (5.)$$

$$\frac{\cotan \alpha - \cotan \alpha'}{\cotan \alpha'} = \frac{\cos x - \cos y}{\cos y}, \quad . \quad . \quad (6.)$$

$$\therefore \frac{\cotan \alpha + \cotan \alpha'}{\cotan \alpha - \cotan \alpha'} = \frac{\cos x + \cos y}{\cos x - \cos y}, \quad . \quad . \quad (7.)$$

But
$$\frac{\cotan \alpha + \cotan \alpha'}{\cotan \alpha - \cotan \alpha'} = \frac{\cos \alpha \cdot \sin \alpha' + \sin \alpha \cos \alpha'}{\cos \alpha \cdot \sin \alpha' - \sin \alpha \cos \alpha'}$$

$$= \frac{\sin (\alpha' + \alpha)}{\sin (\alpha' - \alpha)}.$$

Substituting $u + v$ for x and $u - v$ for y, so that $u = $ half $x + y$ and $v = $ half $x - y$, the equation 7 becomes

$$\frac{\sin (\alpha' + \alpha)}{\sin (\alpha' - \alpha)} = -\frac{\cos u \cos v}{\sin u \sin v}$$

$$= - \cotan \tfrac{1}{2} (x + y) \cdot \cotan \tfrac{1}{2} (x - y).$$

$$\therefore \cotan \tfrac{1}{2} (x - y) = \frac{\sin (\alpha + \alpha')}{\sin (\alpha - \alpha')} \tan \tfrac{1}{2} (x + y)$$

$$= \frac{\sin (\alpha + \alpha')}{\sin (\alpha - \alpha')} \cotan \tfrac{1}{2} \delta, \quad . \quad . \quad (8.)$$

In this, δ represents the value of the angle abc, included by the lines of strike of the two lodes, so that $\tfrac{1}{2} \delta = 90° - \tfrac{1}{2} (x + y)$, and $\tfrac{1}{2} (x + y) = 90° - \tfrac{1}{2} \delta$. The angle δ is known, and x and y are found from these two equations.

The angle of dip ψ of the line of intersection is calculated in the following way:—$h = be \tan \psi$, therefore,

$$\tan \psi = \frac{h}{be} = \frac{h \cdot \cos x}{eq} = \frac{h \cos y}{er}$$

$$= \frac{\cos x}{\cotan \alpha} = \frac{\cos y}{\cotan \alpha'} \quad . \quad . \quad . \quad (9.)$$

In order to employ this formula, the value of the angle x or y

must first have been determined. The angle of dip is found more conveniently from the formula,—

$$\tan \psi = 2 \frac{\sin \alpha \sin \alpha'}{\sin (\alpha + \alpha')} \cdot \sin \tfrac{1}{2} \delta \cos \tfrac{1}{2} (x - y).$$

For example.—The strike of a lode is 101° 15', and its dip 80° towards south; the strike of a second lode is 170° 37½', and its dip 75° towards west; required the strike and the dip of the line of intersection of the two lodes.

By applying the formulæ given, the former will be found to be 62° 27½', and the latter 74° 15' 26".

The Search for Dislocated Lodes.—In following a lode, it frequently happens that a cross-course is met, and, after driving through it, the lode is not to be found on the other side. In such cases it is said to be dislocated or *heaved*. The two intersecting veins seldom form an intersection at right angles; more commonly one is inclined to the other. In Cornwall, of 272 cases of intersection, recorded by Mr. W. S. Henwood,* 22·7 per cent. were intersected but not heaved, 26·2 per cent. were found by driving to the left hand, and 51·1 per cent. to the right hand; 63·5 per cent. were found by driving on the side of the greater angle and 12·9 on the side of the smaller angle. The average distance of dislocation was 16·4 feet.

The first clear views on the subject were put forward in 1810 by Schmidt, who stated that dislocations were to be explained by a sinking of the hanging-wall of the dislocator. Schmidt's rule, as modified by v. Carnall, is as follows:—

If the dislocator is struck on its hanging-wall, it must be passed through, and the driving continued in the hanging-wall of the dislocated lode. If the foot-wall of the dislocator is struck, it must be passed through, and the driving continued in the foot-wall of the dislocated lode. For obtuse angles of dislocation, the rule is reversed. The angle of dislocation is the angle formed by the line of intersection of the two veins, and that portion of the line of strike of the dislocator which enters into the foot-wall of the lode.

On Schmidt's theory, Zimmermann in 1828 based his rule, which is more convenient to use, as it makes no exception of the obtuse angle. His construction is as follows:—

At the point D (or E), Fig. 88, in which the dislocator A is cut, erect, on the line of strike and towards the inside of the dislocator, a perpendicular line D L (E L') lying in a horizontal plane. Determine the position of the line M N (M' N') in which the

* *Trans. R. Geol. Soc., Cornwall,* vol. v., 1843.

planes of the dislocator and of the lode intersect. Prolong the line to N (M') towards the opposite selvage making it D N (E M'). Observe to which side the perpendicular D L (E L') deviates from the line of intersection when it is directed towards the opposite selvage, and after passing through the dislocator, seek the dislocated portion of the lode on the side towards which the perpendicular D L (E L') falls.

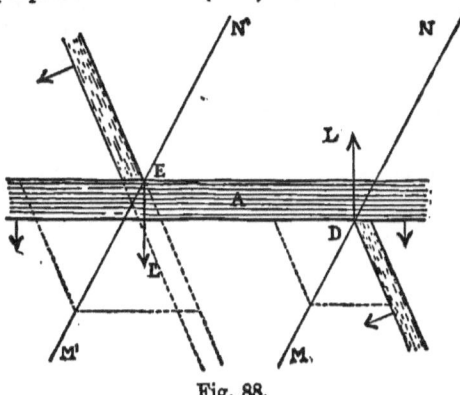

Fig. 88.

The construction is very simple. The line of intersection of the lode and the dislocator is determined by the method described. It is then merely necessary to erect a perpendicular at the point D (or E). If the line of intersection is to be determined by plane trigonometry, formula 8 is employed.

For example.—On driving along a lode, $d\,c$, from d towards c, Fig. 89, it is found that the lode ends at c, having been dislocated by a fissure $a\,b$. The fissure has a strike β of $118°\,7\frac{1}{2}'$, and a dip α' of $55°$ towards the south-west, and the lode has a strike β of $150°$, and a dip α of $82°\,30'$ towards the north-east.

The first problem is to determine the line of intersection of the two veins. The point of intersection i being found by the process previously described, $c\,i$ represents the strike of the line of intersection. By erecting a perpendicular $c\,k$ at the point c, it is evident that

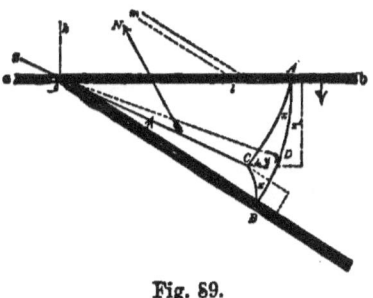

Fig. 89.

MINE-SURVEYING PROBLEMS. 263

the lost vein lm will be found, after the dislocator has been passed through, by driving from c in the direction cb.

If the line of intersection is to be determined by means of plane trigonometry, by employing formula 8, the required line of intersection will be found to have a strike of 145° 6' 23".

If recourse is had to spherical trigonometry, the calculations are more simple. With c as the centre of a sphere, the spherical triangle A B C is described, in which the side A B ($= \varphi = \beta - \beta'$) is in the horizontal plane A c B, A C is in the plane of the fissure ab, and B C in the plane of the lode cd. Again, c D is the horizontal projection of the line of intersection S c C, and C D an arc perpendicular to A B, and from the two right-angled triangles A C D and B C D,

(1.) $\tan y = \sin x \cdot \tan \alpha'$, and
(2.) $\tan y = \sin (\varphi - x) \cdot \tan \alpha$.

From these two equations, it is found that

$$\cotan x = \frac{\tan \alpha'}{\tan \alpha \cdot \sin \varphi} + \cotan \varphi.$$

Numerical values being substituted,

$$\cotan x = \frac{\tan 55°}{\tan 82° 30' \cdot \sin 31° 52\tfrac{1}{2}'} + \cotan 31° 52\tfrac{1}{2}'$$

$$\therefore x = 26° 58' 53''$$

Now, the strike of the fissure ab is 118° 7½'; therefore, the strike of the line of intersection S c C = 118° 7½' + 26° 58' 53" = 145° 6' 23".

If, in the example given, it was found necessary to drive 11 yards from c towards b, in order to reach the lost lode at l, the sinking H of the hanging-wall of the dislocator, must, according to Zimmermann, have amounted to

$$H = \frac{11 \cdot \sin 31° 52\tfrac{1}{2}''}{\cos 55° \cdot \cos 31° 52\tfrac{1}{2}'' + \cotan 82° 30' \cdot \sin 55°}$$

= 9·76381 yards.

Irregularities of Seams and Beds.—Bedded deposits are frequently found to be interrupted by *faults*, causing a cutting-off of the bed, and a displacement of it up or down. A fault of this kind is termed a *hitch* or *trouble*; if on a very large scale, a *dyke*. In order to represent the direction of the displacement, the fault is known as an *up-throw* or *down-throw*.

The alterations in position of stratified deposits undergone

since their deposition, may be divided into three classes—
(1) Faults caused by folding of the strata; (2) throws or faults
caused by fissures; (3) displaced faults. Faults of the first and
third class are only met with in folded strata; faults of the
second class also occur in horizontal strata. All these faults
give rise to dislocation of beds and seams, and rules have been
formulated, like those for lodes, for ascertaining the direction in
which to search for the displaced bed or seam.

Folded faults are, as A. Heim first showed, merely the final
result of folding. In many cases, the progressive steps may be
observed in the strike of the same fault. The mode of formation
of such faults must therefore be considered, not as an hypothesis,
but as an absolute well-established fact. Thus, at the Mansfeld
Mine near Langendreer, a folded fault is very apparent in a
certain cross-cut, whilst 162 feet further north it becomes a
simple folding. Folded faults can only occur in beds and seams,
but not in veins, for these, being filled-up fissures, are of more
recent age than the country rock, and its foldings. With faults
of this kind, the same seam is frequently met several times at
one level. If a fault is recognised as belonging to the folded
class, the direction in which to search for the displaced seam
may easily be decided by means of a sectional sketch.

Throws or fissure faults, are those which have arisen entirely
through the slipping down of the strata on the hanging-wall of
the dislocator. The rule for ascertaining the direction in which
to search for the displaced seam is as follows:—If the dislocating
fissure is met on its hanging-wall, the displaced seam must be
sought in the direction of the hanging-wall of the strata after the
fissure is passed through. Conversely, if the fault is dipping
from you, you must proceed downwards. Zimmermann's construction is applicable to dislocated seams as well as veins.

The third class of faults were first observed by Professor
Koehler in the Westphalian coal-fields, and subsequently in the
lodes of the Harz. Under the term displaced faults (Verschiebungen) are to be understood those dislocations, in which a part
of the previously folded or vertical strata, with the seams
contained therein, was torn away, by the force that caused the
folding, from another part of the strata, and slid or pushed away.
In such cases, the seams and the strata appear curved in the
direction of the movement, and gradually thinned out, though
no folding is to be observed, as is the case with folded faults.
In addition, the plane of disruption exhibits traces of the
movement in the form of slickensides and striations.

These displaced faults may thus be easily distinguished from
other faults. A fault having been recognised as belonging to

this category, the displaced portion of the seam may be found by crossing the plane of disruption, and seeking the shifted portion of the deposit on the side towards which that plane is inclined.*

Subsidence and Draw.—Interesting problems are presented by the surface subsidence caused by the removal of coal in the mine. By means of very accurate levelling, Mr. J. S. Dixon † made a valuable series of observations at Bent Colliery on the subject of the subsidence and draw from working the coal; the facts disclosed upsetting many old rule-of-thumb ideas on the subject. In order to arrive at correct conclusions in an inquiry of this kind, the best way is to select a line for a section on the surface, and peg it off, or have some other means of fixing levels that can be tested from time to time.

The line selected at Bent was at right angles to the advancing workings, and as nearly as possible on the level course of the coal. Pegs were put in at first every 100 feet, and afterwards every 50 feet. The Ell coal at this colliery was worked by the pillar-and-stall method up till the middle of 1881, when the removal of the pillars was commenced. It was, however, some time before this operation reached the line along which the section was taken. The excavation was 5 feet 6 inches in height, and the superincumbent strata were allowed to fall and fill it up. The strata are of a firm nature, and the surface is mostly boulder clay.

The original level of the surface before the pillars were removed is shown by the figures in the table on p. 242. The pillars were removed for a distance of 240 feet back from the solid coal on January 21, 1882, and no subsidence of the surface had ensued. On May 27, 1882, the levels showed the maximum subsidence to have been 1·80 feet at peg 1650, 145 feet back from the face, and the draw, that is, the disturbance at the surface beyond the point of excavation, 60 feet outwards from a point perpendicularly above the working face. On November 14, 1882, the face was 610 feet from the solid, and the subsidence from the original level was as shown in the table. On April 15, 1883, the face was 750 feet from the solid; on November 27, 1883, it was 1060 feet distant; and on October 23, 1884, the removal of the pillars had been completed for some months, and the face was 1230 feet from the solid. The levels were again

---

* On the dislocations of veins, beds, and seams, consult S. C. L. Schmidt, *Theorie der Verschiebungen älterer Gänge*, Frankfurt, 1810 ; C. Zimmermann, *Die Wiederausrichtung verworfener Gänge, Lager und Flötze*, Darmstadt, 1828; R. von Carnall, *Karstens Archiv.*, vol. ix., 1842, p. 3; H. Hoefer, *Oestr. Ztschr.*, 1881., p. 168, translated by R. W. Raymond, *Trans. Amer. Inst. M. E.*, 1882; R. Dannenberg, *Ueber Verwerfungen*, Saarbrucken, 1883; G. Koehler, *Störungen der Gänge, Flötze, und Lager*, Leipzig, 1886.

† *Trans. Mining Inst. Scotland*, vol. vii., 1886., p. 224.

taken on June 17, 1885; the workings being in the same position as they had been for about a year. On December 4, 1885, it was found that the subsidence had practically ceased, and the draw had not altered.

SUBSIDENCE AT BENT COLLIERY.

Peg.	Original Level of Surface.	Subsidence from Original Level at					
	1881.	14th Nov., 1882.	5th April, 1883.	27th Nov., 1883.	23rd Oct., 1884.	17th June, 1885.	4th Dec., 1885.
600	640·6	...	...	...	0·25	0·35	0·45
650	648·9	...	...	...	0·35	0·60	0·60
700	657·2	...	...	...	0·77	0·94	0·94
750	664·6	...	...	...	1·18	1·27	1·40
800	667·5	...	...	0·23	1·37	1·75	2·00
850	673·1	...	...	0·63	1·50	2·24	2·34
900	675·6	...	...	1·13	2·57	2·74	2·82
950	676·0	...	...	1·61	2·97	3·14	3·22
1000	677·1	...	...	2·10	3·27	3·49	3·60
1050	677·3	...	...	2·43	3·32	3·64	3·75
1100	678·8	...	0·50	2·80	3·52	3·80	4·00
1150	679·7	...	0·70	2·93	3·57	3·81	3·92
1200	680·6	...	1·20	...	3·52	3·52	3·52
1250	680·9	0·60	1·60	3·08	3·45	3·45	3·45
1300	679·2	0·40	2·00	3·03	3·42	3·42	3·42
1350	677·9	1·60	2·25	3·00	3·27	3·27	3·27
1400	677·5	1·60	2·45	3·83	3·17	3·17	3·17
1450	680·8	2·30	2·90	3·42	3·42	3·42	3·42
1500	680·1	...	3·05	3·05	3·05	3·05	3·05
1550	677·1	2·90	3·20	3·20	3·20	3·20	3·20
1600	675·5	3·00	3·00	3·00	3·00	3·00	3·00
1750	672·8	2·80	2·80	2·80	2·80	2·80	2·80
1850	663·4	1·70	1·70	1·70	1·70	1·70	1·70
1950	648·6	0·60	0·60	0·60	0·60	0·60	0·60
2000	649·7	0·04	0·04	0·04	0·04	0·04	0·04

The conclusion arrived at is that subsidence from the removal of coal in this case attains its maximum towards the centre of the excavated space, and gradually decreases in each direction. The maximum subsidence was 4·00 feet, and the average from peg 1,000 to peg 1,600 was 3·76 feet, or 73 and 68 per cent. respectively of the height of the excavation. The wave of maximum subsidence regularly followed the working face at an average distance back of 186 feet, or 1 foot horizontal for each 3½ feet perpendicular. The permanent lengths of the draw may be taken as 100 feet (Nov. 14, 1882) on the one side, and 83 feet on the other (Oct. 23, 1884). At these points, the depth to the coal was 650 and 646 feet, representing a draw of 1 horizontal for each 6·5 feet perpendicular, and of 1 horizontal for each 7·78 feet perpendicular respectively.

The coal at Bent, it should be noted, dips at right angles to the line of section at an inclination of about 1 in 20.

The question is one of great importance to mine-surveyors in relation to the effect, on the surface, of mineral workings, and to the area of coal that should be left to prevent damage to buildings. It is consequently highly desirable that similar investigations should be made in other coal-fields.

From a careful study of the subsidence occurring in the Saxon coal-field, R. Hausse,* of the Zaukeroda Colliery, has arrived at some interesting results. The direction of the plane of fracture occurring on the breaking of undermined strata is determined by the angle of fracture—that is, the angle made by the plane of fracture with the horizontal plane. Then if φ is the angle of fracture, and β the dip of the strata, the following equation is obtained:—

$$\tan \varphi = \frac{1 + \cos^2 \beta}{\sin \beta \cos \beta}.$$

Then, if β is equal to 0°, this equation becomes $\tan \varphi = \infty$, and $\varphi = 90°$; in other words, in horizontal strata the plane of fracture coincides with the line of gravity. When $\beta = 90°$, the equation again becomes $\tan \varphi = \infty$, and $\varphi = 90°$; that is to say, in vertical strata, the plane of fracture coincides with the line of gravity. By means of the formula, the angle of fracture may be calculated in any case from the dip of the strata. In this way the following results are obtained:—

* *Saechs. Jahrbuch,* 1886, p. 111.

When β	=	0° then φ	=	90° 00'
		10°		85° 10'
		20°		80° 30'
		30°		76° 10'
		40°		73° 00'
		45°		71° 40'
		50°		70° 50'
		60°		71° 00'
		70°		74° 00'
		80°		80° 50'
		90°		90° 00'

To show how these theoretical results compare with results actually obtained in practice, the following example may be cited:—For supporting the Siemens' glass works at Doehlen in Saxony, a safety pillar of 16 yards horizontal breadth was left, and, in addition to this, the last stall up to that pillar was packed with gob to a horizontal breadth of 16 yards. Assuming that a dense gob-packing is compressed to 0·6 of its original volume by the pressure of the superincumbent strata, the gob-pillar, for purposes of safety, represented a coal-pillar of $16·0 \times 0·6 = 9·6$ yards in breadth. Consequently the coal-pillar and the gob-pillar together had the same effect in supporting the buildings as a coal-pillar of $16·0 + 9·6 = 25·6$ yards in breadth. Notwithstanding the pillars, the surface was found to have sunk considerably.

The thickness of the coal seam was 4 yards. It dipped 12° towards the west, and had a perpendicular depth from the surface of 180 yards. Calculated from this depth and the width of the 25·6-yard pillar, the angle of fracture φ is found to be as follows :—

$$\cotan \varphi = \frac{25·6}{180·0} \; ; \; \varphi = 82° \, 0'$$

The dip β of the strata being 12°, the theoretical formula gives

$$\tan \varphi = \frac{1 + (\cos 12°)^2}{\sin 12° \cdot \cos 12°} \; ; \; \varphi = 84° \, 20'$$

or 2° 20' greater than the result obtained practically.

The theory of subsidence is ably discussed by Callon,[*] who

---

[*] "Lectures on mining delivered at the School of Mines, Paris," by J. Callon, translated by W. Galloway and C. Le Neve Foster, vol. ii., London, 1881, p. 304.

lays down the following proposition:—If the coal has been removed over a certain area, and the space filled up in a seam worked by the methods adopted in Belgium and Northern France, the subsidence of the roof on the filling-up causes fractures along the perimeter of the area at right angles to the plane of stratification. The subsidence of the ground within the cylindrical space indicated by those fractures continues gradually without sensible diminution in amount quite up to the surface, whatever may be the depth of the mine.

CHAPTER XVIII.

Mine Plans.

Plan and Section.—For the representation of mine workings a plan and a vertical section are required. The plan is a projection of the mine workings on a horizontal plane; the section is a projection of the workings on a plane running parallel to the main longitudinal direction of the mine. With complicated and irregular mines, one section is not sufficient. In such a case, several sections have to be made in given directions.

(*a.*) **Metalliferous Mines.**—Four drawings are necessary in order to represent a metalliferous mine—(1) the ground plan; (2) the working plan; (3) a longitudinal section; (4) a transverse section.

The ground plan gives a general representation of the whole concession. It may be on a scale of about 3 chains to the inch, and on it the boundary of the property of every land owner should be distinctly marked, and all the lodes indicated. The working plan gives a general view of the underground workings, as they would be seen from above if the ground was transparent. This plan should be drawn on a large scale, 4, 5, 8, and 10 fathoms to the inch being scales used for the purpose. The longitudinal section is drawn on the supposition that a section of the ground is cut away, and that a side view of the mine is exposed. All the vertical shafts, the stopes, the dip of the ore-courses, and the surface-line with elevations of the mine buildings, will be correctly shown. The levels, diagonal shafts, and winzes will have a false appearance. The levels will appear perfectly straight however crooked their course may be, the diagonal shafts and winzes will appear perpendicular, and the cross-cuts will be represented as open doorways. The transverse section is of great value, as it shows the dip of the ore-courses. In the transverse section, the view is taken at one end of the workings, at right angles to the longitudinal section. Thus, the inclination of the shafts and winzes sunk on the lode is shown. The levels driven on the lode will be represented as open doorways; the cross-cuts are correctly shown; and all variations in the dip of the lode may be seen from the surface to the bottom of the mine.

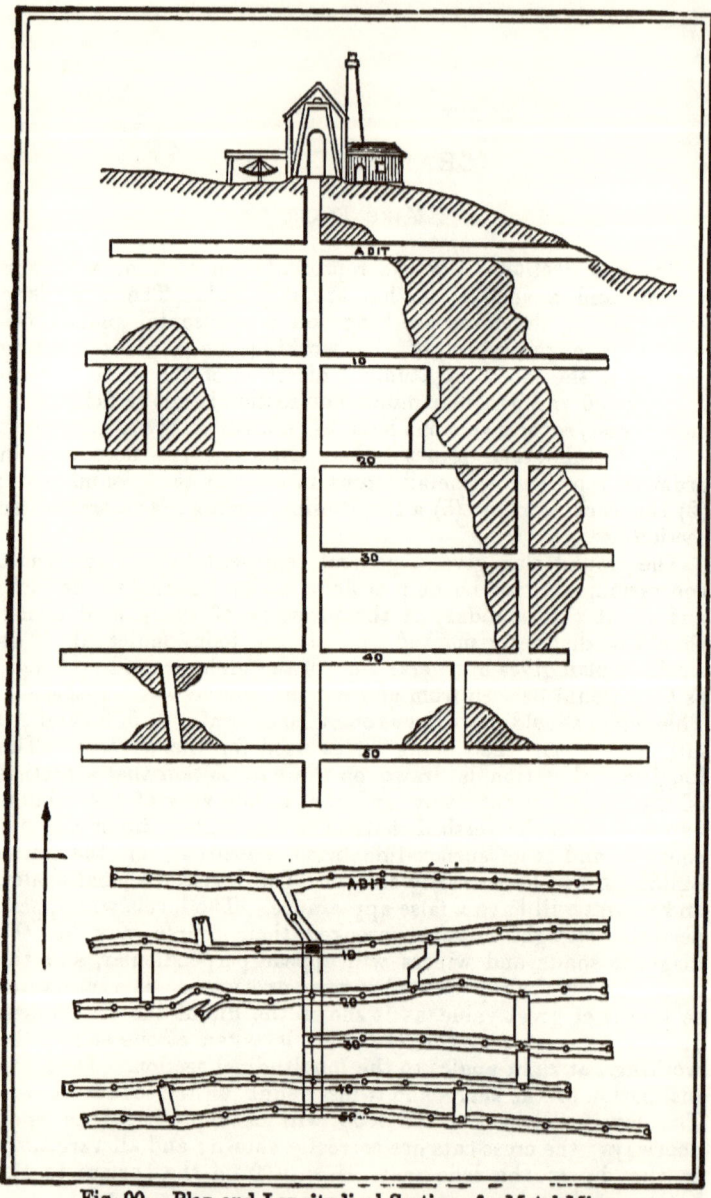

Fig. 90.—Plan and Longitudinal Section of a Metal-Mine.

When the lode is very flat, as at the Cornish mines of Wheal Jane and Wheal Kitty, the section is made along the lode. In this way a true idea is given of the ground worked; but an erroneous one with regard to depth. This method of projecting the section is necessary to enable the ground stoped away to be shown, as when the lode is so very flat, the back of one level in a vertical section would touch the floor of the next. As a rule, lodes are so vertical that a perpendicular plane may be taken for the section.

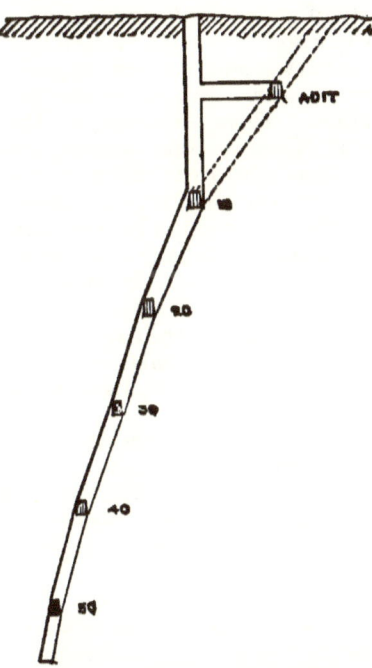

Fig. 91.—Transverse Section.

The workings of a metalliferous mine are represented in Figs. 90, 91, on a scale of about 20 fathoms to the inch. The mine has an adit-level and below that, 10-, 20-, 30-, 40-, and 50-fathom levels. The adit is north of the shaft. The engine shaft contains the pumps which lift the water from the sump or lowest point of the shaft to the adit-level, which comes out to the surface on the adjacent hill side. This shaft was sunk vertically to intersect the lode at the 10-fathom level, a cross-cut being driven to the adit. Then, instead of continuing vertically, necessitating the driving of cross-cuts to the lode, the shaft follows the latter. The shaded portions shown in the longitudinal section represent the projection of the ore masses, removed by stoping. In practice, such portions are not shaded but coloured—purple for tin, green for copper, blue for lead, &c. Between the 10- and 20-fathom levels a mistake arose, the winze and rise did not meet owing to an error of the dialler.

It will be found advisable to colour all the levels on one lode the same tint. Formerly it was the general practice to colour each level a different colour, the adit-level being blue, and the levels below it red, green, yellow, violet, and brown in succession.

No scale is prescribed by law for the plans of the British metalliferous mines. The variety of scales used presents great difficulties with regard to the comparison of the plans of different neighbouring mines. In many districts, the plans are prepared in a slovenly and unsatisfactory manner. This is notably the case in the Derbyshire lead mines. There, according to Mr. A. H. Stokes, H.M. Inspector of Mines for that district, the majority of the mines have no plans whatever. Even at the larger mines which have plans, they are very roughly drawn and rarely indicate the extent to which the ore has been worked. The variable width of the levels is not shown, the latter being represented by a coloured line. The position of the best and most profitable parts of the mine, that is, the width to which the ore has been extracted, is shown as an ordinary narrow heading. In fact, the plans are not true representations of the mine, but merely represent the length of underground tramways. Sections of the mine are seldom made.

(*b.*) Colliery Plans.—By the Coal Mines Regulation Act, 1887, the owner, agent, or manager of every colliery is compelled to keep, in the office at the mine, an accurate plan of the workings of the mine up to a date not more than three months previously, and the general direction and rate of dip of the strata, together with a section of the strata sunk through, or if that be not reasonably practicable, a statement of the depth of the shaft, with a section of the seam. Every such plan must be on a scale not less than that of the Ordnance Survey of 25 inches to the mile.

Representing collieries on a plan is a much more simple operation than representing metalliferous mines. The workings are projected on a horizontal plane. The coal withdrawn is coloured dark, and the direction of the air-current indicated by arrows. The intake air-current is coloured blue, and the return air-current red. The water-courses may be coloured green, drowned waste also green, and faults bright red shaded off on the dip. Main doors may be indicated by a D in blue, main stoppings by blue lines, and caution-boards by a C in red. The heights of the different points above the level of the shaft-bottom should be shown in red figures, and those below the level of the shaft-bottom in blue. The signs shown in Fig. 92 are employed on colliery plans.

When two or more seams are worked one above the other, and are shown on the same plan, they are distinguished by means of colour.

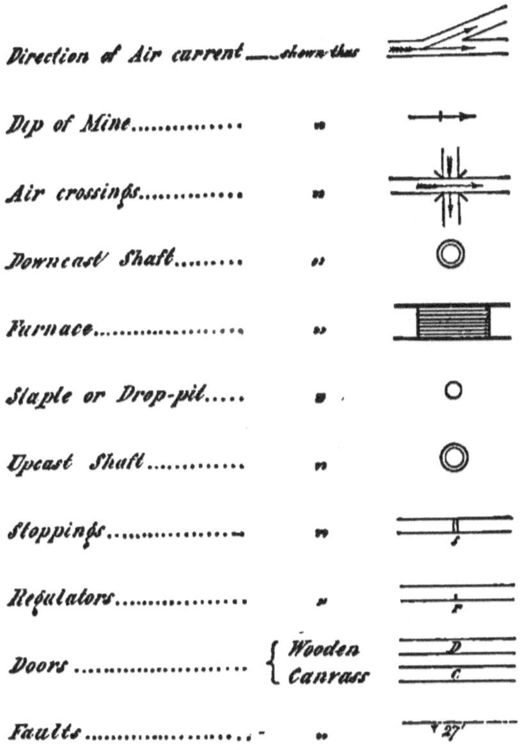

Direction of Air current	shown thus	⇉
Dip of Mine	,,	→
Air crossings	,,	⇅
Downcast Shaft	,,	⊙
Furnace	,,	▬
Staple or Drop-pit	,,	○
Upcast Shaft	,,	⊙
Stoppings	,,	─┼─
Regulators	,,	─┬─
Doors	{ Wooden Canvass	D C
Faults	,,	▼27

Fig. 92.

Admirable illustrations of the manner in which colliery plans should be executed are afforded by the plans which accompany the annual reports of H.M. Inspectors of Mines.

Surface Plans.—The surface plan of a colliery or metalliferous mine requires great distinctness of detail. If the scale of about 25 inches to the mile is adopted, the conventional signs used on the maps of the Ordnance Survey should be employed. If the scale is larger, care must be taken to give the conventional signs such dimensions as will accord with the scale of the plan. Buildings are coloured crimson lake for houses, and dark grey (a light wash of indian ink) for outbuildings. The mine buildings may be distinguished from other buildings shown on the plan by having a darker tint of red. In representing objects on the plan, their natural colours are sometimes adhered to; in other cases a conventional colour is used. Thus, for grass land, a flat tint of green (Hooker's No. 1) is employed; it is made of gamboge and indigo. Cultivated land is represented by a flat tint of burnt sienna. Adjoining fields are slightly varied in tint, furrows sometimes being indicated by coloured strips. Lakes and rivers are coloured light blue (cobalt), with a darker tint on each side. Marshes are represented by the blue of water, with horizontal spots of grass green. Roads are coloured with a light wash of burnt sienna, or yellow ochre. Hedges are represented by green dots for bushes, brick walls by a red line, and wooden fences by lines of a neutral tint. In large scale plans, the Cornish hedge, some 6 feet in width, is shown by two lines the true distance apart, with a wash of neutral tint along each side. In all cases the shadow is put in. The boundaries of the mine concession are indicated by strips of colour.

When the underground workings are drawn on the surface-plan, in the latter there should be no more colouring than necessary. It will be found sufficient to colour the roads, buildings, and water.

(c.) **American Colliery Plans.**—In Pennsylvania the law requires all anthracite colliery owners to prepare maps of all workings on a scale of 100 feet to an inch for the use of the mine-inspector. This scale is rather too large for convenient use, and consequently most of the working maps used for reference are constructed on a scale of 200 or 300 feet to the inch. These maps generally show all the important surface features, buildings, streams, roads, and railways, as well as the underground workings. The latter are commonly drawn in blue, red, or green ink. When several beds are worked, the workings are shown by different colours—a device especially necessary when the workings on one seam are above or below those opened on another bed. In addition to the general map showing all the workings, separate maps showing the workings on each seam are usually made. The survey-lines are plotted with a vernier-protractor, or a protractor of very large size, and the results checked by latitude and departure calculations. Tracings or blue-prints of the workings are supplied from time to time to the viewer. When not in use the plans are stored in large fire-proof vaults. The survey-notes are copied into office record books for future reference. With the exception of the work done by the U.S. Coast Survey, no other surveys in America can compare in accuracy with those of the anthracite mines.

The sharp foldings of the carboniferous strata of the anthracite region of Pennsylvania, have made the study of the structural geology of that region one encompassed with great difficulties. The necessity of having some definite information regarding the structure of the coal beds, before successful mining operations can be prosecuted, induced Mr. C. A. Ashburner* to introduce in 1880 a new method of representing on surface maps the underground structure of the coal beds, from which could be ascertained the situation of the outcrops of the beds, the position of the synclinal and anticlinal axes, their depths in special coal beds below the surface of the ground, and the dip of the bed from the crest of the anticlinal to the bottom of the synclinal. This was accomplished by contour-curve lines drawn along the floor of the coal beds. The contours were obtained from elevations determined in the areas where the coal beds were mined, and from exploring the shafts, bore-holes, and surface exposures in the areas where no extensive mining had been done. In areas where no underground exploration had been made, the positions of the contours along the floors of the coal beds were deduced from surface exposures and an extension of the structure from explored areas.

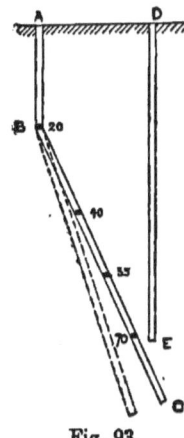

Fig. 93.

Importance of Correct Sections.—The importance of keeping an accurate section of a mine is shown by a serious accident that occurred at Pantgwyn mine. On February 17, 1885, while three men were at work sinking a new shaft, water broke in suddenly and unexpectedly, and drowned them. The exact nature of the casualty will be best understood by means of Fig. 93, representing a cross-section of the mine. A B C is the old pumping and winding shaft, sunk perpendicularly for the first 20 fathoms, and then following the dip of the vein. In 1884, owing to the stoppage of some neighbouring mines, the pumping engine at Pantgwyn was unable to cope with the water, which gradually filled the workings. The owners then resolved to sink a new perpendicular shaft D E, and provide it with more powerful pumping machinery. It was intended that the new shaft should strike the Pantgwyn lode in virgin ground below any of the existing workings, which were to be drained gradually by percolation of the water through the porous veinstone. In February, 1885, the new shaft had reached a perpendicular depth of 62 fathoms from the surface. The old shaft was then supposed to be in the position indicated by the dotted

* *Trans. Amer. Inst. M.E.*, vol. ix., 1881, p. 50.

lines, and the distance between the two shafts at E was reckoned to be 40 feet. On examining the shaft as soon as it had been cleared out, the Government Inspector of Mines, Dr. C. Le Neve Foster, found that the thickness of the barrier was only 9 feet; the section of the mine being incorrect. It naturally appeared to him very strange that such an error should have been made in a small survey of recent date, with two shafts less than 50 yards apart at the surface, until he ascertained that the inclination of the shaft had never been measured below the 40-fathom level. The drivages at the 55-fathom level and the 70-fathom level had been deliberately laid down on the plan just as if the shaft had been correctly dialled. The primary cause of the accident was, without doubt, the want of a correct survey. In reporting on this accident, Dr. Le Neve Foster points out specially that it was not a case of approaching old workings, whose exact position was unknown, or imperfectly known, owing to the abandonment having taken place before there was any statutory obligation as regards the keeping of plans; but here was a new shaft, started by the same company and the same agent, within 50 yards of their own workings, which had been discontinued only a few months before.

Uniformity of Scale and Conventional Signs.—In Belgium and in France the law demands that all mine plans shall be laid down on a scale of 1 : 1000. The surface plan is prepared on the same scale as that of the underground workings. In Prussia, the scale imposed varies in the different mining districts from 1 : 500 for metalliferous mines up to 1 : 1600 for collieries. In Austria, the scale for mine plans is usually 1 : 720. For comparison, it may be added that the scale for colliery plans in Great Britain must not be less than 1 : 2500. Previous to 1888 the smallest scale allowed was 1 : 1584. In America, the scale imposed in Pennsylvania for the anthracite mines is 1 : 1200. The usual scale prescribed in the various States for the preliminary plan of a metalliferous mine-claim is 1 : 2400.

It is desirable to have not only a uniform scale, but also uniformity in the conventional signs used in the plans. With this aim, typical mine plans have been published in Belgium by Mr. J. van Scherpenzeel-Thim; in Germany by Professor Schmidt, of the Freiberg School of Mines; in Hungary by Mr. Péch, the director of the Schemnitz mines, and in Sweden by Mr. G. Nordenström. In Prussia the law demands uniformity in the drawing of mine plans, and special rules are issued by the Government for the purpose. Unfortunately, there is a great want of uniformity in British mine plans in the various mining districts. If plans were always drawn after the same model it is evident that the working would be more uniform, and that each new mine-manager would be enabled to decipher more readily his predecessor's work. The owners, and other persons interested in mineral property, would thus be able to gain a clear understanding of the plans, and successive generations would profit by the stores of information thus recorded. Uniformity of system in the plans, too, greatly facilitates the construction of general maps of mining districts.

Preservation of Plans.—So long ago as 1797 the importance of a systematic mapping of mines was urged at Newcastle by Mr. Thomas, and since that date the value of such a system has frequently been dwelt upon for the purpose of diminishing the probability of the recurrence of fatal accidents in collieries, and of prolonging the duration of the coal resources of the United Kingdom. It is always a matter of regret that faithful records of all underground work in important mining districts have not been carefully preserved. The importance of the preservation of such records was strongly urged by Mr. T. Sopwith in 1844. In the United Kingdom plans of all abandoned mines are now carefully preserved. The Coal Mines Regulation Act (1887) requires that where any mine or seam is abandoned, the owner of the mine or seam at the time of its abandonment shall, within three months after the abandonment, send to a Secretary of State an accurate plan showing the boundaries of the workings of the mine or seam up to the time of the abandonment, and the position of the workings with regard to the surface, and the general direction and rate of dip of the strata, together with a section of the strata sunk through, or if that is not reasonably practicable, a statement of the depth of the shaft, with a section of the seam. Every such plan must be on a scale not less than that of the Ordnance Survey scale of 25 inches to the mile, or on the same scale as the plan used at the mine at the time of its abandonment.

At the Home Office the mine plans are preserved, rolled in cylindrical lacquered tin cases, closed with a lid, on which a number is painted. The cases are placed side by side on shelves, so that their numbers can be at once seen. At Freiberg a similar plan is adopted. This method is very cumbrous. A better method is to keep the plans without being rolled or folded in portfolios. At Przibram, in Bohemia, the plans are kept in a nest of drawers, each drawer forming the frame of a plan placed between two sheets of glass.

Sopwith entirely dispensed with the large and unwieldy rolls of paper on which the workings of collieries and metalliferous mines are usually projected, by drawing the plans on imperial drawing paper. Each sheet was divided into squares of 20 inches, forming an area of 400 square inches. An inch margin was left at the top and bottom of the sheet, and 3 inches at one side for binding a series of plans into a volume. At the other side a margin of 1 inch was left, with a column 5 inches wide for the insertion of written descriptions, scales, titles, references, and other explanations of value as permanent records, with which the plan itself ought to be encumbered as little as possible. In this way, plans are kept perfectly flat, and their accuracy is not affected by the tension of the paper caused by frequent rolling. Rolled plans, on the other hand, soon become so cracked and defaced, as greatly to impair the clearness and accuracy of the plotting, whilst their bulk is a hindrance to frequent inspection and to the plotting of new workings.

Practical Hints for Constructing Mine Plans.—The paper on which the plan is drawn should be the best hard drawing-paper. If plans are required on canvass, the paper should be mounted and carefully dried before the plan is begun, in order that the contraction in drying may not alter the lines. To mount the paper, a piece of linen or calico, rather larger than the plan is required to be, is placed on a tilted table with a flat surface. A strip, 1½ inch wide, at the edges is glued, and pressed on the table, the linen being at the same time pulled tight. With large sheets, two persons pulling at opposite sides are required. The paper is then placed with its right side on the linen. Its back is then pasted until the paper becomes quite limp with the moisture soaked in. The paper is lifted up carefully, and placed with the pasted side on the linen, and pressed from the centre to the edges. The rubbing-down may be done with the hand or with a cloth; in either case a sheet of clean paper is interposed. Paper thus mounted may be drawn upon nearly as well as when stretched on a board. To give an edge for the T-square, if required, a straight edge may be temporarily nailed on.

If several sheets of drawing-paper have to be joined end to end, the edges to be joined should be reduced to half their thickness. This may be done with a knife or with sand-paper.

In mounting and joining drawings, a great deal depends on the paste employed. It must be sufficiently liquid and contain no lumps. To prepare it, a small portion of good starch is completely dissolved in as small a quantity as possible of cold water, and to this solution boiling water is poured with continual stirring of the starch-paste thus formed.

Plans may be varnished by applying several coats of isinglass size, allowing each to dry before applying the next, and finishing with a coat of Canada balsam diluted with oil of turpentine.

The lead-pencil used for plan-drawing should not be very hard nor very soft. The degree of hardness marked H H is the most suitable. The quality may be tested by holding the point in a candle-flame. Good pencils suffer no change in this experiment, whilst bad leads burn away to ash with a sulphurous odour. It is best to use two pencils; one with a flat or chisel point for line drawing, and one with a point in the shape of a perfectly acute cone for sketching.

Short lines should be drawn with the rolling parallel ruler. The plotting scale should never be used for this purpose. Straight edges, used for drawing long lines, may be tested by drawing a line along the edge of the ruler, then laying the ruler on the other side of the line, with the ends exactly upon it, and drawing a line in the same manner. If the straight-edge is true, these lines will exactly coincide; if not, the error is rendered apparent by being doubled.

For inking-in plans, indian ink is always employed, as it does not corrode the steel points of the instrument and preserves its colour unchanged. The best ink, as imported from China, has a finely granular texture and a conchoidal iridescent fracture. When rubbed with water on a slab, it is not gritty, and smells like musk. Inferior ink smells like camphor, and the worst ink smells like soot and glue. The latter is useless for plan-drawing, as it runs when other colours are passed over it. Indian ink is prepared for use by rubbing it with water on a perfectly smooth slab or saucer. It should only be rubbed backwards and forwards, as, for some unexplained reason, rubbing it round and round hardens it. The preparation must be perfectly black; but after it has become black, further mixing renders it viscous.

For removing pencil lines and for cleaning the paper, native india-rubber, vulcanised india-rubber, or stale bread may be employed.

The drawing instruments should be of the best workmanship, as accurate results cannot be obtained with imperfect instruments. Very few instruments are required, a pair of compasses with a steel drawing-pen and a pencil-leg to fit, and a drawing-pen being all that is required for plan-drawing. Bow-compasses are unnecessary. A pair of turn-in compasses constitutes a set of instruments sufficient for most mining purposes.

The best compasses are those which are sector-jointed. The greatest care should be taken to clean steel drawing-pens every time they are put away, and common ink should never be used in them. It will be found desirable to have two of these instruments, one for fine lines and another for thick lines. When the proper opening for fine lines has been found, it is thus unnecessary to change it, as the pen can always be cleaned by passing a piece of paper between the nibs.

The most useful colours for mine plans are—for surface boundaries and underground workings, crimson lake, indigo, cobalt, Prussian blue, burnt sienna, gamboge. Purple, green, and other tints may be obtained by mixing. Opaque colours, such as vermilion, red lead, and ultramarine, should be avoided. The end of the cake of colour is moistened, and rubbed with a drop of water. This is afterwards diluted to the proper tint. The art of laying-on a flat tint consists in allowing the coloured water to flow uniformly over the paper. This is done by applying, with a large camel's-hair brush, kept always moderately full, a tint across the upper part of the portion of the plan to be coloured, and by continuing it downwards from right to left and left to right alternately, never letting the edge dry. The drawing-board should be inclined towards the draughtsman, and the paper is moistened with water before the colour is applied if the portion to be coloured is irregular. A little prepared ox-gall used with the colours obviates the difficulty which often arises from the smoothness or greasiness of the paper. It is, however, almost impossible to use it too sparingly. In drawing the outlines, care should be taken that there is always a piece of clean paper between the hand and the drawing, in order to prevent any greasiness of the paper.

Neat and distinct lettering is very essential in all plans. It frequently happens that a perfectly accurate plan is absolutely spoiled by a badly printed title. The formation of letters requires long practice. Lines drawn in pencil to be afterwards erased, will be found useful as guides. No style of lettering is more effective than the Egyptian or block letters, in which every line is of the same width. By the aid of copper stencil plates a great saving of time is effected. The lettering should be in lines parallel to the bottom of the plan; except the names of lodes, rivers, and roads, of which the general course should be followed.

The plan may be enclosed in a rectangle by a border, which usually consists of two parallel lines, one heavy and the other finer. The simplest border is the best, and time should not be wasted over ornamental corners to embellish the plan.

The plan is usually drawn so that the top of the paper represents the north. Whether this is the case or not, a meridian-line should always be drawn. The north point is sometimes drawn in the form of an ornamental star. When it represents the magnetic meridian, the abbreviation *mag. mer.*, with the date and declination, should be written by the side of it. A scale should invariably be drawn on the plan, with a description of it written above.

Copying Plans.—Plans may be copied by means of geometrical methods employed to determine the points of the plan by intersections or by co-ordinates. The operations are, however, very tedious. In preference to geometrical methods, there are several mechanical methods which should be employed.

1. **Copying by Tracing.**—A large sheet of glass is fixed in a wooden frame, and inclined at an angle of 25° before a window or a lamp. The plan to be copied is covered with drawing-paper, and placed on the pane of glass. The lines of the original can thus be traced with facility.

2. **Copying on Tracing-Paper.**—A sheet of tracing-paper or tracing-cloth is fastened with drawing-pins over the plan to be copied. The lines are then copied in indian ink, a set square being used for ruling the straight lines. The tracing is mounted on white paper, and colour is then applied. If tracing-cloth is used, it will be found advisable to apply the colour to the back of the tracing.

In copying plans on tracing-cloth, considerable difficulty is experienced, owing to the greasy nature of the surface, in getting the ink to run freely. This can easily be obviated by sprinkling the surface of the cloth with finely-powdered chalk or pipeclay.

3. **Copying by Transfer.**—The transfer-paper used for this purpose, is made of very thin paper, one side of which is rubbed with black-lead powder, smoothly spread with a cotton rag. The transfer-paper is placed with its prepared face downwards on the clean paper. Over it is placed the plan to be copied, and all the lines are gone over with an agate point, or other blunt-pointed instrument. If the original cannot be treated in this way, a tracing of it must be employed. In this way, a copy of the original plan is obtained in black lines, which may be afterwards inked in.

4. **Pricking-Through.**—In this method, the clean paper is fixed on a drawing board, and the plan over it. All the angular points in the latter are then pricked through with a very fine needle. The points obtained on the clean paper in this way are joined up, and the plan inked in.

5. **Copying by Photography.**—Photographic processes present the advantages of rapidity and fidelity of reproduction. The apparatus necessary includes thin bluish tracing-paper, printing frames of thick plate-glass hinged at the back, with a piece of thick soft felt for equalising the pressure exerted by the springs or clamps, a developing bath, non-actinic arrangements (yellow window blinds by day, and a ruby lantern by night), and cases for storing paper. Drawings on ordinary paper may

be copied if exposed to light sufficiently long. Instead of springs or clamps on the printing frame, use may be made of Street's pneumatic frame, with an air cushion, inflated by blowing, pressing uniformly over the whole surface of the frame.

The process most commonly used is the cyanotype sensitising process, invented by Sir John Herschel. White lines are produced on a blue ground with a solution of 140 grains of ferric ammonic citrate, 120 grains of potassic ferri-cyanide, and 2 oz. of distilled water. The solution should be kept in a stoneware vessel. This process depends upon the actinic action of light reducing the ferric salts to the ferrous state under certain conditions, one of which is the presence of organic matter, such as the size contained in the paper. The ferrous salt then combines with the potassic salt to form insoluble Prussian blue.

In these processes a sheet of paper, a little larger than the tracing to be copied, is fixed on a board, and with a sponge a thin uniform coating of the liquid is applied as rapidly as possible, and allowed to stand in non-actinic light until perfectly dry. The tracing is placed against the glass of the printing frame, and at the back of the tracing the prepared sheet is placed. The frame is then exposed to light until the prepared sheet becomes of a dark olive-green colour. The sheet is then removed from the frame, and thoroughly washed in pure water for a few minutes until it assumes the required shade of blue.

On the Ordnance Survey, Willis' platinotype process is employed. It gives white lines on a black ground, and is based on the reducing action of a ferrous salt, when exposed to actinic light, on platinum chloride. The sensitising solution is composed of 60 grains of potassic-platinous chloride, 60 grains of ferric oxalate, and 1 oz. of water. The exposure lasts until the paper acquires a dull orange tint. It is then developed in non-actinic light by floating it for 4 seconds in a solution of 130 grains of potassic oxalate and 1 oz. of water at a temperature of 150° to 200° F. When properly developed, the print is washed for 10 minutes in 1 part of hydrochloric acid with 60 parts of water, and finally washed in relays of fresh water, for 15 minutes.*

Reducing and Enlarging Plans.—A plan may be reduced or enlarged, by taking from the original a fraction of the dimensions as required. For this purpose proportional compasses, or scales, may be employed. A very rapid method of reducing or enlarging plans consists in covering the original with a network of

* Eight other processes for the actinic copying of engineering drawings are described by Mr. B. H. Thwaite, *Min. Proc. Inst. C.E.*, vol. lxxxvi., 1886, p. 312.

squares, and the copy with a network of squares having their sides smaller than those of the original squares in the proportion in which the plan is to be reduced. The details may then be sketched in by the eye. This method may also be used for copying plans on the same scale.

Plans may be reduced by mechanism by means of instruments called the *pantograph* and *eidograph*. The pantograph is made in various forms. It always consists essentially of four brass rulers, E D, D B, F G, and G C, Fig. 94, jointed together at F, D, C, and G, so as to form a parallelogram. The two sides D C and D F are extended to double their length. The side F G and the branch F E are marked from D with successive divisions, F P being to D P always in the ratio of F A to D T. Small sockets for holding a pencil or tracing point are placed at P and T. The point A is made the centre of motion and rests on a fulcrum weight. From the property of similar triangles, the three points A, P, and T must range in the same straight line, shown by the dotted line P A T, which is divided at A in the ratio required. Thus, while the point T is moved over the lines of the plan, the point P will trace out a similar figure reduced in the proportion of T A to A P or of D F to F P, the proportion required.

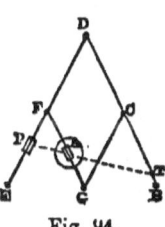

Fig. 94.

The eidograph is more complicated in construction. Although not so frequently used as the pantograph, it is superior to that instrument, within the range of its working powers, which may be considered to be limited to reducing between the full size of the original and one-third of the size. Its great merit is that within its range it reduces accurately in all proportions; for instance, it will reduce in the proportion of 9 to 25 as readily as 1 to 2.*

Plans may be enlarged by any of the methods given for reducing them. It is, however, always better to make a fresh plan from the original notes.

Isometric Plans of Mines.—The kind of drawing adopted for representing the interior of mines, and the vertical surfaces of sections of strata, is that which supposes the eye of the observer to be placed in a direction exactly perpendicular to every part of the plane represented. In this way, two drawings are necessary,— the ground plan and section. By means of isometric projection, these drawings may be embodied in one, in which all the lines of the projection may be measured by a uniform scale.

* A full description of this instrument is given in W. F. Stanley's "*Mathematical Drawing Instruments,*" London, 1866.

A solid body, the chief planes of which are at right angles, the cube for instance, is to be so placed that the three planes which meet together at one corner are equally inclined to the horizontal plane, that is the plane of projection. The three lines which meet at that corner will then be projected so as to form three equal angles of 120° each, and will be the plans of the three edges of the cube. The plans of the opposite edges will be parallel to these, and hence it follows that in isometric projection all angles which are in reality right angles are projected into angles of 120° or 60°.

In making an isometric plan of a mine, three lines must first be drawn, making angles of 120° with one another, for the plans of three edges of the solid, in which it is imagined that the mine is enclosed. An isometric scale must then be constructed, so that the isometric lengths of the required edges may be found. When found, these are measured on the lines drawn from their plans, and the drawing is completed by parallels.

It is known that the relation of a line to its isometric projection is as $\sqrt{3}$ to $\sqrt{2}$. To construct an isometric scale, two lines must therefore be drawn in this ratio. For this purpose, a line 1 unit in length is taken, and at one end of it a perpendicular is erected of the same length, and the ends joined. The hypothenuse of this right-angled triangle will represent $\sqrt{2}$ (Euclid I., 47). If from one end of this line representing $\sqrt{2}$ a perpendicular 1 unit in length is erected, and this triangle completed, the hypothenuse will represent $\sqrt{3}$. Two lines are thus obtained representing $\sqrt{2}$ and $\sqrt{3}$ in the required relation for the scale, and if the real lengths of the edges be measured along $\sqrt{3}$ and perpendiculars dropped from their ends to $\sqrt{2}$, the parts thereby intercepted will be the isometric plans of the required edges.

In making an isometric plan of a mine, it is desirable that a north and south line may form one side of the supposed isometric square that regulates the drawing, the cross-lines being of course east and west. The survey must be plotted by means of the calculated latitudes and departures, the distances being set off along the edges of isometric squares. This method is of great value for elucidating questions of stratigraphy and for solving problems relating to the intersection of lodes. The necessity of referring every object to an isometric plane, however, renders its application to all the minute details of extensive subterranean workings not only tedious and difficult, but also less explanatory than the ground plans and sections in common use.*

* Some excellent isometric plans of mines are given in T. Sopwith's *Treatise on Isometrical Drawing*, London, 2nd ed., 1838.

Relief-Plans and Mine Models.—Instead of use being made of isometric projection for representing the three dimensions of mine-workings on a plan, it is frequently necessary to construct a relief-plan or model of wood, plaster, glass, or wire.

When a plastic material, such as clay, wax, or putty, is used, metal or wooden pins are driven into the base or level datum plane of wood, the top of the pins giving the elevations required. A contour plan, of the same horizontal scale as that selected for the model, is first spread upon the base-board. The pins are then driven firmly through the contour lines into the board, the tops left standing at a sufficient distance from the latter, to represent the height of the various contour lines, according to the vertical scale adopted for the model. After the pins are all properly set, the plastic material is worked into position over and thoroughly covering the pins. This process was employed in the construction of a model, exhibited at the Paris Exhibition of 1878, representing the No. 8 seam of the Loire collieries, which is intersected by an inextricable network of faults of different ages. The model was constructed for the instruction of mine-deputies, who find it difficult to follow the dislocation caused by these faults, more especially the dislocations of faults by faults of different age.

This method was also employed by Mr. C. A. Ashburner in the construction of an interesting model of the Panther Creek Coal Basin, Pennsylvania, showing the shape of the floor of the bed. After the construction of contours in explored areas, the most important aid to the determination of the geological structure of the coal beds in areas where surface exposures cannot be obtained, is the construction of a model with the vertical and horizontal scales the same. The first area so mapped in Pennsylvania was the Panther Creek Basin, one of the most complicated basins of the anthracite district of that State. Many of the difficulties were not understood until a model was made of the floor of the Mammoth coal bed, the thickest and most valuable bed mined in Pennsylvania. A map was first made on a scale of 800 feet to the inch, upon which contour lines were shown along the floor of the Mammoth bed, 50 feet vertically apart, in the areas worked and explored. In the areas included between the two classes, theoretical contour lines were drawn on the map, in accordance with the dip of the exposed strata. Thus, the final model, made in wood and wax, not only formed a graphic representation of the structure of the strata in a highly plicated district, but also proved of great value in the definition of its geological structure, and in the deduction of many conclusions affecting the amount of coal contained in this coal basin, and the proper methods to pursue in its ultimate mining.

The method adopted by Mr. T. Sopwith in the construction of his well-known models was as follows :—A square representing a portion of the mining district, one mile in extent, is divided into 64 squares by parallel lines a furlong apart. Sections along the eighteen lines are drawn and cut out in pasteboard or in thin plates of copper. These are then joined crossways by half-lapping, that is, by cutting each section half-way down, where it crosses another section cut in the same way on the other edge. The model of hollow squares thus formed is placed on a plane surface, and the spaces are filled in with wood or plaster, carved or moulded, so as to represent the surface. The model of part of the lead-mining district of Alston Moor, in Cumberland, exhibited in the Museum of Practical Geology, in London, was constructed by this method by Mr. Sopwith. The model shows the thickness and dip of the limestone, sandstone, and clay beds. The mineral veins are seen on the sides of the model dipping in nearly a vertical direction through the various strata.

Probably the best method of constructing relief plans is that adopted by Mr. M. Moulton in 1876 for a map of the State of New Hampshire. The map was 16 feet long, the highest elevation being $6\frac{1}{2}$ inches above the datum. From a copy of the map of the State on tracing-cloth, the datum sea-level line and the contour line next above it were transferred through the cloth on to a layer of wood, $\frac{1}{4}$ inch in thickness, of the same size as the map. The outside line was drawn in blue and the inside in red. The outer contour was then cut round with a fret-saw, thus breaking off the wood outside the sea-level line. The pedestal on which the map was to be fixed then received the first layer of wood. The next layer was then prepared for sawing, as in the first case, the outside line being the first 500-foot contour and the inside or red line the next above. This having been cut out with the saw, it was nailed and glued to the first layer, its position being fixed by the red line on the latter. Throughout the work the red lines served as guides by which each successive layer was properly placed. After three layers were fixed, the steps were carved off to produce smooth slopes at angles corresponding to those of the map. Each successive group of three layers was treated in the same way.

A complete view of the nature of a mineral vein and of the excavations upon it, is given by a model constructed by Mr. T. B Jordan, in the Museum of Practical Geology. The workings of each successive stage of 10 fathoms, are laid out on a scale of 10 fathoms to the inch on a horizontal frame of light wires crossing at intervals representing 10 fathoms, and the portions of the vein which have been worked between the levels are shown in their true position. Hence, on looking down from above, the eye may trace all the bendings of the lode, and can appreciate the comparative richness and poverty of different parts. The model represents the Holmbush mine, in Cornwall, a mine of a complicated character from the occurrence of workings on cross-courses as well as on lodes. The excavations made are represented in colours, while the solid ground is left blank.

The workings on each vein are distinguished by a special colour. Although affording a perfect view of the general arrangement of a mine, this method is too cumbrous and expensive to be generally employed.

An excellent method of constructing mine models is illustrated by three models of Austrian salt mines exhibited in the Museum of Practical Geology. These models are constructed to a uniform scale of 400 feet to 1 inch. The irregularities of the surface of the ground are represented, and central, transverse, and longitudinal sections are drawn on the sides of each model. On removing the tops of the models, representing the surface, the workings on the different levels are seen plotted on plates of glass, fixed at the proper height, one above the other. The colours of the workings shown on the glass plates, correspond with those of the named levels on the longitudinal sections. An outer line, drawn in discontinuous bars, shows the extent of the deposit of salt at each level.*

At the Stockholm School of Mines, the students are trained in the representation of mine workings on sheets of glass. The advantage of the method is the power of simultaneously representing the underground workings and the surface.

In addition to the practical value and advantage of mine models to the geologist and miner, such models will frequently be found of great advantage in suits at law, in settling mining claims and damages in dispute, when ordinary plans are unavailing.†

* The method of working these mines is fully described by Mr. H. Bauerman in *A Descriptive Catalogue of the Geological, Mining, and Metallurgical Models in the Museum of Practical Geology*, London, 1865.

† On the construction of models, see A. E. Lehman, *Trans. Amer. Inst. M.E.*, vol. xiv., 1886, p. 439; O. B. Harden, *ib.* vol. x., p. 264; L. M. Haupt, *The Topographer*, New York, 1883.

CHAPTER XIX.

APPLICATIONS OF THE MAGNETIC-NEEDLE IN MINING.

Exploring for Iron Ore.—In exploring for magnetic iron ores, the magnetic-needle affords valuable aid, and has been employed for that purpose in Sweden and in the United States.*

The theory of its use is based upon the fact that certain minerals deposited in the earth become magnetic by induction under the influence of the earth's magnetism, and that, consequently, the two poles are fixed in the direction of the magnetic meridian, or, more exactly, in the direction of the magnetic inclination at the opposite ends of the deposit. It is well known that there are substances, such as steel and magnetite, exhibiting polar magnetism; that is to say, they retain the magnetism once acquired even if the inducing force ceases to act. Other substances, such as soft iron and magnetic pyrites, exhibit simple magnetism; in other words, they are magnetic only so long as the induction remains.

The intensity of the magnetism exhibited by deposits of magnetite varies greatly, and is frequently so slight that only delicate instruments and practised observers can detect it; in other cases the needle is affected at considerable distances. It must, of course, be remembered that a given magnetic force affects the needle to exactly the same degree through 100 feet of rock as through the same distance of air.

If the magnetic north pole of the earth is regarded as negative, and the south pole as positive (in the northern hemisphere), the upper end of a vertical mass of ore will be negative, and the lower end positive. Consequently, if a magnetic-needle is brought near the upper or negative pole of the deposit, the north-seeking or positive end of the needle will be attracted. When the point of observation is very near the ore pole the needle will dip downwards. The lower or positive pole of the ore mass, being usually situated at a considerable depth, will not affect the

* See paper on the "Use of the Magnetic-Needle in exploring for Iron Ore," by B. H. Brough, *Journ. Iron and Steel Inst.*, 1887, p. 289.

observation. Other deposits, coursing in a more or less easterly and westerly direction, are less affected by induction; the poles being situated in the long sides of the deposit. Frequently the deposits are faulted and broken. In this case the separate portions behave like fragments of a broken bar magnet, the adjacent ends exhibiting opposite polarity. In exploring for ore, then, if, on advancing from south to north, the free needle is first attracted and then repelled, a fault in the deposit is indicated.

To explore for ore the ordinary miner's dial may be employed. If a straight line is followed with the instrument, the needle will remain directed towards the same point of the dial; or, in other words, will remain in the magnetic meridian as long as it is kept sufficiently far away from iron and magnetic ore masses. But if these are approached, the needle will gradually be deflected. The only case in which there will be no deflection is when the attracting deposit is approached along the meridian passing over its upper pole. It follows that in magnetic surveys the meridian line must first be found, and fixed in the field or on the plan. For this purpose at least two straight lines are set out in the magnetic east and west direction, from 30 to 50 yards apart. These lines will at some point cross the meridian line. If the dial is set up at one end of a line of this kind, at a considerable distance from the magnetic mass, there will, of course, be no attraction. On approaching the meridian the needle will be gradually attracted, and at a certain distance the maximum attraction will be reached. On approaching nearer it will become smaller, until, at the ore meridian itself, it will be inappreciable. The angles of deflection observed at the various stations are noted on pegs driven into the ground, and also in the field-book, or on the plan. Following the same straight line to the other side of the zero point—or, what is the same thing, to the other side of the ore meridian—the same attractions are exhibited, but in reversed order; the needle turning back to the meridian. If similar observations are made along the second east and west line it is easy to fix the ore meridian by joining the two points where there is no deflection. These points are midway between the two points of maximum deflection. This passes over the upper pole of the deposit, and if the pole is approached along the meridian line, the dip of the north-seeking end of the needle will, as a rule, be greater the nearer it comes to the pole. This method is, however, not adapted for fixing the position of the pole exactly. This may be done by determining the isogonic lines—that is to say, by joining the points where the needle has the same deflection.

In order to obtain one or more parallel isogonic lines on both sides of the ore meridian, it is necessary to set out a number of lines parallel to the ore meridian, and from 10 to 30 yards apart. At the points where these lines intersect the east and west lines, the angles of deflection must be observed, and isogonic lines constructed by joining the points of equal deflection. The needle being drawn so much out of its horizontal position that its free play is hindered, it must be weighted and balanced by a piece of wax. If, now, from some point of intersection in the network of squares made on the field of observation, a line is drawn in the direction of the deflection of the magnetic-needle, it will cut the isogonic curve at a second point, and, eventually, the ore meridian. The two points, where the isogonic line is cut, are joined; the joining line is bisected, and at the point of bisection a perpendicular is erected; then, perpendicularly under the point where this cuts the meridian, is the upper ore pole, and at this point it will eventually be found best to sink the shaft, so as to be certain of cutting the ore mass. The ore meridian, it must be noted, need not always be a straight line.

In cases where a better instrument was not available, excellent results have, in this way, been obtained with the ordinary pocket-compass, held in the hand.

For preliminary magnetic surveys, no instrument is better than the Swedish compass. In this instrument, the needle, besides revolving in a horizontal plane in the usual manner, can also turn in a vertical plane to an angle of about 60° with the horizon. The needle is horizontally suspended in a brass case on a long vertical brass pin by means of a long glass cap. The brass terminates above in a short steel point, on which the glass cap rotates. At the bottom of this is a brass stirrup, provided with fine holes, through which pass the horizontal pins supporting the needle. To enable the needle to dip, there is a long slot cut along the middle of it. The compass-box can be suspended by means of three strings passing through three small rings fastened 120° apart on the outside of the box. It can thus be easily carried in the hand. Graduation is not usual, and, indeed, unnecessary. Only the cardinal points are marked, as in using it deviations from the horizontal position alone have to be noticed. This compass was invented in the last century by the celebrated Swedish miner, Daniel Tilas, and is still in general use. The dip of the needle is estimated merely by the eye, and is not actually measured.

The miner's or dip-compass was invented in the United States in 1866, and was adopted by the Geological Survey of New Jersey in the systematic explorations for magnetic iron ore in that State. In this instrument the magnetic-needle is suspended so as to move readily in a vertical direction; the angle of inclination being measured upon the divided rim of a small compass-box. The needle cannot move horizontally. The construction of the instrument is shown in the accompanying figure. When in use, the ring is held in the hand, and the compass-box, by its own weight, takes a vertical position. It must, of course, be held in the plane of the magnetic meridian, which can be determined by holding the instrument horizontally. In this way it serves as an ordinary pocket-compass. Messrs. W. & L. E. Gurley, of Troy, New York, make several different forms of this instrument. One form has a 3-inch needle; its case has the two sides of glass. Another form has a brass back and cover, and a 2½-inch needle. Fig. 95 represents an improved compass by the same makers. It is a modification of the Swedish compass, and has a needle 3 or 4 inches long, resting upon a vertical pivot, so as to move freely in a horizontal plane, and thus place itself in the magnetic meridian; while being attached to the needle-cap by two delicate pivots, one on each side, it is free to dip. It is usually provided with brass covers on both sides.

Fig. 95.

With the dip-compass, whether Swedish or American, perfectly trustworthy results can only be obtained when the observer is acquainted by long experience with the peculiarities of his instrument. Compass explorations being in many cases the sole source of income, it can easily be understood that a skilful operator will be inclined to keep his mode of procedure secret. Consequently the uninitiated are apt to believe that the operator must be specially gifted; and frequently the supernatural properties formerly ascribed to the divining-rod are transferred to the compass. This excess of faith in some is accompanied by scepticism in others. For this, unfortunately, there are good grounds; the compass being so admirably adapted for dishonest purposes. Thus, Mr. T. B. Brooks mentions an American prospector whose compass-needle in the vicinity of an ore mass always showed a dip of 90° when facing west, and the true dip due to local attraction when facing east. The former position, it is said, was very successfully used in selling iron ore grounds, and the latter in buying them. Similarly in Sweden a powerful magnet inserted in a walking-stick has been successfully employed to give a large dip to the needle when it was thought desirable to mislead the purchaser.

As a rule, surveyors assume that the most ore must occur where the dip-compass shows the greatest inclination, or is perpendicular. This assumption, however, is erroneous. The place where the needle is attracted most by a vertical ore bed is not directly above, but to the north of, the south pole of the deposit. For, if the magnetism of the earth is powerful enough, there must be somewhere north of the ore pole a point at which the horizontal components of the magnetism of the earth and of the ore bed are equally powerful, but acting in opposite directions. At this point the horizontal forces neutralise each other, and then the vertical forces of the magnetism of the earth and of the ore bed tend to bring the needle into a vertical position.

The evidences afforded by the needle often lead to error. An unimportant pocket of ore near the surface may have as great an action on the instrument as a larger ore mass situated far below the surface.

It is thus seen that in exploring for iron ore with the magnetic-needle, a purely scientific method is necessary. The compass should be employed for preliminary work, in order to save time and labour; but before a shaft is sunk, recourse should be had to a more accurate method. Improved methods, available for the purpose, have been devised by Brooks, Thalén, and Tiberg.

1. Brooks' Method.—Mr. T. B. Brooks,* of the Geological Survey of Michigan, in exploring for iron ore, determined with a pocket-compass variations east or west; the bearings of a standard line being taken as in ordinary surveys. The inclinations or dips were observed on the dip-compass held in the hand in the plane of the meridian. Sometimes observations were made with the compass held at right angles to this position, that is, facing north and south. The instrument was always held in the hand and levelled by its own weight. The intensity of the magnetic force for the three positions of the compass was measured by the number of oscillations made by the needle in a unit of time, usually taken at a quarter of a minute. No attempt was made to eliminate the earth's attraction by neutralising it with a magnet while the observation was being made, nor by computation; and the great amount of friction in the compass

* *Geological Survey of Michigan*, vol. i., 1873, chap. viii.

renders the number of oscillations only an approximation to the number that would be obtained with a delicately mounted needle. Mr. Brooks has, however, done excellent work with this method in 'the Marquette region and in New York and New Jersey. He also describes another method of working, which he calls magnetic triangulation. The mode of procedure is as follows:—Remote from any magnetic rocks, neutralise, by means of a bar magnet, the earth's influence on the needle of a solar compass. The needle will then stand indifferently in all directions. If the compensated instrument is set up near the magnetic pole to be determined, the needle will point as nearly towards the local pole as its mode of mounting will permit. The operation being repeated at two other points near the magnetic pole, the three lines must intersect in one point, which will be directly over the pole of which the position is sought. By using a dip-compass in a similar manner, data to determine the depth would be obtained. The fact that several local poles often influence the needle at each station renders this method difficult in practice ; a place must be sought where but one strong pole exists.

2. Thalén's Method.—Professor R. Thalén,[*] of the University of Upsala, employs a modification of Weber's portable magnetometer, or of Lamont's theodolite. In its simplest form, Thalén's instrument consists of a compass-box $3\frac{1}{2}$ inches in diameter, divided into degrees or half-degrees. At right angles to the diameter, passing through the zero point of the graduation, an arm extends horizontally. This serves as a sight in setting out lines in the field, and receives the bar magnet for the deviation measurements. A deflection of the needle is caused by means of this magnet, the longitudinal direction of which is parallel to the arm, and the distance of which from the needle always remains unaltered. On the other side of the compass-box there is a socket, into which a rod of soft iron can be placed perpendicularly for inclination measurements. This iron rod, like the magnet, effects a deflection of the needle. The instrument rotates about a vertical axis, and is provided with a spirit-level and levelling screws. In order to simplify the apparatus still further, the compass-box may be fastened to a rectangular board, the edges of which can be used as sights ; whilst the board itself receives the bar magnet, which is fixed by screws or springs in the position that is determined once for all. As support for the instrument, an ordinary surveyor's plane-table may be employed.

The observations with the magnetometer consist for the most

[*] *Jernkontorets annaler*, vol. xxxiv., 1879, p. 17.

part of deviation measurements, for which two different methods may be employed. In one method the instrument is placed so that the needle is directed to the zero point, the bar magnet having been removed from its place. Directly the magnet is replaced, the needle will deviate from its original position, the angle of deviation being read from the graduated circle. In the second method the instrument is turned, while the magnet is in its place, until the needle points to zero. The bar magnet is then removed, and, when the needle has come to rest, the angle is read. In this method, under similar conditions, the angle obtained will be greater than in the former method. Of the two methods, the latter, or *sine method*, is the more delicate; but it requires more time than the former, as the instrument has to be re-adjusted at every observation with the magnet and iron rod. This method has the disadvantage of not being applicable in the extreme north of the ore field, where the magnetism of the ore bed is powerful. In the former, or *tangent method*, the instrument remains unmoved during both measurements. The disadvantage, however, is that the so-called constants of the instrument vary with the angle of deviation. This does not matter if the results are to be arrived at geometrically, since it is then merely necessary to join the points where the same angle is obtained, quite regardless of the magnitude of the angle and of its corresponding constant. If the position of the ore is to be determined by calculation, the sine method must be employed.

Where no ore is present, the needle is acted upon by two forces, one of which is due to the fixed magnet, and the other to the horizontal component of the earth's magnetism. These two forces acting simultaneously, the needle takes up a position in the direction of their resultant. Then if α is the angle of deviation, and H the component of the earth's magnetism, the following formulæ are obtained:—

for the tangent method: $H \tan \alpha = K_1$,
for the sine method: $H \sin \alpha = K_2$,

in which K_1 and K_2 are constants, so long as the size and position of the magnet remain unaltered. If these constants are known, the actual value of H may be found from the magnitude of the observed angle by either of the methods. If the constants are unknown, only the relative value of H may be found. When observations are made near an iron ore field, in both formulæ H must be replaced by R, the resultant of the horizontal component of the earth's magnetism and the magnetism of the deposit. The formulæ then become

$R \tan \alpha = K_1$, and $R \sin \alpha = K_2$.

When the deviations are caused by the soft iron rod instead of by the magnet, somewhat similar formulæ are obtained; but the magnetism of the iron rod being due to induction, its intensity is proportional to the variations of the vertical components of the earth's magnetism. It follows that the constant K of each formula in this case must be replaced by a magnitude that varies with the magnetism of the rod. Observations with the iron rod indicate the inclination of the earth's magnetism; whilst observations with the bar magnet serve for determining the horizontal components of the same terrestrial force. Consequently, by combining the two methods, it is possible to find out the vertical components of the magnetic force.

In order to survey an ore field, it must first be divided into squares with sides 100, 50, or 25 feet in length. Then at every angle of these squares, the deviation must be observed with the magnet and iron rod. Similar observations must be made on ground free from iron, and so far distant from the ore field that the influence of the ore is not felt. It is also advisable to determine the magnetic declination for each point of observation. This may be done by directing the sights along one of the lines that have been set out, and reading the bearing, after the fixed magnet and iron rod have been removed. Observations must also be made along the magnetic meridian north of the supposed ore pole to determine where the north-seeking end of the free needle changes its direction from north to south, or whether it invariably points towards the north.

When these determinations of declination, horizontal intensity, and inclination have been carefully made, and the angles obtained noted on paper divided into squares, lines are drawn for each of the three series of observations, exhibiting equal declination (isogonic lines), equal intensity (isodynamic lines), and equal inclination (isoclinic lines). This is done in each case by joining the points by which equal angles were obtained. The curvature of the lines is drawn as naturally as possible, care being taken to avoid sharp bends. The curves of inclination and intensity thus constructed are closed, and have an approximately circular or elliptical shape, provided that a single isolated ore mass is being dealt with. They are grouped round two points. The one at the north is where the greatest angle of deviation was found, whilst that at the south is where the smallest angle was obtained. Between these two groups of curves is an open curved line representing the neutral angle. In this neutral line the intensity is the same as if no ore was present. The straight line joining the points where the greatest and smallest angles were obtained passes over the centre of the ore mass, and indicates the direction of the magnetic meridian of the ore field. Directly beneath a point in this line, in a vertical ore bed, the greatest mass of ore occurs. The rule that most generally holds good in searching for iron ore is, that the ore mass is to be found immediately beneath the point where the magnetic meridian cuts the neutral line.

The isogonic lines consist of concentric ovals placed, as a rule, symmetrically on both sides of the meridian. From the shape and position of these curves useful indications may be obtained regarding the position of the ore pole, and the shape of the deposit.

3. **Tiberg's Method.**—In exploring for iron ore, Mr. E. Tiberg uses a dip-compass, $3\frac{1}{4}$ inches in diameter, and half an inch deep. The axis of the needle is at right angles to the plane of the box, and rests upon two agate supports. The needle can thus move freely when the compass is placed horizontally or vertically. The instrument differs from other dipping needles in that the centre of gravity of the magnetic-needle is a little below its horizontal axis when the compass is in a vertical position. The needle is compensated for the vertical force of the earth's magnetism by a piece of wax fastened to its south-seeking end.

The instrument is provided with a spirit-level for horizontal adjustment, and with a ring, by means of which it can be suspended vertically. The sighting instrument, used in conjunction with the dip-compass, is a brass plate about a foot in length, provided at one end with four square flanges to receive the dip-compass for horizontal measurements. At right angles to this square, there is a groove in the plate with a sliding receptacle for the bar magnet required for horizontal measurements. Four folding sights are attached to the plate in such a way that their lines of sight form a right angle. The instrument, consequently, can be used as a cross-head. Two special sights are added for levelling operations, and the instrument is provided with a circular spirit-level.

The observations for vertical measurements are made at the surface with the plane-table or by hand. The inclination instrument is fastened to the plane-table, levelled, and turned until the needle points to 90°. The instrument is then raised with the ring at the top, and placed at right angles to the magnetic meridian, and the angle indicated by the needle observed. The same operation has to be done by hand if the plane-table is not available. When the ore appears to be deep, or when the horizontal intensity is powerful, recourse must be had to the plane-table.

The formula for calculating the vertical intensity G is—

$$G = K \tan v,$$

in which v is the angle given by the needle—that is, its deviation from the horizontal—and K a constant varying in different instruments from 0·75 to 1·4 of the earth's horizontal magnetic force. Lines of equal vertical intensity may thus be constructed. In magnetic plans it is usual to employ a blue colour for positive intensity, and a red colour for negative intensity. The accuracy attainable with this method is from 0·2 to 0·1 per cent. of the earth's magnetic force in central Sweden. With the plane-table 250 to 300 observations may be made per day, and 450 to 500 by hand. For each ore field surveyed the needle must be compensated afresh, and a preliminary magnetic survey made. The field is then divided into squares, with sides 40 feet in length. The base-line is as nearly as possible in the middle of the field, and parallel to the direction of the strike of the deposit. In making the survey, observations are made every 10 feet, and in some cases every 5 feet, in the immediate vicinity of the ore, and every 20 to 40 feet or more when farther distant from the ore. The general rule is to make as many observations as may be required to indicate what the appearance of the curves will be. Heights are estimated by the eye, or by a preliminary levelling with the sighting instrument, and the more important topographical details are noted.

The maximum of intensity is generally presented by the point where the ore is nearest to the surface. It may also be situated between two adjacent deposits—in which case the intensity decreases, at first slowly, or not at all, and then comparatively rapidly. The distance to the centre of a vertical ore bed may be taken as at least 0·7 of half the breadth of the north-polar attraction. This rule is, however, not very trustworthy. The vertical distance of the plane of observation from the upper ore pole is equal to the horizontal distance of the point where the needle deviated most from the horizontal from that where $\frac{1}{2}$ of the greatest intensity was found. It is also equal to $1\frac{1}{3}$ of the distance of the point where the needle dipped most from that where half the maximum was found. The latter rule is the best.

Sometimes these calculations enable an opinion to be formed of the relative values of two similar ore beds. For two deposits of a similar character, situated at least 30 feet beneath the surface, it may be assumed that the deposit, for which the product of the greatest intensity and the polar distance is the greater, contains the larger quantity of ore for the same length of deposit. If the polar surfaces of the two beds are limited this product must be replaced by the square of the polar distance.

A good idea of a deposit may be formed from the appearance of the curves of intensity. Regular, long extended, elliptical curves, enclosing a long but narrow district of greatest intensity, always indicate a regular lenticular mass. An asymmetrical bend in the curves indicates parallel deposits. More circular curves may indicate a segregation of ore if the intensity decreases regularly. Irregular curves indicate more or less irregular deposits.

In exploring for courses of ore in the mine, a base-line is marked out in the level, and observations made every 10 feet at least. At each station three observations have to be made :—
(1) To determine the direction of the total horizontal intensity by means of the sighting instrument, the deviation of the magnetic-needle from the base-line being observed. (2) To determine the magnitude of its force by means of the bar magnet. (3) To determine the vertical intensity by means of the inclination instrument. Vertical measurements must also be made at the top and floor of the level, and for this purpose the instrument may be held in the hand. On neutral ground at the surface, the horizontal force of the earth's magnetism and the direction of the earth's magnetic meridian must be determined. The results of all the observations are represented on paper, along the base-line, as arrows showing the horizontal forces of the magnetism of the ore at the points of observation. If all or part of the arrows are directed towards the same point, there the ore may be assumed to be. The ore would be at the level at which the observations were made, if the vertical intensity is negative. When the arrows approach in front or behind, the plane of observation is above or below the magnetic centre of the ore. When the vertical intensity is positive, the ore may be above or below the plane of observation, always assuming that a more or less vertical ore mass is being dealt with.

By applying this method Mr. Tiberg has discovered important deposits of ore at the Swedish mines of Langban and Sikberg.

To illustrate the value of the magnetic-needle in exploring for iron ore, it may be mentioned that, according to the statistics given by Prof. Smock,* there were 115 mines in 1868 in the State of New Jersey, whilst in 1874 the number had increased to 200. All these ore localities were first made known by the use of the magnetic-needle. In fact, the annual production of the State had been increased 50 per cent. by the addition of new producing localities found by the compass. It should also be stated that in many cases there are no visible surface indications of ore.

* *Trans. Amer. Inst. M.E.*, vol. iv., 1876, p. 353.

Use of the Magnetic-Needle in Surveying Bore-holes.—It has been assumed that the diamond drill always bores a perfectly straight hole, even though passing through rocks of different hardness. Actual experience reveals an entirely different state of things, the deviations sometimes being so great as to render a bore-hole misleading. An ingenious plan of correctly ascertaining these deviations has been devised by Mr. E. F. Macgeorge,* an Australian engineer. His plan consists in lowering into the bore-hole clear glass phials filled with a hot solution of gelatine, each containing, in suspension, a magnetic-needle, free to assume the meridian direction. The phials are encased in a brass protecting tube, and let down to the depth required, being allowed to remain for several hours until the gelatine has set.

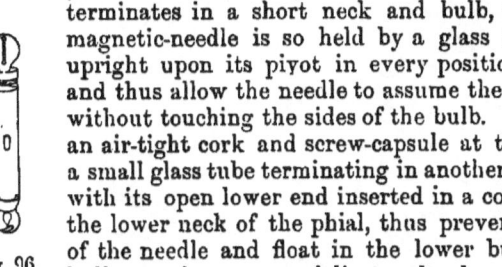

Fig. 96.

The construction of the phials or *clinostats* can be seen from Fig. 96. The clinostat is a true cylinder of glass made to fit accurately within the brass guide-tube. At the lower end it terminates in a short neck and bulb, within which a magnetic-needle is so held by a glass float as to stand upright upon its pivot in every position of the phial, and thus allow the needle to assume the meridian freely without touching the sides of the bulb. Passed through an air-tight cork and screw-capsule at the upper end is a small glass tube terminating in another bulb above and with its open lower end inserted in a cork which enters the lower neck of the phial, thus preventing the escape of the needle and float in the lower bulb. The upper bulb contains a very delicate plumb-rod of glass consisting of a fine rod terminating in a plumb of glass below and a diminutive bulbous float of hollow glass above. It is carefully adjusted to the specific gravity of the gelatine in which it is immersed, so as to insure the rod being truly vertical whatever the position of the phial and bulb may be. When the gelatine is fluid the plummet hangs freely perpendicular, whilst the needle in the lower bulb assumes the magnetic meridian. When, however, the phial is at rest in any position, the contents solidify on cooling, and thus hold fast the indicating plummet and magnet in solid transparent material. On withdrawal from the bore-hole the phials can each be replaced at the same angle at which they cooled, and when the phial is revolved upon the part where the magnetic-needle is seen embedded in the gelatine, until the needle is again in the meridian, the phial is manifestly in the same direction, both as regards inclination and azimuth, as it was when its contents were congealed, and thus the gradient and bearings of the bore-hole can

* *Engineering*, vol. xxxix., 1885, pp. 260, 334.

be determined. By repeating the observations at intervals of every 100 feet, the path of the bore-hole can be accurately mapped.

The inclination and azimuth at the time of cooling is determined exactly by the recording instrument, or *clinometer*, which is a modification of the theodolite. The phial, with its congealed contents, is placed in a sheath of brass tubing (Fig. 97), attached

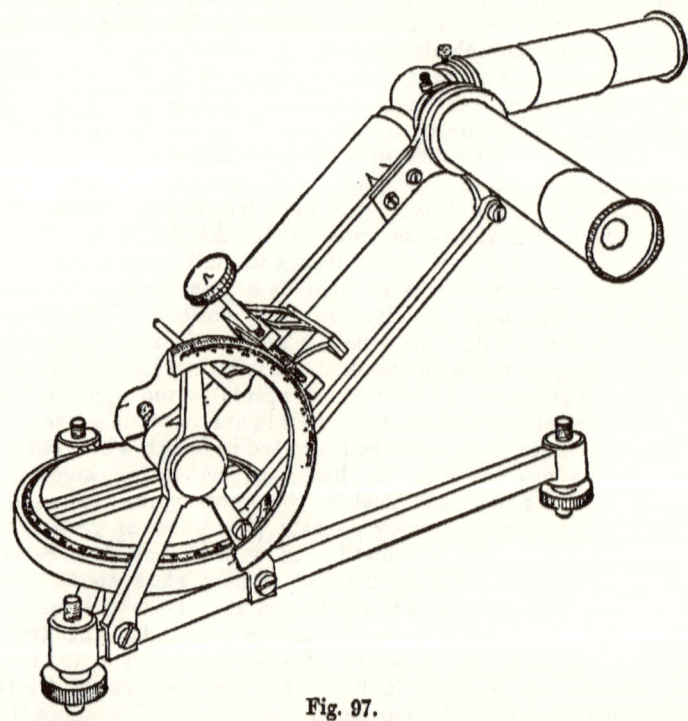

Fig. 97.

to a movable arm carrying the index of a vertical arc. The upper bulb of the phial is brought into the field of two cross-visioned microscopes, carried with the arm round the vertical arc, which are kept truly in the same plane at every angle of inclination by a parallel motion. Upon the object-glass of each microscope vertical lines are drawn. The phial is revolved in its sheath, and the arm is moved along the arc by the tangent screw until the embedded plummet is made perpendicular from each point of view. The phial is now at the angle of inclination at which its contents solidified, and its lower bulb will be found nearly in the axis of the revolving arm, and about an inch above the centre of a horizontal revolving circular mirror, having a system of parallel lines engraved across its face. Reflected in the mirror will be seen the image of the embedded needle, which, of course, pointed north before it was fixed by congelation in the bore-hole. If now the mirror is revolved until the number 270 of the graduated circle is opposite the marked end of the needle, and until the reflected image of the needle is parallel with the engraved lines, an index at the side of the graduated mirror frame will give the exact angle between the needle and the vertical plane of revolution of the phial, which is, in fact, the magnetic bearing of the inclined phial and of the bore-hole it occupied at the time of the application of the test.

This method was first applied at the Scotchman's United Mine at Stawell, in Victoria, and was so effectual as to enable the bore-hole to be found 37 feet away from its supposed position at a depth of 370 feet, a deflection that increased to the large amount of 75 feet at a depth of 500 feet. An exploratory level failed to find the bore-hole at its theoretical position, assuming the drill to have gone straight down. The subsequent search works lasted for more than a year, and cost altogether £3,663. Had the method been available at the commencement, the level driven would have cost only £1,352, and the saving effected would have been no less than £2,311.

Similar experiences have been met with in a number of other bore-holes in the mining districts of Victoria, and the consequence is that mine-proprietors are beginning to distrust the diamond drill altogether. Yet, if accurately surveyed, the most crooked bore is quite as useful as the straightest ever imagined by drill-makers. In view of these facts, the Victorian Government has contracted with the inventor to test all approved bores which have passed through auriferous rock.

By means of the *clinograph*, as the inventor terms his apparatus, a bore may be straightened when so deflected as to endanger the safety of the drill; for, suppose a bore-hole to have deflected suddenly, the depth of the point where the most serious deflection took place can be found. Then, if an india-rubber washer is forced down to 20 feet below this point, and liquid cement run in until it reaches some feet above the point of deflection, and allowed to set, then the drill may be again lowered and started gently, until it has started fairly in its corrected path, when the usual speed of boring may be resumed.

A less satisfactory method for ascertaining the inclination and direction of bore-holes was suggested by G. Nolten.* In the

---

* *Preuss. Zeitschr.*, voL xxviii., 1879, p. 176; Translation by C. Z. Bunning and J. K. Guthrie in *Trans. A. Eng. Inst. M.E.*, vol. xxix., p. 61.

instrument employed, the amount of deviation is etched upon glass by hydrofluoric acid; whilst its direction is found by means of a compass-needle, clamped by the aid of a stop-watch, after sufficient time has been allowed for settling. Notwithstanding the great imperfections of this instrument, its use in Germany has revealed some startling deviations of bore-holes. For example, in a bore-hole at Dienslaken, bored with a rotating drill, the deflection amounted to 47° at a depth of 750 feet. The bore-hole, undertaken by the German Government, at Lieth, in Holstein, was but little better than the preceding; but, by a lucky accident, the deflection of 3° at 984 feet gradually changed to the opposite quarter of the compass at 1,640 and 2,624 feet, and concluded with a deflection of only 1° at 3,280 feet.

Employment of a Powerful Magnet in Cases of Uncertain Holing.—In 1846 Professor Borchers, of Clausthal, first proposed to employ a powerful magnet in cases of uncertain holing from one excavation to another. Since that date, he has improved the method in many ways, and has frequently employed it in practice with great success. In order to ensure a successful holing, the ends of the two levels must not be more than 20 yards apart. The apparatus employed consists of a powerful magnet, with a specially constructed protractor, a compass, and a small auxilary magnet.

The powerful magnet consists of six magnetised steel bars 4 feet in length, enclosed in two wooden boxes, provided with water-tight lids. One of these boxes contains only one magnet; whilst the other box contains the remaining five, separated from one another in the middle and at the ends by pieces of card-board. In the centre of its upper side, the larger box is provided with a pivot, which fits into an aperture in the smaller box. On this

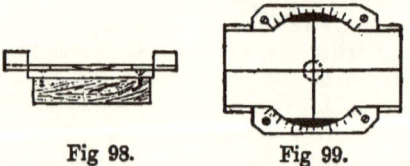

Fig 98.   Fig 99.

pivot, the small box can be rotated, and the north pole of the magnet inside can thus be made to correspond with the south poles of the magnets in the large box. Consequently, a portion of the magnetic force of the latter is neutralised. The powerful magnet must be fixed in such a way that it can be pointed in various directions, without altering the position of its centre.

20

For this purpose, is employed a brass protractor, Figs. 98, 99, which can be screwed on to a thick board. At the centre of the protractor, a brass plate revolves, and between the turned-up edges of this, the principal magnet may be placed. At right angles to the longitudinal axis of the magnet, an index line is engraved. Provided the rock barrier is not more than 6 yards across, an ordinary compass, with a sensitive needle, may be employed. For greater distances, the compass-needle must be suspended by a silk fibre. Under these circumstances the steel pivot is removed from the compass, and a case screwed on to the plate, as shown in Fig 100. The sides are covered with glass to protect the needle from air currents. The upper end of the glass tube, containing the silk fibre, is provided with a contrivance for centering the needle. The latter is somewhat longer than the diameter of the compass dial, and does not require to be centered with mathematical accuracy, provided that both ends are read, and the mean of the two readings taken. The auxiliary magnet is a small magnetised bar 12 to 18 inches in length.

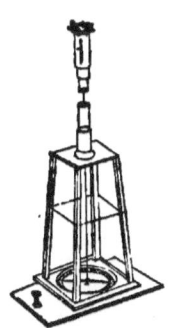

Fig. 100.

The mode of procedure is the following:—
At the end of one of the levels, the protractor is firmly fixed in such a way that its north and south line is in the magnetic meridian. At the end of the other level, the compass is set up, as nearly as possible at the same height as the protractor, and placed so that the needle indicates north. The needle must then be rendered astatic. To effect this, the auxiliary magnet is placed in the direction of the north and south line of the compass, on the side away from the principal magnet in the other excavation, and moved backwards and forwards until the force attracting the needle is neutralised. When these preparations are complete, the principal magnet, with the small box above it, is placed on the movable plate of the protractor, and brought approximately into the direction of holing. The powerful magnet then acts on the astatic needle of the compass, and causes it to take up a direction determined by a law enunciated by Gauss. But as the needle is not perfectly astatic for all directions, what attracting force remains must be again neutralised for the position taken up under the action of the powerful magnet. This is done by revolving on its pivot the small box above the principal magnet, until the north pole of the magnet it contains corresponds with the south poles of the other magnets. The action of the large magnet is thus

diminished. Then if the compass-needle is not perfectly astatic, it will alter its position, as the attracting force of the principal magnet increases or diminishes. If a change in the position of the needle is observed during the action of the weakened magnet, attempts must be made to bring the needle back to the position it occupied when the principal magnet acted with full force, by moving the auxiliary magnet very slightly. The upper bar of the large magnet is then turned back to its original position, and it is ascertained whether the compass-needle alters its position. If this is the case, the process must be repeated until the needle gives the same bearing with the full force and with the diminished force of the large magnet.

From the bearing of the needle and the direction of the large magnet, the direction of holing may be determined by construction, in the following way:—A B C (Fig. 101) is a right-angled triangle, with the right-angle at C; A being the centre of the large magnet, the longitudinal axis of which is in the direction of the hypothenuse A B. At C is the astatic-needle, which, attracted by the large magnet, takes up a position in the line C D. The direction of this line is determined by the equation—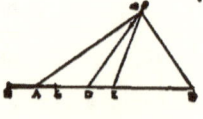

Fig. 101.

A D = ⅓ A B. Strictly speaking, the magnet N S should be very small. For practical purposes, however, this law may be applied without any appreciable error.

The question now arises, in what way should this law be applied. A geometrical method is inconvenient in the mine; and, consequently, it is desirable to calculate the angles α (B A C) and β (A C D), that is, the deviation of the direction of holing A C from the position of the magnet N S, and from that of the compass-needle C D. A, B, and C are situated on the circumference of a circle, the centre of which is E. In the triangle D E C, the angle C D E is equal to $\alpha + \beta$; and, since the triangle A E C is isosceles, the angle A C E is equal to the angle C A E; therefore, the angle D C E is equal to $\alpha - \beta$. The ratio of the sides D E and E C, however, is 1 : 3, and 1 : 3 = sin ($\alpha - \beta$) : sin ($\alpha + \beta$); therefore,

$$\sin (\alpha - \beta) = \tfrac{1}{3} \sin (\alpha + \beta).$$

Suppose, for example, that the bearing given by the protractor of the large magnet was 154°, and that given by the compass 125° 15'; the difference is then 28° 45' = $\alpha + \beta$. Now, sin 28° 45' = 0·48099; one-third of which is 0·16033, which is the sine of the angle 9°.14'. Consequently,

$$\alpha + \beta = 28° \ 45'$$
$$\alpha - \beta = \ 9° \ 14'$$

therefore, $\alpha = 19°$ and $\beta = 9° \ 45'$. The direction of holing A B is, therefore,

$$125° \ 15' + \ 9° \ 45' = 135° \ 0'$$
$$154° \ \ 0' - 19° \ \ 0' = 135° \ 0'$$

This calculated bearing has to be subtracted from 180°, since the north and south line of the compass always remains in the same position throughout the process; the needle being revolved. The direction in which it would be necessary to drive would, consequently, be

$$180° - 135° = 45°.$$

Instructions for carrying out the operations required at the large magnet are given by means of previously arranged signals by the observer at the compass.

A powerful magnet was applied with success in a somewhat similar manner in 1885 by Mr. A. Haddon[*] in seeking a bore-hole, that had diverged from the vertical, at the Holyrood Brewery, Edinburgh. After the bore-hole had gone down 200 feet, it was considered necessary to connect it by a level with a neighbouring well 18 feet 3 inches distant. The miner entrusted with the work having failed to find the bore-hole, Mr. Haddon procured four 8-inch bar-magnets, placed end to end, and secured between two laths of wood. These he lowered into the bore-hole with the south pole downwards, and, by noting the deflection of a compass-needle at different points in the mine, he found that the bore-hole was 8 feet from its expected position.

* *Engineering*, vol. xxxix., p. 31.

CHAPTER XX.

PHOTOGRAPHIC SURVEYING.

Photogrammetry.—The theory of the methods by which plans and sections may be obtained by means of photographs has been termed photogrammetry. The principles of photogrammetry were developed by Lambert as far back as 1759. The first application was made in the years 1791 to 1793 by Beautemps-Beaupré, who constructed topographical plans from his perspective hand-sketches made during his voyage round the world. The first camera constructed for this purpose was used in 1851 by Colonel Laussedat, who in this way surveyed a portion of Paris in 1861. Since then the method has been largely developed in Germany, Austria, and Italy, and the literature of the subject is now considerable.* The principle of the method is simple. If a photograph be taken from a point of which the position is already known, the direction of the axis of the object glass and the focal length of the lens being also known, and the line of the horizon being marked on the picture, the picture can be laid down on a sheet of paper on which it is desired to plot the survey, and will give the direction from the point of observation of all the points the position of which is required. Two photographs of the same object taken from different known points define the position of each object, and also enable altitudes to be calculated or graphically determined. In fact, the method of surveying is exactly that of the plane-table, with the difference that a great portion of the work which, with the plane-table, has to be done in the field is, with the

---

* The following are the principal works on photogrammetry :—Colonel Laussedat's exhaustive articles in the *Mémorial de l'officier du génie*, 1854, No. 16, and 1864, No. 17; "Die Photogrammetrie," by Dr. Stolze, Halle, 1887; "Die Photogrammetrie," by Dr. Koppe, Weimar, 1889; "Photography applied to Surveying," by Lieut. H. A. Reed, New York, 1888; L. P. Paganini's articles in the *Rivista di Topografia*, 1889; "Die Photographie im Dienste des Ingenieurs," by F. Steiner, Vienna, 1891; "Die Photographische Terrainaufnahme," by V. Pollack, Vienna, 1891; "Die Photographische Messkunst," by F. Schiffner, Halle, 1892; "Das Photographische Aufnehmen zu wissenschaftlichen Zwecken," by A. Meydenbauer, Berlin, 1892; "Éléments de Photogrammétrie," by V. Legros, Paris, 1892; and E. Monét's article in the *Mémoires de la société des ingénieurs civils*, 1894, p. 216.

photographic method, done in the office. The degree of accuracy obtainable is obviously not excessive. The method is, however, well adapted for such topographical surveys as mining engineers are sometimes called upon to execute.

Instruments Used.—There are many types of phototheodolites in use. The principle is, however, the same in all. The instrument consists of an ordinary theodolite in which the telescope is replaced by a camera, whose optic axis is accurately parallel to that of a telescope placed at the side. A graduated horizontal circle and a vertical circle enable the angles to be read with accuracy, and a spirit level fixed to the camera serves to ensure the horizontality of the instrument. The holder for the plates is provided with points of thin sheet metal which mark the horizontal and vertical lines on the picture. The point of intersection of the marking should coincide with point sighted at the cross-wires of the telescope. The leading maker of phototheodolites is R. Lechner of Vienna.

A compact instrument for photographic surveying has been designed by Mr. J. Bridges Lee for use in geological surveys. It was described by him in a paper read before the Geological Society on December 5, 1894. The instrument consists essentially of a photographic camera fitted inside with a magnetic needle, which carries a vertical transparent scale divided and numbered to 360°, and also with cross fibres which intersect at right angles. The fittings and adjustments of the instrument are of such a character that the camera can be accurately levelled and directed towards any point in a horizontal direction, and when a photograph is taken in an ordinary way the bearing of the meridian vertical plane which bisects the instrument through the protographic lens will be recorded automatically on the face of the photograph. The vertical fibre (and its image on the photograph) serves as an index to read the bearing; and the same fibre marks by its shadow a line right across the photograph, which marks the meridian vertical plane on the image. The horizontal fibre is adjusted to mark on the image the horizontal plane which bisects the photographic lens. The camera rests on a divided horizontal circle, which can be adjusted to a truly horizontal position by levelling screws. There is a tripod stand and head, with suitable appliances for supporting and adjusting the instrument in position. The camera is provided with a rectilinear doublet lens, and iris diaphragm and rack and pinion focussing adjustment. It is made of aluminium, and it is surmounted by a telescope adjustable in altitude, and fitted with vertical and horizontal webs; and it is also surmounted by a revolvable tubular level.

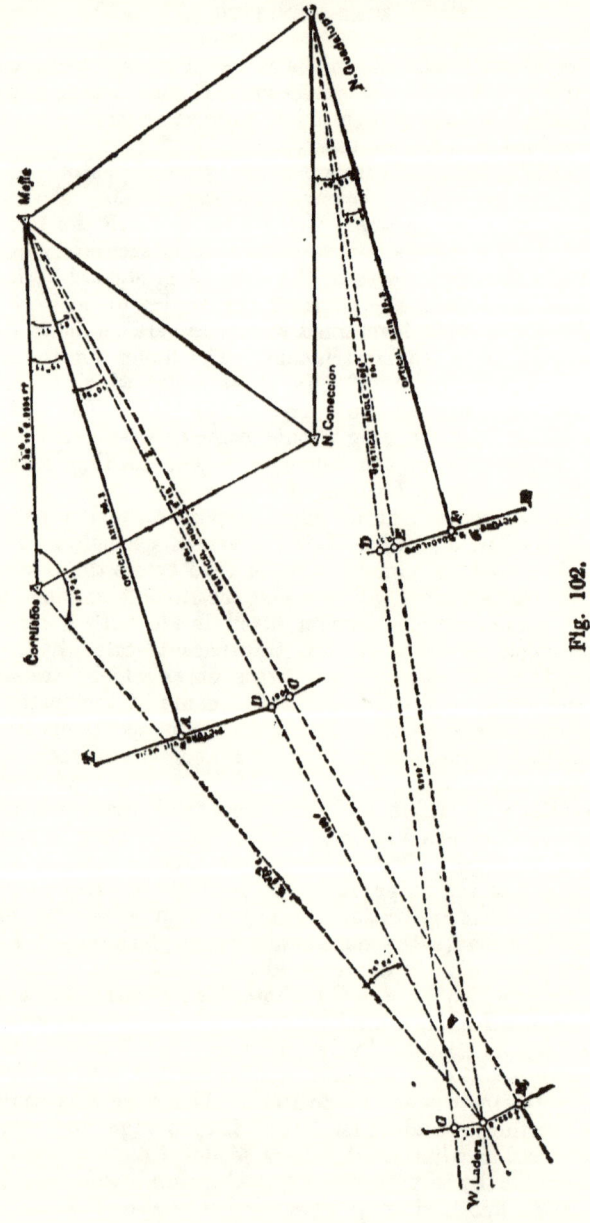

Fig. 102.

Application to Mining Work.—Mr. H. M. Stanley, of Arizona,[*] successfully employed the photographic method in a survey of the properties of the Plata-Reina de Senora Mining and Milling Company, situated in the mining district of Las Planchas, Mexico. The area surveyed comprised about 6 square miles in broken mountainous country. In order to carry out the work as quickly and as accurately as possible, it was decided to triangulate the area, and to complete the work by photographic surveying; an 8 by 10 Eastman camera being used. The first picture was taken to the north, and to the right of the meridian. The others were taken round the circle, one after another, so as to slightly overlap, care being taken to note the height of the instrument and the index number for each picture.

The method of plotting employed by Mr. Stanley is illustrated in Fig. 102. The points marked "Corruscos," "Mejia," "N. Coneccion," and "N. Guadalupe" are points established by triangulation, at each of which pictures were taken. This sketch was originally constructed on a scale of $\frac{1}{2}$ inch to 150 feet. The focal distance of the lens used is 20·3 half-inches.

In order to fix the point "W. Ladera," it was found on examining the pictures that this point is on VIII. Mejia and I. North Guadalupe. The first operation is to orient these pictures —*i.e.*, find and plot the position of the optical axis and of the picture in each case. On VIII. Mejia, the point "Corruscos" is known. Mark it (1) on the back of the negative. With the dividers measure carefully the horizontal distance from this point to the vertical axis. From a diagonal scale of equal parts constructed on a half-inch, the horizontal distance is found to be + 5·53 half-inches, or units, and as it is to the right of the vertical axis it is marked plus. This distance is the altitude of a right-angled triangle whose base is the focal distance of the lens. The hypothenuse is the distance from the optical centre of the lens to the image of the known point on the picture, in this case "Corruscos." The tangent of the angle at the base of the right-angled triangle is equal to

$$\frac{+\ 5\cdot 53}{20\cdot 3} = +\ 0\cdot 27241.$$

The orientation angle is therefore + 15° 15′.

This result is placed in the proper column of a table ruled as follows:—

[*] *Trans. Amer. Inst. M.E.*, vol. xx., 1891, p. 740.

PHOTOGRAPHIC SURVEYING. 311

Photographic Survey of...

SCALE, ½ inch = 150 ft.   FOCAL DISTANCE, 20·3.

Station.	View No.	Point No.	Co-ordinates		Orientation Angle.	Location Angle.	Vertical Angle.	Height of Point above or below Station.	Height of Station above or below Datum.	Height of Point above or below Datum.	Distance.	Remarks.
			Horizontal.	Vertical.								
Mejia, ...	VIII.	1	+5·53	..	+15° 15′	..	..	..	..	..	..	Oriented on Corruscos Flag.
N. Guadalupe,	I.	1	+5·47	..	+15° 04′	..	..	..	..	..	..	Oriented on N. Coneccion Flag.
Mejia, ...	VIII.	2	−3·60	+0·81	..	−10° 36′	+2° 15′	+222·8	+500·0	+722·8	5668′	Location of W. Ladera Flag.
N. Guadalupe,	I.	2	+2·35	−0·51	..	+ 6° 36′	−1° 26′	−157·3	+880·1	+722·8	6292′	Location of W. Ladera Flag.

To plot the position of the optical axis, draw a line through the station Mejia, making with the hypothenuse, Mejia-Corruscos, an angle equal to −15° 15′—*i.e.*, to the left. Make this line equal to 20·3 half-inches or units and it will be the optical axis. A line perpendicular to it at its extremity will be the position of the picture VIII. Mejia. In the same manner the picture I. N. Guadalupe may be oriented as shown on the sketch, using for the purpose point (1) of that picture, which is the flag at N. Coneccion. The calculation in this case is:—

$$\text{Tangent of the angle} = \frac{+ 5·47}{20·3} = + 0·26945.$$

Orientation angle = + 15° 04′.

The two pictures having been oriented, the positions of all points common to them both may be determined. On picture VIII. Mejia, it is seen that the point W. Ladera, point (2), is − 3·80 units to the left of the vertical axis, and + 0·81 unit above the horizontal axis. The same point (2) on the picture I. N. Guadalupe, is + 2·35 units to the right of the vertical axis, and − 0·51 unit below the horizon. These results are recorded on the calculation-sheet. Now,

$$\frac{-3·80}{20·3} = \text{tangent of angle} = - 0·18719.$$

Location-angle = − 10° 36′.

312   MINE-SURVEYING.

At the point Mejia draw the line Mejia-W. Ladera, making with the optical axis an angle equal to − 10° 36'—that is, to the left of the optical axis.

From picture I. N. Guadalupe it is found that

$$\frac{+\ 2\cdot 35}{20\cdot 3} = \text{tangent of angle} = +0\cdot 11576.$$

Location-angle = + 6° 36'.

At the point N. Guadalupe draw the line N. Guadalupe-W. Ladera, making an angle with the optical axis of picture I. N. Guadalupe, equal to + 6° 36'—that is, to the right of the optical axis. The intersection of the two lines Mejia-W. Ladera and N. Guadalupe-W. Ladera is the position of the point W. Ladera which was required.

This point could have been determined graphically. On the line L A B lay off A B = − 3·80. Through B and Mejia draw the line Mejia-W. Ladera. On the line D F N lay off F E = + 2·35, and draw N. Guadalupe-E-W. Ladera. These two lines will intersect at W. Ladera. The distance Mejia-W. Ladera, and also N. Guadalupe-W. Ladera are scaled from the map and placed in the proper column of the calculation-sheet.

To find the elevation of W. Ladera, or its depression above or below Mejia and N. Guadalupe, the procedure is:—Through the point, B, draw BC perpendicular to B-Mejia, and make it equal to + 0·81 unit. Through Mejia and C draw the line Mejia-C-M. At W. Ladera draw W. Ladera-M perpendicular to Mejia-W. Ladera. Then the line W. Ladera-M is the elevation of W. Ladera above Mejia, and it may be scaled and placed on the calculation-sheet.

At E draw D E perpendicular to the line N. Guadalupe-W. Ladera and equal to − 0·51 unit and at W. Ladera draw W. Ladera-G perpendicular to the same line. Through N. Guadalupe and D draw N. Guadalupe-D-G. Then W. Ladera-G is the depression of W. Ladera below N. Guadalupe. Scale this, and place it on the calculation-sheet.

To calculate the elevation—

In the right-angled triangle Mejia-A-B, the side Mejia-B $= \dfrac{20\cdot 3}{\cos 10°\ 36'} = 20\cdot 6$ units.

In the right-angled triangle Mejia-B-C, the tangent of angle at base $= \dfrac{0\cdot 81}{20\cdot 6} = 0\cdot 03932$; the angle of elevation = 2° 15'.

In the triangle Mejia-W. Ladera-M, the side W. Ladera-M = $5668 \times \tan 2° 15' = 222·8$ feet.

In the triangle N. Guadalupe-F-E, the side N. Guadalupe-E $= \dfrac{20·3}{\cos 6° 36'} = 20·4$ units.

In the triangle N. Guadalupe-D-E, the tangent of angle at base $= \dfrac{-0·51}{20·4} = -0·02500$; the angle of depression $= -1° 26'$.

In the triangle N. Guadalupe-W. Ladera-G, the side W. Ladera-G = $6292 \times \tan 1° 26' = 157·3$ feet.

Therefore, W. Ladera is 222·8 feet above Mejia, and 157·3 feet below N. Guadalupe. If Mejia is 500 feet above the datum plane, then W. Ladera is 722·8 feet and N. Guadalupe 880·1 feet above the same plane. In the same manner any other point on these two photographs may be determined graphically or by calculation.

The point W. Ladera may be determined from one photograph thus :—

The side Corruscos-Mejia is known from the triangulation, and the bearing of Corruscos-W. Ladera from the field notes. Then in the triangle Corruscos-Mejia-W. Ladera, the angle at Corruscos = 139° 45'. From the photograph VIII. Mejia, the angles 15° 15' and 10° 36' may be found as before. Their sum 25° 51' is the angle at Mejia. The angle at W. Ladera is equal to $180° - (139° 45' + 25° 51') = 14° 24'$. The triangle can now be solved by the ordinary sine-formula, and the distances from Mejia and N. Guadalupe to W. Ladera and their bearings can be determined.

Photographic surveying has also been successfully adopted in other mining districts. Lieut. H. A. Reed in his work on photography applied to surveying reproduces an excellent French photographic map of an area of 13·6 square miles in the vicinity of Sainte-Marie-aux-Mines. The field work was plotted to the scale of $\frac{1}{5000}$. The contours have an equidistance of 5 metres. The field-work occupied 10 days, the number of photographic stations was 31, of prints 52, and of points determined 1,400.

In 1880 the Carrara marble quarries were successfully surveyed by L. P. Paganini by the aid of photography, the mountainous character of the district having rendered the use of the plane table inconvenient. The method was also used by V. Pollack in 1890 for a survey required in connection with the construction of a mountain railway at the Eisenerz-Vordernberg iron mines in Styria.

Advantages of Photogrammetry. — From the foregoing description it is evident that, with the camera as a surveying instrument, the field-work may be performed with great rapidity. The reduction to a minimum of the time occupied in field-work is the chief advantage of the method. The survey of a length of 3 miles of the Windischgarsten-Spital railway in Austria, covering the entire width of the valley and including the heights on the right side, recorded in 24 pictures by Hafferl, occupied in favourable weather four and a-half hours. With the climatic conditions obtaining at the Arlberg in 1889, it was absolutely impossible to use any other method of surveying the precipitous peaks. It is thus evident that the method is specially useful in the unhealthy malarious districts that a mining engineer is often called upon to survey. It is also well adapted in mountainous and difficult country for laying out rack-railways or aerial wire ropeways. The successful photographic surveys of the Arlberg and of the Rosstrappe mountain in the Harz show that inaccessible regions may easily be surveyed. It follows that it is possible to survey regions that cannot be traversed without danger, such as railways in operation, glaciers, ground above mines where subsidence has set in, or areas to which access is forbidden by the owners. There is, too, the further advantage that additions may at any time be made to the plan without a fresh survey being necessary. The plotting of the survey is not attended by difficulty, as the plan results from an application of the simple method of intersections, whilst the representation of surface-forms and of heights is effected either mechanically or by the use of tabular values that are easily applied. With carefully constructed instruments, the results exceed in precision those obtained with the compass or with the plane-table. As addenda to the plans, the photographs recording the survey will, for the purposes of mine reports, often supply useful information.

APPENDIX I.

EXAMINATION QUESTIONS.

The following examination questions will be found useful to those students who have not the advantage of regular instruction in mine-surveying, affording them a means of personally testing their knowledge :—

1. Give the length of a link, and of a chain. How many chains are there in a mile, and how many acres in a square mile ? (*Colliery Managers' Examination, Bristol.*)

2. In chaining over sloping ground, how do you correct for the inclination? Give a simple rule when the inclination is expressed either in angular measure or as a gradient, *e.g.*, 1 in 6, 1 in 15. (*City and Guilds of London Institute, Examination in Mine-Surveying*, 1885.)

3. Describe the miner's dial, and note the improvements recently introduced into its construction. (*Royal School of Mines, Examination in Mine-Surveying*, 1884.)

4. Give a copy of a page of a survey-book recording an imaginary underground-survey. How may you approximately ascertain the date of the workings of an old undated plan? (*Colliery Managers' Examination, West Lancashire*, 1887.)

5. Describe the Henderson dial, and state its supposed advantages over the rack instrument. (*R.S.M.*, 1883.)

6. Give a short description of the miner's dial, with its usual appliances, especially when it is used as a theodolite, the needle being thrown off. (*City Guilds*, 1880.)

7. Describe a Gunter's or land measuring chain. (*City Guilds*, 1881.)

8. What is meant by the term true meridian? Describe a simple method for approximately determining it. (*City Guilds*, 1885.)

9. State the present deviation. In what manner is the deviation usually found to vary from year to year, also in travelling from one locality to another at a considerable distance ? (*City Guilds*, 1885.)

10. Sketch on paper the following bearings of a survey :—N. 82° E., 68 links ; S. 51° E., 95 links ; N. 63° E., 78 links ; N. 20° E., 97 links ; N. 35° W., 87 links ; N. 87° W., 140 links ; S. 52° W., 140 links ; S. 48° E., 85 links. (*Colliery Managers, Derby.*)

11. Explain the traverse tables. (*Colliery Managers, South Wales.*)

12. Suppose you were driving towards an old waste, which is shown on a plan 20 years old, explain the precautions to be taken as regards the meridian. (*Colliery Managers, Derby.*)

13. You are required to traverse over a level in which rails are laid down. How would you proceed to use an ordinary miner's dial under the circumstances, the dial being without a rack, but supplied with two sets of legs? The only true bearing was one taken in a cross-cut north, at a distance of, say, 5 fathoms off the main level, where the traverse is being made; this cross-cut occurring about half way in the traverse. Rule a supposed page of your underground book suited to this purpose, and give, say, six drafts or bearings all supposed to be affected by the attraction of the rails, the polarity of the whole being governed by the true bearing in the cross-cut north. If time will permit, insert distances and prove your work by plotting. (*City Guilds*, 1883.)

14. Explain by writing and sketching how to make a loose needle survey. (*Yorkshire College, Leeds*, 1886.)

15. The three sides of a triangle measure 144, 192, and 240 links respectively. Find the area of the triangle in square yards, and the angle opposite to the shortest side. (*City Guilds*, 1885.)

16. What is the area in statute acreage of a triangular field whose sides measure 2420, 1860, and 2005 links respectively? A sketch may be given, but not to scale. Logarithms are recommended for the calculation. (*City Guilds*, 1883.)

17. Explain by writing and sketching how to make and book a fast needle survey. (*Yorkshire College, Leeds*, 1886.)

18. The area, in acres, roods, and poles, is required of an irregular field, which was surveyed by running one line through it from end to end (A to B), with offsets taken as under:—

No plan to be drawn.

Left	B / Centre	Right
	B	
150	15·50 ☉	0
182	13·00	
	12·48	175
	11·59	55
	9·80	183
280	8·65	
202	3·93	92
	1·50	75
145	0·45	
0	☉	0
	A	

Length of line, 15·50 chains. (*City Guilds*, 1883.)

APPENDIX I.   317

19. Give a general description of the theodolite, and explain the method in which you would use it in making an underground-survey. (*City Guilds,* 1887.)

20. What are the special advantages and disadvantages in the use of the ordinary miner's compass as compared with the theodolite? (*City Guilds,* 1887.)

21. Lay down the underground-survey given on page 38, on the scale of 3 chains to an inch. Trigonometrical calculations may be used. (*City Guilds,* 1887.)

22. Find the horizontal distance and direction of the Station H from the shaft. Also the approximate difference of level between these points. (*City Guilds,* 1887.)

23. Work out the following series of levels, showing the height, above the Station A of each point taken :—

Distance.	Back-Sight.	Intermediate.	Fore-Sight.
A	12·63	...	...
0·40	...	9·16	...
1·00	...	7·43	...
1·50	...	5·31	...
2·00	...	4·06	...
3·50	...	2·16	...
4·50	9·06	...	0·42
5·50	...	7·50	...
6·50	...	6·15	...
8·00	...	3·60	...
9·00	...	2·12	...
10·50	10·15	...	0·75
11·20	...	8·70	...
13·00	...	4·45	...
14·60	...	...	3·23

—(*City Guilds*, 1887.)

24. Explain by writing how to level and plot a section. (*Yorkshire College, Leeds*, 1886.)

25. Find the quantity of coal in 1 acre of a seam of the following section:—Top coal, 2 feet 4 inches; band, 0 feet 10 inches; bottom coal, 1 feet 8 inches; total, 4 feet 10 inches, taking the specific gravity of coal at 1·25. (*Colliery Managers, Newcastle-on-Tyne.*)

26. Find the quantity of coal in an acre of a seam 5 feet 6½ inches thick, taking the specific gravity at 1·25. (*Newcastle-on-Tyne.*)

27. If pillars are left 30 by 21, and winnings 32 by 26, what percentage is got in the first working? (*Colliery Managers, Newcastle-on-Tyne.*)

28. How much coal might be expected to be available in an area of 150 acres of a 4-feet seam, allowing one-fifth for faults and waste? (*Science and Art Department, Examination in Mining*, 1884.)

29. The solid contents of a lode are in volume per cent.:—

Galena, ...	30
Zinc-blende,...	15
Iron pyrites, ...	20
Quartz, ...	35

What is the weight per cubic fathom of the stuff and of its different constituents? (*S. and A. D.*, 1884.)

30. A copper lode is 14 inches thick, containing copper pyrites and fluorspar in the proportion of 2 parts of fluorspar to 1 part of copper pyrites. What is the weight of a square fathom of the lode, allowing one-thirtieth for hollows? (*Rickard.*)

31. A level 7 feet high is driven on a tin lode 8 inches thick, of which one-tenth is oxide of tin, the remainder being quartz. How many tons of tin stuff will be obtained per fathom in length, if the lode is quite solid? (*Rickard.*)

32. In working to the full rise of a seam of which the inclination is 1 in 12 you meet with a rise fault of 10 yards. What will be the length of a rise tunnel to be drawn at the inclination of 1 in 6 between the seam at the low side of the fault, and the seam on its rise side, supposing the fault to be vertical? (*Colliery Managers, West Lancashire*, 1887.)

33. Plot on a scale of 8 fathoms to the inch the following underground traverse, taken with the ordinary miner's "left-hand" dial:—

No.			Bearing.	Distance.			
				fms.	ft.	in.	
A	...	...	355° 30'	10	4	9	From centre of pp. shaft. A at crossing of East level.
B	...	...	84° 26'	7	3	2	
C	...	...	92° 04'	8	1	9	C At x cut N.
[D²	...	...	342° 09'	7	3	0	D² END do.
D	...	...	96° 05'	3	5	9	END.

—(*City Guilds*, 1883.)

APPENDIX I.

34. Describe the ordinary method of using the theodolite in making an underground-survey. Also any special method which may be adopted where great accuracy is required. (*City Guilds*, 1887.)

35. Lay down the following underground-survey on the scale of 2 chains to an inch:—

Distance, Chains.		Vertical Inclination.	Horizontal Angles.
Shaft to A	1·90	0° 0′	A = 145° 15′
A B	6·75	4° 35′	B = 177° 30′
B C	4·30	3° 13′	C = 213° 54′
C D	9·77	0° 0′	D = 97° 20′
D E	3·90	6° 46′	E = 130° 13′
E F	6·13	0° 0′	F = 167° 30′
F G	3·01	2° 20′	...

The horizontal angles are those on the left hand of a person travelling in the direction of the survey, and the magnetic bearing of the line F G is 30° east of north. (*City Guilds*, 1887.)

36. The difference of level of two points several miles apart is required with great exactness, and a levelling-instrument of high power is used for the purpose.

Under what circumstances would it be necessary to allow for the spherical form of the earth, and in what manner would you make the proper corrections? (*City Guilds*, 1887.)

37. A colliery waggon way is laid down in a straight line from A, near the shaft, to a point B, in a direction 40° east of north, and is to be extended to join a main line of railway towards the east, running due north and south. The distance from B to the main line is 30 chains, measured due east, and the junction is to be made by a curve 60 chains radius.

Show how the waggon way must be set out, and find what length of line will be required beyond the point B.

In setting out the curve from the straight portion of railway, what offset must be made at the end of the first chain? (*City Guilds*, 1887.)

38. It is intended to sink a shaft on the end of a level driven from Pendarves' shaft, and the following is the survey by J. Budge from the centre of the shaft to the eastern end of the level:—

MINE-SURVEYING.

No.	Bearing.	Distance.	
		fms. ft. ins.	
A	357° 00'	7 3 0	from centre of shaft.
B	82° 45'	4 0 6	
C	81° 30'	3 0 0	
D	90° 00'	8 1 1	
E	102° 00'	5 0 0	
F	96° 45'	4 3 0	
G	105° 00'	2 4 5	
H	85° 00'	3 3 0	
J	77° 45'	2 2 7	
K	351° 00'	4 4 0	END.

As absolute accuracy was required a reverse or proof course of dialling was made from the end back to the shaft, with the following results :—

No.	Bearing.	Distance.	
		fms. ft. ins.	
A	171° 30'	4 2 10	from eastern END.
B	259° 00'	2 3 0	
C	265° 15'	3 1 6	
D	283° 15'	3 2 0	
E	279° 30'	8 4 3	
F	268° 45'	7 2 0	
G	263° 00'	4 2 0	
H	260° 15'	3 4 8	
J	177° 45'	7 1 10	centre of shaft.

Calculate the distance and bearing, from Pendarves' shaft, of the point at the surface at which the new shaft must be sunk.

39. Sketch and describe a hanging compass, state in which way it is tested and repaired, and describe the manner of its application. (*Tokio University, Japan*, 1879.)

40. Give a short description of the German dial, and what you consider to be its merits or demerits as compared with the English miner's dial. (*City Guilds*, 1880.)

41. Describe the continental method of surveying mines by means of the hanging compass, giving sketches of the instruments employed. (*R.S.M.*, 1886.)

42. What methods have been used to determine the deviation of bore-holes from the vertical? (*Science and Art Department*, 1887.)

43. At the Scotchman's United Mine, Stawell, and in various other places, it has been found that bores made by the diamond drill have deviated so seriously from their initial direction as to imply errors amounting to from 30 to 75 feet in bore-holes of 500 feet. Describe a method of making a survey of such bore-holes, and assuming the errors to have been detected, how is it possible to straighten a bore which has been so deflected as to endanger the safety of the drill? (*R.S.M.*, 1885.)

44. How should the compass be used in exploring for iron ores? (*R.S.M.*, 1887.)

45. Two parallel lodes were discovered at the surface, which was level, 30 yards apart underlying south, the south lode making an angle with the horizon of 65 degrees, the north lode of 52 degrees. Required the perpendicular depth from the surface to their point of intersection; and how far south of the south lode would the centre of a perpendicular shaft have to be placed to come down to the same point? Illustrate by a sketch, not necessarily to scale, but a scale is recommended in order to roughly test the accuracy of the calculations. (*City Guilds*, 1883.)

46. Illustrate in colours the following parts of a finished plan, scale 8 fathoms to the inch :—A road 25 feet wide bounded on each side by a hedge or bank 6 feet wide, showing a gateway, with a cross hedge or two. also a house 30 feet by 20 feet abutting on the road, with a pond adjoining open to the road, but with the hedge continued round its other sides. The pond not to be less than 58 feet long and 25 feet wide, and of an oval but irregular shape. A shaft 10 feet by 6 feet to be shown in one of the fields, surrounded by a burrow or rubbish heap which is to be sketched in with pen and indian ink. The whole drawing to be about 1 foot in length. (*City Guilds*, 1883.)

47. Without the application of a protractor, lay off the following angles from the same base, viz.:—20, 30, and 62 degrees, using a table of natural sines for the purpose. Describe the process. (*City Guilds*, 1883.)

48. In the triangle A B C, the angle $A = 37° 45'$, $B = 72° 15'$, and the side $A B = 437$. Find the sides A C, B C, and the perpendicular distance from C to A B. (*City Guilds*, 1887.)

49. In the triangle A B C, the side $A B = 365$, $A C = 180$, and the angle $B = 25° 30'$. Determine the angles A and C, and the side B C. (*City Guilds*, 1887.)

50. What do you understand by the word traversing? Where is this form of surveying necessary? How would you use an angular instrument in the

operation, and how would you check the accuracy of the plotting of the work by trigonometry? (*City Guilds*, 1883.)

51. Describe the true meridian, as compared with the magnetic meridian. How does the adoption of the latter affect plans made from compass observations and added to, as in mine plans, from year to year? (*City Guilds*, 1882.)

52. It is desired to know the exact distance and bearing of an imaginary line between the centre of a perpendicular shaft A and a point B in a level underground, over which it is intended to sink another perpendicular shaft, the dialling of the level commencing from A. Sketch the supposed drafts underground, marking each with its length and bearing, and proceed to describe the best and most accurate method of laying down, at the surface, the line required, and the position of the proposed new shaft over B. (*City Guilds*, 1881.)

53. Describe the ordinary process of levelling, stating any precautions required to ensure accuracy. (*City Guilds*, 1885.)

54. Work out the following series of levels and plot in the form of a section. Horizontal scale 1 chain to the inch, vertical scale 20 feet to the inch. Datum-line 50 feet.

Distance.	Back-Sight.	Fore-Sight.	
Chains.	Feet.	Feet.	
0·70	1·30	8·85	
1·50	8·85	2·30	
2·45	13·96	5·40	
3·60	5·40	0·52	
4·05	12·62	8·80	
5·40	8·80	1·12	
7·00	2·32	7·05	
9·40	1·33	9·96	
10·20	3·34	5·87	
11·35	5·87	9·10	

—(*City Guilds*, 1885.)

55. Plot, on a scale of 2 chains to an inch, the following survey:—

APPENDIX I. 323

	Chains.	Bearing.	Inclination. Rise.	
A	2·50	119° 45'	...	
B	7·47	137° 16'	3° 50'	
C	13·03	141° 32'	...	
D	3·40	196° 50'	...	
E	6·50	189° 24'	9° 36'	
F	11·66	266° 36'	7° 30'	
G	5·25	272° 22'	...	

—(*City Guilds*, 1885.)

56. A straight draft is required to be driven of uniform inclination between C and G. How must it be set out from each end? (*City Guilds*, 1885.)

57. Describe the method of using the transit-theodolite in order to measure horizontal and vertical angles with great precision. (*City Guilds*, 1885.)

58. Explain the principle of the vernier, and describe the manner in which you would construct a vernier for a circle to read 30 seconds, when the arc is divided into quarter degrees. (*R. S. M.*, 1884.)

59. How may the underground- and surface-surveys of a mine be connected? (*R. S. M.*, 1887.)

60. In a 20-fathom level driven on an east and west lode, underlying north, a winze has been commenced bearing due north, and it is determined to pitch a rise against it in the 40-fathom level; the 30-fathom level not having been driven far enough east for the purpose. How would you determine the exact point in the 40-fathom level to start from? (*R. S. M.*, 1886.)

61. Calculate trigonometrically the bearing and distance of C from the centre of the shaft in the following traverse:—

No.	Angle.	Bearing.	Distance.			Remarks.
			fms.	ft.	in.	
A	0° 00'	351° 29'	10	4	8	From centre of shaft.
B	90° 21'	...	9	3	2	
C	175° 12'	...	12	0	0	END.

—(*R. S. M.*, 1886.)

62. Lay down, on a scale of 1 chain to the inch, the survey given on page 36, representing a four-sided field connected with the shaft of a mine. Calculate the area. (*City Guilds*, 1885.)

63. Plot the following survey, by W. Rickard, of a Cornish mine:—
From pp. line in Williams' shaft at the 60-fathom level.

No.	Bearing.	Distance.			Inclination.	Inclined Length.			Remarks.
		fm.	ft.	in.		fm.	ft.	in.	
A	176° 00'	3	2	6	...	...			...
B	77° 30'	4	1	9	...	...			...
C	82° 45'	5	3	3	...	...			...
D	97° 15'	3	2	9	...	...			to Vivian's winze.
E²	4° 15'	...			F.75° 45'	10	5	6	...
F²	285° 00'	7	2	9	...	...			...
G²	263° 00'	6	3	3	...	...			to Williams' shaft.
H²	171° 00'	...			R.74° 11'	5	3	6	Up shaft to pp. line.
E	79° 15'	6	3	6	...	...			...
F	57° 00'	7	2	9	...	...			...
G	65° 30'	2	4	6	...	...			At × cut drive to regain the lode.
H	183° 00'	5	2	9	...	...			On lode.
J	94° 45'	6	4	6	...	...			to John's rise.
K²	182° 30'	...			R.67° 30'	11	3	0	Up rise to 50 fm. level.
L²	84° 15'	5	4	9	...	...			...
M²	75° 30'	6	2	8	...	...			to Mitchell's shaft.
K	79° 15'	8	5	4	...	...			END.

64. State the nature of the dislocations or *heaves* of lodes, their probable origin, their appearance vertically and on a horizontal plane; and the various rules that have been recommended for regaining the severed portion. (*R.S.M. Examination in Mining*, 1879.)

65. A, B, and C are three bore-holes; the depths of which from the same horizontal plane to a seam of coal are respectively 100, 106, and 108 yards.

From A to B is 100 yards, and from A to C 120 yards. The angle in a horizontal plane between AB and AC is 30°. What is the direction of the dip of the seam, and the angle of dip? (*Merivale's Notes and Formulæ*.)

66. Name the permanent adjustments of the transit theodolite, and state how they are made. (*Edinburgh University*, 1888.)

67. Explain fully the process of setting out a tunnel in the driving of which a number of shafts have to be employed. (*Edinburgh University*, 1888.)

68. Suppose you were required to take levels along an underground roadway in order to plot a section showing both roof and floor, state what instruments you would use and how you would proceed. (*Colliery Managers, West Lancashire*, 1887.)

69. State approximately the declination of the magnetic needle for the year 1888, and the average annual variation. How is the declination found to vary in amount as you travel northwards or eastwards? (*City Guilds*, 1888.)

70. Describe the Hedley dial. (*City Guilds*, 1888.)

71. Explain what is meant by the true meridian. How may the true meridian be determined by simple observations of some well-known stars? (*City Guilds*, 1888.)

72. Describe the method of measuring horizontal angles with the theodolite by the process of repetition, and point out the special advantages of this mode of using the instrument. (*City Guilds*, 1888.)

73. Explain the method of reducing and plotting a survey by rectangular co-ordinates. What are the advantages of this method as compared with the ordinary mode of plotting with the scale and protractor? (*City Guilds*, 1889.)

74. What is meant by the term "error of collimation" as applied to a transit-theodolite? How may this error be detected and rectified? Assuming that a considerable error of collimation is allowed to remain uncorrected, in what manner will it affect the measurement of an angle? Can the instrument be used in such a manner as to neutralise this error? (*City Guilds*, 1889.)

75. It is required to determine the position of a distant point, C, in the workings of a colliery, with reference to the surface. For this purpose a survey is made with the theodolite above and underground, from the shaft A to C, and also to a second shaft B, by which means the underground and surface-surveys are connected. Show how you would carry out the survey so as to obtain the most accurate result.

Give your idea as to the degree of accuracy attainable by this method; and how far it will depend upon the relative positions of the points A, B, and C, and the nature of the surveys between these points. (*City Guilds*, 1889.)

76. Describe the slide rule. (*City Guilds*, 1890.)

77. A line is measured on a uniform slope of 1 in 17. What allowance per chain must be made for the inclination?

78. What is meant by the declination of the needle, and what is the amount of it at Greenwich now, and what was it ten years ago? What precautions must be constantly taken to insure the accuracy of mining plans in consequence of the variation of declination? (*City Guilds*, 1893.)

79. In the case of a mine with only one shaft, which is vertical, and where there is iron, which cannot be removed, in every part, explain how to connect the underground with the surface survey. (*City Guilds*, 1893.)

80. The sides of a triangle are 1,200, 1,100, and 1,000 links in length respectively, what is its area in acres, roods, and perches? Suppose this area to be in a horizontal plane, and to be covered by a seam of coal lying at an inclination of 34° from the horizontal, the thickness of the coal being uniform and measuring, at right angles to the dip, 3 feet in thickness, what is the tonnage of coal in the seam over the above area? (*City Guilds*, 1894.)

81. What errors in direction are likely to arise in surveys made with the magnetic-needle, and how can such errors be controlled and corrected? (*S. and A. D.*, 1895.)

82. In what manner and on what principles can the measurement of the distances and the levels of a series of points in rugged country be expedited? Give examples with sketches of the application of the method. (*University College*, 1895.)

APPENDIX II.

BIBLIOGRAPHY.

The following is a list of the principal treatises published on mine-surveying:—

AGRICOLA, G.—" De re metallica libri duodecim," folio. Basel, 1556.
REINHOLD, E.—"Grundlicher und wahrer Bericht vom Feldmessen." Saalfeld, 1574.
HOUGHTON, T.—"Rara avis in terris, or the compleate miner," 12mo. London, 1681.
VOIGTEL, N.—"Geometria subterranea," folio. Eisleben, 1686. Also 1692, 1714.
WEIDLER, J. F.—"Institutiones geometriæ subterranæ," 8vo. Wittenberg, 1726.
JUGEL, J. G.—"Geometria subterranea," 4to. Berlin, 1744. 2nd Edition, Leipzig, 1773.
BEYER, A.—"Gründlicher Unterricht vom Bergbau nach Anleitung der Markscheidekunst," 4to. Altenburg, 1749. 2nd Edition, 4to. Edited by C. F. Lempe, 1785.
OPPEL, F. W. VON.—"Anleitung zur Markscheidekunst," 4to. Dresden, 1749.
DUHAMEL, J. P. F. G.—"Géométrie souterraine," 4to. Paris, 1787.
FENWICK, T.—" A Theoretical and Practical Treatise on Subterraneous Surveying," 8vo. Newcastle-upon-Tyne, 1804. A reprint of this work is published with additions by T. Baker.
HECHT, D. F.—" Lehrbuch der Markscheidekunst," 8vo. Freyberg, 1829.
BUDGE, J.—"The Practical Miner's Guide," 8vo. London, 1825. 2nd Edition, 1845.
HANSTADT, J. N. L. VON.—"Anleitung zur Markscheidekunst," 4to. Pest, 1835.
WEISBACH, J.—"Die neue Markscheidekunst," 2 vols., 4to. Brunswick, 1851-59.
ADRIANY, J.—"Leitfaden seiner Vorträge über Markscheidekunde," 8vo. Vienna, 1852. 2nd Edition, 1861.
BEER, A. H.—" Lehrbuch der Markscheidekunst," 8vo. Prague, 1856.
HOSKOLD, H. D.—" A Practical Treatise on Mining, Land, and Railway Surveying," 8vo. London, 1863.
SARRAN, M. E.—" Manuel du géomètre souterrain," 2 vols., 8vo. Paris, 1868.
MILLER-HAUENFELS, A. VON.—" Höhere Markscheidekunst," 8vo. Vienna, 1868.
BORCHERS, E.—" Die praktische Markscheidekunst," 8vo. Hanover, 1870.
LINTERN, W.—"The Mineral Surveyor and Valuer's Complete Guide," 12mo. London 1872.
LIEBENAM, A.—" Lehrbuch der Markscheidekunst," 8vo. Leipzig, 1876.
BRATHUHN, O.—" Lehrbuch der praktischen Markscheidekunst," 8vo. Leipzig, 1884. 2nd edition, 1894.
VILLET, F.—"Traité pratique du lever des plans souterrains," 8vo. St. Etienne, 1885.
SCHMIDT, M.—" Zwölf Musterblätter für Grubenrisszeichnen." Freiberg, 1887.

328   APPENDIX II.

The following works contain chapters on Mine-Surveying:—

PRYCE, W.—"Mineralogia cornubiensis," folio. London, 1778 (pp. 202-213).
HAUSMANN, J. F. L.—" Reise durch Scandinavien," 5 vols., 8vo. Göttingen, 1811-18. [An account is given of the methods of surveying mines in Sweden, vol. v., pp. 115-126.]
VILLEFOSSE, A. M. HÉRON DE LA.—" De la richesse minérale," 3 vols., 4to, with folio atlas. Paris, 1819.
SOPWITH, T.—" A Treatise on Isometric Drawing," 8vo. London, 1834.
WILLIAMS, B.—" Practical Geodesy," 8vo. London, 1842.
COMBES, C.—"Traité de l'exploitation des mines," 3 vols., 8vo, with 4to, atlas. Paris, 1844.
DEGOUSÉE, J.—" Guide du sondeur," 2 vols., 8vo. Paris, 1847.
PONSON, A. T.—"Traité de l'exploitation des mines de houille," 4 vols., 8vo, with folio atlas. Liége, 1852. 2nd edition, 1870.
BAUERNFEIND, C. M.—" Elemente der Vermessungskunde," 2 vols., 8vo. Munich, 1856. 7th edition, 1890.
RICKARD, W.—" The Miner's Manual of Arithmetic and Surveying, containing the usual Calculations Employed by the Miner," 8vo. Truro, 1859.
GILLESPIE, W. M.—" A Treatise on Levelling, Topography, and higher Surveying," 8vo. New York, 1871.
ANDRÉ, G. G.—" The Draughtsman's Handbook of Plan and Map Drawing," 4to. London, 1874.
HYSLOP, J.—" Colliery Management," 2nd edition, 2 vols., 8vo. London, 1876.
DAVIES, C.—" Elements of Surveying and Levelling." Revised by J. H. van Amringe, 8vo. New York, 1883. The chapter on Mine-Surveying was revised by J. G. Murphy.
HABETS, A.—"Cours de topographie," 8vo. Liége, 1883.
HUNT, R.—" British Mining, a Treatise on the Metalliferous Mines of the United Kingdom," 8vo. London, 1884.
CHANCE, H. M.—"Report on Coal Mining. Pennsylvania Second Geological Survey," 8vo. Philadelphia, 1885.
JOHNSON, J. B.—" The Theory and Practice of Surveying," 8vo. New York, 1886. The chapter on Mine-Surveying was written by C. A. Russell.
WARDLE, W.—" Reference Book on Practical Coal Mining," 8vo. London, 1887.
STANLEY, W. F.—" Surveying and Levelling Instruments," 8vo. London, 1890.
PELLETAN, A.—" Traité de Topographie," 8vo. Paris, 1893.
LASKA, W.—" Lehrbuch der Vermessungskunde," 8vo. Stuttgart, 1894.

INDEX.

ABNEY'S level, 183.
Accuracy obtainable in spirit-levelling, 183.
  ,, of linear measurements, 24.
Adit level, 6.
Adjustments of the level, 166.
  ,, of the theodolite, 98.
Agricola, G., 3, 26.
Aita, L., 186.
American mining claims, 127.
  ,, transit, 95.
Amsler's planimeter, 159.
Anallatism, 220.
Aneroid barometer, 192.
Angular measures, 8.
Apex, 5.
Arrows, 12.
Artificial horizon, 213.
Ashburner, C. A., 276, 286.
Azimuth, 59.

BACK-OBSERVATIONS, 31.
Balancing, 147.
Ball and socket joint, 31.
Barometer, aneroid, 192.
  ,, mountain, 191.
Base-line, 120.
Base of verification, 120.
Basset, 5.
Bauerman, H., 288.
Beanlands, A., 208.
Bearing of a line, 31.
Bed, 5.
Bench-marks, 180.
Bibliography, 327.
Boning staves, 164.
Borchers, E., 303.
  ,, measuring rods, 194.
  ,, portable magnetometer, 216.
  ,, vane rod, 171.
Bord, 70.
Bore-holes, strike and dip of a seam found from, 248.
  ,, surveying, 300.

Bowie, A. J., 200.
Boys, C. V., 149.
Bramwell, Sir F., 159.
Brathuhn, O., 110.
Brooks, T. B., 293.
Brough, B. H., 229, 289.
Bunning, C. Z., 187, 302.
Burt's solar compass, 103.

CALCULATING machines, 149.
  ,, scales, 149.
Calculation of areas, 154.
Callon, J., 268.
Candle-holder, 238.
Cape rood, 132.
Casella's theodolite, 97.
Chain, 11.
  ,, only, surveying with the, 18.
  ,, in trigonomet. surveys, 20.
Chaining on slopes, 13.
Chains converted into feet, 12.
Chords, plotting by, 142.
Chorobates, 185.
Chree, C., 51.
Chrismàr's, O., 111, 194.
Chrismàr's theodolite stand, 108.
Circumferenter, 59.
Claim, 7.
Claims, survey of, 127.
Clark, E., 207.
Clinograph, 300.
Clinometer for bore-holes, 300.
  ,, for exploratory work, 190.
  ,, German, 79.
  ,, G. P. Evelyn's, 237.
Clinostats, 300.
Coal mines regulation act (1887), 273, 278.
Coal-seams, produce of, 160.
Colby's compensating bars, 21.
Colliery surveys with the dial, 37.
  ,, with the rack-dial, 67.
  ,, with the theodolite, 112.
Collimation, 99.

INDEX.

Collimation method of levelling, 179.
Colouring plans, 281.
Combes, C., 52.
Compensating bars, 21.
Computing the sides of triangles, 123.
Concession, 7.
Conder, Major, 243.
Connection of underground- and surface-surveys, 201.
Contour lines, 196, 257.
Conventional signs for mine plans, 277.
Co-ordinates, plotting by, 142, 151.
Copying plans, 282.
Correction for chaining on slopes, 14.
Corresponding altitudes, 45.
Country, 5.
Course, 5.
Coxe, E. B., 22, 114.
Craven, A., 241.
Cross-course, 5.
Cross-cut, 6.
Cross-sections, 235.
Cross-staff, 15.
Croton aqueduct, 241.
Curvature of the earth's surface, 172.
Curves for engine planes, 237.
Curves, ranging, by means of angles at the circumference, 233.
" by means of offsets, 231.
Cushing's reversible level, 167.

DATUM line, 175.
Davis's dial, 63.
Dawson, W. B., 228.
Declination of the magnetic needle, 40.
Depth of shafts, 193.
Diagonal eye piece, 211.
" scales, 137.
Dial joint, 64.
Dialling book, 35.
" " for surveying in presence of iron, 54.
" definition of, 1.
Dickinson, J., 5.
Diopter, 2.
Dip, 5, 246.
Direction of mineral deposits, 246.
Direct vernier, 60.
Dislocated lodes, 261.
Distance-measuring by telescope, 217.
Distances, measurement of, 11.
Diurnal variation of the magnetic needle, 42.

Divining rod, 3.
Dixon, J. S., 265.
Down-throw, 263.
Drawing-plans, 279.
Drift, 7.
Driving levels underground, 235.
Dump heap, cubical content of, 258.
Dumpy level, 165.
Dyke, 263.

EARTH's magnetism, directive action of the, 26.
Eccentric telescope for transit-theodolite, 212.
Eccentricity of magnetic needle, 30.
Eckhold's omnimeter, 217.
Eidograph, 284.
Electric light for surveying purposes, 111.
End, 6.
Enlarging plans, 283.
Equalising, 155.
Errors in compass surveys, 57.
" spirit-levelling, 183.
Evelyn's clinometer, 237.
Everest theodolite, 92.
Examination questions, 315.
Exploring for iron ore, 289.

FACE, 71.
Fairley's gradometer, 246.
Fast-needle surveying, 59.
Faults, 263.
Feet converted into links, 12.
Field-book for chain surveys, 20.
Field-compasses, 22.
Fixed-needle surveying, 59.
Floor, 5.
Flying levels, 174.
Follower in chaining, 13.
Foot-wall, 5.
Forebreast, 6.
Fore-observations, 31.
Foster, C. Le Neve, 5, 268, 277.

GAERTNER, E. G., 148.
Galloway, T. L., 187.
Galloway, W., 268.
Gangue, 5.
Gate roads, 7.
German dial, 78.
Gilbert, G. K., 192.
Giving and taking, 155.
Gnomon, 45.
Gradienter screw, 217.

Gradometer, 246.
Graefe, M., 195
Gravatt's level, 165.
,, staff, 168.
Gurden, R. L., 150.
Gurley's solar attachment, 104.
Guthrie, J. K., 302.

HADE, 5.
Hanging compass, 78.
,, wall, 5.
Harden, J. H., 94.
,, O. B., 288.
Hausse, R., 267
Heading, 7.
Headway, 71.
Hedley's dial, 34.
Henderson, J., 35, 51.
,, dial, 62.
,, rapid traverser, 149.
Henwood, W. S., 261.
Hero of Alexandria, 2.
Hildebrand's compass, 215.
History of the miner's dial, 26.
,, mining-theodolite, 87.
,, surveying, 1.
Hitch, 71, 263.
Hoffman joint, 64.
,, tripod head, 93.
Holing from one excavation to another, 252.
Holing use of magnet in, 303.
Hoosac tunnel, 242.
Horizontal circle of theodolite, 88.
Hoskold, H. D., 203, 211.
Hoskold's transit-theodolite, 91.
Houghton, T., 27, 186.
Howard, W. F., 76, 109, 197.
Huebner, H., 109.
Hughes, H. W., 180, 161.
Hunt, R., 2.
Hydraulic mining ditches, 199.
Hypsometer, 193.

ILL-CONDITIONED triangles, 120.
Illumination of cross-wires of theodolite, 111.
Inclination of colliery roads, 236.
,, magnetic-needle, 50.
Inclined shafts, surveying in, 75.
Index-error, 100.
Interior angles of a traverse, 112.
Intermediate sights, 176.
Intersection of two veins, 258.
Iron ore, exploring for, 289.

Iron rails, influence of, 52.
,, surveying in the presence of, 54.
Irregular deposits, 5.
,, variations of the magnetic-needle, 44.
Irregularities of seams and beds, 263.
Isogonic lines, 42.
Isometric plans of mines, 284.

JACKSON, L. D., 235.
Jee's levelling-staff, 169.
Johnson, F. R., 200.
,, G. R., 85.
,, J. B., 228, 229.
Jordan, T. B., 287.
,, W., 23.
Junge, A., 53.
Jurisch, C. L. H. M., 151.

KOEHLER, G., 265.

LATCHING, definition of, 1.
Leader in chaining, 13.
Lean's dial, 61.
Least reading of a vernier, 60.
Lechner, R., 308.
Lee, J. B., 308.
Lehigh Valley Coal Co., 196.
Lehman, A. E., 288.
Lettering of the miner's dial, 33.
,, on plans, 281.
Levelling, 164; -book, 175, 177, 178, 179, 181, 182; -staff, 167.
Levels of a mine, 6.
Limb of theodolite, 89.
Lighting verniers, 110.
Linear measurements, accuracy of, 24.
,, rolling planimeter, 160.
Local attraction in the mine, 53.
Lodes, 5.
Long compass-box, 214.
Long-wall, 7.
Lorber, F., 24, 160.
Lyman, B. S., 229.

MACGEORGE, E. F., 300.
Magnet used in cases of uncertain holing, 303.
Magnetic meridian, 40.
,, -needle, declination of, 41.
,, ,, for exploring for iron ore, 289.
,, ,, shape of, 29.
Magnetometer, 216.
Map, determination of meridian by, 49.

Marquard, L., 151.
Marquois scales, 185.
Mason's level, 164.
Masses, 6.
Measures of area, 154.
,, length, 7.
Measuring-tape, 15.
,, -wheel, 23.
Meridian line, setting-out, 49.
Merivale, J. H., 161.
Miller-Hauenfels, A. von, 80.
Mine models, 286.
Mineral deposits, 5.
Miner's dial, 28.
Models of mines, 286
Moinot's tacheometer, 221.
Morgen, 132.
Moulton, M., 287.
Murphy, J. G., 161.

NATURAL scale, 135.
Newall, R. S., 216.
Newton's tripod, 31.
New York target rod, 168.
Nolten, G., 302.
Norris, R., 116.

OBLIQUE offsets, 16.
Obstacles in chaining, 16.
Offset rod, 15.
Offsets, 15.
Oldest mine plan, 1.
Omnimeter, 217.
Optical square, 15.
Ordnance bench mark, 180.
,, survey, 122.
Ore-reserves, calculation of, 161.
Orientation, line of, 50.
Osterland's hanging compass, 81.
Outcrop, 5.

PACING, 23.
Pantograph, 284.
Parallax, 98.
Passometer, 23.
Pedometer, 23.
Penkert's hanging compass, 85.
Physical levelling, 191.
Photogrammetry, 307.
Photography, 282, 307.
Pierce, J., 126.
Plane-table, 126.
Plane theodolite, 89.
Planimeters, 158.
Plans of colleries, 273, 275.

Plans of metalliferous mines, 270.
Plate of theodolite, 89.
Plotting-scales, 139.
,, sections, 184.
,, surveys, 134.
,, ,, with the German dial, 83.
,, the underground traverse on the surface, 231.
Plumb-bob, 107, 196, 236.
Plummet lamp, 109.
Point at surface directly above one underground, 250.
Pole star, determination of meridian by, 48.
Porro's lens, 220.
,, tacheometer, 221.
Post and stall, 7.
Preservation of plans, 278.
Prismatic compass, 111, 126.
Prolongation of base-line, 121.
Protractor, 140, 222.
Pryce, W., 28.
Przyborski, 111.

QUICK levelling tripod, 95.

RACK dial, 59.
Racking, 60.
Railways to mines, setting-out, 231.
Ramsay, J. A., 180.
Ranges, 132.
Ranging rods, 230.
,, straight lines, 230.
Rankine, W. J. M., 235.
Rapid traverser, 149.
Raymond, R. W., 97, 265.
Record of colliery survey, 39.
,, ,, with fixed needle, 68.
,, surface-survey with the dial, 37.
Reducing plans, 283.
Reflecting level, 183.
Relief plans, 286.
Repetition, 101.
Reservoir, cubical content of, 257.
Retrograde vernier, 60.
Rhodius, A., 259.
Ridding, 71.
Rise, 6.
Rods, 21.
Roessler's hanging compass, 81.
Rolley ways, 7.
Roof, 5.
Royalty, 7.
Rücker, A. W., 51.

Sayce, Prof., 242.
Scales, 134.
„ for mine plans, 277.
Schmidt, M., 170, 204.
Schmidt's rule, 261.
Scotland, plotting surveys in, 150.
Seam, 5.
Section corner, 132.
Secular variations of the magnetic needle, 41.
Seibt, W., 183.
Sett, 7.
Setting-out, 230.
Severn tunnel, 210.
Shadow-method of determining the true meridian, 44.
Shaft, 6.
„ surveying, 75.
Shafts, depth of, 193.
„ sunk from several levels, 256.
Siloam inscription, 242.
Simply divided scales, 134.
Simms, F. W., 238.
Slide-rule, 149, 222.
Slope, ratio of, 235.
Slopes, chaining on, 13.
Smock, J. G., 299.
Smyth, Sir W. W., 4.
Solar attachment, 103.
Sopwith, T., 285, 287.
Sopwith's staff, 168.
South Africa, surveying in, 132, 151.
Southern hemisphere stars, 49.
Spherical excess, 121.
Spirit-level, 165.
Spirit-levels of the miner's dial, 30.
Split-sight, 62.
Stadia, 218.
„ and theodolite, 226.
Stampfer's distance-measurer, 217.
Stanley, H. M., 310.
„ W. F., 111, 169, 223, 284.
Station-lines, 19; measuring, 78.
Stations, 19.
Steel band, 22.
Stenton, 71.
Stepping, 15.
Stockwork, 6.
Stokes, A. H., 273.
Stope, 6.
Stoup and room, 7.
Strike, 5.
Stuart-Menteath, P. W., 5.
Subsidence and draw, 265.
Sump, 6.

Surface-plans of mines, 274.
Surface-surveys with the dial, 35.
„ „ theodolite, 120.
Surveying, definition of, 1.
„ with the chain only, 18.
Suspended planimeter, 160.

Tabular deposits, 5.
Tacheometer, 223.
Telemeter, 226.
Telescope, 90.
Telescopic measurement of distances, 217.
Telescopic measurements underground, 228.
Thalén, R., 294.
Theodolite and compass compared, 118.
„ levelling with, 187.
„ surveys in Pennsylvania, 114.
Thill, 71.
Thornton's dial, 66.
„ staff, 169.
Thwaite, B. H., 283.
Tiberg, E., 297.
Tie-line, 19.
Topographical stadia, 225.
Township corner, 132.
Tracing, 282.
Transit-instrument, 208.
„ theodolite, 89; for connecting surveys, 210.
Transvaal, surveys in, 133.
Trautwine, J. C., 235.
Traverse, 67.
„ tables, 149.
Traversing underground, 67, 107.
Trianglation, 120.
Trigonometer, 148.
Trigonometrical formulæ, 9.
„ levelling, 187.
Tripod of the miner's dial, 31.
Trouble, 263.
Troughton's level, 166.
True meridian, 40.
„ determination of, 44.
Tubular compass, 214.
Tunnel, 6.
„ driven through a hill, 255.
Tunnels, setting-out, 237.

Underlie, 5.
Units of length, 7.
Up-throw, 263.

INDEX TO AUTHORS.

	PAGE
ALLINGHAM (W.), Navigation and Meteorology,	19
ANGLIN (S.), Design of Structures,	4
BARKER (D. WILSON-), Navigation and Seamanship,	19
BERINGER (J. J. & C.), Assaying,	6
BLACKMORE (E.), British Mercantile Marine,	19
BLOUNT (B.) and BLOXAM (A. G.), Chemistry for Engineers and Manufacturers,	5
BLYTH (A. Wynter), Foods and Poisons,	7
BROTHERS (A.), Photography,	6
BROUGH (B. H.), Mine-Surveying,	8
BROWNE (W. R.), Student's Mechanics,	8
—— Fuel and Water,	41
BUCK (R. C.), Algebra,	19
BUTTERFIELD (W. J. A.), Gas Manufacture,	9
COLE (Prof.), Practical Geology,	10
—— Open Air Studies,	10
CRIMP (W. S.), Sewage Disposal Works,	11
DAVIES (Surgeon-Major), Hygiene,	12
DAVIS (Prof.), Biology,	13
—— The Flowering Plant,	13
—— Zoological Pocket-Book,	13
DONKIN (Bryan), Gas, Oil, and Air Engines,	14
DUERR (Geo.), Bleaching and Calico-Printing,	12
DUPRÉ & HAKE (Manual of Chemistry),	14
ETHERIDGE (R.), Stratigraphical Geology,	30
EWART (Prof.), Preservation of Fish,	14
FIDLER (Prof.), Bridge-Construction,	15
FOSTER (Prof. C. le Neve), Ore and Stone Mining,	16
GIBB (Thos.), Copper,	38
GRIFFIN (J. J.), Chemical Recreations,	17
GRIFFIN'S Electrical Price-Book,	17
GRIFFIN'S ENGINEERING PUBLICATIONS,	18
GRIFFIN'S GEOLOGICAL and METALLURGICAL SERIES,	20
GRIFFIN'S NAUTICAL SERIES,	19
GRIFFIN'S SANITARY PUBLICATIONS,	20
GRIFFIN'S TECHNOLOGICAL PUBLICATIONS,	21
GURDEN (R.), Traverse Tables,	17
GUTTMANN (O.), Blasting,	21
HARBORD (F. W.), Steel,	38
HUGHES-GIBB (E.), How Plants Live,	15
HUGHES (H. W.), Coal Mining,	22
HURST (G. H.), Colours and Varnishes,	23
—— Garment Dyeing and Cleaning	23
JAMIESON (Prof.), MANUALS, Advanced and Elementary,	24
—— Steam Engine,	24
—— Applied Mechanics,	24
—— Magnetism and Electricity,	24
JENKINS (H. C.), Metallurgical Machinery,	38
JOHNSON (J. C. F.), Getting Gold,	26
KNECHT & RAWSON, Dyeing,	25
LAWN (J. G.), Mine Accounts,	26
MACKENZIE (T.), Applied Mechanics,	19, 28
M'MILLAN (W. G.), Electro-Metallurgy,	27
—— Electric Smelting,	27
MILLAR (W. J.), Latitude and Longitude,	19, 28
MUNRO & JAMIESON'S Electrical Pocket-Book,	29
MUNRO (Dr.), Agricultural Chemistry,	29
MUNRO (R. D.), Steam-Boilers,	28
—— Kitchen Boiler Explosions,	28
NYSTROM'S Pocket-Book for Engineers,	29
PHILLIPS & BAUERMAN, Metallurgy,	31
POYNTING (Prof.), Mean Density of the Earth,	31
RANKINE'S Applied Mechanics,	32
—— Civil Engineering,	32
—— Machinery and Millwork,	32
—— Steam Engine & other Prime Movers,	32
—— Useful Rules and Tables,	32
—— A Mechanical Text-Book,	32
—— Miscellaneous Scientific Papers,	33
REDGRAVE (G. R.), Cements,	33
REDWOOD (Boverton), Petroleum,	34
REED (Sir E. J.), Stability of Ships,	35
REID (Geo., M.D.), Practical Sanitation,	36
RICHMOND (H. D.), Dairy Chemistry,	35
RIDDELL (Dr. Scott), Ambulance,	37
RIDEAL (S., D.Sc.), Disinfection,	36
ROBERTS-AUSTEN (Prof.), Metallurgy and Alloys,	38
ROBINSON (Prof.), Hydraulics,	39
ROSE (T. K.), Gold, Metallurgy of,	40
ROTHWELL, (C. F. Seymour), Textile Printing,	41
SEATON (A. E.), Marine Engineering,	42
SEATON & ROUNTHWAITE, Marine Engineers' Pocket-Book,	42
SEELEY (Prof.), Physical Geology,	30
SEXTON (Prof.), Elementary Metallurgy,	43
—— Quantitative & Qualitative Analysis,	43
SHELTON (W. V.), Mechanic's Guide,	41
SMITH, (Johnson), Shipmaster's Medical Help,	19, 37
SMITH (Prof. R. H.), Measurement Conversions,	44
—— Calculus for Engineers,	44
THOMSON & POYNTING (Profs.) Text-Book of Physics,	45
TRAILL (T. W.), Boilers, Land and Marine,	45
TURNER (Thos.), Iron,	46
WALTON (T.), Know Your Own Ship,	19, 47
WATKINSON (Prof. W. H.), Gas and Oil Engines,	47
WELLS (S. H.), Engineering Drawing,	49
WRIGHT (Dr. Alder), The Threshold of Science,	48
—— Oils and Fats, Soaps and Candles,	48
YEAMAN (C. H.), Elec. Measurements,	49
YEAR-BOOK of Scientific Societies,	50

INDEX TO SUBJECTS.

	PAGE
AGRICULTURAL CHEMISTRY,	29
AIR ENGINES,	14
ALGEBRA,	19
ALLOYS,	38
AMBULANCE,	87
ASSAYING,	6
BIOLOGY,	13
BLASTING,	21
BLEACHING,	12
BOTANY,	13, 15
BRIDGE-CONSTRUCTION,	15
BOILERS, Construction,	45
—— Kitchen, Explosions of,	28
—— Management,	28
CALCULUS FOR ENGINEERS,	44
CALICO-PRINTING,	12, 41
CEMENTS,	33
CHEMICAL ANALYSIS, Qualitative and Quantitative,	43
CHEMICAL RECREATIONS,	17, 48
CHEMISTRY FOR ENGINEERS,	5
—— for Manufacturers,	5
—— Inorganic,	14
COAL-MINING,	22
COLOURS,	23
COPPER, Metallurgy of,	38
DAIRY CHEMISTRY,	35
DENSITY OF THE EARTH,	31
DESIGN (Engineering),	49
—— of Structures,	4
DISINFECTION and DISINFECTANTS,	36
DRAWING (Engineering),	49
DYEING,	23, 25
ELECTRIC SMELTING,	27
ELECTRICAL MEASUREMENTS,	49
—— Pocket-Book,	29
—— Price-Book,	17
ELECTRICITY and MAGNETISM,	24
ELECTRO-METALLURGY,	27
ENGINEERS, Pocket-books for,	29, 42
—— Useful Rules for,	18, 32
ENGINEERING, Civil,	32
—— Marine,	42
—— Drawing and Design,	49
FISH, Preservation of,	14
FOODS, Analysis of,	7
FUEL and WATER,	41
GAS ENGINES,	14, 47
GAS MANUFACTURE,	9
GEOLOGY, Introduction to,	10
—— Physical,	30
—— Practical,	10
—— Stratigraphical,	30
GOLD, Getting,	26
—— Metallurgy of,	40
HYDRAULICS,	39
HYGIENE,	11, 12, 36

	PAGE
IRON, Metallurgy of,	46
KITCHEN BOILER EXPLOSIONS,	28
LATITUDE and LONGITUDE, To Find,	19, 28
MACHINE DESIGN,	49
MACHINERY and MILLWORK,	32, 38
MAGNETISM,	24
MARINE BOILERS,	45
—— Engineering,	42
MECHANICS, Applied—	
—— Elementary,	19, 24, 28
—— Student's,	8
—— Advanced,	24, 32
MEASUREMENTS, Conversion of, from French to English, and vice versâ,	44
—— Electrical,	49
MEDICINE and SURGERY, Domestic,	51
—— for Shipmasters,	87
MERCANTILE MARINE, British,	19
METALLURGY, Elementary,	43
—— Introduction to,	38
—— Advanced,	31
—— of Gold,	40
—— of Iron,	46
MINING—	
—— Blasting,	21
—— Book-keeping,	26
—— Coal,	22
—— Ore and Stone,	16
—— Surveying,	8
NAVIGATION,	19
OILS and FATS,	48
OIL ENGINES,	14, 47
ORE MINING,	16
PETROLEUM,	84
PHOTOGRAPHY,	6
PHYSICS,	24, 45, 48
POISONS, Detection of,	7
SANITATION,	11, 12, 36
SCIENCE, Popular Introduction to,	48
SEAMANSHIP,	19
SEWAGE, Disposal of,	11
SHIPS, Loading, &c., of,	47
—— Stability of,	35, 47
SHIPMASTER'S MEDICAL GUIDE,	37
SOAPS, Manufacture of,	48
SOCIETIES, Year-book of,	50
STEAM ENGINE, Elementary,	24
—— Advanced,	24, 42
STEEL, Metallurgy of,	38
—— VESSELS,	19
SURVEYING, Mine,	8
TRAVERSE TABLES,	17
TEXTILE PRINTING,	12, 41
VARNISHES,	23
ZOOLOGY,	13

THE DESIGN OF STRUCTURES:

Practical Treatise on the Building of Bridges, Roofs, &c.

By S. ANGLIN, C.E.,

Master of Engineering, Royal University of Ireland, late Whitworth Scholar, &c.

With very numerous Diagrams, Examples, and Tables.
Large Crown 8vo. Cloth.

SECOND EDITION, *Revised*. 16s.

The leading features in Mr. Anglin's carefully-planned "Design of Structures" may be briefly summarised as follows:—

1. It supplies the want, long felt among Students of Engineering and Architecture, of a concise Text-book on Structures, requiring on the part of the reader a knowledge of ELEMENTARY MATHEMATICS only.

2. The subject of GRAPHIC STATICS has only of recent years been generally applied in this country to determine the Stresses on Framed Structures; and in too many cases this is done without a knowledge of the principles upon which the science is founded. In Mr. Anglin's work the system is explained from FIRST PRINCIPLES, and the Student will find in it a valuable aid in determining the stresses on all irregularly-framed structures.

3. A large number of PRACTICAL EXAMPLES, such as occur in the every-day experience of the Engineer, are given and carefully worked out, some being solved both analytically and graphically, as a guide to the Student.

4. The chapters devoted to the practical side of the subject, the Strength of Joints, Punching, Drilling, Rivetting, and other processes connected with the manufacture of Bridges, Roofs, and Structural work generally, are the result of MANY YEARS' EXPERIENCE in the bridge-yard; and the information given on this branch of the subject will be found of great value to the practical bridge-builder.

"Students of Engineering will find this Text-Book INVALUABLE."—*Architect*.

"The author has certainly succeeded in producing a THOROUGHLY PRACTICAL Text-Book."—*Builder*.

"We can unhesitatingly recommend this work not only to the Student, as the BEST TEXT-BOOK on the subject, but also to the professional engineer as an EXCEEDINGLY VALUABLE book of reference."—*Mechanical World*.

"This work can be CONFIDENTLY recommended to engineers. The author has wisely chosen to use as little of the higher mathematics as possible, and has thus made his book of REAL USE TO THE PRACTICAL ENGINEER. . . . After careful perusal, we have nothing but praise for the work."—*Nature*.

LONDON: EXETER STREET, STRAND.

CHEMISTRY FOR ENGINEERS AND MANUFACTURERS.

A PRACTICAL TEXT-BOOK.

BY

BERTRAM BLOUNT, AND **A. G. BLOXAM,**
F.I.C., F.C.S.,   F.I.C., F.C.S.,
Consulting Chemist to the Crown Agents for the Colonies.   Consulting Chemist, Head of the Chemistry Department, Goldsmiths' Inst., New Cross.

With Numerous Illustrations. In Two Volumes, Large 8vo.
Sold Separately.

VOLUME I. Price 10s. 6d.
CHEMISTRY OF ENGINEERING, BUILDING, AND METALLURGY.

GENERAL CONTENTS.

I. INTRODUCTION.
  1. Chemistry of the Chief Materials of Construction.
  2. Sources of Energy.
  3. Chemistry of Steam-raising.
  4. Chemistry of Lubrication and Lubricants.
II. METALLURGICAL PROCESSES used in the Winning and Manufacture of Metals.

"PRACTICAL THROUGHOUT . . . an ADMIRABLE TEXT-BOOK, useful not only to Students, but to ENGINEERS and MANAGERS OF WORKS in PREVENTING WASTE and IMPROVING PROCESSES."—*Scotsman.*
"EMINENTLY PRACTICAL."—*Glasgow Herald.*
"A book worthy of HIGH RANK . . . its merit is great . . . treatment of the subject of GASEOUS FUEL particularly good. . . . WATER GAS and its production clearly worked out. . . . Altogether a most creditable production. We WARMLY RECOMMEND IT, and look forward with keen interest to the appearance of Vol. II."—*Journal of Gas Lighting.*

VOLUME II. Price 16s.
THE CHEMISTRY OF MANUFACTURING PROCESSES.

GENERAL CONTENTS.

I. Sulphuric Acid Manufacture.
II. Manufacture of Alkali, &c.
III. Destructive Distillation.
IV. Artificial Manure Manufacture.
V. Petroleum.
VI. Lime and Cement.
VII. Clay Industries and Glass.
VIII. Sugar and Starch.
IX. Brewing and Distilling.
X. Oils, Resins, and Varnishes.
XI. Soap and Candles.
XII. Textiles and Bleaching.
XIII. Colouring Matters, Dyeing, and Printing.
XIV. Paper and Pasteboard.
XV. Pigments and Paints.
XVI. Leather, Glue, and Size.
XVII. Explosives and Matches.
XVIII. Minor Chemical Manufactures.

LONDON: EXETER STREET, STRAND.

ASSAYING (A Text-Book of):
For the use of Students, Mine Managers, Assayers, &c.

By C. BERINGER, F.C.S.,
Late Chief Assayer to the Rio Tinto Copper Company, London,
And J. J. BERINGER, F.I.C., F.C.S.,
Public Analyst for, and Lecturer to the Mining Association of, Cornwall.

With numerous Tables and Illustrations. Crown 8vo. Cloth, 10/6.
THIRD EDITION; Revised.

GENERAL CONTENTS. — PART I. — INTRODUCTORY; MANIPULATION: Sampling; Drying; Calculation of Results—Laboratory-books and Reports. METHODS: Dry Gravimetric; Wet Gravimetric—Volumetric Assays: Titrometric, Colorimetric, Gasometric—Weighing and Measuring—Reagents—Formulæ, Equations, &c.—Specific Gravity. PART II.—METALS: Detection and Assay of Silver, Gold, Platinum, Mercury, Copper, Lead, Thallium, Bismuth, Antimony, Iron, Nickel, Cobalt, Zinc, Cadmium, Tin, Tungsten, Titanium, Manganese, Chromium, &c.—Earths, Alkalies. PART III.—NON-METALS: Oxygen and Oxides; The Halogens—Sulphur and Sulphates—Arsenic, Phosphorus, Nitrogen—Silicon, Carbon, Boron—Useful Tables.

"A REALLY MERITORIOUS WORK, that may be safely depended upon either for systematic instruction or for reference."—*Nature.*
"This work is one of the BEST of its kind. . . . Essentially of a practical character. . . . Contains all the information that the Assayer will find necessary in the examination of minerals."—*Engineer.*

PHOTOGRAPHY:
ITS HISTORY, PROCESSES, APPARATUS, AND MATERIALS.
Comprising Working Details of all the More Important Methods.

By A. BROTHERS, F.R.A.S.

WITH TWENTY-FOUR FULL PAGE PLATES BY MANY OF THE PROCESSES DESCRIBED, AND ILLUSTRATIONS IN THE TEXT.

In 8vo, Handsome Cloth. Price 18s.

GENERAL CONTENTS. — PART. I. INTRODUCTORY — Historical Sketch; Chemistry and Optics of Photography; Artificial Light.—PART II. Photographic Processes.—PART III. Apparatus.—PART IV. Materials.—PART V.—Applications of Photography; Practical Hints.

"Mr. Brothers has had an experience in Photography so large and varied that any work by him cannot fail to be interesting and valuable. . . . A MOST COMPREHENSIVE volume, entering with full details into the various processes, and VERY FULLY illustrated. The PRACTICAL HINTS are of GREAT VALUE. . . . Admirably got up."—*Brit. Jour. of Photography.*
"For the Illustrations alone, the book is most interesting; but, apart from these, the volume is valuable, brightly and pleasantly written, and MOST ADMIRABLY ARRANGED."—*Photographic News.*
"Certainly the FINEST ILLUSTRATED HANDBOOK to Photography which has ever been published. Should be on the reference shelves of every Photographic Society."—*Amateur Photographer.*
"A handbook so far in advance of most others, that the Photographer must not fail to obtain a copy as a reference work."—*Photographic Work.*
"The COMPLETEST HANDBOOK of the art which has yet been published."—*Scotsman.*

LONDON: EXETER STREET, STRAND.

SCIENTIFIC AND TECHNOLOGICAL WORKS.

WORKS BY A. WYNTER BLYTH, M.R.C.S., F.C.S.,
Barrister-at-Law, Public Analyst for the County of Devon, and Medical Officer of Health for St. Marylebone.

FOODS:
THEIR COMPOSITION AND ANALYSIS.

In Demy 8vo, with Elaborate Tables, Diagrams, and Plates. Handsome Cloth. FOURTH EDITION. Price 21s.

GENERAL CONTENTS.

History of Adulteration—Legislation, Past and Present—Apparatus useful to the Food-Analyst—"Ash"—Sugar—Confectionery—Honey—Treacle—Jams and Preserved Fruits—Starches—Wheaten-Flour—Bread—Oats—Barley—Rye—Rice—Maize—Millet—Potato—Peas—Chinese Peas—Lentils—Beans—MILK—Cream—Butter—Oleo-Margarine—Butterine—Cheese—Lard—Tea—Coffee—Cocoa and Chocolate—Alcohol—Brandy—Rum—Whisky—Gin—Arrack—Liqueurs—Absinthe—Principles of Fermentation—Yeast—Beer—Wine—Vinegar—Lemon and Lime Juice—Mustard—Pepper—Sweet and Bitter Almond—Annatto—Olive Oil—WATER—Standard Solutions and Reagents. *Appendix:* Text of English and American Adulteration Acts.

PRESS NOTICES OF THE FOURTH EDITION.

"Simply INDISPENSABLE in the Analyst's laboratory."—*The Lancet.*

"THE STANDARD WORK on the subject. . . . Every chapter and every page gives abundant roof of the strict revision to which the work has been subjected. . . . The section on MILK is, we believe, the most exhaustive study of the subject extant. . . . An INDISPENSABLE MANUAL for Analysts and Medical Officers of Health."—*Public Health.*

"A new edition of Mr. Wynter Blyth's Standard work, ENRICHED WITH ALL THE RECENT DISCOVERIES AND IMPROVEMENTS, will be accepted as a boon."—*Chemical News.*

POISONS:
THEIR EFFECTS AND DETECTION.

THIRD EDITION. In Large 8vo, Cloth, with Tables and Illustrations. Price 21s.

GENERAL CONTENTS.

I.—Historical Introduction. II.—Classification—Statistics—Connection between Toxic Action and Chemical Composition—Life Tests—General Method of Procedure—The Spectroscope—Examination of Blood and Blood Stains. III.—Poisonous Gases. IV.—Acids and Alkalies. V.—More or less Volatile Poisonous Substances. VI.—Alkaloids and Poisonous Vegetable Principles. VII.—Poisons derived from Living or Dead Animal Substances. VIII.—The Oxalic Acid Group. IX.—Inorganic Poisons. *Appendix:* Treatment, by Antidotes or otherwise, of Cases of Poisoning.

"Undoubtedly THE MOST COMPLETE WORK on Toxicology in our language."—*The Analyst (on the Third Edition).*

"As a PRACTICAL GUIDE, we know NO BETTER work."—*The Lancet (on the Third Edition).*

*** In the THIRD EDITION, Enlarged and partly Re-written, NEW ANALYTICAL METHODS have been introduced, and the CADAVERIC ALKALOIDS, or PTOMAINES, bodies playing so great a part in Food-poisoning and in the Manifestations of Disease, have received special attention.

LONDON: EXETER STREET, STRAND.

MINE-SURVEYING (A Text-Book of):
For the use of Managers of Mines and Collieries, Students at the Royal School of Mines, &c.

BY BENNETT H. BROUGH, F.G.S.,
Late Instructor of Mine-Surveying, Royal School of Mines.

With Diagrams. FIFTH EDITION. Crown 8vo. Cloth, 7s. 6d.

GENERAL CONTENTS.

General Explanations—Measurement of Distances—Miner's Dial—Variation of the Magnetic-Needle—Surveying with the Magnetic-Needle in presence of Iron—Surveying with the Fixed Needle—German Dial—Theodolite—Traversing Underground—Surface-Surveys with Theodolite—Plotting the Survey—Calculation of Areas—Levelling—Connection of Underground- and Surface-Surveys—Measuring Distances by Telescope—Setting-out—Mine-Surveying Problems—Mine Plans—Applications of Magnetic-Needle in Mining—*Appendices*.

"It is the kind of book which has long been wanted, and no English-speaking Mine Agent or Mining Student will consider his technical library complete without it."—*Nature*.

"SUPPLIES A LONG-FELT WANT."—*Iron*.

"A valuable accessory to Surveyors in every department of commercial enterprise."—*Colliery Guardian*.

WORKS
BY WALTER R. BROWNE, M.A., M. INST. C.E.,
Late Fellow of Trinity College, Cambridge.

THE STUDENT'S MECHANICS:
An Introduction to the Study of Force and Motion.

With Diagrams. Crown 8vo. Cloth, 4s. 6d.

"Clear in style and practical in method, 'THE STUDENT'S MECHANICS' is cordially to be recommended from all points of view."—*Athenæum*.

FOUNDATIONS OF MECHANICS.
Papers reprinted from the *Engineer*. In Crown 8vo, 1s.

FUEL AND WATER:
A Manual for Users of Steam and Water.
BY PROF. SCHWACKHÖFER AND W. R. BROWNE, M.A. (See p. 41.)

LONDON: EXETER STREET, STRAND.

GAS MANUFACTURE
(THE CHEMISTRY OF).

A Hand-Book on the Production, Purification, and Testing of Illuminating Gas, and the Assay of the Bye-Products of Gas Manufacture. For the Use of Students.

BY

W. J. ATKINSON BUTTERFIELD, M.A., F.C.S.,
Head Chemist, Gas Works, Beckton, London, E.

With Numerous Illustrations.   Handsome Cloth.   Price 9s.

"The BEST WORK of its kind which we have ever had the pleasure of reviewing."—*Journal of Gas Lighting.*

GENERAL CONTENTS.

I. Raw Materials for Gas Manufacture.
II. Coal Gas.
III. Carburetted Water Gas.
IV. Oil Gas.
V. Enriching by Light Oils.
VI. Final Details of Manufacture.
VII. Gas Analysis.
VIII. Photometry.
IX. Applications of Gas.
X. Bye-Products.

*** This work deals primarily with the ordinary processes of GAS MANUFACTURE employed in this country, and aims especially at indicating the *principles* on which they are based. The more modern, but as yet subsidiary, processes are fully treated also. The Chapters on *Gas Analysis* and *Photometry* will enable the consumer to grasp the methods by which the quality of the gas he uses is ascertained, and in the Chapter on *The Applications of Gas*, not only is it discussed as an illuminant, but also as a ready source of heat and power. In the final Chapter, an attempt has been made to trace in a readily-intelligible manner the extraction of the principal derivatives from the crude BYE-PRODUCTS. The work deals incidentally with the most modern developments of the industry, including *inter alia* the commercial production and uses of acetylene and the application of compressed gas for Street Traction. The needs of the Students in Technical Colleges and Classes have throughout been kept in view.

LONDON: EXETER STREET, STRAND.

Works by GRENVILLE A. J. COLE, M.R.I.A., F.G.S.,
Professor of Geology in the Royal College of Science for Ireland.

PRACTICAL GEOLOGY
(AIDS IN):
WITH A SECTION ON PALÆONTOLOGY.

SECOND EDITION, Revised. With Illustrations. Cloth, 10s. 6d.

GENERAL CONTENTS.—PART I.—SAMPLING OF THE EARTH'S CRUST. PART II.—EXAMINATION OF MINERALS. PART III.—EXAMINATION OF ROCKS. PART IV.—EXAMINATION OF FOSSILS.

"Prof. Cole treats of the examination of minerals and rocks in a way that has never been attempted before . . . DESERVING OF THE HIGHEST PRAISE. Here indeed are 'Aids' INNUMERABLE and INVALUABLE. All the directions are given with the utmost clearness and precision."—*Athenæum.*
"To the younger workers in Geology, Prof. Cole's book will be as INDISPENSABLE as a dictionary to the learners of a language."—*Saturday Review.*
"That the work deserves its title, that it is full of 'AIDS,' and in the highest degree 'PRACTICAL,' will be the verdict of all who use it."—*Nature.*
"This EXCELLENT MANUAL . . . will be a VERY GREAT HELP. . . . The section on the Examination of Fossils is probably the BEST of its kind yet published. . . . FULL of well-digested information from the newest sources and from personal research."—*Annals of Nat. History.*

New and Attractive Work by Prof. COLE.

OPEN-AIR STUDIES:
An Introduction to Geology Out-of-doors.

With 12 Full-Page Illustrations from Photographs. *Cloth. 8s. 6d.*

GENERAL CONTENTS.—The Materials of the Earth—A Mountain Hollow—Down the Valley—Along the Shore—Across the Plains—Dead Volcanoes—A Granite Highland—The Annals of the Earth—The Surrey Hills—The Folds of the Mountains.

"The FASCINATING 'OPEN-AIR STUDIES' of PROF. COLE give the subject a GLOW OF ANIMATION . . . cannot fail to arouse keen interest in geology."—*Geological Magazine.*
"EMINENTLY READABLE . . . every small detail in a scene touched with a sympathetic kindly pen that reminds one of the lingering brush of a Constable."—*Nature.*
"The work of Prof. Cole combines ELEGANCE of STYLE with SCIENTIFIC THOROUGHNESS."—*Petermann's Mittheilungen.*
"The book is worthy of its title: from cover to cover it is STRONG with bracing freshness of the mountain and the field, while its ACCURACY and THOROUGHNESS show that it is the work of an earnest and conscientious student. . . . Full of picturesque touches which are most welcome."—*Natural Science.*
"A CHARMING BOOK, beautifully illustrated."—*Athenæum.*

LONDON: EXETER STREET, STRAND.

SCIENTIFIC AND TECHNOLOGICAL WORKS. 11

SEWAGE DISPOSAL WORKS:
A Guide to the Construction of Works for the Prevention of the Pollution by Sewage of Rivers and Estuaries.

BY

W. SANTO CRIMP, M.Inst.C.E., F.G.S.,

Late Assistant-Engineer, London County Council.

With Tables, Illustrations in the Text, and 37 Lithographic Plates. Medium 8vo. Handsome Cloth.

SECOND EDITION, REVISED AND ENLARGED. 30s.

PART I.—INTRODUCTORY.

Introduction.
Details of River Pollutions and Recommendations of Various Commissions.
Hourly and Daily Flow of Sewage.
The Pail System as Affecting Sewage.
The Separation of Rain-water from the Sewage Proper.

Settling Tanks.
Chemical Processes.
The Disposal of Sewage-sludge.
The Preparation of Land for Sewage Disposal.
Table of Sewage Farm Management.

PART II.—SEWAGE DISPOSAL WORKS IN OPERATION—THEIR CONSTRUCTION, MAINTENANCE, AND COST.

Illustrated by Plates showing the General Plan and Arrangement adopted in each District.

Map of the LONDON Sewage System.
Crossness Outfall.
Barking Outfall.
Doncaster Irrigation Farm.
Beddington Irrigation Farm, Borough of Croydon.
Bedford Sewage Farm Irrigation.
Dewsbury and Hitchin Intermittent Filtration.
Merton, Croydon Rural Sanitary Authority.
Swanwick, Derbyshire.
The Ealing Sewage Works.
Chiswick.
Kingston-on-Thames, A. B. C. Process.
Salford Sewage Works.

Bradford, Precipitation.
New Malden, Chemical Treatment and Small Filters.
Friern Barnet.
Acton, Ferozone and Polarite Process.
Ilford, Chadwell, and Dagenham Works.
Coventry.
Wimbledon.
Birmingham.
Margate.
Portsmouth.
BERLIN Sewage Farms.
Sewage Precipitation Works, Dortmund (Germany).
Treatment of Sewage by Electrolysis.

*** From the fact of the Author's having, for some years, had charge of the Main Drainage Works of the Northern Section of the Metropolis, the chapter on LONDON will be found to contain many important details which would not otherwise have been available.

"All persons interested in Sanitary Science owe a debt of gratitude to Mr. Crimp. . . . His work will be especially useful to SANITARY AUTHORITIES and their advisers . . . EMINENTLY PRACTICAL AND USEFUL . . . gives plans and descriptions of MANY OF THE MOST IMPORTANT SEWAGE WORKS of England . . . with very valuable information as to the COST of construction and working of each. . . . The carefully-prepared drawings permit of an easy comparison between the different systems."—*Lancet.*

"Probably the MOST COMPLETE AND BEST TREATISE on the subject which has appeared in our language . . Will prove of the greatest use to all who have the problem of Sewage Disposal to face."—*Edinburgh Medical Journal.*

LONDON: EXETER STREET, STRAND.

Pocket Size. Leather. With Illustrations. 12s. 6d.

HYGIENE (A Hand-Book of),
BY
SURGEON-MAJOR A. M. DAVIES, D.P.H.Camb.,
Late Assistant-Professor of Hygiene, Army Medical School.

General Contents.

Air and Ventilation—Water and Water Supply—Food and Dieting—Removal and Disposal of Sewage—Habitations—Personal Hygiene—Soils and Sites—Climate and Meteorology—Causation and Prevention of Disease—Disinfection.

"This ADMIRABLE HANDBOOK . . . gives FULL information compressed into the smallest possible bulk."—*Edin. Med. Journal.*
"The elegant dress of the little volume before us is but the outer covering of A TRULY RICH KERNEL, and justly merits the praise it spontaneously calls forth. Attractive to the eye, Surgeon-Major DAVIES' volume is equally attractive to the mind. Students will find that its 590 pages comprise ALL information necessary. COMPACT, HANDY, COMPREHENSIVE, it certainly merits a high place among the text-books of the day."—*Sanitary Record.*
"We are glad to welcome Surgeon-Major Davies' book . . . he has had ample opportunity to make himself A MASTER OF THE SCIENCE, and he has a right to speak. . . . WONDERFULLY WELL UP TO DATE, well and clearly written, pleasant to read."—*The Lancet.*
"Really an ADMIRABLE BOOK. . . . A MOST HANDY WORK OF REFERENCE full of information."—*The Hospital.*
"A singularly compact and elegant volume . . . contains an admirable *précis* of everything relating to Hygiene CLEARLY and LOGICALLY ARRANGED and easy of reference. Likely, we think, to be the favourite text-book."—*Public Health.*

Large 8vo. Handsome Cloth. 12s. 6d.

BLEACHING & CALICO-PRINTING.
A Short Manual for Students and Practical Men.

By GEORGE DUERR,
Director of the Bleaching, Dyeing, and Printing Department at the Accrington and Bacup Technical Schools; Chemist and Colourist at the Irwell Print Works.

ASSISTED BY WILLIAM TURNBULL
(of Turnbull & Stockdale, Limited).

With Illustrations and upwards of One Hundred Dyed and Printed Patterns designed specially to show various Stages of the Processes described.

"When a READY WAY out of a difficulty is wanted, it is IN BOOKS LIKE THIS that it is found."—*Textile Recorder.*
"Mr. DUERR'S WORK will be found MOST USEFUL. . . . The information given of GREAT VALUE. . . . The Recipes THOROUGHLY PRACTICAL."—*Textile Manufacturer.*

LONDON: EXETER STREET, STRAND.

WORKS
By J. R. AINSWORTH DAVIS, B.A.,
PROFESSOR OF BIOLOGY, UNIVERSITY COLLEGE, ABERYSTWYTH;
EXAMINER IN ZOOLOGY, UNIVERSITY OF ABERDEEN.

DAVIS (Prof. Ainsworth): BIOLOGY (An Elementary Text-Book of). In large Crown 8vo, Cloth. SECOND EDITION.

PART I. VEGETABLE MORPHOLOGY AND PHYSIOLOGY. With Complete Index-Glossary and 128 Illustrations. Price 8s. 6d.
PART II. ANIMAL MORPHOLOGY AND PHYSIOLOGY. With Complete Index-Glossary and 108 Illustrations. Price 10s. 6d.

EACH PART SOLD SEPARATELY.

*** NOTE—The SECOND EDITION has been thoroughly Revised and Enlarged, and includes all the leading selected TYPES in the various Organic Groups.

"Certainly THE BEST 'BIOLOGY' with which we are acquainted. It owes its pre-eminence to the fact that it is an EXCELLENT attempt to present Biology to the Student as a CORRELATED AND COMPLETE SCIENCE. The glossarial Index is a MOST USEFUL addition."—*British Medical Journal.*

"Furnishes a CLEAR and COMPREHENSIVE exposition of the subject in a SYSTEMATIC form."—*Saturday Review.*

"Literally PACKED with information."—*Glasgow Medical Journal.*

DAVIS (Prof. Ainsworth): THE FLOWERING PLANT, as Illustrating the First Principles of Botany. Large Crown 8vo, with numerous Illustrations. 3s. 6d. SECOND EDITION.

"It would be hard to find a Text-book which would better guide the student to an accurate knowledge of modern discoveries in Botany. . . . The SCIENTIFIC ACCURACY of statement, and the concise exposition of FIRST PRINCIPLES make it valuable for educational purposes. In the chapter on the Physiology of Flowers, an *admirable résumé* is given, drawn from Darwin, Hermann Müller, Kerner, and Lubbock, of what is known of the Fertilization of Flowers."

DAVIS and SELENKA: A ZOOLOGICAL POCKET-BOOK; Or, Synopsis of Animal Classification. Comprising Definitions of the Phyla, Classes, and Orders, with Explanatory Remarks and Tables. By Dr. Emil Selenka, Professor in the University of Erlangen. Authorised English translation from the Third German Edition. In Small Post 8vo, Interleaved for the use of Students. Limp Covers, 4s.

"Dr. Selenka's Manual will be found useful by all Students of Zoology. It is a COMPREHENSIVE and SUCCESSFUL attempt to present us with a scheme of the natural arrangement of the animal world."—*Edin. Med. Journal.*

"Will prove very serviceable to those who are attending Biology Lectures. . . . The translation is accurate and clear."—*Lancet.*

LONDON: EXETER STREET, STRAND.

GAS, OIL, AND AIR ENGINES:

A Practical Text-Book on Internal Combustion Motors without Boiler.

By BRYAN DONKIN, M.Inst.C.E.

SECOND EDITION, Revised throughout. With numerous Illustrations. Large 8vo. 25s.

GENERAL CONTENTS.—**Gas Engines:**—General Description—History and Development—British, French, and German Gas Engines—Gas Production for Motive Power—Theory of the Gas Engine—Chemical Composition of Gas in Gas Engines—Utilisation of Heat—Explosion and Combustion. **Oil Motors:**—History and Development—Various Types—Priestman's and other Oil Engines. **Hot-Air Engines:**—History and Development—Various Types: Stirling's, Ericsson's, &c., &c.

"The BEST BOOK NOW PUBLISHED on Gas, Oil, and Air Engines. . . . Will be of VERY GREAT INTEREST to the numerous practical engineers who have to make themselves familiar with the motor of the day. . . . Mr. Donkin has the advantage of LONG PRACTICAL EXPERIENCE, combined with HIGH SCIENTIFIC AND EXPERIMENTAL KNOWLEDGE, and an accurate perception of the requirements of Engineers."—*The Engineer.*

"The intelligence that Mr. BRYAN DONKIN has published a Text-book should be GOOD NEWS to all who desire reliable, up-to-date information. . . . His book is MOST TIMELY, and we welcomed it at first sight as being just the kind of book for which everybody interested in the subject has been looking. . . . We HEARTILY RECOMMEND Mr. Donkin's work. . . . A monument of careful labour. . . . Luminous and comprehensive. . . . Nothing of any importance seems to have been omitted."—*Journal of Gas Lighting.*

INORGANIC CHEMISTRY (A Short Manual of).

By A. DUPRÉ, Ph.D., F.R.S., AND WILSON HAKE,

Ph.D., F.I.C., F.C.S., of the Westminster Hospital Medical School.

SECOND EDITION, Revised. Crown 8vo. Cloth, 7s. 6d.

"A well-written, clear and accurate Elementary Manual of Inorganic Chemistry. . . . We agree heartily in the system adopted by Drs. Dupré and Hake. WILL MAKE EXPERIMENTAL WORK TREBLY INTERESTING BECAUSE INTELLIGIBLE."—*Saturday Review.*

"There is no question that, given the PERFECT GROUNDING of the Student in his Science, the remainder comes afterwards to him in a manner much more simple and easily acquired. The work IS AN EXAMPLE OF THE ADVANTAGES OF THE SYSTEMATIC TREATMENT of a Science over the fragmentary style so generally followed. BY A LONG WAY THE BEST of the small Manuals for Students."—*Analyst.*

HINTS ON THE PRESERVATION OF FISH,

IN REFERENCE TO FOOD SUPPLY.

By J. COSSAR EWART, M.D., F.R.S.E.,

Regius Professor of Natural History, University of Edinburgh.

In Crown 8vo. Wrapper, 6d.

LONDON: EXETER STREET, STRAND.

SCIENTIFIC AND TECHNOLOGICAL WORKS.

SECOND EDITION, *Revised.* Royal 8vo. With numerous Illustrations and 13 *Lithographic Plates.* Handsome Cloth. Price 30s.

BRIDGE-CONSTRUCTION

(A PRACTICAL TREATISE ON):

Being a Text-Book on the Construction of Bridges in Iron and Steel.

FOR THE USE OF STUDENTS, DRAUGHTSMEN, AND ENGINEERS.

BY T. CLAXTON FIDLER, M. INST. C. E.,

Prof. of Engineering, University College, Dundee.

"Mr. FIDLER'S SUCCESS arises from the combination of EXPERIENCE and SIMPLICITY OF TREATMENT displayed on every page. . . . Theory is kept in subordination to practice, and his book is, therefore, as useful to girder-makers as to students of Bridge Construction."—("*The Architect*" *on the Second Edition.*)

"Of late years the American treatises on Practical and Applied Mechanics have taken the lead . . . since the opening up of a vast continent has given the American engineer a number of new bridge-problems to solve . . . but we look to the PRESENT TREATISE ON BRIDGE-CONSTRUCTION, and the Forth Bridge, to bring us to the front again."—*Engineer.*

"One of the VERY BEST RECENT WORKS on the Strength of Materials and its application to Bridge-Construction. . . Well repays a careful Study."—*Engineering.*

"An INDISPENSABLE HANDBOOK for the practical Engineer."—*Nature.*

HOW PLANTS LIVE AND WORK:

A Simple Introduction to Real Life in the Plant-world, Based on Lessons originally given to Country Children.

BY ELEANOR HUGHES-GIBB.

With Illustrations. Crown 8vo. Cloth. 2s. 6d.

⁎ The attention of all interested in the Scientific Training of the Young is requested to this DELIGHTFULLY FRESH and CHARMING LITTLE BOOK. It ought to be in the hands of every Mother and Teacher throughout the land.

"The child's attention is first secured, and then, in language SIMPLE, YET SCIENTIFICALLY ACCURATE, the first lessons in plant-life are set before it."—*Natural Science.*

"In every way well calculated to make the study of Botany ATTRACTIVE to the young."—*Scotsman.*

LONDON: EXETER STREET, STRAND.

ORE & STONE MINING.

BY

C. LE NEVE FOSTER, D.Sc., F.R.S.,

PROFESSOR OF MINING, ROYAL COLLEGE OF SCIENCE; H.M. INSPECTOR OF MINES.

In Large 8vo. With Frontispiece and 716 Illustrations. 34s.

"Dr. Foster's book was expected to be EPOCH-MAKING, and it fully justifies such expectation. . . . A MOST ADMIRABLE account of the mode of occurrence of practically ALL KNOWN MINERALS. Probably stands UNRIVALLED for completeness."—*The Mining Journal.*

GENERAL CONTENTS.

INTRODUCTION. Mode of Occurrence of Minerals: Classification: Tabular Deposits, Masses—Examples: Alum, Amber, Antimony, Arsenic, Asbestos, Asphalt, Barytes, Borax, Boric Acid, Carbonic Acid, Clay, Cobalt Ore, Copper Ore, Diamonds, Flint, Freestone, Gold Ore, Graphite, Gypsum, Ice, Iron Ore, Lead Ore, Manganese Ore, Mica, Natural Gas, Nitrate of Soda, Ozokerite, Petroleum, Phosphate of Lime Potassium Salts, Quicksilver Ore, Salt, Silver Ore, Slate, Sulphur, Tin Ore, Zinc Ore. Faults. **Prospecting**: Chance Discoveries—Adventitious Finds—Geology as a Guide to Minerals—Associated Minerals—Surface Indications. **Boring**: Uses of Bore-holes—Methods of Boring Holes: i. By Rotation, ii. By Percussion with Rods, iii. By Percussion with Rope. **Breaking Ground**: Hand Tools—Machinery—Transmission of Power—Excavating Machinery: i. Steam Diggers, ii. Dredges, iii. Rock Drills, iv. Machines for Cutting Grooves, v. Machines for Tunnelling—Modes of using Holes—Driving and Sinking—Fire-setting—Excavating by Water. **Supporting Excavations**: Timbering—Masonry—Metallic Supports—Watertight Linings—Special Processes. **Exploitation**: Open Works:—Hydraulic Mining—Excavation of Minerals under Water—Extraction of Minerals by Wells and Bore-holes—Underground Workings—Beds—Veins—Masses. **Haulage or Transport**: Underground: by Shoots, Pipes, Persons, Sledges, Vehicles, Railways, Machinery, Boats—Conveyance above Ground. **Hoisting or Winding**: Motors, Drums, and Pulley Frames—Ropes, Chains, and Attachments—Receptacles—Other Appliances—Safety Appliances—Testing Ropes—Pneumatic Hoisting. **Drainage**: Surface Water—Dams—Drainage Tunnels—Siphons—Winding Machinery—Pumping Engines above ground—Pumping Engines below ground—Co-operative Pumping. **Ventilation**: Atmosphere of Mines—Causes of Pollution of Air—Natural Ventilation—Artificial Ventilation: i. Furnace Ventilation, ii. Mechanical Ventilation—Testing the Quality of Air—Measuring the Quantity and Pressure of the Air—Efficiency of Ventilating Appliances—Resistance caused by Friction. **Lighting**: Reflected Daylight—Candles—Torches—Lamps—Wells Light—Safety Lamps—Gas—Electric Light. **Descent and Ascent**: Steps and Slides—Ladders—Buckets and Cages—Man Engine. **Dressing**: i. Mechanical Processes: Washing, Hand Picking, Breaking Up, Consolidation, Screening—ii. Processes depending on Physical Properties: Motion in Water, Motion in Air—Desiccation—Liquefaction and Distillation—Magnetic Attraction—iii. Chemical Processes: Solution, Evaporation and Crystallisation, Atmospheric Weathering, Calcination, Cementation, Amalgamation—Application of Processes—Loss in Dressing—Sampling. **Principles of Employment of Mining Labour**: Payment by Time, Measure, or Weight—By Combination of these—By Value of Product. **Legislation affecting Mines and Quarries**: Ownership—Taxation—Working Regulations—Metalliferous Mines Regulation Acts—Coal Mines Regulation Act—Other Statutes. **Condition of the Miner**: Clothing—Housing—Education—Sickness—Thrift—Recreation. **Accidents**: Death Rate of Miners from Accidents—Relative Accident Mortality Underground and Above-ground—Classification of Accidents—Ambulance Training.

"This EPOCH-MAKING work . . . appeals to MEN OF EXPERIENCE no less than to students . . . gives numerous examples from the MINING PRACTICE of EVERY COUNTRY. Many of its chapters are upon subjects not usually dealt with in text books. . . . Of great interest. . . . Admirably illustrated."—*Berg- und Hüttenmännische Zeitung.*

"This SPLENDID WORK."—*Oesterr. Ztschrft. für Berg- und Hüttenwesen.*

LONDON : EXETER STREET, STRAND.

EDITION for 1896.
Cloth, for Office use, 8s. 6d. Leather, for the Pocket, 8s. 6d.

GRIFFIN'S ELECTRICAL PRICE-BOOK.

For Electrical, Civil, Marine, and Borough Engineers, Local Authorities, Architects, Railway Contractors, &c., &c.

EDITED BY H. J. DOWSING,

Member of the Institution of Electrical Engineers; of the Society of Arts; of the London Chamber of Commerce, &c.

PART I.—PRICES AND DETAILS OF MACHINERY AND APPARATUS.
PART II.—USEFUL INFORMATION CONCERNING THE SUPPLY OF ELECTRICAL ENERGY; Complete Estimates; Reports, Rules and Regulations, Useful Tables, &c.; and General Information regarding the carrying out of Electrical Work.

"The ELECTRICAL PRICE-BOOK REMOVES ALL MYSTERY about the cost of Electrical Power. By its aid the EXPENSE that will be entailed by utilising electricity on a large or small scale can be discovered. . . . Contains that sort of information which is most often required in an architect's office when the application of Electricity is being considered."—*Architect.*

"The value of this Electrical Price-Book CANNOT BE OVER-ESTIMATED. . . . Will save time and trouble both to the engineer and the business man."—*Machinery.*

*** The Publishers beg to call attention to the New Edition of the ELECTRICAL ENGINEERS' PRICE-BOOK. It is gratifying to learn that the work has been found USEFUL and VALUABLE by the general body of Engineers, Architects, Builders, and others. The prices given for work carried out have been acknowledged FAIR, and such as provide for RELIABLE AND GOOD WORKMANSHIP, and they have proved of use in Arbitrations, Appeals, and Assessment Cases.

GRIFFIN (John Joseph, F.C.S.):

CHEMICAL RECREATIONS: A Popular Manual of Experimental Chemistry. With 540 Engravings of Apparatus. *Tenth Edition.* Crown 8vo. Cloth. Complete in one volume, cloth, gilt top, 12/6.

Part I.—Elementary Chemistry, 2/.
Part II.—The Chemistry of the Non-Metallic Elements, 10/6.

GURDEN (Richard Lloyd, Authorised Surveyor
for the Governments of New South Wales and Victoria):

TRAVERSE TABLES: computed to Four Places Decimals for every Minute of Angle up to 100 of Distance. For the use of Surveyors and Engineers. *Third Edition.* Folio, strongly half-bound, 21/.

*** *Published with Concurrence of the Surveyors-General for New South Wales and Victoria.*

"Those who have experience in exact SURVEY-WORK will best know how to appreciate the enormous amount of labour represented by this valuable book. The computations enable the user to ascertain the sines and cosines for a distance of twelve miles to within half an inch, and this BY REFERENCE TO BUT ONE TABLE, in place of the usual Fifteen minute computations required. This alone is evidence of the assistance which the Tables ensure to every user, and as every Surveyor in active practice has felt the want of such assistance, few knowing of their publication will remain without them."—*Engineer.*

LONDON: EXETER STREET, STRAND.

Griffin's Standard Publications

FOR

ENGINEERS, ELECTRICIANS, ARCHITECTS, BUILDERS, NAVAL CONSTRUCTORS, AND SURVEYORS.

		PAGE
Applied Mechanics,	Rankine, Browne, Jamieson,	32, 8, 24
Civil Engineering,	Prof. Rankine,	32
Bridge-Construction,	Prof. Fidler,	15
Design of Structures,	S. Anglin,	4
Sewage Disposal Works,	Santo Crimp,	11
Traverse Tables,	R. L. Gurden,	17
Marine Engineering,	A. E. Seaton,	42
Stability of Ships,	Sir E. J. Reed,	35
The Steam-Engine,	Rankine, Jamieson,	32, 24
Chemistry for Engineers,	Blount & Bloxam,	5
Gas, Oil, and Air-Engines,	Bryan Donkin,	14
Boiler Construction,	T. W. Traill,	45
,, Management,	R. D. Munro,	28
Fuel and Water (for Steam Users),	Schwackhöfer and Browne,	41
Machinery and Millwork,	Prof. Rankine,	32
Hydraulic Machinery,	Prof. Robinson,	39
Metallurgical Machinery,	H. C. Jenkins,	38
Nautical Text-Books,	Captain Blackmore (Ed.),	3
Useful Rules and Tables for Engineers, &c.,	Profs. Rankine and Jamieson,	32
Electrical Pocket-Book,	Munro and Jamieson,	29
Electrical Price-Book,	H. J. Dowsing,	17
Graphic Tables for Conversion of Measurements,	Prof. Robt. H. Smith,	44
Marine Engineers' Pocket-Book,	Seaton and Rounthwaite,	42
Nystrom's Pocket-Book,	Dennis Marks,	29

LONDON: EXETER STREET, STRAND.

SCIENTIFIC AND TECHNOLOGICAL WORKS.

GRIFFIN'S NAUTICAL SERIES.
EDITED BY EDW. BLACKMORE,
Master Mariner, First Class Trinity House Certificate, Assoc. Inst. N.A.;
AND WRITTEN, MAINLY, by SAILORS for SAILORS.

In Crown 8vo. With Illustrations and Plates.

"A VERY USEFUL SERIES."—*Nature.* "This ADMIRABLE SERIES."—*Fairplay.*
"The volumes of MESSRS. GRIFFIN'S NAUTICAL SERIES may well and profitably be read by ALL interested in our NATIONAL MARITIME PROGRESS."—*Marine Engineer.*
"EVERY SHIP should have the WHOLE SERIES as a REFERENCE LIBRARY. HANDSOMELY and STRONGLY BOUND, CLEARLY PRINTED and ILLUSTRATED."—*Liverpool Journ. of Commerce.*

Know Your Own Ship: A Simple Explanation of the Stability, Construction, Tonnage, and Freeboard of Ships. By THOS. WALTON, Naval Architect, Lecturer to Ships' Officers, Government Navigation School, Leith. With numerous Illustrations. SECOND EDITION. 5s.
"MR. WALTON'S book removes a want, and will be found VERY USEFUL."—*The Engineer.*
"Will attain LASTING SUCCESS . . . EXCEEDINGLY HANDY."—*Shipping World.*

Latitude and Longitude: How to find them. By W. J. MILLAR, M.Inst.C.E., late Sec. to the Inst. of Engineers and Shipbuilders in Scotland. 2s.
"Cannot but prove an acquisition to those studying Navigation."—*Marine Engineer.*
"Young Seamen will find it HANDY and USEFUL, SIMPLE and CLEAR."—*The Engineer.*

Practical Mechanics: Applied to the requirements of the Sailor. By THOS. MACKENZIE, Master Mariner, F.R.A.S. 3s. 6d.
"THIS EXCELLENT BOOK . . . contains a LARGE AMOUNT of information."—*Nature.*
"WELL WORTH the money . . . EXCEEDINGLY HELPFUL."—*Shipping World.*
"NO SHIPS' OFFICERS' BOOKCASE will henceforth be complete without CAPTAIN MACKENZIE'S 'PRACTICAL MECHANICS.' Notwithstanding my many years' experience at sea, it has told me *how much more there is to acquire.*"—(Letter to the Publishers from a Master Mariner).

The British Mercantile Marine; An Historical Sketch of its Rise and Development. By the EDITOR.

Elementary Seamanship. By D. WILSON-BARKER, Master Mariner, F.R.S.E., F.R.G.S. With Numerous Plates, two in Colours, and Frontispiece.

Navigation: Theoretical and Practical. By D. WILSON-BARKER, Master Mariner, &c., and WILLIAM ALLINGHAM.

Ocean Meteorology: For Officers of the Merchant Navy. By WILLIAM ALLINGHAM, First Class Honours, Navigation, Science and Art Dep.

Practical Algebra and Trigonometry: For the Young Sailor, &c. By RICH. C. BUCK, of the Thames Nautical Training College, H.M.S. "Worcester."

The Construction and Maintenance of Vessels built of Steel. By a Practical Engineer and Shipwright.

A Medical and Surgical Help for Shipmasters and Officers IN THE MERCHANT NAVY. Including First Aid at Sea. By WM. JOHNSON SMITH, F.R.C.S., Principal Medical Officer, Seaman's Hospital, Greenwich. With Illustrations and Coloured Plates. Handsome Cloth, 6s. (See p. 37.)
"SOUND, JUDICIOUS, REALLY HELPFUL."—*The Lancet.*

LONDON: EXETER STREET, STRAND.

Griffin's Standard Publications
FOR
GEOLOGISTS, MINE-MANAGERS, AND METALLURGISTS.

		PAGE
Geology (Stratigraphical),	R. ETHERIDGE,	30
,, (Physical),	PROF. SEELEY,	30
,, (Practical),	PROF. COLE,	10
,, (Introduction to),	,,	10
Mine-Surveying,	B. H. BROUGH,	8
Mining, Coal,	H. W. HUGHES,	22
,, Ore and Stone,	PROF. LE NEVE FOSTER,	16
Blasting and Explosives,	O. GUTTMANN,	21
Assaying,	C. & J. J. BERINGER,	6
Metallurgy,	PHILLIPS AND BAUERMAN,	31
,, (Introduction to),	PROF. ROBERTS-AUSTEN,	38
,, (Elementary),	PROF. SEXTON,	43
Copper, Metallurgy of,	THOS. GIBB,	38
Gold, ,,	T. K. ROSE,	40
Iron and Steel, ,,	PROF. TURNER,	46
Alloys,	PROF. ROBERTS-AUSTEN,	38

Griffin's "Health" Publications.

Ambulance,	DR. RIDDELL,	37
Disinfection and Disinfectants,	DR. RIDEAL,	36
First Aid at Sea,	DR. JOHNSON SMITH,	37
Foods and Poisons,	A. WYNTER BLYTH,	7
Hygiene,	SURGEON-MAJOR DAVIES,	12
Practical Sanitation,	DR. GEO. REID,	36
Sewage Disposal Works,	SANTO CRIMP,	11
Hygienic Prevention of Consumption,	{ DR. SQUIRE. [*See Medical Catalogue.*]	

LONDON: EXETER STREET, STRAND.

SCIENTIFIC AND TECHNOLOGICAL WORKS.

Griffin's Chemical and Technological Publications.

		PAGE
Chemistry for Engineers, Builders, and Manufacturers,	MM. BLOUNT AND BLOXAM,	5
Agricultural Chemistry,	PROF. J. M. H. MUNRO,	29
Bleaching and Calico-Printing,	GEO. DUERR,	12
Cements,	G. R. REDGRAVE,	33
Dairy Chemistry,	H. D. RICHMOND,	35
Disinfectants,	DR. RIDEAL,	36
Dyeing,	MM. KNECHT AND RAWSON,	25
,,	G. H. HURST,	23
Electro-Metallurgy,	W. G. M'MILLAN,	27
Foods, Analysis of,	WYNTER BLYTH,	7
Gas Manufacture,	W. ATKINSON BUTTERFIELD,	9
Oils, Soaps, Candles,	DR. ALDER WRIGHT,	48
Painters' Colours, Varnishes,	G. H. HURST,	23
Petroleum,	MM. REDWOOD AND HOLLOWAY,	34
Photography,	A. BROTHERS,	6
Poisons, Detection of,	WYNTER BLYTH,	7
Textile Printing,	SEYMOUR ROTHWELL,	41

In Large 8vo, with Illustrations and Folding-Plates. 10s. 6d.

BLASTING:

A Handbook for the Use of Engineers and others Engaged in Mining, Tunnelling, Quarrying, &c.

BY OSCAR GUTTMANN, Assoc. M. INST. C.E.

Member of the Societies of Civil Engineers and Architects of Vienna and Budapest, Corresponding Member of the Imp. Roy. Geological Institution of Austria, &c.

GENERAL CONTENTS.—Historical Sketch—Blasting Materials—Blasting Powder—Various Powder-mixtures—Gun-cotton—Nitro-glycerine and Dynamite—Other Nitro-compounds—Sprengel's Liquid (acid) Explosives—Other Means of Blasting—Qualities, Dangers, and Handling of Explosives—Choice of Blasting Materials—Apparatus for Measuring Force—Blasting in Fiery Mines—Means of Igniting Charges—Preparation of Blasts—Bore-holes—Machine-drilling—Chamber Mines—Charging of Bore-holes—Determination of the Charge—Blasting in Bore-holes—Firing—Straw and Fuze Firing—Electrical Firing—Substitutes for Electrical Firing—Results of Working—Various Blasting Operations—Quarrying—Blasting Masonry, Iron and Wooden Structures—Blasting in earth, under water, of ice, &c.

"This ADMIRABLE work."—*Colliery Guardian.*
"Should prove a *vade-mecum* to Mining Engineers and all engaged in practical work."
—*Iron and Coal Trades Review.*

LONDON: EXETER STREET, STRAND.

COAL-MINING (A Text-Book of):
FOR THE USE OF COLLIERY MANAGERS AND OTHERS ENGAGED IN COAL-MINING.

BY

HERBERT WILLIAM HUGHES, F.G.S.,
Assoc. Royal School of Mines, Certificated Colliery Manager.

THIRD EDITION. *In Demy 8vo, Handsome Cloth. With very Numerous Illustrations, mostly reduced from Working Drawings.* 18s.

"The details of colliery work have been fully described, on the ground that collieries are more often made REMUNERATIVE by PERFECTION IN SMALL MATTERS than by bold strokes of engineering. . . . It frequently happens, in particular localities, that the adoption of a combination of small improvements, any of which viewed separately may be of apparently little value, turns an unprofitable concern into a paying one."—*Extract from Author's Preface.*

GENERAL CONTENTS.

Geology: Rocks—Faults—Order of Succession—Carboniferous System in Britain. **Coal**: Definition and Formation of Coal—Classification and Commercial Value of Coals. **Search for Coal**: Boring—various appliances used—Devices employed to meet Difficulties of deep Boring—Special methods of Boring—Mather & Platt's, American, and Diamond systems—Accidents in Boring—Cost of Boring—Use of Boreholes. **Breaking Ground**: Tools—Transmission of Power: Compressed Air, Electricity—Power Machine Drills—Coal Cutting by Machinery—Cost of Coal Cutting—Explosives—Blasting in Dry and Dusty Mines—Blasting by Electricity—Various methods to supersede Blasting. **Sinking**: Position, Form, and Size of shaft—Operation of getting down to "Stone-head"—Method of proceeding afterwards—Lining shafts—Keeping out Water by Tubbing—Cost of Tubbing—Sinking by Boring—Kind-Chaudron, and Lipmann methods—Sinking through Quicksands—Cost of Sinking. **Preliminary Operations**: Driving underground Roads—Supporting Roof: Timbering, Chocks or Cogs, Iron and Steel Supports and Masonry—Arrangement of Inset. **Methods of Working**: Shaft, Pillar, and Subsidence—Bord and Pillar System—Lancashire Method—Longwall Method—Double Stall Method—Working Steep Seams—Working Thick Seams—Working Seams lying near together—Spontaneous Combustion. **Haulage**: Rails—Tubs—Haulage by Horses—Self-acting Inclines—Direct-acting Haulage—Main and Tail Rope—Endless Chain-Endless Rope—Comparison. **Winding**: Pit Frames—Pulleys—Cages—Ropes—Guides—Engines—Drums—Brakes—Counterbalancing—Expansion—Condensation—Compound Engines—Prevention of Overwinding—Catches at pit top—Changing Tubs—Tub Controllers—Signalling. **Pumping**: Bucket and Plunger Pumps—Supporting Pipes in Shaft—Valves—Suspended lifts for Sinking—Cornish and Bull Engines—Davey Differential Engine—Worthington Pump—Calculations as to size of Pumps—Draining Deep Workings—Dams. **Ventilation**: Quantity of air required—Gases met with in Mines—Coal-dust—Laws of Friction—Production of Air-currents—Natural Ventilation—Furnace Ventilation—Mechanical Ventilators—Efficiency of Fans—Comparison of Furnaces and Fans—Distribution of the Air-current—Measurement of Air-currents. **Lighting**: Naked Lights—Safety Lamps—Modern Lamps—Conclusions—Locking and Cleaning Lamps—Electric Light Underground—Delicate Indicators. **Works at Surface**: Boilers—Mechanical Stoking—Coal Conveyors—Workshops. **Preparation of Coal for Market**: General Considerations—Tipplers—Screens—Varying the Sizes made by Screens—Belts—Revolving Tables—Loading Shoots—Typical Illustrations of the arrangement of Various Screening Establishments—Coal Washing—Dry Coal Cleaning—Briquettes.

"Quite THE BEST BOOK of its kind . . . as PRACTICAL in aim as a book can be . . . touches upon every point connected with the actual working of collieries. The illustrations are EXCELLENT."—*Athenæum.*

"A Text-book on Coal-Mining is a great desideratum, and Mr. HUGHES possesses ADMIRABLE QUALIFICATIONS for supplying it. . . . We cordially recommend the work."—*Colliery Guardian.*

"Mr. HUGHES has had opportunities for study and research which fall to the lot of but few men. If we mistake not, his text-book will soon come to be regarded as the STANDARD WORK of its kind."—*Birmingham Daily Gazette.*

*** *Note.*—The first large edition of this work was exhausted within a few months of publication.

LONDON: EXETER STREET, STRAND.

WORKS BY GEORGE H. HURST, F.C.S.,

Member of the Society of Chemical Industry; Lecturer on the Technology of Painters' Colours, Oils, and Varnishes, the Municipal Technical School, Manchester.

PAINTERS' COLOURS, OILS, AND VARNISHES:

A Practical Manual.

SECOND EDITION, *Revised and Enlarged. With Numerous Illustrations.*
Price 12s. 6d.

GENERAL CONTENTS.—Introductory—THE COMPOSITION, MANUFACTURE, ASSAY, and ANALYSIS of PIGMENTS, White, Red, Yellow and Orange, Green, Blue, Brown, and Black—LAKES—Colour and Paint Machinery—Paint Vehicles (Oils, Turpentine, &c., &c.)—Driers—VARNISHES.

"This useful book will prove MOST VALUABLE. We feel bound to recommend it to ALL engaged in the arts concerned."—*Chemical News.*

"A *practical* manual in every respect . . . EXCEEDINGLY INSTRUCTIVE. The section on Varnishes the most reasonable we have met with."—*Chemist and Druggist.*

"VERY VALUABLE information is given."—*Plumber and Decorator.*

"A THOROUGHLY PRACTICAL book, . . . constituting, we believe, the ONLY English work that satisfactorily treats of the manufacture of oils, colours, and pigments."—*Chemical Trades' Journal.*

"Throughout the work are scattered hints which are INVALUABLE to the intelligent reader."—*Invention.*

BY THE SAME AUTHOR.

GARMENT DYEING AND CLEANING.

A Practical Book for Practical Men.

With Numerous Illustrations. 4s. 6d.

GENERAL CONTENTS.—Technology of the Textile Fibres—Garment Cleaning—Dyeing of Textile Fabrics—Bleaching—Finishing of Dyed and Cleaned Fabrics—Scouring and Dyeing of Skin Rugs and Mats—Cleaning and Dyeing of Feathers—Glove Cleaning and Dyeing—Straw Bleaching and Dyeing—Glossary of Drugs and Chemicals—Useful Tables.

"An UP-TO-DATE hand book has long been wanted, and Mr. Hurst, who has produced several admirable works, has done nothing more complete than this. An important work, the more so that several of the branches of the craft here treated upon are almost entirely without English Manuals for the guidance of workers. The price brings it within the reach of all."—*Dyer and Calico-Printer.*

"Mr. Hurst's work DECIDEDLY FILLS A WANT . . . ought to be in the hands of EVERY GARMENT DYER and cleaner in the Kingdom."—*Textile Mercury.*

LONDON: EXETER STREET, STRAND.

WORKS BY
ANDREW JAMIESON, M.Inst.C.E., M.I.E.E., F.R.S.E.,
Professor of Electrical Engineering, The Glasgow and West of Scotland Technical College.

PROFESSOR JAMIESON'S ADVANCED MANUALS.
In Large Crown 8vo. Fully Illustrated.

1. STEAM AND STEAM-ENGINES (A Text-Book on).
For the Use of Students preparing for Competitive Examinations. With over 200 Illustrations, Folding Plates, and Examination Papers. ELEVENTH EDITION. Revised and Enlarged, 8/6.

"Professor Jamieson fascinates the reader by his CLEARNESS OF CONCEPTION AND SIMPLICITY OF EXPRESSION. His treatment recalls the lecturing of Faraday."—*Athenæum.*
"The BEST BOOK yet published for the use of Students."—*Engineer.*
"Undoubtedly the MOST VALUABLE AND MOST COMPLETE Hand-book on the subject that now exists."—*Marine Engineer.*

2. MAGNETISM AND ELECTRICITY (An Advanced Text-Book on). Specially arranged for Advanced and "Honours" Students.

3. APPLIED MECHANICS (An Advanced Text-Book on).
Vol. I.—Comprising Part I.: The Principle of Work and its applications; Part II.: Gearing. Price 7s. 6d. SECOND EDITION. [*Now ready.*

"FULLY MAINTAINS the reputation of the Author—more we cannot say."—*Pract. Engineer.*

Vol. II.—Comprising Parts III. to VI.: Motion and Energy; Strength of Materials; Graphic Statics; Hydraulics and Hydraulic Machinery.
[*In active preparation.*

PROFESSOR JAMIESON'S INTRODUCTORY MANUALS.
With numerous Illustrations and Examination Papers.

1. STEAM AND THE STEAM-ENGINE (Elementary Text-Book on). For First-Year Students. FIFTH EDITION. 3/6.
"Quite the RIGHT SORT OF BOOK."—*Engineer.*
"Should be in the hands of EVERY engineering apprentice."—*Practical Engineer.*

2. MAGNETISM AND ELECTRICITY (Elementary Text-Book on). For First-Year Students. THIRD EDITION. 3/6.
"A CAPITAL TEXT-BOOK . . . The diagrams are an important feature."—*Schoolmaster.*
"A THOROUGHLY TRUSTWORTHY Text-book. . . . Arrangement as good as well can be. . . . Diagrams are also excellent. . . . The subject throughout treated as an essentially PRACTICAL one, and very clear instructions given."—*Nature.*

3. APPLIED MECHANICS (Elementary Text-Book on).
Specially arranged for First-Year Students. SECOND EDITION. 3/6.
"Nothing is taken for granted. . . . The work has VERY HIGH QUALITIES, which may be condensed into the one word 'CLEAR.'"—*Science and Art.*

A POCKET-BOOK of ELECTRICAL RULES and TABLES.
FOR THE USE OF ELECTRICIANS AND ENGINEERS.
Pocket Size. Leather, 8s. 6d. *Twelfth Edition,* revised and enlarged.

LONDON: EXETER STREET, STRAND.

SCIENTIFIC AND TECHNOLOGICAL WORKS.

"The MOST VALUABLE and USEFUL WORK on Dyeing that has yet appeared in the English language . . . likely to be THE STANDARD WORK OF REFERENCE for years to come."—*Textile Mercury.*

In Two Large 8vo Volumes, 920 pp., with a SUPPLEMENTARY Volume, containing Specimens of Dyed Fabrics. Handsome Cloth, 45s.

A

MANUAL OF DYEING:

FOR THE USE OF PRACTICAL DYERS, MANUFACTURERS, STUDENTS, AND ALL INTERESTED IN THE ART OF DYEING.

BY

E. KNECHT, Ph.D., F.I.C.,
Head of the Chemistry and Dyeing Department of the Technical School, Manchester; Editor of "The Journal of the Society of Dyers and Colourists;"

CHR. RAWSON, F.I.C., F.C.S.,
Late Head of the Chemistry and Dyeing Department for the Technical College, Bradford; Member of Council of the Society of Dyers and Colourists;

And **RICHARD LOEWENTHAL, Ph.D.**

GENERAL CONTENTS.—Chemical Technology of the Textile Fabrics—Water—Washing and Bleaching—Acids, Alkalies, Mordants—Natural Colouring Matters—Artificial Organic Colouring Matters—Mineral Colours—Machinery used in Dyeing—Tinctorial Properties of Colouring Matters—Analysis and Valuation of Materials used in Dyeing, &c., &c.

"This MOST VALUABLE WORK . . . will be widely appreciated."—*Chemical News.*
"This authoritative and exhaustive work . . . the MOST COMPLETE we have yet seen on the subject."—*Textile Manufacturer.*
"The MOST EXHAUSTIVE and COMPLETE WORK on the subject extant."—*Textile Recorder.*
"The distinguished authors have placed in the hands of those daily engaged in the dye-house or laboratory a work of EXTREME VALUE and UNDOUBTED UTILITY . . . appeals quickly to the technologist, colour chemist, dyer, and more particularly to the rising dyer of the present generation. A book which it is refreshing to meet with."—*American Textile Record.*

LONDON: EXETER STREET, STRAND.

GETTING GOLD:
A GOLD-MINING HANDBOOK FOR PRACTICAL MEN.

BY

J. C. F. JOHNSON, F.G.S., A.I.M.E.,
Life Member Australian Mine-Managers' Association.

Crown 8vo, Extra. With Illustrations. Cloth, 3s. 6d.

NEW VOLUME OF GRIFFIN'S MINING SERIES.

Edited by C. LE NEVE FOSTER, D.Sc., F.R.S.,
H.M. Inspector of Mines, Professor of Mining, Royal School of Mines.

Mine Accounts and Mining Book-keeping,

A Manual for the Use of Students, Managers of Metalliferous Mines and Collieries, and others interested in Mining.

With very Numerous Examples taken from the Actual Practice of leading Mining Companies throughout the world.

BY

JAMES G. LAWN, Assoc.R.S.M.,
Professor of Mining at the South African School of Mines, Capetown, Kimberley, and Johannesburg.

In Large 8vo.

LONDON: EXETER STREET, STRAND.

WORKS BY
WALTER G. M'MILLAN, F.I.C., F.C.S.,
Lecturer in Metallurgy at Mason College, Birmingham.

ELECTRIC SMELTING AND REFINING:
A PRACTICAL MANUAL OF
THE EXTRACTION·AND TREATMENT OF METALS BY ELECTRICAL METHODS.
Being the "ELEKTRO-METALLURGIE" of Dr. W. BORCHERS.
Translated from the Second German Edition
BY WALTER G. M'MILLAN, F.I.C., F.C.S.
In large 8vo. With Numerous Illustrations and Three Folding-Plates.

*** THE PUBLISHERS beg to call attention to this valuable work. Dr. BORCHERS' treatise is PRACTICAL throughout. It confines itself to ONE branch of Electro-Chemistry, viz.:—ELECTROLYSIS, a subject which is daily becoming of more and more importance to the Practical Metallurgist and Manufacturer. Already in the extraction of Aluminium, the refining of Copper, the treatment of Gold and other metals, electrical processes are fast taking the place of the older methods. Dr. BORCHERS' work is acknowledged as the standard authority on the subject in Germany, and the English version, from the able pen of Mr. W. G. M'MILLAN (author of the well-known Treatise on Electro-Deposition and Electro-Plating) will, it is believed, take equal rank in English-speaking countries.

ELECTRO-METALLURGY (A Treatise on):
Embracing the Application of Electrolysis to the Plating, Depositing, Smelting, and Refining of various Metals, and to the Reproduction of Printing Surfaces and Art-Work, &c.
BY WALTER G. M'MILLAN, F.I.C., F.C.S.
With numerous Illustrations. Large Crown 8vo. Cloth 10s. 6d.

GENERAL CONTENTS.—Introductory—Sources of Current—General Condition to be observed in Electro-Plating—Plating Adjuncts and Disposition of Plant—Cleansing and Preparation of Work for the Depositing-Vat, and Subsequent Polishing of Plated Goods—Electro-Deposition of Copper—Electrotyping—Electro-Deposition of Silver—of Gold—of Nickel and Cobalt—of Iron—of Platinum, Zinc, Cadmium, Tin, Lead, Antimony, and Bismuth; Electro-chromy—Electro-Deposition of Alloys—Electro-Metallurgical Extraction and Refining Processes—Recovery of certain Metals from their Solutions or Waste Substances—Determination of the Proportion of Metal in certain Depositing Solutions—Appendix.

"This excellent treatise, . . . one of the BEST and MOST COMPLETE manuals hitherto published on Electro-Metallurgy."—*Electrical Review.*
"This work will be a STANDARD."—*Jeweller.*
"Any metallurgical process which REDUCES the COST of production must of necessity prove of great commercial importance. . . . We recommend this manual to ALL who are interested in the PRACTICAL APPLICATION of electrolytic processes."—*Nature.*

LONDON: EXETER STREET, STRAND.

MACKENZIE (Thos., Master Mariner, F.R.A.S.):

PRACTICAL MECHANICS: APPLIED to the REQUIREMENTS of the SAILOR. Crown 8vo, with numerous Illustrations. Handsome Cloth. 3s. 6d. [*Griffin's Nautical Series.*

" Calculated to be of GREAT PRACTICAL service."—*Fairplay.*
" THIS EXCELLENT BOOK . . . contains a LARGE AMOUNT of information."
—*Nature.*
" WELL WORTH the money . . . will be found EXCEEDINGLY HELPFUL."—*Shipping World.*
" No SHIPS' OFFICERS' BOOKCASE will henceforth be complete without CAPTAIN MACKENZIE'S 'PRACTICAL MECHANICS.' Notwithstanding my many years' experience at sea, it has told me *how much more there is to acquire.*"—(Letter to the Publishers from a Master Mariner).

MILLAR (W. J., M.Inst.C.E., late Secretary to the Inst. of Engineers and Shipbuilders in Scotland):

LATITUDE AND LONGITUDE: HOW TO FIND THEM. Crown 8vo, with Diagrams. 2s. [*Griffin's Nautical Series.*

" CONCISELY and CLEARLY WRITTEN . . . cannot but prove an acquisition to those studying Navigation."—*Marine Engineer.*
" Young Seamen will find it HANDY and USEFUL, SIMPLE and CLEAR."—*The Engineer.*

SECOND EDITION. *Enlarged, and very fully Illustrated.* Cloth, 4s. 6d.

STEAM - BOILERS:
THEIR DEFECTS, MANAGEMENT, AND CONSTRUCTION.
By R. D. MUNRO,
Chief Engineer of the Scottish Boiler Insurance and Engine Inspection Company.

This work, written chiefly to meet the wants of Mechanics, Engine-keepers, and Boiler-attendants, also contains information of the first importance to every user of Steam-power. It is a PRACTICAL work written for PRACTICAL men, the language and rules being throughout of the simplest nature.

" A valuable companion for workmen and engineers engaged about Steam Boilers, ought to be carefully studied, and ALWAYS AT HAND."—*Coll. Guardian.*
" The subjects referred to are handled in a trustworthy, clear, and practical manner. . . . The book is VERY USEFUL, especially to steam users, artisans, and young engineers."—*Engineer.*

BY THE SAME AUTHOR.

KITCHEN BOILER EXPLOSIONS: Why
they Occur, and How to Prevent their Occurrence? A Practical Handbook based on Actual Experiment. With Diagrams and Coloured Plate, Price 3s.

LONDON: EXETER STREET, STRAND.

MUNRO & JAMIESON'S ELECTRICAL POCKET-BOOK.

TWELFTH EDITION, Revised and Enlarged.

A POCKET-BOOK
OF
ELECTRICAL RULES & TABLES
FOR THE USE OF ELECTRICIANS AND ENGINEERS.
BY
JOHN MUNRO, C.E., & PROF. JAMIESON, M.INST.C.E., F.R.S.E.
With Numerous Diagrams. Pocket Size. Leather, 8s. 6d.

GENERAL CONTENTS.

UNITS OF MEASUREMENT.	ELECTRO-METALLURGY.
MEASURES.	BATTERIES.
TESTING.	DYNAMOS AND MOTORS.
CONDUCTORS.	TRANSFORMERS.
DIELECTRICS.	ELECTRIC LIGHTING
SUBMARINE CABLES.	MISCELLANEOUS.
TELEGRAPHY.	LOGARITHMS.
ELECTRO-CHEMISTRY.	APPENDICES.

"WONDERFULLY PERFECT. . . . Worthy of the highest commendation we can give it."—*Electrician.*
"The STERLING VALUE of Messrs. MUNRO and JAMIESON'S POCKET-BOOK."— *Electrical Review.*

MUNRO (J. M. H., D.Sc., Professor of Chemistry,
Downton College of Agriculture):

AGRICULTURAL CHEMISTRY AND ANALYSIS: A PRACTICAL HAND-BOOK for the Use of Agricultural Students.

NYSTROM'S POCKET-BOOK OF MECHANICS
AND ENGINEERING. Revised and Corrected by W. DENNIS MARKS, Ph.B., C.E. (YALE S.S.S.), Whitney Professor of Dynamical Engineering, University of Pennsylvania. Pocket Size. Leather, 15s. TWENTIETH EDITION, Revised and greatly enlarged.

LONDON: EXETER STREET, STRAND.

Demy 8vo, Handsome Cloth, 18s.

Physical Geology and Palæontology,
ON THE BASIS OF PHILLIPS.

BY

HARRY GOVIER SEELEY, F.R.S.,
PROFESSOR OF GEOGRAPHY IN KING'S COLLEGE, LONDON.

With Frontispiece in Chromo=Lithography, and Illustrations.

"It is impossible to praise too highly the research which PROFESSOR SEELEY'S 'PHYSICAL GEOLOGY' evidences. IT IS FAR MORE THAN A TEXT-BOOK—it is a DIRECTORY to the Student in prosecuting his researches."—*Presidential Address to the Geological Society*, 1885, *by Rev. Prof. Bonney, D.Sc., LL.D., F.R.S.*

"PROFESSOR SEELEY maintains in his 'PHYSICAL GEOLOGY' the high reputation he already deservedly bears as a Teacher."—*Dr. Henry Woodward, F.R.S., in the "Geological Magazine."*

"PROFESSOR SEELEY'S work includes one of the most satisfactory Treatises on Lithology in the English language. . . . So much that is not accessible in other works is presented in this volume, that no Student of Geology can afford to be without it."—*American Journal of Engineering.*

Demy 8vo, Handsome Cloth, 34s.

Stratigraphical Geology & Palæontology,
ON THE BASIS OF PHILLIPS.

BY

ROBERT ETHERIDGE, F.R.S.,
OF THE NATURAL HIST. DEPARTMENT, BRITISH MUSEUM, LATE PALÆONTOLOGIST TO THE GEOLOGICAL SURVEY OF GREAT BRITAIN, PAST PRESIDENT OF THE GEOLOGICAL SOCIETY, ETC.

With Map, Numerous Tables, and Thirty=six Plates.

*** PROSPECTUS *of the above important work—perhaps the* MOST ELABORATE *of its kind ever written, and one calculated to give a new strength to the study of Geology in Britain—may be had on application to the Publishers.*

"No such compendium of geological knowledge has ever been brought together before."—*Westminster Review.*

"If PROF. SEELEY'S volume was remarkable for its originality and the breadth of its views, Mr. ETHERIDGE fully justifies the assertion made in his preface that his book differs in construction and detail from any known manual. . . . Must take HIGH RANK AMONG WORKS OF REFERENCE."—*Athenæum.*

LONDON: EXETER STREET, STRAND.

THIRD EDITION. With Folding Plates and Many Illustrations.
Large 8vo. Handsome Cloth. 36s.

ELEMENTS OF METALLURGY:
A PRACTICAL TREATISE ON THE ART OF EXTRACTING METALS FROM THEIR ORES.

By J. ARTHUR PHILLIPS, M.Inst.C.E., F.C.S., F.G.S., &c.
And H. BAUERMAN, V.P.G.S.

GENERAL CONTENTS.

Refractory Materials.	Antimony.	Iron.
Fire-Clays.	Arsenic.	Cobalt.
Fuels, &c.	Zinc.	Nickel.
Aluminium.	Mercury.	Silver.
Copper.	Bismuth.	Gold.
Tin.	Lead.	Platinum.

⁎ Many NOTABLE ADDITIONS, dealing with new Processes and Developments, will be found in the Third Edition.

"Of the THIRD EDITION, we are still able to say that, as a Text-book of Metallurgy, it is THE BEST with which we are acquainted."—*Engineer.*

"The value of this work is almost *inestimable.* There can be no question that the amount of time and labour bestowed on it is enormous. . . . There is certainly no Metallurgical Treatise in the language calculated to prove of such general utility."—*Mining Journal.*

"In this most useful and handsome volume is condensed a large amount of valuable practical knowledge. A careful study of the first division of the book, on Fuels, will be found to be of great value to every one in training for the practical applications of our scientific knowledge to any of our metallurgical operations."—*Athenæum.*

"A work which is equally valuable to the Student as a Text-book, and to the practical Smelter as a Standard Work of Reference. . . . The Illustrations are admirable examples of Wood Engraving."—*Chemical News.*

POYNTING (J. H., Sc.D., F.R.S., late Fellow of Trinity College, Cambridge; Professor of Physics, Mason College, Birmingham):
THE MEAN DENSITY OF THE EARTH: An Essay to which the Adams Prize was adjudged in 1893 in the University of Cambridge. In large 8vo, with Bibliography, Illustrations in the Text, and seven Lithographed Plates. 12s. 6d.

"An account of this subject cannot fail to be of GREAT and GENERAL INTEREST to the scientific mind. Especially is this the case when the account is given by one who has contributed so considerably as has Prof. Poynting to our present state of knowledge with respect to a very difficult subject. . . . Remarkably has Newton's estimate been verified by Prof. Poynting."—*Athenæum.*

POYNTING and THOMSON: TEXT-BOOK OF PHYSICS. (See under *Thomson*.)

LONDON: EXETER STREET, STRAND.

WORKS BY
W. J. MACQUORN RANKINE, LL.D., F.R.S.,
Late Regius Professor of Civil Engineering in the University of Glasgow.

THOROUGHLY REVISED BY

W. J. MILLAR, C.E.,
Late Secretary to the Institute of Engineers and Shipbuilders in Scotland.

I. A MANUAL OF APPLIED MECHANICS:
Comprising the Principles of Statics and Cinematics, and Theory of Structures, Mechanism, and Machines. With Numerous Diagrams. Crown 8vo, cloth, 12s. 6d. FOURTEENTH EDITION.

II. A MANUAL OF CIVIL ENGINEERING:
Comprising Engineering Surveys, Earthwork, Foundations, Masonry, Carpentry, Metal Work, Roads, Railways, Canals, Rivers, Waterworks, Harbours, &c. With Numerous Tables and Illustrations. Crown 8vo, cloth, 16s. NINETEENTH EDITION.

III. A MANUAL OF MACHINERY AND MILLWORK:
Comprising the Geometry, Motions, Work, Strength, Construction, and Objects of Machines, &c. Illustrated with nearly 300 Woodcuts. Crown 8vo, cloth, 12s. 6d. SEVENTH EDITION.

IV. A MANUAL OF THE STEAM-ENGINE AND OTHER PRIME MOVERS:
With Numerous Tables and Illustrations, and a Diagram of the Mechanical Properties of Steam. Crown 8vo, cloth, 12s. 6d. THIRTEENTH EDITION.

V. USEFUL RULES AND TABLES:
For Architects, Builders, Engineers, Founders, Mechanics, Shipbuilders, Surveyors, &c. With APPENDIX for the use of ELECTRICAL ENGINEERS. By Professor JAMIESON, F.R.S.E. SEVENTH EDITION. 10s. 6d.

VI. A MECHANICAL TEXT-BOOK:
A Practical and Simple Introduction to the Study of Mechanics. By Professor RANKINE and E. F. BAMBER, C.E. With Numerous Illustrations. Crown 8vo, cloth, 9s. FOURTH EDITION.

*** *The* "MECHANICAL TEXT-BOOK" *was designed by Professor* RANKINE *as an* INTRODUCTION *to the above Series of Manuals.*

LONDON: EXETER STREET, STRAND.

SCIENTIFIC AND TECHNOLOGICAL WORKS.

PROF. RANKINE'S WORKS—(*Continued*).

VII. MISCELLANEOUS SCIENTIFIC PAPERS.

Royal 8vo. Cloth, 31s. 6d.

Part I. Papers relating to Temperature, Elasticity, and Expansion of Vapours, Liquids, and Solids. Part II. Papers on Energy and its Transformations. Part III. Papers on Wave-Forms, Propulsion of Vessels, &c.

With Memoir by Professor TAIT, M.A. Edited by W. J. MILLAR, C.E. With fine Portrait on Steel, Plates, and Diagrams.

"No more enduring Memorial of Professor Rankine could be devised than the publication of these papers in an accessible form. . . . The Collection is most valuable on account of the nature of his discoveries, and the beauty and completeness of his analysis. . . . The Volume exceeds in importance any work in the same department published in our time."—*Architect*.

CALCAREOUS CEMENTS:
THEIR NATURE, PREPARATION, AND USES.
With some Remarks upon Cement Testing.

BY GILBERT R. REDGRAVE, ASSOC. INST. C.E.

With Illustrations. 8s. 6d.

GENERAL CONTENTS.—Introduction—Historical Review of the Cement Industry—The Early Days of Portland Cement—Composition of Portland Cement—PROCESSES OF MANUFACTURE—The Washmill and the Backs—Flue and Chamber Drying Processes—Calcination of the Cement Mixture—Grinding of the Cement—Composition of Mortar and Concrete—CEMENT TESTING — CHEMICAL ANALYSIS of Portland Cement, Lime, and Raw Materials — Employment of Slags for Cement Making — Scott's Cement, Selenitic Cement, and Cements produced from Sewage Sludge and the Refuse from Alkali Works — Plaster Cements — Specifications for Portland Cement—Appendices (Gases Evolved from Cement Works, Effects of Seawater on Cement, Cost of Cement Manufacture, &c., &c.)

"A work calculated to be of GREAT and EXTENDED UTILITY."—*Chemical News*.
"INVALUABLE to the Student, Architect, and Engineer."—*Building News*.
"A work of the GREATEST INTEREST and USEFULNESS, which appears at a very critical period of the Cement Trade."—*Brit. Trade Journal*.
"Will be useful to ALL interested in the MANUFACTURE, USE, and TESTING of Cements."—*Engineer*.

LONDON: EXETER STREET, STRAND.

PETROLEUM
AND ITS PRODUCTS:
A PRACTICAL TREATISE.

BY

BOVERTON REDWOOD,
F.R.S.E., F.I.C., Assoc. Inst. C.E.,

Hon. Corr. Mem. of the Imperial Russian Technical Society; Mem. of the American Chemical Society; Consulting Adviser to the Corporation of London under the Petroleum Acts, &c., &c.

ASSISTED BY GEO. T. HOLLOWAY, F.I.C., Assoc. R.C.S.,
And Numerous Contributors.

In Two Volumes, Large 8vo. Price 45s.

With Numerous Maps, Plates, and Illustrations in the Text.

GENERAL CONTENTS.

I. General Historical Account of the Petroleum Industry.
II. Geological and Geographical Distribution of Petroleum and Natural Gas.
III. Chemical and Physical Properties of Petroleum.
IV. Origin of Petroleum and Natural Gas.
V. Production of Petroleum, Natural Gas, and Ozokerite.
VI. The Refining of Petroleum.
VII. The Shale Oil and Allied Industries.
VIII. Transport, Storage, and Distribution of Petroleum.
IX. Testing of Petroleum.
X. Application and Uses of Petroleum.
XI. Legislation on Petroleum at Home and Abroad.
XII. Statistics of the Petroleum Production and the Petroleum Trade, obtained from the most trustworthy and official sources.

"The MOST COMPREHENSIVE AND CONVENIENT ACCOUNT that has yet appeared of a gigantic industry which has made incalculable additions to the comfort of civilised man.... The chapter dealing with the arrangement for STORAGE and TRANSPORT of GREAT PRACTICAL INTEREST.... The DIGEST of LEGISLATION on the subject cannot but prove of the GREATEST UTILITY."—*The Times.*
"A SPLENDID CONTRIBUTION to our technical literature."—*Chemical News.*
"This THOROUGHLY STANDARD WORK ... in every way EXCELLENT ... most fully and ably handled ... could only have been produced by a man in the very exceptional position of the Author.... INDISPENSABLE to all who have to do with Petroleum, its APPLICATIONS, MANUFACTURE, STORAGE, or TRANSPORT."—*Mining Journal.*
"We must concede to Mr. Redwood the distinction of having produced a treatise which must be admitted to the rank of THE INDISPENSABLES. It contains THE LAST WORD that can be said about Petroleum in any of its SCIENTIFIC, TECHNICAL, and LEGAL aspects. It would be difficult to conceive of a more comprehensive and explicit account of the geological conditions associated with the SUPPLY of Petroleum and the very practical question of its AMOUNT and DURATION."—*Journ. of Gas Lighting.*

LONDON: EXETER STREET, STRAND.

SCIENTIFIC AND TECHNOLOGICAL WORKS. 35

Royal 8vo, Handsome Cloth, 25s.

THE STABILITY OF SHIPS.

BY

SIR EDWARD J. REED, K.C.B., F.R.S., M.P.,

KNIGHT OF THE IMPERIAL ORDERS OF ST. STANILAUS OF RUSSIA; FRANCIS JOSEPH OF AUSTRIA; MEDJIDIE OF TURKEY; AND RISING SUN OF JAPAN; VICE-PRESIDENT OF THE INSTITUTION OF NAVAL ARCHITECTS.

With numerous Illustrations and Tables.

THIS work has been written for the purpose of placing in the hands of Naval Constructors, Shipbuilders, Officers of the Royal and Mercantile Marines, and all Students of Naval Science, a complete Treatise upon the Stability of Ships, and is the only work in the English Language dealing exhaustively with the subject.

In order to render the work complete for the purposes of the Shipbuilder, whether at home or abroad, the Methods of Calculation introduced by Mr. F. K. BARNES, Mr. GRAY, M. REECH, M. DAYMARD, and Mr. BENJAMIN, are all given separately, illustrated by Tables and worked-out examples. The book contains more than 200 Diagrams, and is illustrated by a large number of actual cases, derived from ships of all descriptions, but especially from ships of the Mercantile Marine.

The work will thus be found to constitute the most comprehensive and exhaustive Treatise hitherto presented to the Profession on the Science of the STABILITY OF SHIPS.

" Sir EDWARD REED'S 'STABILITY OF SHIPS' is INVALUABLE. In it the STUDENT, new to the subject, will find the path prepared for him, and all difficulties explained with the utmost care and accuracy; the SHIP-DRAUGHTSMAN will find all the methods of calculation at present in use fully explained and illustrated, and accompanied by the Tables and Forms employed; the SHIPOWNER will find the variations in the Stability of Ships due to differences in forms and dimensions fully discussed, and the devices by which the state of his ships under all conditions may be graphically represented and easily understood; the NAVAL ARCHITECT will find brought together and ready to his hand, a mass of information which he would otherwise have to seek in an almost endless variety of publications, and some of which he would possibly not be able to obtain at all elsewhere."—*Steamship.*

"This IMPORTANT AND VALUABLE WORK . . . cannot be too highly recommended to all connected with shipping interests."—*Iron.*

"This VERY IMPORTANT TREATISE, . . . the MOST INTELLIGIBLE, INSTRUCTIVE, and COMPLETE that has ever appeared."—*Nature.*

"The volume is an ESSENTIAL ONE for the shipbuilding profession."—*Westminster Review.*

RICHMOND (H. Droop, F.C.S., Chemist to the
Aylesbury Dairy Company):

DAIRY CHEMISTRY FOR DAIRY MANAGERS: A Practical Handbook. (*Griffin's Technological Manuals.*)

LONDON: EXETER STREET, STRAND.

GRIFFIN'S SANITARY PUBLICATIONS.

THIRD EDITION, REVISED. With Additional Illustrations. Price 6s.

PRACTICAL SANITATION:
A HAND-BOOK FOR SANITARY INSPECTORS AND OTHERS INTERESTED IN SANITATION.

By GEORGE REID, M.D., D.P.H.,
Fellow of the Sanitary Institute of Great Britain, and Medical Officer, Staffordshire County Council.

With an Appendix on Sanitary Law
By HERBERT MANLEY, M.A., M.B., D.P.H.,
Medical Officer of Health for the County Borough of West Bromwich.

GENERAL CONTENTS.—Introduction—Water Supply: Drinking Water, Pollution of Water—Ventilation and Warming—Principles of Sewage Removal—Details of Drainage; Refuse Removal and Disposal—Sanitary and Insanitary Work and Appliances—Details of Plumbers' Work—House Construction—Infection and Disinfection—Food, Inspection of; Characteristics of Good Meat; Meat, Milk, Fish, &c., unfit for Human Food—Appendix: Sanitary Law; Model Bye-Laws, &c.

"A VERY USEFUL HANDBOOK, with a very useful Appendix. We recommend it not only to SANITARY INSPECTORS, but to HOUSEHOLDERS and ALL interested in Sanitary matters."—*Sanitary Record.*

In Large 8vo, Handsome Cloth. 12s. 6d.

DISINFECTION & DISINFECTANTS
(AN INTRODUCTION TO THE STUDY OF).
Together with an Account of the Chemical Substances used as Antiseptics and Preservatives.

By SAMUEL RIDEAL, D.Sc.LOND., F.I.C., F.C.S.,
Examiner in Chemistry to the Royal College of Physicians; formerly Lecturer on Chemistry, St. George's Hospital Medical School, &c., &c.

With Folding-Plate and Illustrations of the most Approved Modern Appliances.

*** "Notwithstanding the rapid development of Sanitary Science in this country, there does not exist at the present time in the English language any book which deals exclusively with the composition of DISINFECTANTS. The present volume will, therefore, supply a want which has been felt not only by the chemist and bacteriologist, but also by those who are concerned with the practical work of disinfection. . . ."—EXTRACT FROM AUTHOR'S PREFACE.

"DR. RIDEAL'S volume is bound to prove of GREAT VALUE, both as a PRACTICAL GUIDE and as a WORK OF REFERENCE."—*Pharmaceutical Journal.*

"AN EXHAUSTIVE TREATISE, dealing with the WHOLE RANGE of the subject:—Disinfection by Heat, Chemical Disinfectants, Practical Methods, Personal Disinfection, Legal Regulations, and Methods of Analysis . . . so very well done and so USEFUL that it will be valued by ALL connected with Sanitation and Public Health."—*Chemist and Druggist.*

"A book that has long been wanted . . . will prove of VERY GREAT VALUE."—*Local Government Journal.*

LONDON: EXETER STREET, STRAND.

GRIFFIN'S "FIRST AID" PUBLICATIONS.

On Land.

THIRD EDITION, REVISED. *Large Crown 8vo. Handsome Cloth.* 4s.

A MANUAL OF AMBULANCE.

By J. SCOTT RIDDELL, C.M., M.B., M.A.,

Assistant-Surgeon, Aberdeen Royal Infirmary; Lecturer and Examiner to the Aberdeen Ambulance Association; Examiner to the St. Andrew s Ambulance Association, Glasgow, and the St. John Ambulance Association, London.

With Numerous Illustrations and Full Page Plates.

General Contents.—Outlines of Human Anatomy and Physiology—The Triangular Bandage and its Uses—The Roller Bandage and its Uses—Fractures—Dislocations and Sprains—Hæmorrhage—Wounds—Insensibility and Fits—Asphyxia and Drowning—Suffocation—Poisoning—Burns, Frost-bite, and Sunstroke—Removal of Foreign Bodies from (*a*) The Eye; (*b*) The Ear; (*c*) The Nose; (*d*) The Throat; (*e*) The Tissues—Ambulance Transport and Stretcher Drill—The After-treatment of Ambulance Patients—Organisation and Management of Ambulance Classes—Appendix: Examination Papers on First Aid.

"A CAPITAL BOOK. . . . The directions are SHORT and CLEAR, and testify to the hand of an able surgeon."—*Edin. Med. Journal.*

"This little volume seems to us about as good as it could possibly be. . . . Contains practically every piece of information necessary to render First aid. . . . Should find its place in EVERY HOUSEHOLD LIBRARY."—*Daily Chronicle.*

"So ADMIRABLE is this work, that it is difficult to imagine how it could be better."—*Colliery Guardian.*

At Sea.

Crown 8vo, Extra. Handsome Cloth. 6s.

A MEDICAL AND SURGICAL HELP
FOR SHIPMASTERS AND OFFICERS
IN THE MERCHANT NAVY.
INCLUDING
FIRST AID TO THE INJURED.

By WM. JOHNSON SMITH, F.R.C.S.,
Principal Medical Officer, Seamen's Hospital, Greenwich.

With Coloured Plates and Numerous Illustrations.

*** The attention of all interested in our Merchant Navy is requested to this exceedingly useful and valuable work. It is needless to say that it is the outcome of many years' PRACTICAL EXPERIENCE amongst Seamen.

"SOUND, JUDICIOUS, REALLY HELPFUL."—*The Lancet.*

"It would be difficult to find a Medical and Surgical Guide more clear and comprehensive than Mr. JOHNSON SMITH, whose experience at the GREENWICH HOSPITAL eminently qualifies him for the task. . . . A MOST ATTRACTIVE WORK. . . . We have read it from cover to cover. . . . It gives clearly written advice to Masters and Officers in all medical and surgical matters likely to come before them when remote from the land and without a doctor. . . . We RECOMMEND the work to EVERY Shipmaster and Officer."—*Liverpool Journal of Commerce.*

LONDON: EXETER STREET, STRAND.

Griffin's Metallurgical Series.
STANDARD WORKS OF REFERENCE
FOR

Metallurgists, Mine-Owners, Assayers, Manufacturers, and all interested in the development of the Metallurgical Industries.

EDITED BY

W. C. ROBERTS-AUSTEN, C.B., F.R.S.,
CHEMIST AND ASSAYER OF THE ROYAL MINT; PROFESSOR OF METALLURGY IN THE ROYAL COLLEGE OF SCIENCE.

In Large 8vo, Handsome Cloth. With Illustrations.

VOLUMES ALREADY PUBLISHED.

1. **INTRODUCTION to the STUDY of METALLURGY.** By the EDITOR. THIRD EDITION. 12s. 6d.

"No English text-book at all approaches this in the COMPLETENESS with which the most modern views on the subject are dealt with. Professor Austen's volume will be INVALUABLE, not only to the student, but also to those whose knowledge of the art is far advanced."—*Chemical News.*

"INVALUABLE to the student. . . . Rich in matter not to be readily found elsewhere."—*Athenæum.*

"This volume amply realises the expectations formed as to the result of the labours of so eminent an authority. It is remarkable for its ORIGINALITY of conception and for the large amount of information which it contains. . . . We recommend every one who desires information not only to consult, but to STUDY this work."—*Engineering.*

"Will at once take FRONT RANK as a text-book."—*Science and Art.*

"Prof. ROBERTS-AUSTEN's book marks an epoch in the history of the teaching of metallurgy in this country."—*Industries.*

2. **GOLD (The Metallurgy of).** By THOS. KIRKE ROSE, D.Sc., Assoc. R.S.M., F.I.C., of the Royal Mint. SECOND EDITION, 21s. (See p. 40).

3. **IRON (The Metallurgy of).** By THOS. TURNER, Assoc. R.S.M., F.I.C., F.C.S. 16s. (See p. 46).

Will be Published at Short Intervals.

4. **STEEL (The Metallurgy of).** By F. W. HARBORD, Assoc R.S.M., F.I.C.

5. **COPPER (The Metallurgy of).** By THOS. GIBB, Assoc. Royal School of Mines. [*At Press.*

6. **METALLURGICAL MACHINERY:** the Application of Engineering to Metallurgical Problems. By HENRY CHARLES JENKINS, Wh.Sc., Assoc. R.S.M., Assoc. M.Inst.C.E., of the Royal Mint.

7. **ALLOYS.** By the EDITOR.

*** Other Volumes in Preparation.

LONDON: EXETER STREET, STRAND.

SCIENTIFIC AND TECHNOLOGICAL WORKS. 39

SECOND EDITION, Revised and Enlarged.
In Large 8vo, Handsome cloth, 34s.

HYDRAULIC POWER
AND
HYDRAULIC MACHINERY.

BY

HENRY ROBINSON, M. Inst. C.E., F.G.S.,

FELLOW OF KING'S COLLEGE, LONDON; PROF. OF CIVIL ENGINEERING,
KING'S COLLEGE, ETC., ETC.

With numerous Woodcuts, and Sixty=nine Plates.

General Contents.

Discharge through Orifices—Gauging Water by Weirs—Flow of Water through Pipes—The Accumulator—The Flow of Solids—Hydraulic Presses and Lifts—Cyclone Hydraulic Baling Press—Anderton Hydraulic Lift—Hydraulic Hoists (Lifts)—The Otis Elevator—Mersey Railway Lifts—City and South London Railway Lifts—North Hudson County Railway Elevator—Lifts for Subways—Hydraulic Ram—Pearsall's Hydraulic Engine—Pumping-Engines—Three-Cylinder Engines—Brotherhood Engine—Rigg's Hydraulic Engine—Hydraulic Capstans—Hydraulic Traversers—Movable Jigger Hoist—Hydraulic Waggon Drop—Hydraulic Jack—Duckham's Weighing Machine—Shop Tools—Tweddell's Hydraulic Rivetter—Hydraulic Joggling Press—Tweddell's Punching and Shearing Machine—Flanging Machine—Hydraulic Centre Crane—Wrightson's Balance Crane—Hydraulic Power at the Forth Bridge—Cranes—Hydraulic Coal-Discharging Machines—Hydraulic Drill—Hydraulic Manhole Cutter—Hydraulic Drill at St. Gothard Tunnel—Motors with Variable Power—Hydraulic Machinery on Board Ship—Hydraulic Points and Crossings—Hydraulic Pile Driver—Hydraulic Pile Screwing Apparatus—Hydraulic Excavator—Ball's Pump Dredger—Hydraulic Power applied to Bridges—Dock-gate Machinery—Hydraulic Brake—Hydraulic Power applied to Gunnery—Centrifugal Pumps—Water Wheels—Turbines—Jet Propulsion—The Gerard-Barré Hydraulic Railway—Greathead's Injector Hydrant—Snell's Hydraulic Transport System—Greathead's Shield—Grain Elevator at Frankfort—Packing—Power Co-operation—Hull Hydraulic Power Company—London Hydraulic Power Company—Birmingham Hydraulic Power System—Niagara Falls—Cost of Hydraulic Power—Meters—Schönheyder's Pressure Regulator—Deacon's Waste-Water Meter.

" A Book of great Professional Usefulness."—*Iron.*

*** The SECOND EDITION of the above important work has been thoroughly revised and brought up to date. Many new full-page Plates have been added—the number being increased from 43 in the First Edition to 69 in the present. Full Prospectus, giving a description of the Plates, may be had on application to the Publishers.

LONDON: EXETER STREET, STRAND.

GRIFFIN'S METALLURGICAL SERIES.

THE METALLURGY OF GOLD.

BY

T. KIRKE ROSE, D.Sc., Assoc.R.S.M., F.I.C.,

Assistant Assayer of the Royal Mint.

SECOND EDITION. Revised and partly Re-written. Including the most recent Improvements in the Cyanide Process, and a new Chapter on Economic Considerations (Management, Cost, Output, &c.). With Frontispiece and additional Illustrations. Large 8vo. Handsome Cloth. 21s.

LEADING FEATURES.

1. Adapted for all who are interested in the Gold Mining Industry, being free from technicalities as far as possible; of special value to those engaged in the industry—viz., mill-managers, reduction-officers, &c.

2. The whole ground implied by the term "Metallurgy of Gold" has been covered with equal care; the space is carefully apportioned to the various branches of the subject, according to their relative importance.

3. The MACARTHUR-FORREST CYANIDE PROCESS is fully described for the first time. By this process over £2,000,000 of gold per annum (at the rate of) is now being extracted, or nearly one-tenth of the total world's production. The process, introduced in 1887, has only had short newspaper accounts given of it previously. The chapters have been submitted to, and revised by, Mr. MacArthur, and so freed from all possible inaccuracies.

4. Among other new processes not previously described in a text-book are— (1) The modern barrel chlorination process, practised with great success in Dakota, where the Black Hills district is undergoing rapid development owing to its introduction. (2) New processes for separating gold from silver—viz., the new Gutzkow process, and the Electrolytic process; the cost of separation is reduced by them by one-half.

5. A new feature is the description of EXACT METHODS employed in particular extraction works—Stamp-batteries of South Africa, Australia, New Zealand, California, Colorado, and Dakota; Chlorination works also, in many parts of the world; Cyanide works of S. Africa and New Zealand. These accounts are of special value to practical men.

6. The bibliography is the first made since 1882.

"Dr. ROSE gained his experience in the Western States of America, but he has secured details of gold-working from ALL PARTS of the world, and these should be of GREAT SERVICE to practical men. . . . The four chapters on *Chlorination*, written from the point of view alike of the practical man and the chemist, TEEM WITH CONSIDERATIONS HITHERTO UNRECOGNISED, and constitute an addition to the literature of Metallurgy, which will prove to be of classical value."—*Nature.*

"The most complete description of the chlorination process which has yet been published. —*Mining Journal.*

LONDON: EXETER STREET, STRAND.

NEW AND IMPORTANT WORK.

Companion-Volume to MM. Knecht and Rawson's "Dyeing."

TEXTILE PRINTING:

A PRACTICAL MANUAL.

Including the Processes Used in the Printing of
COTTON, WOOLLEN, and SILK FABRICS.

BY

C. F. SEYMOUR ROTHWELL, F.C.S.,

Mem. Soc. of Chemical Industries; late Lecturer at the Municipal Technical School, Manchester.

In Large 8vo, with Illustrations in the text and Specimens of Printed Patterns.

SCHWACKHÖFER and BROWNE:

FUEL AND WATER: A Manual for Users of Steam and Water. By Prof. FRANZ SCHWACKHÖFER of Vienna, and WALTER R. BROWNE, M.A., C.E., late Fellow of Trinity College, Cambridge. Demy 8vo, with Numerous Illustrations, 9/.

GENERAL CONTENTS.—Heat and Combustion—Fuel, Varieties of—Firing Arrangements: Furnace, Flues, Chimney—The Boiler, Choice of—Varieties—Feed-water Heaters—Steam Pipes—Water: Composition, Purification—Prevention of Scale, &c., &c.

"The Section on Heat is one of the best and most lucid ever written."—*Engineer.*
"Cannot fail to be valuable to thousands using steam power."—*Railway Engineer.*

SHELTON-BEY (W. Vincent, Foreman to the Imperial Ottoman Gun Factories, Constantinople):

THE MECHANIC'S GUIDE: A Hand-Book for Engineers and Artizans. With Copious Tables and Valuable Recipes for Practical Use. Illustrated. *Second Edition.* Crown 8vo. Cloth, 7/6.

LONDON: EXETER STREET, STRAND.

CHARLES GRIFFIN & CO.'S PUBLICATIONS.

Thirteenth Edition. Price 21s.
Demy 8vo, Cloth. With Numerous Illustrations, reduced from Working Drawings.

A MANUAL OF
MARINE ENGINEERING:
COMPRISING THE DESIGNING, CONSTRUCTION, AND WORKING OF MARINE MACHINERY.

By A. E. SEATON, M. Inst. C. E., M. Inst. Mech. E., M.Inst.N.A.

GENERAL CONTENTS.

Part I.—Principles of Marine Propulsion.
Part II.—Principles of Steam Engineering.
Part III.—Details of Marine Engines: Design and Calculations for Cylinders, Pistons, Valves, Expansion Valves, &c.
Part IV.—Propellers.
Part V.—Boilers.
Part VI.—Miscellaneous.

*** The THIRTEENTH EDITION includes a Chapter on WATER-TUBE BOILERS, with Illustrations of the leading Types.

"In the three-fold capacity of enabling a Student to learn how to design, construct, and work a Marine Steam-Engine, Mr. Seaton's Manual has NO RIVAL."—*Times.*
"The important subject of Marine Engineering is here treated with the THOROUGHNESS that it requires. No department has escaped attention. . . . Gives the results of much close study and practical work."—*Engineering.*
"By far the BEST MANUAL in existence. . . . Gives a complete account of the methods of solving, with the utmost possible economy, the problems before the Marine Engineer."—*Athenæum.*
"The Student, Draughtsman, and Engineer will find this work the MOST VALUABLE HANDBOOK of Reference on the Marine Engine now in existence."—*Marine Engineer.*

THIRD EDITION. With Diagrams. Pocket-Size, Leather. 8s. 6d.

A POCKET-BOOK OF
MARINE ENGINEERING RULES AND TABLES,
FOR THE USE OF
Marine Engineers, Naval Architects, Designers, Draughtsmen, Superintendents and Others.

BY.

A. E. SEATON, M.I.C.E., M.I.Mech.E., M.I.N.A.,

AND

H. M. ROUNTHWAITE, M.I.Mech.E., M.I.N.A.

"ADMIRABLY FULFILS its purpose."—*Marine Engineer.*

LONDON: EXETER STREET, STRAND.

WORKS BY A. HUMBOLDT SEXTON, F.I.C., F.C.S.,
Professor of Metallurgy in the Glasgow and West of Scotland Technical College.

In Large Crown 8vo, Handsome Cloth, 6s.

ELEMENTARY METALLURGY
(A TEXT-BOOK OF).
Including the Author's PRACTICAL LABORATORY COURSE.

With Numerous Illustrations.

GENERAL CONTENTS.—Introduction—Properties of the Metals—Combustion—Fuels—Refractory Materials—Furnaces—Occurrence of the Metals in Nature—Preparation of the Ore from the Smelter—Metallurgical Processes—Iron: Preparation of Pig Iron—Malleable Iron—Steel—Mild Steel—Copper—Lead—Zinc and Tin—Silver—Gold—Mercury—Alloys—Applications of ELECTRICITY to Metallurgy—LABORATORY COURSE WITH NUMEROUS PRACTICAL EXERCISES.

" The volume before us FULLY ENHANCES and confirms PROF. SEXTON's reputation. . . . Just the kind of work for Students COMMENCING the study of Metallurgy, or for ENGINEERING Students requiring a GENERAL KNOWLEDGE of it, or for ENGINEERS in practice who like a HANDY WORK OF REFERENCE. To all three classes we HEARTILY commend the work."—*Practical Engineer.*

" EXCELLENTLY got-up and WELL-ARRANGED. . . . Iron and copper well explained by EXCELLENT diagrams showing the stages of the process from start to finish. . . . The most NOVEL chapter is that on the many changes wrought in Metallurgical Methods by ELECTRICITY."—*Chemical Trade Journal.*

" Possesses the GREAT ADVANTAGE of giving a COURSE OF PRACTICAL WORK."—*Mining Journal.*

Sexton's (Prof.) Outlines of Quantitative Analysis.
FOR THE USE OF STUDENTS.

With Illustrations. FOURTH EDITION. Crown 8vo, Cloth, 3s.

" A COMPACT LABORATORY GUIDE for beginners was wanted, and the want has been WELL SUPPLIED. . . . A good and useful book."—*Lancet.*

Sexton's (Prof.) Outlines of Qualitative Analysis.
FOR THE USE OF STUDENTS.

With Illustrations. THIRD EDITION. Crown 8vo, Cloth, 3s. 6d.

" The work of a thoroughly practical chemist."—*British Medical Journal.*
" Compiled with great care, and will supply a want."—*Journal of Education.*

LONDON: EXETER STREET, STRAND.

WORKS BY PROF. ROBERT H. SMITH, Assoc.M.I.C.E.,
M.I.M.E., M.I.El.E., M.Fed.L.Mi.E., Whit. Sch., M.Ord.Meiji.

MEASUREMENT CONVERSIONS
(English and French):

28 GRAPHIC TABLES OR DIAGRAMS.

Showing at a glance the MUTUAL CONVERSION of MEASUREMENTS in DIFFERENT UNITS

Of Lengths, Areas, Volumes, Weights, Stresses, Densities, Quantities of Work, Horse Powers, Temperatures, &c.

For the use of Engineers, Surveyors, Architects, and Contractors.

In 4to, Boards. 7s. 6d.

---

* Prof. SMITH'S CONVERSION-TABLES form the most unique and comprehensive collection ever placed before the profession. By their use much time and labour will be saved, and the chances of error in calculation diminished. It is believed that henceforth no Engineer's Office will be considered complete without them.

"The work is INVALUABLE."—*Colliery Guardian.*

"Ought to be in EVERY office where even occasional conversions are required. . . . Prof. SMITH'S TABLES form very EXCELLENT CHECKS on results. . . . A VERY USEFUL and good set of diagrams."—*Electrical Review.*

"Prof. Smith deserves the hearty thanks, not only of the ENGINEER, but of the COMMERCIAL WORLD, for having smoothed the way for the ADOPTION of the METRIC SYSTEM of MEASUREMENT, a subject which is now assuming great importance as a factor in maintaining our HOLD upon FOREIGN TRADE. There can be no doubt that the antiquated system of Weights and Measures used in this country is doomed to be superseded by the much simpler method of DECIMAL MEASUREMENT. The sooner this is recognised, the better."—*The Machinery Market.*

THE CALCULUS FOR ENGINEERS,
WITH EXTENSIVE
CLASSIFIED REFERENCE LIST OF INTEGRALS.

By PROF. ROBERT H. SMITH.

ASSISTED BY

ROBERT FRANKLIN MUIRHEAD,

M.A., B.Sc. (Glasgow), B.A. (Cambridge),

Formerly Clark Fellow of Glasgow University, and Lecturer on Mathematics at Mason College.

In Crown 8vo, extra, with Diagrams and Folding-Plate.

LONDON : EXETER STREET, STRAND.

SCIENTIFIC AND TECHNOLOGICAL WORKS.

By PROFESSORS J. J. THOMSON & POYNTING.

In Large 8vo. Fully Illustrated.

A TEXT-BOOK OF PHYSICS:

COMPRISING

PROPERTIES OF MATTER; HEAT; SOUND AND LIGHT; MAGNETISM AND ELECTRICITY.

BY

J. H. POYNTING,
SC.D., F.R.S.,
Late Fellow of Trinity College, Cambridge; Professor of Physics, Mason College, Birmingham.

AND

J. J. THOMSON,
M.A., F.R.S.,
Fellow of Trinity College, Cambridge; Prof. of Experimental Physics in the University of Cambridge.

THIRD EDITION, *Revised and Enlarged.* Pocket-Size, Leather, also for Office Use, Cloth, 12s. 6d.

BOILERS, MARINE AND LAND:
THEIR CONSTRUCTION AND STRENGTH.

A HANDBOOK OF RULES, FORMULÆ, TABLES, &C., RELATIVE TO MATERIAL, SCANTLINGS, AND PRESSURES, SAFETY VALVES, SPRINGS, FITTINGS AND MOUNTINGS, &C.

For the Use of all Steam-Users.

BY T. W. TRAILL, M. INST. C. E., F. E. R. N.,
Late Engineer Surveyor-in-Chief to the Board of Trade.

*** TO THE THIRD EDITION MANY NEW TABLES have been added.

"Very unlike any of the numerous treatises on Boilers which have preceded it. . . . Really useful. . . . Contains an ENORMOUS QUANTITY OF INFORMATION arranged in a very convenient form. . . . Those who have to design boilers will find that they can settle the dimensions for any given pressure with almost no calculation with its aid. . . . A MOST USEFUL VOLUME . . supplying information to be had nowhere else."—*The Engineer.*

"As a handbook of rules, formulæ, tables, &c., relating to materials, scantlings, and pressures, this work will prove MOST USEFUL. The name of the Author is a sufficient guarantee for its accuracy. It will save engineers, inspectors, and draughtsmen a vast amount of calculation."—*Nature.*

"By such an authority cannot but prove a welcome addition to the literature of the subject. . . . We can strongly recommend it as being the MOST COMPLETE, eminently practical, work on the subject."—*Marine Engineer.*

"To the engineer and practical boiler-maker it will prove INVALUABLE. The tables in all probability are the most exhaustive yet published. . . . Certainly deserves a place on the shelf in the drawing office of every boiler shop."—*Practical Engineer.*

LONDON: EXETER STREET, STRAND.

GRIFFIN'S METALLURGICAL SERIES.

THE METALLURGY OF IRON.

BY

THOMAS TURNER, Assoc.R.S.M., F.I.C.,

Director of Technical Instruction to the Staffordshire County Council.

IN LARGE 8VO, HANDSOME CLOTH, WITH NUMEROUS ILLUSTRATIONS (MANY FROM PHOTOGRAPHS). PRICE 16s.

GENERAL CONTENTS.

Early History of Iron.
Modern History of Iron.
The Age of Steel.
Chief Iron Ores.
Preparation of Iron Ores.
The Blast Furnace.
The Air used in the Blast Furnace.
Reactions of the Blast Furnace.
The Fuel used in the Blast Furnace.

Slags and Fluxes of Iron Smelting.
Properties of Cast Iron.
Foundry Practice.
Wrought Iron.
Indirect Production of Wrought Iron.
The Puddling Process.
Further Treatment of Wrought Iron.

Corrosion of Iron and steel.

"A MOST VALUABLE SUMMARY of useful knowledge relating to every method and stage in the manufacture of cast and wrought iron down to the present moment . . . particularly rich in chemical details. . . . An EXHAUSTIVE and REALLY NEEDED compilation by a MOST CAPABLE and THOROUGHLY UP-TO-DATE metallurgical authority."—*Bulletin of the American Iron and Steel Association.*

"This is A DELIGHTFUL BOOK, giving, as it does, reliable information on a subject becoming every day more elaborate. . . . The account of the chief iron ores is, like the rest of this work, RICH in detail. . . . Foundry Practice has been made the subject of considerable investigation by the author, and forms an interesting and able chapter."—*Colliery Guardian.*

"Mr. Turner's work comes at an opportune moment and in answer to a REAL DEMAND. . . . A THOROUGHLY USEFUL BOOK, which brings the subject UP TO DATE. The author has produced an EMINENTLY READABLE BOOK. . . . Whatever he describes, he describes well. . . . There is much in the work that will be of GREAT VALUE to those engaged in the iron industry."—*Mining Journal.*

IN PREPARATION.

COMPANION-VOLUME ON

THE METALLURGY OF STEEL.

By F. W. HARBORD, Assoc.R.S.M., F.I.C.

LONDON: EXETER STREET, STRAND.

SCIENTIFIC AND TECHNOLOGICAL WORKS.

KNOW YOUR OWN SHIP.
By THOMAS WALTON, Naval Architect.

SPECIALLY ARRANGED TO SUIT THE REQUIREMENTS OF

Ships' Officers, Shipowners, Superintendents, Draughtsmen, Engineers, and others. Explains, in a simple manner, such important subjects as:—

Displacement, Deadweight, Tonnage, Freeboard, Moments, Buoyancy, Strain, Structure, Stability, Rolling, Ballasting, Loading, Shifting Cargoes, Admission of Water, Sail Area, &c., &c.

SECOND EDITION. *With Numerous Illustrations.* Handsome Cloth. 5s.

"The little book will be found EXCEEDINGLY HANDY by most officers and officials connected with shipping. . . . Mr. Walton's work will obtain LASTING SUCCESS, because of its unique fitness for those for whom it has been written."—*Shipping World.*

"An EXCELLENT WORK, full of solid instruction and INVALUABLE to every officer of the Mercantile Marine who has his profession at heart."—*Shipping.*

"Not one of the 242 pages could well be spared. It will admirably fulfil its purpose . . . useful to ship owners, ship superintendents, ship draughtsmen, and all interested in shipping."—*Liverpool Journal of Commerce.*

"A mass of VERY USEFUL INFORMATION, accompanied by diagrams and illustrations, is given in a compact form."—*Fairplay.*

"A large amount of MOST USEFUL INFORMATION is given in the volume. The book is certain to be of great service to those who desire to be thoroughly grounded in the subject of which it treats."—*Steamship.*

"We have found no one statement that we could have wished differently expressed. The matter has, so far as clearness allows, been admirably condensed, and is simple enough to be understood by every seaman."—*Marine Engineer.*

GAS AND OIL ENGINES:

An Introductory Text-book on the Theory, Design, Construction, and Testing of Internal Combustion Engines without Boiler.

FOR THE USE OF STUDENTS.

BY

PROF. W. H. WATKINSON, WHIT. SCH., M.INST.MECH.E.,
Glasgow and West of Scotland Technical College.

In Crown 8vo, extra, with Numerous Illustrations. [*Shortly.*

LONDON: EXETER STREET, STRAND.

WORKS BY DR. ALDER WRIGHT, F.R.S.

FIXED OILS, FATS, BUTTERS, AND WAXES:

THEIR PREPARATION AND PROPERTIES,

And the Manufacture therefrom of Candles, Soaps, and Other Products.

BY

C. R. ALDER WRIGHT, D.Sc., F.R.S.,

Late Lecturer on Chemistry, St. Mary's Hospital School; Examiner in "Soap" to the City and Guilds of London Institute.

In Large 8vo. Handsome Cloth. With 144 Illustrations. 28s.

"Dr. WRIGHT'S work will be found ABSOLUTELY INDISPENSABLE by every Chemist. TEEMS with information valuable alike to the Analyst and the Technical Chemist."—*The Analyst.*

"Will rank as the STANDARD ENGLISH AUTHORITY on OILS and FATS for many years to come."—*Industries and Iron.*

SECOND EDITION. With very Numerous Illustrations. Handsome Cloth, 6s. Also Presentation Edition, Gilt and Gilt Edges, 7s. 6d.

THE THRESHOLD OF SCIENCE:

Simple and Amusing Experiments (over 400) in Chemistry and Physics.

*** To the NEW EDITION has been added an excellent chapter on the Systematic Order in which Class Experiments should be carried out for Educational purposes.

"Any one who may still have doubts regarding the value of Elementary Science as an organ of education will speedily have his doubts dispelled, if he takes the trouble to understand the methods recommended by Dr. Alder Wright. The Additions to the New Edition will be of great service to all who wish to use the volume, not merely as a 'play-book,' but as an instrument for the TRAINING of the MENTAL FACULTIES."—*Nature.*

"Step by step the learner is here gently guided through the paths of science, made easy by the perfect knowledge of the teacher, and made flowery by the most striking and curious experiments. Well adapted to become the TREASURED FRIEND of many a bright and promising lad."—*Manchester Examiner.*

LONDON: EXETER STREET, STRAND.

SCIENTIFIC AND TECHNOLOGICAL WORKS.

Engineering Drawing and Design

(A TEXT-BOOK OF):

In Two Parts, Published Separately.

VOL. I.—PRACTICAL GEOMETRY, PLANE, AND SOLID. 3S.
VOL. II.—MACHINE AND ENGINE DRAWING AND DESIGN. 4S. 6D.

BY

SIDNEY H. WELLS, WH.SC.,
A.M.INST.C.E., A.M.INST.MECH.E.,

Principal of, and Head of the Engineering Department in, the Battersea Polytechnic Institute; formerly of the Engineering Departments of the Yorkshire College, Leeds; and Dulwich College, London.

With many Illustrations, specially prepared for the Work, and numerous Examples, for the Use of Students in Technical Schools and Colleges.

"A THOROUGHLY USEFUL WORK, exceedingly well written. For the many Examples and Questions we have nothing but praise."—*Nature.*

"A CAPITAL TEXT-BOOK, arranged on an EXCELLENT SYSTEM, calculated to give an intelligent grasp of the subject, and not the mere faculty of mechanical copying. . . . Mr. Wells shows how to make COMPLETE WORKING-DRAWINGS, discussing fully each step in the design."—*Electrical Review.*

"The first book leads EASILY and NATURALLY towards the second, where the technical pupil is brought into contact with large and more complex designs."—*The Schoolmaster.*

Electrical Measurements & Instruments.

A Practical Hand-book of Testing for the Electrical Engineer.

BY CHARLES H. YEAMAN,

Assoc. Inst. E.E., formerly Electrical Engineer to the Corporation of Liverpool.

The author has had an extensive experience in the use of Electrical Measuring Instruments of various types in the Laboratory, Testroom, and Workshop.
The following subjects of practical importance are dealt with:—

SUPPLY METERS. | POTENTIOMETERS.
GALVANOMETERS.

The testing of Supply Meters is a subject upon which very little has been published. The Potentiometer has not been systematically treated in any recent book on electrical measurement, and although Galvanometers are considered by many writers, there still remains the want for a connected description of the different types and their uses.
The Electrical Engineer is particularly concerned with—

ALTERNATING CURRENT MEASUREMENTS.
FAULTY LOCATION.
DYNAMO AND TRANSFORMER EFFICIENCY TESTS.
LOW RESISTANCES. | MEDIUM RESISTANCES.
HIGH RESISTANCES.
BATTERY TESTING. | MAGNETIC TESTS.
DESCRIPTION OF TEST-ROOMS AND ELECTRO-TECHNICAL LABORATORIES.

This work is written by an Electrical Engineer for Electrical Engineers. It forms an excellent text-book for students proceeding to the "Electrical Instruments" section of the Honours Grade Examinations in Electrical Engineering of the City and Guilds of London Institute.
The majority of the illustrations have not been published before, and have been specially prepared for this work.

LONDON: EXETER STREET, STRAND.

Thirteenth Annual Issue. Handsome cloth, 7s. 6d.

THE OFFICIAL YEAR-BOOK

OF THE

SCIENTIFIC AND LEARNED SOCIETIES OF GREAT BRITAIN AND IRELAND.

COMPILED FROM OFFICIAL SOURCES.

Comprising (together with other Official Information) LISTS of the PAPERS read during 1895 before all the LEADING SOCIETIES throughout the Kingdom engaged in the following Departments of Research:—

§ 1. Science Generally: *i.e.*, Societies occupying themselves with several Branches of Science, or with Science and Literature jointly.
§ 2. Mathematics and Physics.
§ 3. Chemistry and Photography.
§ 4. Geology, Geography, and Mineralogy.
§ 5. Biology, including Microscopy and Anthropology.
§ 6. Economic Science and Statistics.
§ 7. Mechanical Science and Architecture.
§ 8. Naval and Military Science.
§ 9. Agriculture and Horticulture.
§ 10. Law.
§ 11. Literature.
§ 12. Psychology.
§ 13. Archæology.
§ 14. Medicine.

Of the TWELFTH ISSUE (for 1895), *The Engineer* says—"Every year of publication of this book has ADDED to the PROOFS of its USEFULNESS. . . . The Year-books of past years form a VERY HANDY CONSECUTIVE INDEX of the work done by the Societies."

"The YEAR-BOOK OF SOCIETIES is a Record which ought to be of the greatest use for the progress of Science."—*Sir Lyon Playfair, F.R.S., K.C.B., M.P., Past-President of the British Association.*

"It goes almost without saying that a Handbook of this subject will be in time one of the most generally useful works for the library or the desk."—*The Times.*

"British Societies are now well represented in the 'Year-Book of the Scientific and Learned Societies of Great Britain and Ireland.'"—(Art. "Societies" in New Edition of "Encyclopædia Britannica," vol. xxii.)

Copies of the FIRST ISSUE, giving an Account of the History, Organization, and Conditions of Membership of the various Societies, and forming the groundwork of the Series, may still be had, price 7/6. *Also Copies of the following Issues.*

The YEAR-BOOK OF SOCIETIES forms a complete INDEX TO THE SCIENTIFIC WORK of the year in the various Departments. It is used as a ready HANDBOOK in all our great SCIENTIFIC CENTRES, MUSEUMS, and LIBRARIES throughout the Kingdom, and has become an INDISPENSABLE BOOK OF REFERENCE to every one engaged in Scientific Work.

LONDON: EXETER STREET, STRAND.

A BOOK NO FAMILY SHOULD BE WITHOUT.

THIRTY-FIRST EDITION. *Royal 8vo, Handsome Cloth,* 10s. 6d.

A DICTIONARY OF
Domestic Medicine and Household Surgery,

BY

SPENCER THOMSON, M.D., EDIN., L.R.C.S.,

REVISED, AND IN PART RE-WRITTEN, BY THE AUTHOR,

BY

JOHN CHARLES STEELE, M.D.,

LATE OF GUY'S HOSPITAL,

AND BY

GEO. REID, M.D., D.P.H.,

MED. OFFICER, STAFFS. COUNTY COUNCIL.

With Appendix on the Management of the Sick-room, and many Hints for the Diet and Comfort of Invalids.

In its New Form, DR. SPENCER THOMSON'S "DICTIONARY OF DOMESTIC MEDICINE" fully sustains its reputation as the "Representative Book of the Medical Knowledge and Practice of the Day" applied to Domestic Requirements.

The most recent IMPROVEMENTS in the TREATMENT OF THE SICK—in APPLIANCES for the RELIEF OF PAIN—and in all matters connected with SANITATION, HYGIENE, and the MAINTENANCE of the GENERAL HEALTH—will be found in the New Issue in clear and full detail; the experience of the Editors in the Spheres of Private Practice, of Hospital Treatment, and of Sanitary Supervision respectively, combining to render the Dictionary perhaps the most thoroughly practical work of the kind in the English Language. Many new Engravings have been introduced—improved Diagrams of different parts of the Human Body, and Illustrations of the newest Medical, Surgical, and Sanitary Apparatus.

*** *All Directions given in such a form as to be readily and safely followed.*

FROM THE AUTHOR'S PREFATORY ADDRESS.

"Without entering upon that difficult ground which correct professional knowledge and educated judgment can alone permit to be safely trodden, there is a wide and extensive field for exertion, and for usefulness, open to the unprofessional, in the kindly offices of a *true* DOMESTIC MEDICINE, the timely help and solace of a simple HOUSEHOLD SURGERY, or, better still, in the watchful care more generally known as 'SANITARY PRECAUTION,' which tends rather to preserve health than to cure disease. 'The touch of a gentle hand' will not be less gentle because guided by knowledge, nor will the *safe* domestic remedies be less anxiously or carefully administered. Life may be saved, suffering may always be alleviated. Even to the resident in the midst of civilisation, the 'KNOWLEDGE IS POWER,' to do good; to the settler and emigrant it is INVALUABLE."

" Dr. Thomson has fully succeeded in conveying to the public a vast amount of useful professional knowledge."—*Dublin Journal of Medical Science.*
" The amount of useful knowledge conveyed in this Work is surprising."—*Medical Times and Gazette.*
" WORTH ITS WEIGHT IN GOLD TO FAMILIES AND THE CLERGY."—*Oxford Herald.*

LONDON: CHARLES GRIFFIN & CO., LIMITED, EXETER STREET, STRAND.

FIRST SERIES—THIRTY-SIXTH EDITION.
SECOND SERIES—TENTH EDITION.

MANY THOUGHTS OF MANY MINDS:

A Treasury of Reference, consisting of Selections from the Writings of the most Celebrated Authors. FIRST AND SECOND SERIES.

COMPILED AND ANALYTICALLY ARRANGED

By HENRY SOUTHGATE.

♦

Each Series is complete in itself, and sold separately.

Presentation Edition, Cloth and Gold, . . . 12s. 6d. each volume.
Library Edition, Half Bound, Roxburghe, . . 14s.   ,,
Do.,   Morocco Antique, . . . 21s.   ,,

In Square 8vo, elegantly printed on toned paper.

"'MANY THOUGHTS,' &c., are evidently the produce of years of research."—*Examiner.*
"Many beautiful examples of thought and style are to be found among the selections."—*Leader.*
"There can be little doubt that it is destined to take a high place among books of this class."—*Notes and Queries.*
"A treasure to every reader who may be fortunate enough to possess it. Its perusal is like inhaling essences; we have the cream only of the great authors quoted. Here all are seeds or gems."—*English Journal of Education.*
"Mr. Southgate's reading will be found to extend over nearly the whole known field of literature, ancient and modern."—*Gentleman's Magazine.*
"We have no hesitation in pronouncing it one of the most important books of the season. Credit is due to the publishers for the elegance with which the work is got up, and for the extreme beauty and correctness of the typography."—*Morning Chronicle.*
"Of the numerous volumes of the kind, we do not remember having met with one in which the selection was more judicious, or the accumulation of treasures so truly wonderful."—*Morning Herald.*
"The selection of the extracts has been made with taste, judgment, and critical nicety."—*Morning Post.*
"This is a wondrous book, and contains a great many gems of thought."—*Daily News.*
"As a work of reference, it will be an acquisition to any man's library."—*Publishers' Circular.*
"This volume contains more gems of thought, refined sentiments, noble axioms, and extractable sentences, than have ever before been brought together in our language."—*The Field.*
"All that the poet has described of the beautiful in nature and art, all the axioms of experience, the collected wisdom of philosopher and sage, are garnered into one heap of useful and well-arranged instruction and amusement."—*The Era.*
"The collection will prove a mine rich and inexhaustible, to those in search of a quotation."—*Art Journal.*

"Will be found to be worth its weight in gold by literary men."—*The Builder.*
"Every page is laden with the wealth of profoundest thought, and all aglow with the loftiest inspirations of genius."—*Star.*
"The work of Mr. Southgate far outstrips all others of its kind. To the clergymen, the author, the artist, and the essayist, 'Many Thoughts of Many Minds' cannot fail to render almost incalculable service."—*Edinburgh Mercury.*
"We have no hesitation whatever in describing Mr. Southgate's as the very best book of the class. There is positively nothing of the kind in the language that will bear a moment's comparison with it."—*Manchester Weekly Advertiser.*
"There is no mood in which we can take it up without deriving from it instruction, consolation, and amusement. We heartily thank Mr. Southgate for a book which we shall regard as one of our best friends and companions."—*Cambridge Chronicle.*
"This work possesses the merit of being a MAGNIFICENT GIFT-BOOK, appropriate to all times and seasons; a book calculated to be of use to the scholar, the divine, and the public man."—*Freemason's Magazine.*
"It is not so much a book as a library of quotations."—*Patriot.*
"The quotations abound in that *thought* which is the mainspring of mental exercise."—*Liverpool Courier.*
"For purposes of apposite quotation, it cannot be surpassed."—*Bristol Times.*
"It is impossible to pick out a single passage in the work which does not, upon the face of it, justify its selection by its intrinsic merit."—*Dorset Chronicle.*
"We are not surprised that a SECOND SERIES of this work should have been called for. Mr. Southgate has the catholic tastes desirable in a good Editor. Preachers and public speakers will find that it has special uses for them."—*Edinburgh Daily Review.*
"The SECOND SERIES fully sustains the deserved reputation of the FIRST."—*John Bull.*

LONDON: CHARLES GRIFFIN & CO., LIMITED, EXETER STREET, STRAND.

www.ingramcontent.com/pod-product-compliance
Lightning Source LLC
Chambersburg PA
CBHW020106010526
44115CB00008B/709